Decolonising
Colonial Education:
Doing Away with Relics and Toxicity Embedded in the Racist Dominant Grand Narrative

Nkwazi Nkuzi Mhango

Langaa Research & Publishing CIG
Mankon, Bamenda

Publisher:
Langaa RPCIG
Langaa Research & Publishing Common Initiative Group
P.O. Box 902 Mankon
Bamenda
North West Region
Cameroon
Langaagrp@gmail.com
www.langaa-rpcig.net

Distributed in and outside N. America by African Books Collective
orders@africanbookscollective.com
www.africanbookcollective.com

ISBN-10: 9956-550-27-2

ISBN-13: 978-9956-550-27-2

As a thinker and member of a human family, I truly envisage a pivotally collective dream-cum-vision for peace and development for the human family through the decolonisation and detoxification of colonial education as espoused by the current dominant grand narrative. I envisage the world in which all grand narrative matters; and are treated equally in constructing a world grand narrative made after dialogues and agreement of the human family that will reconcile the well off and the worse off of the world.

Nkwazi Mhango
University of Manitoba
Winnipeg
Canada

Table of Contents

List of Images

Acknowledgements

As ever, I acknowledge my wife Nesaa who contributed immensely in writing this tome. Her unconditional and unwavering support has always been second to none. So, too, our children mainly Ng'ani, Nkuzi and Nkwazi Jr, the youngest, do bear the brunt sometimes, especially when I am out for my researches and readings which lead to missing me at home at the normal times and occasions as their father. I hugely acknowledge my mentor, Professor Sean Byrne, has also been so instrumental to remind me not to stop writing apart from contributing some ideas as far as writing is concerned. Again, Byrne is the one who pushed me to the limits to write academic books after teaching me in my grad studies. I also would like to acknowledge Professor Jessica Senehi who has also been instrumental to me, especially *vis-a-vis* how to tell the story nicely. From these two professors and friends, I learned how to use a simplified language in telling my stories. No way can I thank my brother professor Eliakim Sibanda who enriched my knowledge, especially as the guru of History.

There is no way I can complete my acknowledgements without mentioning the name of my brother, Professor Munyaradzi Mawere who has always encouraged me to think about Africa; and thus, do something about it. As well, my friends and readers Sirili Akko and Salih Hassan are acknowledged for their unwavering support.

Lastly, I would like to acknowledge all academics, practitioners and readers who will pick up from where I ended in my quest for the decolonisation and detoxification of colonial education as it is embedded in the current dominant grand narrative.

Preface

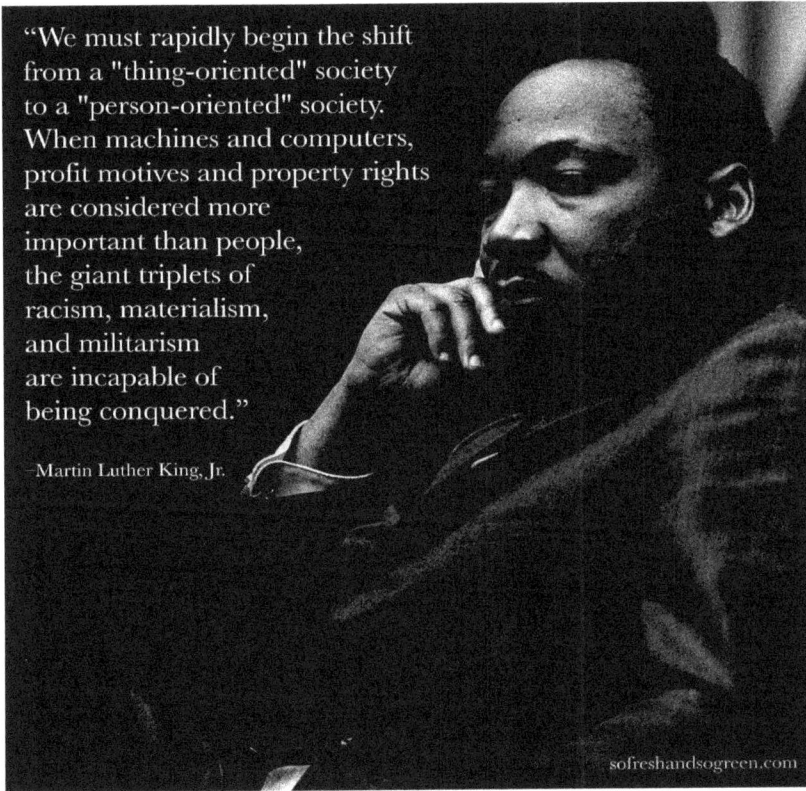

"We must rapidly begin the shift from a "thing-oriented" society to a "person-oriented" society. When machines and computers, profit motives and property rights are considered more important than people, the giant triplets of racism, materialism, and militarism are incapable of being conquered."

-Martin Luther King, Jr.

sofreshandsogreen.com

Figure 1 photo; courtesy of sofreshaandsogreen.com

One of the forces and reasons behind writing this volume rests on the fact that Western cultures, practices, theories, ways of doing things and thinking have dominated the world intellectually for many decades so as to declare themselves as universal even where they are only a handful of people who have hijacked and *la-di-da* almost everything. Carney, Rappleye & Silova (2012) note that many world culture scholars have been involved in identifying and advocating for diffusional education models based on Western ideals as a way of legitimising dominant epistemological paradigms which compromise the possibilities of understanding actual processes of global convergence in education.

The volume aims at challenging such internalised myths, lies, fabrications and hegemonic dominance in knowledge.

The second reason is the fact that Africa has always been a recipient so as to become a dumpster for almost everything including academic impetus such as ideas, books and rules. Abhorred by such unnecessary dependency and the fact that Africa once lived independently without any godfather, I had to search my soul and ask myself what can be done to, at least, make a U-turn and revisit Africa's past in order to salvage what is left of its epistemes and grand narratives. In my soul searching I found that the way forward is not to just go back. Instead, it is to negotiate the regime of what we currently have, especially as far as colonial and toxic epistemes are concerned as espoused by the current Western dominant grand narrative. This undertaking asks for critical and rebellious thinking. *Ipso facto*, one of my duties as a contribution to the dialogue is to challenge such thinking; and show how it is aimed at, of course, undermining others; thereby belittling, even making them look like they have no inputs in the matters pertaining to the world. Truly, dependency makes those on the receiving end to be perceived as intellectually impotent, if I may use the term however ugly it may look. Equally, when a few or one part of the world usurps the powers from the majority, chances of abusing and misusing such powers and exploiting those excluded are high, particularly if we revisit the role and era of slavery, colonialism, and now, neoliberalism all enacted and applied to benefit the West at the detriment of the rest. This is, especially true when we consider some approaches the so-called developed countries take towards the so-called underdeveloped countries as Adeleke (2015) asserts that European powers claimed that they were geared by the mission of universalising; and thereby civilising Africa so that it could benefit from "superior European civilisation" under what England claimed to bear the white man's burden or France's mission civilisatrice or civilising mission. However, Mhango (2015) makes a good question asking if slavery and colonialism were civilisation or devilisation of others and their civilisations and methods (Johnson, 2009).

Even the term third world is in itself offensive, pejorative, parochial and prejudiced. The above quote speaks volume as far as the current dominant grand narrative–espoused and maintained by the West–is concerned. With regard to treating others, there is no equality or equity or parity not to mention addressing the needs of both parties in this pact. Even the sense of dignity–for all human beings–is amiss in such an assertion as evidenced in world politics, *realpolitik* and international laws. To do away with such self-aggrandisement towards the belittled others namely non-Western societies, we need to observe some ethics which can bring us together in order to dialogue and negotiate our differences, needs, likes, dislikes, prejudices even histories ready to face the future together as equal partners. This is only possible if we willingly agree to decolonise and vacuum clean the current toxic episteme. Battersby & Siracusa (2009) in their book, *Globalization and Human Security* propose global moral which they define to mean the capacity to mediate between national cultures, communities of fate and alternative styles of life which aims at disclosing the basis for dialogue with the traditions and discourses of others with the aim of expanding the horizon of one's own framework of meaning and prejudice.

If anything, since the inception of Western colonised and hegemonic education as espoused by the current dominant Western-grand narrative, almost all fields of education have been hugely held and totally dominated by Western intellectualism which ignores other cultures by relegating them to peripheries. Countries or societies outside of the Western hegemonic-grand narrative–purposely, and by all means and purposes–have been left out in education except for a few areas in some fields that were partly incorporated such as Satyagraha or 'persistence for truth' (India) (Joshi, 2012), Ubuntu or 'human quality' (South Africa) (Gade, 2012), Ho'oponopono or 'rightly right' (Hawaii) (Duprée, 2012) in CRS and a few others. Even when such artificially accommodated facets of education are mentioned or being referred to, it is just in a passing and a casual manner but not foundational one. They just play complementary roles but not taking a center stage. Such philosophies and models are mere intellectual subsidiaries that have to receive knowledge and education from the mother thinker, namely Western intellectualism that knows and owns almost everything as far as education is concerned. This is not fair; and it cannot remain unchanged without causing more conflicts and problems to the world. If anything, such subsidiarity the non-Western disciplines of education play means nothing but intellectual colonisation that needs to be dealt with shall, the world want to do justice; and live peacefully and equally. And such intellectual colonisation can be decisively dealt with by decolonising education. How do you call a system that excludes others if not colonial and hegemonic? For, other disciplines rooted in Non-Western Schools of thoughts are not treated equally to Western ones. This begs many questions whose answers academic, mainly from sidelined civilisations and grand narratives need to provide. Arguably, one day, or some days, some thinkers will rise up and take the challenge up proposing the decolonisation of all fields just as this volume espouses. Maybe, they have already started. Again, how much consideration and importance does such a move receive? Basically, I decided to introduce; and tackle this issue so as to contribute to an intellectual dialogue that aims at providing a space for all human beings, cultures and civilisations to fully participate in shaping our peaceful world that we all badly need and want. Basically, I underscore the importance of all narratives and their epistemes regardless they are modern or traditional. Logically, the way humans use their intelligence is currently measured through academic standards such as examinations, researches and the way one can define experiential knowledge. This being the case, those who control education systems have an upper hand in deciding who should qualify and who should not all depending on their targets and intentions as in the rating of the university globally. Such cannot be real education that superimposes truth to anybody. Scolnicov (2013) maintains that "there is thus no point in teaching others, if by "teaching" one means conveying the truth about the way things are" (p. 5) but not the way one either manipulates or wants things to look the way he wants but not the way they are. The truth about the way things are has no cloud of any form concerning with interpreting what truth is. Neither does it accommodate the exploitation of one another as it currently is under toxic episteme. Logically, everybody has his or her way of seeing the truth. The end product of this process is what is called episteme. This is why graduate and post graduate students spend more and much time in dialoguing and arguing instead of writing, cramming or reading only. They need to cultivate the culture, academic culture, of arguing, analysing, disputing, defending and whatnots of whatever put before them. However, all such academic practices are done in the *diktat* of Western colonised education. If such education would fully and truthfully accommodate all views and grand narratives, it surely would be referred as true education. But when it comes to theories so hypothesised and discussed, most of them are Western. True episteme is about seeking and telling the Truth with capital letter. It is a naked education that does not have any baggage with it is what is needed in addressing our problems of which one is terrorism this corpus unpacks though briefly. We need the type of episteme that allows critical thinking based on reality; decolonised education that can poke holes in the *status quo*.

In a nutshell, this is the genesis of this volume. We need to debunk the myth of Western hegemonic dominance by questioning and deconstructing its toxic education which is embedded in West dominant-grand narrative. However, it does not mean that Western world does not have anything good to offer. Through an eye of scrutiny, it has a lot that we need to retain as we add the inputs of other grand narratives of the world. Notably, all evil things, especially such as slavery, colonialism and imperialism which were used to lay foundations of the current education regime all over the world need to be revisited and those who benefited from them must be forced to redress those they colonised and exploited. Thus, we need to sieve the inputs of the current dominant grand narrative in order to pick good things as we discard the evil ones. In solving the problem of colonial and toxic education, we must avoid to be fooled by good things it has done *ad interim*. What is obvious is that we are not going to start from a clean slate. For, we will need to scrutinise all grand narratives in order to sieve and winnow them so that we can displace chaff and garbage they have. And so, the same *modus operandi* will be applied in all civilisations, disciplines and schools of thoughts the world over. Here the aim is to negotiate our future together so that we can live equitably and peacefully as a human family. We need to put down the burdens Western intellectualism has maliciously placed on our heads so as to keep on dominating and bullying us whether consciously or otherwise. We need to recapture our golden era however distant, *inferior* or out of touch it may seem to others. We need to reclaim our place in this planet as equally intelligent humans. This planet is for all of us equally, consistently and interdependently. To address all issues raised, the author has taken a Conflict Resolution slant due to his predisposition as an academic in the field.

List of Abbreviations

AD	Anno Domini
ANC	African National Congress
ATC	American Trade Center
AU	African Union
AUT	Association of University Teachers
BCE	Before Common Era
CAR	Central African Republic
CE	Common Era
CIA	Central Intelligence Agency
CRS	Conflict Resolution Studies
DRC	Democratic Republic of Congo
DSAE	Dictionary of South African English on Historical Principles
EPA	Environmental Protection Agency
FAO	Food and Agriculture Organisation
GBV	Gender-based Violence
GDP	Gross Domestic Product
GM	Genetically Modified
GPI	Global Peace Index
GWOT	Global War on Terror
GWOTA	Global War on Terra Africana
ICC	International Criminal Court
ICISS	International Commission on Intervention and State Sovereignty
ICU	Intensive Care Unit
IFIs	International Financial Institutions
IMF	International Monetary Fund
ISIL	Islamic State of Iraq and Levant
LRA	Lord Resistance Army
LTTE	Liberation Tigers of Tamil Eelam
MP	Member of Parliament
MPLA	Popular Movement for Liberation of Angola
NDTV	New Delhi Television
OPEC	Organisation for Petroleum Exporting Countries
PEACS	Peace and Conflict Studies

PhD	Doctor of Philosophy
PHS	Public Health Service
R2P	Right to Protect
SPLA	Sudan People's Liberation Army
SSA	Sub-Saharan Africa
TEK	Traditional Education Knowledge
UDHR	Universal Declaration of Human Rights
UK	United Kingdom
UN	United Nations
UNEP	United Nations Environment Programme
UNITA	União Nacional para a Independência Total de Angola
URT	United Republic of Tanzania
US	United States
USSR	Union of Soviet Socialist Republics
WB	World Bank
WMD	Weapons of Mass Destruction
WTC	World Trade Center
WW	World War

1

Detoxifying Toxic and Hegemonic Education as Step to True Peace and Reconciliation of the World based on Equality

According to the unanimous testimony of the Ancients, first the Ethiopians and then the Egyptians created and raised to an extraordinary stage of development all the elements of civilization, while other people especially the Eurasians were still deep in barbarism Amélineau cited in Diop (1989).

It is not an overstatement to note that Africa–since the inception of colonialism–has been operating under a wrong and misleading education system just like many victims of colonialism elsewhere. This can be seen on how Africa has been viewed as a backward continent of dependency and melancholies. All started when African education and ways of life and doing things were altered. Arguably, toxic and colonial education as espoused by the West, Africa's former colonial masters–as it is embedded in their current dominant grand narrative–has ruined the lives of the victims of colonialism and other isms. After over fifty years of political or flag independence, Africa has the duty to itself which is to deconstruct, decolonise and detoxify the current regime of education; it has in place. Africa is taught almost everything including things that it used to teach others such as, *inter alia*, interconnectedness, interdependence, equality, equity, humanity and human rights. This cannot continue unabatedly. African academics need to make their case *vis-à-vis* decolonising colonial and toxic education that has left Africa lagging behind as far as development, prosperity and technological advancement–as they are defined by the current dominant grand narrative–are concerned. It boggles the mind to note that Africa has always been a recipient as if it is inhabited by brainless creatures. Africa's history has been misconstrued, misrepresented and, above all, destroyed just because its adopted toxic epistemes have not been able to rectify the anomalies the colonial powers created. Maanga (2015) notes that

African heroes and heroines are purposely left out in historical accounts of the world due to the fact that some foreign writers and local-brainwashed historians are used to internalise such mental colonialism.

What pains even more is the fact that when colonial thinkers misconstrued, and thereby misrepresented Africa's history, did so purposely by maliciously by negating and supressing all beauties, bounties and truths found in the said history. Yet, they shamelessly came calling their twisted history a body of knowledge while it actually was, and still is, a body of lies. Time for reclaiming Africa's robbed and lost glory has now arrived after some brave African academics embarked on the journey of self-reinvention. It is only through decolonising and detoxifying education Africa can truly reclaim its lost glory. Mhango (2015) suggests that African academics should take on what he calls "foul-smelling trickery" of demolishing, demonising and *develising* Africa carried out by Western media and toxic education Africa inherited from its colonial powers.

Fundamentally, this chapter aims at challenging other African academics and some pro-African Western academics to join hands and decolonise Africa's education systems. It is from this milieu that the author of this book invites all African academics from a range of disciplines to offer their expertise all aimed at academically emancipating Africa, and possibly, other Aboriginal people of the world from intellectual dependence and infancy; if I may use the terms. Is it fair, for example, for Africans to be taught about humanity or human rights while they are the ones who practically showed Europeans how these two concepts work? Under the concept of Ubuntu, every human being was presumed to be a human regardless her or his race, gender or economic status. Didn't colonial powers violate this philosophy when they enslaved and colonised Africans? Didn't colonial agents enjoy this philosophy when they first arrive to end up violating it? Kunene (1996) cited in Makgoro (2017) notes that "Ubuntu is the very quality that guarantees not only a separation between men, women and the beasts, but the very fluctuating gradations that determine the relative quality of that essence" (p. 9).

Furthermore, in this chapter, I will show how Africa was not lagging behind in civilisation and development as colonial writers alleged after writing pseudo history of Africa that Maanga (*op.cit.*) notes. In so doing, I seek to challenge the current grand narrative epistemologically; and thereby act as catalysts of embarking on positive change aimed at emancipating Africa so as to contribute to the world's affairs instead of remaining a passive player. A major argument I make here is that knowledge is a God-given tool that enables any human or animal society to function in its own environment. So, deconstructing, decolonising and detoxifying the current education regime are a *sine qua non* for African academics, especially those who are cognisant of the true meaning of education. Despite being a stinking racist, John Dewey notes an important thing. Dewey (2004) cited in Lambert (2009) notes that "there is the standing danger that the material of formal instruction will be merely the subject matter of the schools, isolated from the subject matter of life- experience (p. 121). Dewey underscores the weakness of the Western-superimposed education on others. We can see this reality in climate change, global warming, arms race, conflict, exploitation, capitalism and colonialism. The writings are all over the place, so to speak. Said (1978) cited in Annamalai (2005) views colonial education as a product of experience based on the construction of orientalism.

This book seeks, *inter alia*, to address evocative issues resulting from colonial legacies revolving around colonial education that it seeks to decolonise, deconstruct and make education an emancipatory tool for those left abaft in the current regime of colonial and toxic education. It epistemologically challenges the general experiments, theories and practices of the current crop of education, especially in Africa where knowledge is imported but not exported as if Africa is intellectually impotent if not moribund. Africa is treated–and thereby treats itself–as if it has never had its own knowledge or grand narrative. In principle, the author seeks to deconstruct and decolonise toxic and colonial education–the West has always espoused for its interests as opposed to the interests of others–in order to accommodate, and incorporate other non-Western epistemes based on their visions and grand narratives. Such a move aims at making non-Western epistemes partners of the current dominant Western grand narrative which has been in place for many decades without delivering non-Western societies the same way it did in serving Western countries. Thus, my *a priori* argument is that such education must be decolonised and deconstructed so as to benefit all human beings by incorporating other grand narratives of the world so that they can equally contribute in running the world. Basically, the book seeks to do away with the dominance of one grand narrative that has–for a long time and by all means–ignored and excluded other grand narratives as if they are not the part of world civilisation. Further, the volume explores, *inter alia*, education as one of the means the dominant grand narrative has always used to exploit and intimidate other grand narratives. Therefore, before delving into other issues, we need to define education. By and large, Education can be defined as a process (Bruner, 2009) or a continuum (Leijen, 2006; and Kusurkar & Croiset, 2015) that involves human interpretation or attempts to make sense of her or his surroundings in order to control them for her or his improvement and the improvements and interests of others. It is a behavioural process that involves multi-processes such as investigation, observation, adaption and, above all, curiosity all aimed at solving some problems a particular human encounters. Fromm (1966, p. 52) cited in Vargas (2014) defines education as "freedom to create and to construct, to wonder and to venture. Such freedom requires that the individual be active and responsible, not a slave or a well-fed cog in the machine" (p. 93) without confining oneself to methodologies and complexities of the said education. Essentially, education is a tool with which the oppressed can liberate themselves, not just individually but collectively and enormously as it used to be in the so-called African traditional societies in which education was the right of every member of the society to use in building and helping the society. You can see how emancipatory education is on the lives of those who acquired it currently. However, you wonder to see *academic goons* aka *elites* living large by robbing the poor. Such people are not truly educated; if we consider the fact that education is an emancipatory tool for those who acquired it and their societies. This is amiss in Africa. It shocks to find that, for example, venal and inept rulers who presided over corrupt regimes that felled economy and social services to constitutionally have free medical services where in power and after retiring or exiting power. What for if they are the ones that felled social services? How many such criminals does Africa have, feed and keep under the guise of former presidents who did nothing but robbing their countries?

Importantly, if Africa and the countries that have such systemic theft enshrined in their constitutions would have decolonised education, they would not be wasting humongous sums of money in keeping such fat cats who happen to be the root causes of the miseries many people in these countries are suffering now. Smith (2013) maintains that education must aim at emancipation of the people by creating opportunities for material conditions. Smith's definition however is narrow and Eurocentric. For, it lacks moral aspect, conditions and underpinnings by concentrating on material conditions. Arguably, it imperatively right to argue that any type of education–call it modern or traditional–must intentionally create opportunities aimed at improving human life materially and morally. Such a well-rounded education was found in many African societies among others. For, regarding the type of education that the so-called African traditional society produced and offered compared to the so-called modern education, the differences are basically the aims of the said education and methodology of how to impart it. Likewise, another difference can be found on the fact that the so-called modern education is imparted through oral and written media while the latter was only imparted through oral and practical media. Therefore, what is needed is nothing but to change the methodologies by just modernising them but not condemning and looking down at them as the current toxic and colonial education has always done. I would argue that, education as any science, cannot be static. It is dynamic by nature due to the needs of time and changes human society always goes through or undergoes. Primarily, education is not something colonial, manipulative or static that aims at making one section of the population better than another or an individual better than another for the purpose of exploitation. True education allows and involves competition which aims at the betterment of all people but not some people at the detriment or expenses of others. Education that accommodates or once accommodated exploitation, racism, subservience among people is cancerous, dangerous, toxic, and useless. It needs to be decolonised and detoxified. For, true education makes whoever that acquires it a better person in the sense that he or she makes her or his life better as well the lives of others. Education is for the betterment of people's lives but not for ruining them as it has been for some people under the current grand narrative. For example, one who makes a gun to protect others is well educated compared to the other who makes or acquires the same to rob, threaten, colonise or intimidate others.

Fundamentally, the major aim of decolonised education–this volume envisages and espouses–is to make a human more a human than a consuming machine (Mhango, 2015) for the benefits of all but not turning her or him into a mere consuming machine or an object of whatever experimentation for imperilling others. Also, the essence of education espoused by decolonisation and deconstruction is *a posteriori* to free humans and societies from exploitation of each other. Profoundly, the aim of this type of education is to bring about total and true change and harmony among human family as the force of emancipation. Indeed, this education is an antithetic to the current regime of toxic education that espouses neoliberal policies with the aim of enabling one part of the globe to exploit others by using the achievement gotten from corrupted, rotten and toxic education.

By deconstructing, and thereby decolonising the current academic regime of education *a fortiori,* I seek to reconcile unnecessary differences and incongruities resulting from the dominance of one society over others by using its hegemonic grand narrative. In deconstructing and detoxify the current toxic-cum-colonial education, I will address issues such as racism, environmental degradation, history and the importance of the so-called Traditional Ecological Knowledge (TEK). More so, the book seeks to locate some glitches that colonial education caused, and still causes to the victims of colonialism so that it can be easier for them to decolonise it and themselves on top of seeking redress for the sufferings this regime of education has caused them as a way of making things right ready to move forward equally and harmoniously as a human family.

Berkes, Colding & Folke (2000, p. 1252) cited in Eijck & Roth (2007) define TEK as "a cumulative body of knowledge, practice and belief, evolving by adaptive processes and handed down through generations by cultural transmission, about the relation of living beings (including humans) with one another and with their environment" (p. 2). Without romanticising it, indeed, this is the very knowledge that aimed at serving the society without imposing itself upon, doubling down on or humiliating other civilisations. This sort of education goes far wide by incorporating spiritual teachings without manipulating them as opposed to exploitative spirituality that Africa and other colonised people received from the colonisers by the way of religions which demonised and killed their grand narratives in order to quell; and thereby exploit them. Again, why is non-Western education called traditional but not just mere education just like western one as if it comes from no knowledge or experience, observation and human efforts to know in order to rule the environment? The answer is simple that the current dominant grand narrative sought to distinguish and distance itself from other grand narrative by promoting its own version of education that has always been referred to as modern one. Doing so—however dubious it is—would not succeed without belittling, copying without attribution, demonising, denying and excluding others. TEK is seen as *informal* knowledge compared to *formal* Western one. Is it or is it not depends on how you look at the aim and meaning of education on their practicality and totality. Again, as for formality or informality of anything, it all depends on the culture that defines it. One may argue that if the so-called TEK is informal by nature, even the so-called Modern Education is informal in the eyes of traditional societies due to the manner in which the duo is offered and interpreted based on their purpose to the world. Pennycook (2017) maintains that the introduction of the so-called modern education aims at superimposing a hidden curriculum based on the dominance of positivism and structuralism for the benefit of the West which is true based on results of such education to the victims of colonialism and toxic education. Try to imagine how the so-called modern education altered and destroyed the lives of the victims of colonialism all over the world by robbing their good things without accrediting them.

And this is very true due to the fact that the so-called formal or modern education was introduced in many places during colonialism whereby religion, especially Christianity was used as a vehicle of penetrating other cultures so as to destroy or subdue them. This was before the introduction of Islam which did the same to its victims. This cannot be true education that destroys the lives, ways of life, cultures and the general wellbeing of other people simply because to benefit those doing so. Historically, education in Africa was controlled and provided by the church before colonial governments took over from it. Refer to how many post-colonial African leaders were trained by mission schools and the fact that when they received their freedom there was no formal and free structure governing education other than missionary schools they had to make do with. Apart from leaving education in the hands of colonial agents after acquiring independence for a long time, unfortunately, even when post-colonial African governments took over the reins of power, they did not decolonise or overhaul the said education by creating their own decolonised curricula. This is why the West has always been mistakenly viewed as more advanced and civilised than the victims of its toxic education based on colonial grand narrative this volume seeks to debunk and challenge. Up until now, many African countries are spending billions of dollars sending their people to Western countries to acquire this colonised education that has never freed them from mental enslavement and vulnerability as a people. The West has become a citadel of education and almost everything reasonable. Africa is always viewed as an inchoate continent before the eyes of the current grand narrative. By maintaining colonial education, post-colonial governments purposely or accidentally allowed their people to keep on being poisoned with colonial education whose products can be seen today in terms of corruption and West worshipping in African countries that is always regarded as barren of anything good as far as thinking is concerned. Such leaders and people could not challenge the *status quo* except maintain it as it happened thereafter up until now when the drive of decolonising education is evidently looming however for a few free thinkers. You can see this on how Africa is divided linguistically based on who colonised it. Mhango (2015) argues that many African countries are abler to communicate with their colonial masters than their neighbours. With all such docility and toxicity, still such colonial and toxic education is still referred to as formal, advanced and civilised. Even what is referred to as modernity, is not, particularly if we consider the fact that its pillars of expansion namely, colonialism and cultural imperialism perpetrated by religions is no longer new or modern in modern times. How can something of seventeen century keep on being modern in the twenty-first century? This reminds us of the virginity of Mary even after giving birth to Jesus and his siblings. I do not see how my grandmother can remain a girl or a virgin after giving birth to my parents. For the education that does not accept or accommodate a simple fact that everything is subject to change is irrelevant, especially for the continent that aspires to change so that it catches up with others who duped and exploited it. Henceforth, when I talk about education, knowledge, formality, informality and modernity, it must be underscored the fact that I am purposely talking about culture and civilisations. Nobody knows accurately when the universe came into being and how. Apart from myths of creation and estimation by Western science, nobody can accurately pin down the exact date life started in this universe. I wonder a people who did not know even the existence of the Americas up until the 15th century could know the origin of the whole world. However, the difference, as for whose version of the origin of things we should take, is that in the current toxic and colonial education, it is only the determinant and dominant culture espoused under the expenses of other non-dominant culture that defines everything wantonly and undeservedly. Even the world civilisation is currently measured by using the yardstick of the dominant culture. You can see this in almost everything from governing systems, economic paradigms, intellectual settings, beauty, development have always been biasedly defined by the dominant culture to its advantage.

There are crucial areas that need to be explored and straightened up. For example, since African countries acquired their political independence, they have allowed Western countries to fund and supervise their elections, while to the contrary; African countries do not supervise the elections of those who supervise theirs as the way of reciprocity and respect. There is no way one can explain this phenomenon without touching on colonial legacies that enabled the West to dominate African countries thanks to colonial education. Also, this brings the understanding of those whose elections are funded and supervised to question. To put it simply, the person who allows another to enter his bedroom without the other opening his for him is not normal. It is like stripping before another person who does not strip as the sign of reciprocity. A good thing about the *business* of stripping is that it takes two to tango failure to which the one stripping in front of the one who is suited is regarded as self-degrading and self-belittling. What makes Western dominance over African countries is the whole issues of exploitation and destabilisation that trace their roots in colonial and toxic education that this volume seeks to decolonise by forcing it to treat other grand narratives equally and fairly. For example, whenever elections are conducted in many Africa countries, instead of depending on the voters to make a verdict, they depend on Western donors and observers to decide whether the said elections were credible, free and fair or otherwise. Sometimes, Western countries employ such dominance to favour the candidates or parties or stooges they believe can protect their interests even at the detriment of the citizens. What happened in Egypt soon after deposing Hosni Mubarak speaks volume. After the majority of Egyptians voted the Muslim Brotherhood in power in 2012, the West did not like this choice. Therefore, one year after Mohamed Morsi of the Muslim Brotherhood was sworn in as president, the military–backed by the West–toppled him; simply because the West did not approve or respect Egyptians' choice of the party to rule them. Profoundly, no elections in Africa can be deemed credible without being supervised and verified by Western poll observers. And thanks to this incongruity, most of democratically-elected governments serve two masters namely, the voters and their Western masters. Ironically, once Western observers give their verdict, thanks to colonial legacy and bad education, you will see those declared winners say that the elections were credible just because Western observers said so. This shows how African countries are not self-confident and how dependent they are even on deciding what is wrong and right. Who is questioning or condemning this democratic colonialism by the West? Some scholars testify to dependence that African countries have created due to colonial legacy and the dominance of Western grand narrative as espoused through education which Luce (2016) argues that forces and reinforces the stereotypification that is a simplification not only because it produces a false representation of reality, but also because it fixes it, denying difference.

Notably, this book deals with the imminent need and drive which is aimed at decolonising the current crop of education that the colonial powers left behind to work as their tool of entrenching and elongating colonialism over their ex-colonies for their advantage. I, thus, will seek to unpack and elucidate some facts and views on how to decolonise the said colonial and toxic education based on our experience as the victims of colonialism, imperialism and neocolonialism altogether. To get a hunch on the whole concept, I have defined education above and I will try as much as I can to define all terms used in this tome in order to enable the reader to grasp what we are intending to put across. We need to look at the purpose[s] of the said education in order to help the readers to be on the same page with us. Apart from defining education, the purpose of education can be defined by asking the question that Fielding & Moss (2010) ask: "What is the purpose of education?" Further, Fielding & Moss answer their question observing that "an education [is *this is mine*)] for survival and flourishing, living well and within limits; environmental, societal and individual well-being....in context of reduced inequality" (p. 15). I fully concur with this definition as far as the essence and the purpose of education are concerned. The definition contrasts the tragic-cum-toxic education colonialists introduced and thereby superimposed on their colonies and ex-colonies so as to leave behind more colonised elites who, up until now, still go cap in hand begging from their former colonial masters without feeling any guilty or shame. Therefore, the purpose of this tome is to try to help such toxic academics, politicians and the victims at large to become aware of the duty they have which is to free themselves from the limbo-cum-*cul-de-sac* they are in as the means of competently and fully participate in all activities as humans and societies. I particularly wonder, for instance, to see some African presidents, some with PhDs in in various fields, going cap in hand begging while their countries sit on huge quantities of resources such as fertile land, minerals, hardworking and health population, favourable weather you name it. You do not get it. You just wonder; how such a person can fail to constructively and effectively utilise his or her education to change this circle of intellectual bankruptcy-cum-impotence that has always resulted into many suffering to the people such an individual misrules. To me, such an education is nothing but tragic-cum-toxic; and is aimed at self-degradation, self-destruction and self-hate but not self-and total emancipation. If anything, this where the whole conceptualisation of the decolonisation and detoxification of the current colonial, hegemonic and toxic education system in all fields comes into play.

Apart from politics, education has virtually dominated, and it indeed, does, all aspects of life in the world for many generations. Every country strives to educate its citizens so that they can competently participate in its daily life, interrelate and stand among the countries of the world. There is no way one can claim legality to occupy certain positions in many professions nationally and internationally without proving her or his academic fitness. Since the world embarked on Western system of doing things, education has become a *sine qua non* as far as gaining a job legality is concerned. This is the cardinal rule-cum-standard almost everywhere on earth. The situation worsened after Africans embraced and subscribed to colonial ways of doing things such as addressing each other and, above all, thinking. Due to colonial intellectual impotence-cum-relic, Africa has had, and still has, many preposterous titles, *inter alia*, such as sir, sheik, and honourable even if those bearing those titles do no act or look like them. Despite this being the general rule, there are some exceptions to it in that people still forge their academic credentials; and thanks to corruption; such criminals get away with murder. This being the case, how, for example, a corrupt Member of Parliament (MP) or president who forged his or her academic credentials or underuses or fails to use his academic fitness can be honourable while he or she does horribly dishonorable things such as asking and taking bribes? It is a common sight, especially in corrupt and poor countries, wherein uneducated or wrongly educated people to rule others.

Moreover, academic unfitness can be traced on how people identify themselves. For example, in the cities of East Africa where Islamic culture, accidentally took precedence it is not an anomaly to hear an old man being referred to as sheik which in Swahili means *Mzee* or old man. Why using sheik instead of *Mzee* which is traditionally a Swahili title that fits elders without denoting religious denomination one is affiliated with. Again, many people–especially those who subscribe to such imported-colonial relics–would feel at home with being addressed to as sheik but not *Mzee*. Why? The answer is simple. They received colonised and toxic education this volume seeks to decolonise and detoxify. It is only the late *Mwalimu* or teacher, Julius Nyerere, Tanzania's founding father, who revolutionarily institutionalised the title of *Ndugu* which means brother[s] or sister[s] or relative[s] to typically signify equality among Tanzanians. However, he took the title of *Mwalimu* or teacher to signify that he was teaching his people, something he did to the letter. After exiting power; and his socialistic policies thereof being felled, Tanzanians are no long prone to and proud of referring to each other as *Ndugu* to signify equality, oneness and love among themselves. Instead, they are now devouring titles such as honourable, sheik, tycoon so and so and many more as a sign of divorcing brotherhood and sisterhood that Nyerere created and inculcated in them for the entire time he was in power.

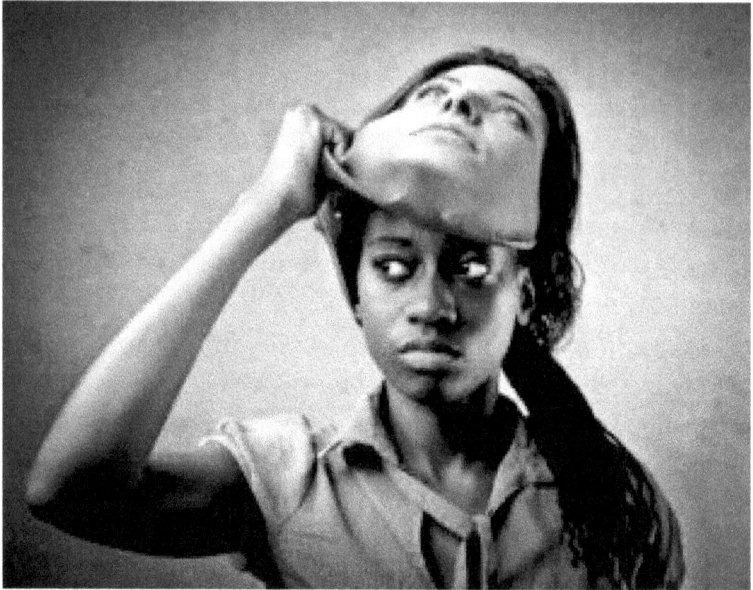

Figure 1 courtesy of readingthemaps.blogspot.com

If we look at Africa in general, apart from adopting ridiculous foreign titles, is not out of the woods yet *vis-a-vis* internalising and using fake identification. Although Africa no longer tangibly colonised, has Sirs and other colonial hangovers; and there is trend of the same magnitude whereby some people in high position of power forge academic credentials in order to be referred to or viewed as educated while they are not. Africa has many bogus professors and doctors currently who do not have any gist of such merits and qualifications they pretend and portend to have simply because the common people subscribe to such braggadocios not to mention financial entitlements that go with them. No doctor can be allowed and accepted to offer services to patients without proving that he or she has attained a required level of education. No pilot can fly a plane without proving he or she attained the required level of education, *inter alia*. But, in politics, anybody can claim to be whatever he or she wants to be and get away with murder. Apart from dupery and forgery in the modern world, education is inevitable for whoever want to occupy certain positions. The question we need to ask is: Does the current education truly serve the purpose a true education is supposed to? In some countries, there are some requirements for attaining a certain level of education for one who wants to run for some political position. However, it is not necessary that someone must be affiliated to certain political ideology.

So, you can see how education is even more vital than politics despite the fact that politics plays a great role in human's day-to-day life. Again, despite underscoring the cardinality of education *vis-à-vis* our modern lives, we need to ask ourselves: What type of education do we have and do we need to live a decent life? Does it have intellectual multivocality in that it represents all grand narratives of the world or it is just *monofocal*, monopolar and unipolar sort of education that benefits one side as it abuses another? What of multimodality as far as the inputs from everybody is concerned? Due to the inevitable nature of education, we need to carefully analyse and assess what the current regime and type of education does and offers in emancipating or making us slaves of others whose views are dominant in this education. Wright & Lubensky (2009) think that it is important to embark on collective efforts to understand and do away with or reduce prejudices in order to change the attitudes that can bring about equality. To successfully do away with injustices and prejudices, we need underscore the fact that "change in perception promoted by education and reconciliation have to proceed alongside structural reforms to prevent a return to dominant relationships" (Jeong, 2005, p. 4). Arguably, this approach needs to be taken universally in pragmatically addressing the anomalies that exist in post-colonial education in former colonies (which is a conflict in itself) where elites have become a new group of colonisers or homegrown colonialists (Mhango, 2016). I concur with the idea of decolonising education by inveigling others to understand that education should be functional in the environment of those receiving it. Adeyimi & Adeyinka (2002, 2003) cited in Mutamba (2012) and Chirwa & Naidoo (2014) underscore the role education played in precolonial African society wherein a few exceptions educational practices, African education was holistically utilitarian and was imparted through various media such as imitation, initiation ceremonies, work, play, oral literature among others. This means, precolonial African education was more of problem-solving, and was more practicable than theoretical by nature. And if you look at this type of education critically, you make sense of it. Why, for example, should one strive to know the type of the soil in the moon while he or she does not know his or her own body or the soil of his or her own planet, farm or village? How practical and utilitarian African education was can be found in the nonepareility of the person simply because one person carried many function at one time. For example, an herbalist was the same doctor, leader, artist and pharmacist whereby under Western education such roles need more than three people to carry them out. One person would have knowledge of herbs, he or she would go to the forest to identify and collect them to end up prescribing them. Coming back home from the forest, the same person (African traditional doctor) would process the herbs, prescribe and distribute them after listening to patients and do some diagnostic works. The same person would fully participate in other unrelated social activities of the day.

Also, for such multifaceted activities aimed at helping the society, African medicine people and other professionals did not charge much money as it currently is wherein many African skills were demonised and wantonly destroyed so as to depend on expensive Western medicines. Behind this whole hike and deceit, there is education which seems not to meet the test of serving all humanity equally and equitably. There is an education that does not enable people to function in their environment. If anything, one cause of Africa's dependence can be traced on the type of education it has used soon after its original education was felled.

Regarding its practicability, practicality and authenticity, African education makes more sense in that a person had to prove his or her skill[s] based on performance but not documentation. Instead of studying for certificates as it currently is whereby some people go through the system and come out without any expected knowledge, African education provided the tools and skills one wanted. And to prove that the person was qualified or educated he or she had to prove it by actions but not interviews or theoretical underpinnings. Former Zanzibar president, Abeid Karume, used to say that there is no need for interviewing those who were looking for jobs. Instead, you just give them the job to do so that you can assess them and thereafter decide either to hire them or not. Likewise, African education was foul proof in that there was no person who would forge it as it currently is in many corrupt countries. Due its availability, functionality, integrity and practicality to everybody, nobody would contemplate about forging qualifications. For, whenever anybody wanted to apply his or her skill, he or she had to exhibit it by performing what one was expected of. So, I can argue that African education was advantageous and innocuous; because it was not easy to fake. What is the situation currently under toxic education? How many fake doctors and professors do you know? Paradoxically, while Europe was groaning in diseases such as smallpox and bubonic plague, Africans, with their despised, education, were so healthy that Europeans envied them and decided to enslave them on the basis that they were stronger than Europeans. There are many traditional healers who cure injuries, especially bone fractures without taking any x-ray or metal gadgets.

In Dar es Salaam, Tanzania, sometimes in 1990s, people referred to orthopedists for amputation were smuggled out of hospitals to be cured by traditional healers in cases where Western-trained expert doctors failed. Evidentially, such practices still prove how the utilitarian nature of Africa education practically works. Mawere (2011) notes that "there is monumental literature by philosophers like David Hume, George W.F. Hegel, Immanuel Kant, Lucien Levy Bruhl & Diedrich Westermann that describe Africans as 'tabula rasa', a people with no reason/rationality; hence without a history and worse still philosophy" (p. 1). It nauseates and goads whoever comes across such nonsense not to mention how it boggles the mind, and abhors the rationale of the so-called modernity which, in actual fact, denotes Western ways of doing things–that keeps on maintaining the same stance even when things have changed to empirically show that Africans had knowledge, science and philosophy just like any other community. Mhango (2015) argues that nobody can export intellect to another. Instead, everybody can export and import some skills and knowledge but not intellect. He, too, goes further arguing that no society has its unique self-dependent skills in entirety. For, all societies on earth have been copying from; and lending some skills, science and technologies to each other since time immemorial.

I argue that African education was based on the African environment and African culture. This is why I strongly propose that Africa needs to salvage what is left of what African education systems used to be before the coming of colonial toxic education system that left Africans tarnished, confused and typically stereotyped as ignorant and backward. The retrieval of precolonial African education can give us a clue of how African traditional education (as it is sadly called) was, and the way it benefited the society. For, there was no joblessness or desperation for its recipients. African society did not have any prejudice with the colonialists when they arrived. Even when they butchered African epistemes, Africans did not immediately react with counter-violence. Instead, through what African societies thought would be mutual understanding; they welcomed colonialists and their ways. However, the double-faced colonialists did not reciprocate. Also, this means: all human beings have their inherent knowledge however different it seems from others. To understand how Africans functioned well before the introduction of colonialism and its toxic and hegemonic education, we need to firstly appreciate the fact that they had their ways of educating one another suitable to their needs, time, and environment. Thus, it is noteworthy to interrogate the type of education Africa had instead of denying, ignoring or oversimplifying its existence. African or traditional education system was intended to deliver results quickly due to the needs of the time. I think to try to force African education system to look like Western is to miss a point given that the two societies lived in different environments and their needs and goals were different too as were their epistemes. So, too, forcing the similarity is a colonial tendency. Even Muslim world's education from which Western education loaned was not the same as the latter. Due to being written by colonisers, there are some important aspects of education from Africa that were left out purposely in order to portray Africa as uncivilised. As I shall show later, the art of writing as a medium of communication is not new to Africa. Apart from African writing systems, there were so many sites with parietal art that showed how Africans lived and passed their information to the next generations. Famous rock paintings can be found in Kondoa-Irangi (Tanzania) (Ndembwike, 2006); Chongoni (Malawi), wall paintings Chisungu, Malawi; and Mbala (Zambia) (Zubieta Calvert, 2010). Historically, Africa produced the first written language. This is because Egypt, the first human civilisation is found in Africa; and thus Egyptian scripts are among the most ancient writing systems in the world (Barton, 2017).

True, African education system might have concentrated more on praxis than theories and written epistemological niceties, and of course, complexities to make it sound like or compete with the hegemonic Eurocentric one. Some people might wrongly translate education as the art of writing and reading only while it is more than that. However, this is not the case with many African societies. Evidentially, Africans had their own scripts as I will prove later; they did not espouse the art of writing as their only means of representing their views and knowledge. They crammed and repeated by feats almost everything that was vital for their livelihood and survival. Apart from Africans, arguably, Arabs had more advanced written knowledge than Europeans who scoped many inventions from them.

Again, after the introduction of colonial education which, is, basically aimed at breaking down the social division by producing labourers and workers for colonialism but not liberation (Chisholm & Leyendecker, 2008). The utilitarianism of African education was purposely felled and gave room to toxic and colonial education which would make Africans wantonly and pointlessly dependent as it later happened indolent so as to force us contemplate about deconstructing the current education. African education was aimed at solving day-to-day problems as it envisaged future ones; and it produced self-sufficiency and self-reliance to the individuals and the society. To the contrary, in most cases in Africa, the current regime of education produces dependent and inept professionals who cannot perform the same roles the product of utilitarian education produced. Refer to how Africa has always lagged behind as far as advancement and development are concerned. It is simple; Africa has never used its grand narrative to define its advancement and development. Instead, it is using West's yardsticks. It becomes even harder now—many African countries have to heavily depend on the West for almost all of their needs—for example, medicines after butchering their multipurpose-medical practices resulting from

African education. There is evidence that utilitarian education system in Africa made it prosperous and self-sufficient but not rudderless as its detractors define it. Refer to how Africa was more stable and stronger economically than after being colonised. Refer to how Africans were healthier than others because slave masters tried to enslave other peoples in other continents to no avail so as to settle on Africans. Refer to how Africa survived without begging or borrowing. There are those who claim that the coming of colonialism improved the lives of Africans, especially in wellbeing which is totally wrong. If Africans were sick and diseased as the West has always strove to portray them, how would they be sick and be able to provide slaves where others failed? Economically, Africa had never lived by depending on anybody except itself. Such evidence cannot be easily concealed, erased, gainsaid or ignored forever.

I chose the above statements and facts to suitably represent my views on the theme on what type of education we should buy into in our efforts to decolonise the current education system the West had dominated for many years. I, therefore, for example, espouse education that is ontologically and epistemologically based on the environment and needs of the recipients. This is what African education system used to be before the introduction of colonial-cum-toxic education system that rendered our people academically impotent so much that it left them tarnished, confused and typically stereotyped as ignorant and backward. When I claim that our people were left impotent, it must be clear that colonisers gave them knowledge and skills that they could not use to be self-reliant; and that failed them from applying such knowledge and skills to emancipate Africa from the dependency it has been since acquiring independence. I am talking of the type of education and skills that many Africans acquired without making them rebel against colonialism and whatever *status quo ante*. This is why such education is called to question as far as the emancipation of Africa is concerned. Apart from presenting the weakness of the toxic-colonial system of education, the above statements give us a clue on how African or traditional education–as it is sadly called–was; and the way it benefited the society as far as "mutual understanding" and reduction of prejudice are concerned. There was no joblessness or desperation in Africa for those who acquired it before the introduction of colonialism and its brand of toxic education that taught Africans to hate and abuse their own ways of life. Practically, African society did not have any prejudice against the colonialists when they arrived. This is because their education was rooted on equality, humanity, mutuality and justice as opposed to the latter which espoused, *inter alia*, colonialism, racism, slavery and exploitation. Even when they butchered its educations system, Africa did not suspect anything. Instead, through what African societies thought would be mutual understanding based on reciprocity; welcomed colonialists and their ways. However, double-faced colonialists did not reciprocate positively. Also, this testifies to the fact that wherever there are human beings there is knowledge however different it may seem from others. To understand how Africans functioned well before the introduction of colonialism and its toxic and hegemonic education, we need to firstly appreciate the fact that they had their ways of educating one another that were suitable to attending their needs at the time, and in their environment.

Moreover, it is noteworthy to interrogate the type of education Africa had instead of denying, ignoring or oversimplifying its existence. Secondly, African or traditional education system–as colonial education called it–was intended to be an education for actions not for theories due to the needs of the time. I think to try to force African education system to look like Western is to miss a point given that the two societies lived in different environments and had different aspirations and needs. And in consequence, their needs and goals were different too as were their education systems. To know how difficult, it is to use one's yardstick to evaluate another education, try to evaluate Western education using African educational yardstick and vice versa.

Arguably, African education system might lack theoretical underpinnings, written epistemological niceties, and of course, complexities to make it sound like or compete with the hegemonic Eurocentric one. Again, it is not supposed be measured by Western yardstick that needs to be de-essentialised. For, it is a superimposition whose vision creates the othering of others (Bekerman & Zembylas, 2011). Education must be evaluated and measured by its applicability and functionality in addressing and solving the problem of those espousing it in their environment. Jaundiced people and detractors might wrongly translate education as the art of writing by ignoring the fact that education is the way of imparting, inculcating, transferring and acquiring some new skills and knowledge from; and based on whatever media and source given that such skills and knowledge help in addressing and solving some needs and problems respectably. Education can be obtained through studying in the class, observing without necessarily attending the class and through experience of living a certain life which enables a person to acquire experience, expertise and savviness in certain areas of study or challenges. Poignantly, much emphasis is currently put on education by way of attending classes and getting certification thereby. However, this was not the case with many African societies before the arrival of colonialism in which education was obtained by the means of living and experiencing the challenges the societies faced. Despite the fact that there are some African societies that had their own scripts as I will prove later, Africans did not espouse the art of writing as their only means of representing their views and knowledge due to being able to cram and memorise almost everything that was vital for their survival and livelihood. It was possible for Africans to keep the knowledge because they applied their knowledge and skills every day in their daily challenges and chores. Even if we consider the importance of written scripts, I can argue that Arabs had more advanced written script as means of keeping knowledge than Europeans who scoped many inventions from them. Africans were not alone in keeping their knowledge at their chests.

Like Africans, Eskimos, too, did not institutionalise the use of written means of acquiring education or communication due to the ways they kept their history and information. Alia (2008) maintains that the Eskimo preserved the vestiges of their families and society through memorisation, which was the same situation in Africa despite having some writing systems as indicated above. Such an observation makes sense however not to everybody. For those coming from the societies that keep their knowledge at heart, such a thing is logical, normal and possible. To the contrary, for people from the societies that put everything in writing, it can be a whole new ball game. For example, close-knit societies did not need writing skills or say to read identity cards for its bearer to be recognised because everybody knew everybody. Thus, identification was based more on knowledge and connection of another than carrying Identity Cards, which can be seen as a weird thing today. Similarly, the IDs can nowadays be forged as opposed to interconnectivity and interdependency that cannot be tampered with in any form. Again, if we ask ourselves why we have to carry IDs, we might understand why other did not carry them and vice versa. Firstly, with a small and close-knit; and interconnected population–in which everybody knows everybody–there was no need for a person to have to carry an ID. Secondly, trust among people–who actually and truly know one another–is likely to be higher than big centers or cities where it is impossible to know all residents. So, we need to appreciate that carrying IDs is not a sign of advancement but the necessity of time and lifestyle in a certain environment which is now the *sine qua non* for matters of security and functionality of the society however forgeable they are. Here the population dictates what to use for identification. Why is carrying readable IDs is seen as advancement and education while being able to recognise almost all members of the society is not? To me, both ways of operating in the society are acceptable all depending on the needs and the setting of a particular society. There is no way one can laugh at a person who knows her or his way but doesn't know how to read a written map? We need maps because we do not know the way; and we do not need the map because we know the way.

If we consider Eskimo's example above, we will find that in spite of having no scripts, they were able to memorise and differentiate many names of snow which non-Eskimos are unable to conceptualise apart from just taking snow for granted by calling it just one name, snow. Even by writing such names down, it still is hard for such people in regards to understanding them. If one of the characteristics of modern education is the complexity of its setting, why doesn't this apply to Eskimo's way of conceptualising, *inter alia*, one concept snow? I think Eskimos purposely want their knowledge and the way it can be imparted to be simple as much as it can be for them to understand and utilise it. The situation was the same for

Africa. This is why the two societies made education available for whoever wanted it without charging whoever seeks it or complicating it as it is in Eurocentric education. To me, having many names for the same things has some more scientific underpinnings even if the said concept is not recorded anywhere except in the heads, hearts and minds of the user[s] than not. This is striking. It is ridiculous that those who portray their education as complexified fail to see such complexity. Don't they see it; or they just pretend not to see it in order to justify their assertion not to mention making their own *advanced* and *complexified*? You cannot underestimate such a people with such unwritten and complicated way of keeping records simply because it does not look like yours, or it does not justify your dubious assertion. It baffles to learn that Eskimos have many words for snow. Boaz (1966) cited in Lupyan (2012) posits that "even if there were a large number of [word] roots for different snow types in some Arctic language" (p. 262) it will be harder for non-Arctic people to comprehend. There is no way anybody can know snow more than Eskimos who, since their creation, have been surrounded by it. This is the feature that is living in their environment. They know snow more than anybody who is not living in their environment. Consequently, nobody can teach Eskimos how to define the snow. Instead, Eskimos can teach non-Eskimos about the snow and their environment. However, just like the Eskimo's naming of snow, "primitive" and "underdeveloped" African education system–as colonialists like to derogatorily call it–may be wrongly conceptualised, it still had some many important aspects that we cannot gainsay or non-African pretend to know more than African themselves. It is argued that through their education, Africans were able to live peacefully without states as Lonsdale (1981) cited in Schatzberg (2014) notes that the art of living together peacefully is Africa's contribution to the world; also see Justice (2011). Such a prerogative makes sense given that the said states were superimposed on Africa and ended up dividing Africans. Obviously, Lonsdale does not hide his ignorance about how African empires or kingdoms, and nations were made. Africans had their system of ruling based on kingdoms and communities all depending on what a society chose to govern itself.

Evidentially, Africans lived in nations which Europeans wrongly narrowed down to kingdoms such as Mwenemutapa, Buganda, Bunyoro-Kitara, Asante, Songhay, Luba-Lunda and many more. To Africans, the so-called kingdoms by Europeans were but nations just like Queendoms like Britain and Holland are today. It is sad to note that many academics fail to appreciate the concept of nation, *inter alia*, in African context compared to European one due to undermining the orality of many African epistemological concepts. This is why I encourage African historians to document this aspect in order to bring to the fore many concepts African philosophy has that are not well known or misconstrued currently.

To do away with the current academic crudity, rigidity and toxicity, worthy education needs to dig deeper down history and come up with the true history of the world so that stereotyping of one society by another could be ended as means of creating equality and equity aimed at reducing tensions that generate cultural conflicts whose results have been the rise and surge of terrorism currently. It defeats the meaning of academia when one epistemological sources or settings are seen as being better than or superior to others. Sometimes, it boggles the mind to find that half-baked and doctored findings such as those despising and demonising African history are accepted as researches while true researches would not alter the findings. Instead, as per the rule, any true research has to present the facts as found *mutatis mutandis* but not otherwise. I wonder to find that the so-called enlightened European elites are the same that called other civilisations uncouth or savagery and whatnot something that has produced many conflicts, especially after those originating from these cultures or societies realise the hoax behind the current history written by the current hegemonic grand narrative of the West that demonises others, particularly Aboriginal people in various parts of the world. Such a desire to decolonise episteme is, especially indispensable now. In addressing this anomaly in this chapter, I am going to use questions, storytelling and other means to show the importance and the needs for decolonising the current education.

The decolonisation of education provides an impetus for seeing things the way they are instead of seeing them with the lenses of toxic education as it dictates us to do. We will be able to see a clear picture of the conflict this volume seeks to address for the good of the whole world. We stand to learn from a new version of decolonised education, mainly in conflict resolution for example. And this is important given that we will be able to erase all anomalies, bigotry, lies and fabrications the current regime has inculcated in many people, specifically its prescriptive nature as opposed to elicitive model of conflict resolution education (Loode, 2011), utilitarian and observatory approaches under a new regime of decolonised education.

Again, this is a challenge of its kind given that we are dealing with an established system posed to gain from its existence even if it means to achieve that through victimising others as it has been the case since its introduction to the world. Normative as it may seem, decolonised education needs to turn a page and focus on how to objectively treat those anomalies marring it due to its nature of drawing from many discipline which also are mudded by bigotry, lies, fabrications and stereotypical things as I will show later. I, basically will base my findings and questions on history among others. History will play a great role in proving the point that Indigenous people–who were, and still are affected by the current regime of toxic education–indeed, had their own functioning educational systems based on their aspirations and environment. We understand that the current regime of education has failed because it has created more problems than solutions. Such problems can be seen on many faces such as the increase of violence, poverty, exploitation, ecological degradation consumerism and whatnots. New deconstructed education based on the needs of all in the world, will be nourished by the desire to live in a just, equitable, equal and peaceful world. So, whatever is argued in this chapter, however it might be regarded or misconstrued, is aimed at finding the truth by facing reality in order to successfully make the case that might attract, provoke or make some feel guilty. In so doing, this volume seeks to make many African academics create the need of embarking on the journey of decolonising education as harbingers for decolonisation of other fields.

Education that undoubtedly leads to peaceful life and peacefulness is more important than the one that leads to chaos and violence however "civilised" and "advanced" it may wrongly and arrogantly portend to be as the current hegemonic education is. Ngugi cited in Smith (2013) notes that even the language of disseminating knowledge has been universally colonised and maintained since colonial time; and the West would like this chicanery to remain uninterrupted and uninjured as it is so as to keep on exploiting, impinging and imposing on others. To crown it all, whatever the West does is referred to as modern, academic, scientific, universal and well researched even if it is not true. You can see this in their religion. Is Christianity scientific and modern with all its baggage of improbable and provable ignorance? Even colonialism was; and still is barbaric but not civilisation or modernity or anything near.

I am trying to prove how hegemonic-cum-toxic the current education is. In so doing, I will briefly touch on the concept of research that has been used to dupe and hoodwink many people in colonised countries including academics and politicians. My experience in post-graduate studies in Canada informs me that the dominant grand narrative, by using its education system which is biased, seeks to extract data from non-Western countries by putting more emphasis on how to conduct research but not on why conducting research and export it to Western countries or institutions which is theft be it academic, intellectual or just mere research. I may argue. Currently, the West is still colonising other non-Western world intellectually by robbing it of its data. You can even argue that such intellectual conspiracy enhanced by spying Africa, for example, under the pretext of research which is purposely aimed at not only colonising it but also bullying and degrading it, especially in this century of the so-called advancement and globalisation. Mamdani (2011) nicely observes that "the global market tends to relegate Africa to providing raw material ("data") to outside academics who process it and then re-export their theories back to Africa" (p. 13). Notably, Mamdani is not a skinny academic. He is one of the gurus in social science that has contributed immensely. This is the man who has authored over a hundred renowned academic pieces of work. So, his claims are credibly from the person who has lived and seen it all as far as academics robbery

27

is concerned. Considering the title of his work, fundamentally, Mamdani's argument is about the life Mhango (2015) refers to as the chicken life whereby the chicken produces what it does not eat and eats what it does not produce. Once such data are taken out of Africa and being processed by injecting poison and be brought back to Africa, you cannot call it the original thing it was before being extracted and being exported so as to be imported back to where to it was mined. Thanks to toxic education, our academics and leaders do not query and stop such an anomaly which is negatively impact on Africa as far as intellectual future is concerned. If the West has always hidden and exorbitantly charged whoever who want to conduct research there, why is Africa allowing the same to come and rob us wantonly? You wonder to see Western pharmaceutical companies coming to Africa and use Africans as guinea pigs. Once the same succeed in developing a cure of the diseases researched on for free, they sell their products exorbitantly to the same continent whose guinea pigs enable them to discover whatever medicine. I wonder why many African academics and politicians can make do with such criminality in the name of research.

Regarding global market involving research, let us make it clear. What Mamdani means with global market is nothing but Western intellectual conspiracy against other non-Western countries, chiefly the so-called third countries. This appeals very strongly; particularly if we consider that almost all markets of everything internationally are based in the West. Such abuses and misuses of education cannot be left to continue without questioning even deconstructing the very education. The world is now pregnant with researches. Some consumed a lot of money; and they have never been worked on. Some of the researches are influenced by those funding the projects they seek to probe. Lesser, Ebbeling, Goozner, Wypij & Ludwig (2007) disclose that industry funding of nutrition-related scientific articles may determine the results of the researches. This means that the so-called research in such circumstances is nothing but a hoax referred to as research while in the matter of fact it is the will of the companies that is dressed as research in order to dupe the consumers. And this is obvious that toxic education always aims at making money which is different from African education that aimed at providing services as the right of every member of the society. People educated under African education were not allowed to sell their services because everything belonged to the society which was basically collectivistic by nature.

As for corrupt research and cooked results based on either extracting data from other countries, there is another ugly side, especially where pharmaceutical companies want to dubiously and easily mint and print money. Laurie & Wolfe (2012) argue that poor people in postcolonial countries whose majority are the people of colour need to be protected from such exploitative and harmful researches. This is the reality of today's research under exploitative and toxic education. To do away with biases resulting from research funding and the production of contrived results, there must be agreed standards of conducting research. This will help poor countries to do away with endangerment and exploitation many pharmaceutical companies have always perpetrated against them. Thanks to such corrupt and imperial researches, poor countries are easily turned into guinea pigs for the benefits of the so-called developed world which is done at the detriment of poor countries or the so-called third world countries. Again, once such criminality committed under the banner of research is committed, it is called science. Sometimes, it becomes useless to blame without putting measures in place to counter such a "form of scientific misconduct" (Okonta & Rossouw, 2013) as espoused by toxic education the dominant grand narrative champions. If we really face it, what type of science is this that is exploitative and discriminative? One may wonder and ask; why they do this. Petras (1993) cited in Terrebonne (2008) provides an answer by defining cultural imperialism as "the systematic penetration and domination of the cultural life of the popular classes by the ruling class of the West in order to reorder the values, behavior, institutions, and identity of oppressed peoples to conform to the interests of the imperial classes" (p. 3). Petras' observation is crystal clear that the current regime of education will never benefit Africa without being decolonised and detoxified altogether. And this duty is squarely on the shoulders of African and pro-African academics only, especially due to the fact that African politicians have failed completely in addressing this anomaly. However, Smith (2013) argues that recently, some researches have started to document some of Indigenous nuggets such as education however slowly and a few. If anything, this is the hunch that African academics need to seize and use to emancipate their continent. Bishop (1990) provides an example of some societies such as Igbo, and Incas which were able to "handle large numbers in sophisticated ways if the societal needs" (p. 54). When science is mentioned, the first thought goes to Greece. Ironically, there was no way Greece would excel in mathematics and science in general without the help of Egypt (Joseph, 2010). I do not think that many pupils in African schools know such a reality, especially those majoring mathematics and science. One of the ways of detoxifying the current education system is to bring such hidden fact to the fore by promoting them in order to build self-confidence in African youth and coming academics. For, such nontoxic researches show that every society has its science and way of solving problems. This can be seen on the fact that all colonised societies used to live independently before the introduction of colonialism. Despite such realities being out there, they are not taught in African schools due to the fear that toxic education inculcated in African leaders and academics. Again, it is a few researches, especially in social science that aim at emancipating the oppressed. Academics such as Berg and Lune aim at telling the truth about traditional ways of doing things as the means of empowering the victims.

As I will later show, there is not only greed and rust with regards to concealing true Africa history and science but also racism as far as some researches are concerned. This can address another issue as to why many policies forced into African countries by the International Monetary Fund (IMF) and the World Bank (WB) *vis-à-vis* structurally adjusting their economies have always failed despite being touted that they were researched on. Despite such oft-failures, African countries–thanks to fake and toxic education–have never questioned why such *researched policies* have always failed. Instead, they have always been blamed whenever things went wrong. This is the juncture at which you can see the irrationality of importing experts from Western countries without exporting any as the way of reciprocity in order to exchange experience. No society can solely know everything or all things as if it is the society of gods. Similarly, no society can be ignorant of everything or all things as if it is the society of zombies or stones. Even the society of simple creatures such as insects knows something because of having knowledge and its way of solving its problems. Why don't recipient countries question the anomaly of being dependent? The right answer lies in toxic education that has turned some of its recipients into zombies who are perpetually at home with the disgrace of being recipients without questioning it or asking themselves as to when they will reciprocate to those offering handouts they call aid. Once again, the current toxic education creates a society of chickens on the one hand and the society of saviours on the other hand. This is wrong for both sides arguably. For, it reinforces colonialism, slavery and racism that allow one part to use another as guinea pigs in its researches as indicated above.

In a word, true scientific researches are supposed to know no colour or economic status; they are supposed to empowering but not disempowering and exploitative. Fundamentally, this is what true education must mean and be about. It is supposed to show positive and constructive differences between who attained and who did not attain it. Education is supposed to act as the soap or a cleansing agent to differentiate those who went through and those who did not go through it. Scientific researches are supposed to be based on neutrality but not commercial interests. Characteristically, any research must purposely aim at empowering people; but not exploiting or using them as guinea pigs in order, for those funding the research, to make a killing even if doing so results to suffering for other innocent people. Despite such assertion being the way forward in social science, the International Financial Institutions (IFIs) mentioned above, have not done so; and they are not ready to do so. As argued above, the victims who are led by the so-called academics and enlightened ones do not have guts to question such an incompatibility that has–for a long time of course–negatively affected their countries in almost all spheres of life. For, when the economy of a certain country is negatively affected, all spheres of live are equally affected. What the IFIs superimpose on poor countries is a disaster. Despite alleging that their policies are researched, they tied in what Mamdani (2007) argues that:

31

The World Bank's notion of a flat world, sans history, can only entrench a global division of knowledge whereby research is concentrated in a few technologically advanced countries—the knowledge-driven economies—with its results disseminated to the majority of humanity living in market-driven economies and therefore fit to be no more than passive consumers of knowledge with no other future to look forward to than that of clones (xvi).

When knowledge is concentrated–as it has been under the current dominant grand narrative–in the hands of a few technologically advanced countries, what surely follows is academic neocolonialism. You can see this not only on dissemination of or education systems but also in practices and researches whether conducted by academics or independent firms such as the IMF or the WB. *Exempli gratia*, you can see this in the IMF's or the WB's policies. Whatever good name such disastrous policies may be given, it is nothing but exploitative and toxic research. Its results, typically testify to that. What the IMF and the WB have done to poor countries makes me concur with Smith (*Ibid.*) who argues that exploitative research cannot replace exploitative research because doing so is nothing but a replication of the same even if it is given good and bold names. Therefore, thinking that such an action is fair is nothing but toxic and dangerous understanding-cum-undertaking. Again, those cheating others that their dominant grand narrative has answers to all the problems of the world while it is but a problem in itself, force them to swallow their lies; and thereafter, they say that justice in academia or whatever field or matter has been done. It needs the deconstruction of the current regime of education to have guts to face it; and bluntly and openly tell it to its face that what is going in is not constructive, desirable and fair. This section reminds me the discussion I had with a PhD holder friend of mine about the American Central Intelligence Agency (CIA). We were talking about terrorism after the September 11th attacks. My *enlightened* friend mentioned something that left me shocked. He said that the CIA would round up all terrorists, and hence get rid the world of this cancer. I asked him how and when. He summarily said that the CIA's mightier power as an agent of the security of the world–not the tool of the United States used to sabotage others–enables it to do just that! Nothing would have irked me just like asserting that the CIA was the agency of security for the world while it indeed is the opposite, especially if we consider the fact that the same CIA assassinated many free-thinking leaders such as Patrice Lumumba (DRC), Salvador Allende (Chile) and Jacobo Albenz (Guatemala) to mention but a few (Mhango, 2015, 2016). Due to the annoyance and disregard I showed to my friend, our discussion did not take long before, he excused himself after noticing how gullible he was. I wondered what my friend researched on in his dissertation that awarded him a PhD despite being ignorant of such simple matters. How many of such illiterates regarded as educated do we have currently? This reality aside, what transpired between 1932 and 1972 in Tuskegee, Alabama in the United States (US) on the study of the effects of syphilis in Alabama speaks volumes. Boulware, Cooper, Ratner, LaVeist & Powe (2016) note that federal funded investigators withheld available treatment from African-Americans suffering from syphilis just because of racial discrimination.

Another recent casualty of the current dominant grand narrative that espouses capitalism and despotism was Captain Thomas Sankara who staged a successful *coup d'état* in the then Upper Volta on 4 August, 1983. He changed the name to Burkina Faso or the "country of upright people" (Brezinski, 2012, p. 15) who recently proved to be upright people (not men) indeed, after toppling the stooge who toppled Sankara. On 15th October, 1987 Sankara was toppled and killed by his best friend who was stooge of the West, Blaise Compaore (Turner, 2013). Sankara's sin was the introduction of the government that wanted to make Burkina Faso self-reliant as the means of cutting down or doing away with dependence on foreign handouts. Such a move, apart from offending corrupt officials in his country, did not augur well with former colonial masters, France and other African countries whose rulers were the stooges of the West such as Ivory Coast. These three cases are but the tip on the iceberg as far as Africa's past-political landscape is concerned. Africa still has many rulers who take and obey orders of former colonial masters at the detriment of their own people. This way, Africa cannot forge ahead; and therefore true peace cannot exist in Africa without redressing colonial legacy by imposing financial fines under criminal liability on former colonial masters. Again, without decolonising education, Africa will not get brave and well brains and manpower that will stand to agitate for its rights. If the situation goes on as it currently is, the world should expect many conflicts in Africa. This is why decolonising education becomes a non-negotiable matter shall Africa aspire to forge ahead. Sometimes, I wonder how a president can go to another president to beg and feel comfortable about it. Africa's dependency arguably is manmade due to colonial and toxic education that many African leaders got so as to blind them from seeing bemoaning naked reality.

Again, if the US, which has an upper hand on the IFIs, can commit such criminality on its own people based on the so-called and perceived as scientific research, what of other countries that it is not constitutionally responsible for? All this can be attributed to toxic education. It informs us that countries must–whose grand, narratives are not incorporated in the running of the world especially in education–not trust such countries. Again, does it make sense for the world to keep on trusting such a country without having alternative measures put in place or agitating that other grand narratives be incorporated in the international superstructure? In the coming chapters I will–scantly though based on the effects of toxic education–touch on some practices related to research although they are not purely research whereby Western countries and institutions exploit poor and innocent people from pauperised countries referred to as the third world countries. What I intend to show is the fact that such exploitation has being ongoing and neither academics nor policy makers in both exploiting or exploited countries raised eyebrows either due to the double standard of toxic education or just mere ignorance if not fear inculcated in those who received the said education.

Fundamentally, all stinking dependence that the so-called poor countries have created emanates from this toxic education. Mhango (2015) queries why countries with immense resources are categorised as poor while they have such resources which are running the economies of the world. It baffles. Why–for example; if we face it– the Democratic Republic of Congo (DRC) is categorised as poor compared to the so-called superpowers simply because they have the power of weapons as opposed to resources such as those found in the DRC and in many African countries. Mhango argues academics–especially African–to rebel against this colonial system that has always shackled them based on abracadabra enshrined in toxic education.

2

The Role of True and Decolonised Education to Justice in the World Today Based on Historical Realities

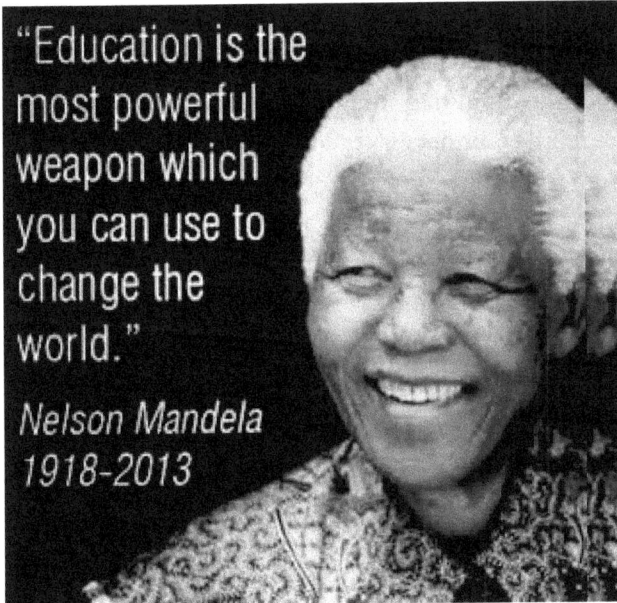

Figure 2 photo: courtesy of definyourgrid.com

Decolonisation, as we know, is a historical process: that is to say it cannot be understood; and it cannot become intelligible or clear to itself except in the exact measures that we can discern the movements which give it historical form and content Fanon, the Wretched of the Earth (1963, p. 36) cited in Tuck & Yang (2012).

This chapter is about the detoxification of colonial education which cannot come as a result of magical practices, conjectures or natural shock all devoid of facing historical realities and the realities of the time. Although the so-called modern education has contributed immensely in many areas in the world, it still needs to be decolonised in that it must accommodate other views, theories and practices from other cultures of the world. This is crucial since the contributions and successes of this sort of education, among others, were enhanced by its dominance. Had this dominance happened naturally without trampling and demonising other cultures, nobody would bother to suggest any decolonisation. We all know. Colonialism superimposed almost everything on the colonies. So, the first thing the deconstruction and detoxification of the current dominant toxic education is to do justice to its victims even to itself. By decolonising it, blames and suspicions will go away; and in their place, cooperation and trust will germinate. When such things occur, the world will work together and minimise unnecessary conflicts that have cost a lot of time and money for the world today.

To do away with the current educational toxicity, African education needs to dig deeper down history and come up with the true history of the world so that stereotyping of one society by another could be ended as means of creating equality and equity aimed at reducing or completely ending tensions resulting to cultural conflicts whose results have been the rise and surge of terrorism currently. Calling other civilisations uncouth or savage ones and whatnots is likely to produce many conflicts, especially after those originating from these cultures or societies realise the hoax behind the current history written by the current hegemonic-grand narrative of the West that demonises others, especially Aboriginal people in various parts of the world. Such a desire to decolonise the so-called modern education is, especially indispensable now when conflicts are rife in many countries that the current Western education system has always excluded so as to have no inputs in education.

In addressing cultural toxicity resulting from the feeling of superiority in this volume, I am going to address many areas in which stereotyping and negligence are high. I am doing this in order to show the importance and the needs for decolonising education based on historical realities of today as it is based, conceived and nourished by Eurocentric and hegemonic education as it was purposely created by colonialism. To avoid being regarded as anachronistic or parsimonious, I will touch on both sides namely, the colonisers and the colonised, and the dominant and the dominated in order to forge a new and mutual relationship aimed at addressing this matter intellectually, truthfully, and honestly for the good of the world. More importantly, through decolonisation of education, practitioners, professionals and academics, will be able to clearly and transparently deal with some protracted conflicts, especially in the areas not represented by the current educational regime as enacted by colonialists to suite their agendas. Consequently, there must be a need to start by revisiting the history of the victims of colonial education. The toxicity of this sort of education is still at work even today. You can, see the toxicity of colonial education even today, by any stretch, in unexpected areas as Omboki (2016) reports that:

> Students at a boys' boarding school burnt down seven of their 12 dormitories after their teachers refused to allow them to watch a football match on television on Saturday night. The Itierio Boys High School students reacted in anger after learning that they would not be allowed to watch the game between Portugal and Croatia in the ongoing European championships, Euro 2016.

It is sad to note the students who set their dormitories on fire do not know how poor their parents and country are. To them, sports are better than their future. This is the type of education this volume seeks to decolonise and detoxify so that those acquiring it must be able to become self-conscious not only about themselves but also about their surroundings. This sort of education seeks to rejuvenate utilitarianism African education had before being destroyed and poisoned after the introduction of colonialism.

Can European students replicate this simply because they were refused to watch an African football match? When I assert that African education is colonised and toxic thanks to propagandist methods its grand narrative has always employed through media and pop culture, I exactly mean this. Such pufferies revolving around fictional and mythical things have claimed many lives and minds of its victims.

To better human endeavour, decolonisation of education provides an impetus for seeing things the way they are instead of looking at them the way the lenses of toxic education dictate us to do. Through decolonised education, those who receive it will be able to see a clearer and bigger picture of the issues they want to address for the good of the whole world based on the decolonisation of education. The world stands to learn from a new version of decolonised education. And this is important given that through decolonised education Africa will be able to erase all anomalies, bigotry, lies and fabrication the current *doctored* education has, specifically its prescriptive nature as opposed to elicitive and observatory undertaking under a new regime of decolonised education. Again, this is a challenge of its kind given that the victims are dealing with an established system posed to gain from its existence even if it means achieving that through victimising others as it has been the case since its introduction to the world. Sometimes, those who it did not contaminate see things those corruptly made by this system do not see. Later, I will cite the words of the poorest and humblest president Jose Pepe Mujica of Uruguay as far as environmental menace is concerned since he can be regarded as an illiterate by Western standards simply because he does not poses certificates he would have gotten from class, yet he is a very animated philosopher many so-called educated people cannot match or rival.

Importantly, if we explore or consider African society before the coming of colonialism, for example, we find that the society was functional thanks to its type of education that sadly though is not accommodated in the current dominant grand narrative. When anybody ponders on education, he or she need to avoid Western or colonial mentality that dictates and wants everything to either subscribe to or look the way Western schools of thoughts want or the way they perceive everything. People have different lenses and understanding of things based on who they are and why they look at these things. We live in the same world; however we have many different world views of the same. Mountain for an Eskimo might have different meaning from an African living nearby humongous and tall mountains such as Kilimanjaro, Kenya or Ruwenzori to mention a few. The same applies to snow or islands in the middle of oceans and seas. As you can see, African education, as well as Indigenous epistemes that remained invisible (Kuokkanen, 2010) in various areas of the world, was utilitarian all depending on the purpose such education served.

Generally speaking, African education enabled the members of the respective societies to function in their environment swiftly according to their needs of the time. This is why colonial governments did not have to bother to bring workers to Africa to carry out their day-to-day functions. If there was a lack of workers or people to carry on day-to-day business of the government, obviously, the colonial governments would have imported their workers from home countries. This did not happen; and proves beyond any doubt that colonies had what it takes in delivering services. Again, the contributions that colonised people rendered to colonial governments were not appreciated. Instead, colonial administrators, thinkers and agents denied the existence of any kind of civilisation in Africa. Brantlinger (2004) cited in Fantina (2010) notes that "for middle- and upper-class Victorians, dominant over a vast working-class majority at home and over increasing millions of "uncivilized" peoples of "inferior" races abroad, power was self-validating" (p. 147). So, it is obvious that the British geared by their ignorance of others, bigotry, greed and lack of knowledge, purposely decided to recant any sense of humanity in the areas they colonised in order to be seen as the ones who brought civilisation while they actually exported their barbarity and duplicity. Mhango (2015) offers a good critique asking if colonialism and slavery were civilisation; and if they were, what type of civilisation is this. To him, civilisation is on and about humanity, justice, peace, truth and, above all, equality as humans or Ubuntu but not otherwise.

Even if we face the so-called modern education, where did it acquire its dominance and skills out of its traditional education system in Europe that they arrogantly baptised to be modern while it is not? Historically, colonial powers maintained their state of denial arguing that the colonies were backward; and this is why they were colonised without underscoring the truth that colonisation was enhanced by lies and the fact that Africans and other colonised people thought that colonisers were able to reciprocally do justice as their hosts were. If anything, this speaks volume as far as competence and applicability of their knowledge and education are concerned. Despite denial and fabrications, there are some truths that cannot be eternally hidden or suppressed. It is true that Africans and other colonised people taught their guests almost everything about their environment expecting them to positively reciprocate. Here the detriment for colonised people is that education was a one-way traffic wherein colonisers gained knowledge from the colonised without teaching their subject about themselves. Even where they did, they did not teach the truth but instead, they taught fabrications based on their superiority as opposed to the inferiority of the colonised.

Furthermore, to prove that African education produced competent and skilled manpower that could proficiently serve the society, colonial government did not deploy any armies of workers other than the colonised. How could colonial governments bother to bring their workers while Indigenous people were there to carry on all types of jobs that made colonial governments function well? Sadly though, this is not appreciated; and was done–*sui generis*–and deliberately in order to undermine traditional education system to sound as if it did not exist, and if it did, it was irrelevant and useless. How would colonial governments appreciate and credit such a system that saved them money and time–that would be spent on importing workers in foreign lands out of Europe–while it even failed to appreciate an already advanced system of education in their colonies in Africa? There is evidence that Africa was sometimes technologically ahead or at par with Europe as Evans (2015) notes in their book *Africa Undermined* that in the first millennium BCE which is the onset of the sub-Saharan Iron Age coincided with the equivalent development in Western Europe.

Lanning & Mueller (1979) note that when Dr. David Livingstone arrived in Africa was stunned to find that iron technology in Mozambique was way far more advanced than Britain's whose products of iron seemed "rotten" comparably. Where did this go and who felled it? Again, if the most "civilised" nation of the world admits this, how would it supposedly lead others in its deceit evidenced in colonialism and colonisation?

Britain that had many colonies, for example, is renowned for not appreciating the contributions others made to its successes based on exploiting others. This lugubrious behavior did not only apply on Africa but also others including her European cousins in Northern Ireland. Britain will never admit that Northern Ireland was as developed as Britain was before it invaded and occupied it. If you want to kill a dog just give it a bad name. Indeed, colonial academy did not only give Aboriginal people a bad name but also demonised them in every aspect of life. As if that was not enough, it gave them toxic education that perpetuated colonialism even after the colonial powers left the colonies. Colonised people were called barbarians, beasts and all bad names just because of their ways of life, culture and–of course–their land would not yield to colonialism if they were told who they actually were. If this is not corrected, identity-based conflicts are likely to emanate from them, especially at this time Africans and other Aboriginal people are more aware of themselves than they were under colonialism.

Basically, the straw that broke the camel's back for Africans came when the colonisers decided to write their history as a way of telling their stories. In telling the story of pre-colonial Africa and other colonised people, colonial writers and spin doctors–no doubts– purposely ignored the contribution Africans and Aboriginal people made all over the world. For example, it took time for the United States to admit that it learned the art of confederacy from Aboriginal people of the Americas who used this system to rule themselves as sign of democratic system. History has it that the confederacy we evidence today in Canada and the US were copied from Iroquois (Mhango, 2015) despite the US constitution and other instruments remaining silent about crediting the First Nations for helping them to reach this milestone that has defined the powers and prowess of this nation. Despite hiding and avoiding this reality, it is still there. Despite hiding and avoiding this reality, it is still there. The US had never appreciated the contribution black slaves made to its development. If there is anything hegemonic and toxic colonial education is good at is none other than copying and concealing that it copied such toxic education is good at demonising others as it glorifies itself. Amélineau cited in Diop (1989) notes:

> I then realised, and realized clearly, that the most famous Greek systems, notably those of Plato and Aristotle, had originated in Egypt. I also realized that the lofty genius of the Greeks had been able to present Egyptian ideas incomparably, especially in Plato; but I thought

that what we loved in the Greeks, we should not scorn or simply disdain in the Egyptians. Today, when two authors collaborate, the credit for their work in common is shared equally by each. I fail to see why ancient Greece should reap the entire honor for ideas she borrowed from Egypt (page not provided).

Consecutive American governments tried to conceal the contribution by the Aboriginal peoples of the US for years but they lastly decided to come out of the closet and admit how they copied confederation science from the Aboriginal peoples of the Americas they used to refer to as savages. Who is actually savage between the ones who copied and concealed and the ones who allowed others to copy and share? I am wondering. What if this type of governance that the Aboriginal peoples of the Americas used was continued without any suppression or interference? Maybe, many conflicts resulting from the aped-confederacies and constitutions would not have occurred. Maybe, the US would not have participated in dirty politics all over the world wherein many innocent leaders were toppled and killed. Maybe, the US would not have perpetrated and supported apartheid for many years. Maybe, the world would have more security and democracy today than it currently has. Why don't we go back and salvage what is left to see how it can help us to forge ahead in decolonising the current Eurocentric epistemes and techne? Again, why did the US government plagiarised the concept from others while knowing that doing so was against neoliberal ethos governed by copy rights?

It is only in Africa where the mummified bodies that have endured the punishment of the element for thousands of years are found, in Egypt. King Tutankhamun (Tut) is a living example of how Africa was advanced scientifically. Remember king Tut ruled Egypt before it was conquered by modern times Arabs who destroyed the noses of the mummies in order to erase African heritage. Those who deem Africa uncivilised tried to arabise everything that has to do with ancient civilisation in Egypt. Again, they forgot one fact that pyramids were not only in Egypt. The *Encyclopaedia of Ancient Myths and Culture* (2003) notes that "there are in fact remains of about 80 pyramids in Egypt, while there are well over 100 later, less substantial ones in the Sudan" (p. 512) not to mention the great houses of stones of Zimbabwe. Additionally Granville (2008) discloses that "the Nubian region, an ancient civilization with palaces, temples, and pyramids (tombs) flourished as long ago as 7000 B.C.E. As many as 223 Nubian pyramids were discovered in the ancient cities along the Nile in Sudan (Kerma, Napata, Nuri, Naga, and Meroe), which is twice the number of pyramids in Egypt" (p. 472). Although biased Western and Arab writers tend to credit Egypt for its civilisation, the truth is that Sudanese too must be credited for participating in building such ancient civilisation. For, sometimes, in the history of the two countries, kings from both sides conquered and defeated each other. Habashi (2015) notes that

> Around 1000 BC, following the collapse of the New Kingdom of Egypt (1555-1090 BC), the Nubian kingdom of Kush emerged as a great power in the south on the Nile. Sudanese kings conquered and ruled Egypt. They seized Thebes and eventually the Nile Delta. By about 300 BC the center of the kingdom had shifted south to the Meroe (p. 88).

In concurring with Habash (*Ibid.*), Bonnet & Valbelle (2008); Draper (2008); Cornelius (2010); and Morkot (2013), *inter alia*, note that Nubian or black pharaohs once ruled Egypt. Evidently, Western science scooped from Egypt so as to come up with temporal embalmment that cannot be equated with the traditional Egyptian mummification. So, too, this testifies to the truth that Africa helped others, especially the current hegemonic regime of knowledge of which the West boasts.

Moreover, Buncombe (2010) notes that Al Karaouine in Fez, Morocco—founded in 859 AD and considered the world's oldest, continually-operating university, and Cairo's Al Azhar University (975 AD), were established in Africa and they are predated by a Buddhist university of Nalanda. And this is not the end of Africa's indelible marks on the so-called modern science. The Egyptian pyramids and the mummies in them are another stunning mystery that, up until now, has never been resolved. Arguably, there is no modern-scientifically advanced building on earth that is at par with the pyramids. Equally, the chemicals that were applied on the mummies have never been deciphered. Belmonte (2001) maintains that "hieroglyphic in the tombs of nobles and workmen offers little information about the pyramids themselves, about how they were built, or about the corpus of beliefs surrounding it" (p. 4). Basically, the pyramids are still mythological and cosmological wonders to the modern world of *advanced* science. What makes the pyramids a hard nut to crack for modern scientists is the fact that there is no evidence of whatever type of machinery that was used to mount mega blocks of rocks on top of others. As for the mummies, Byyny & Houston-Ludlam (2016) disclose that:

> Ancient Egyptians, led by Imhotep, recorded details of their medical procedures on papyrus, and made important observations in human anatomy. They performed surgeries, set fractured bones in place, performed amputations, sutured large gaping wounds, and bandaged injuries and wounds. They immobilized injuries using splints, plaster, and tape, and incised and drained abscesses. They knew the properties of many plants that could be extracted and used to treat maladies—many of which are still used today. (p. 7); also see Baker & Judd (2012).

Those accusing Africa of being backward scientifically, without underscoring such findings, must have their knowledge and motives called to question. Patil (2012) cites Kahun; Edwin Smith; Ebers, Hearst; Erman; London, Berlin; and Chester Beatty who note that there are eight major ancient Egyptian medical papyri or volumes dating from 1900BCE to c 1200BCE (p. 23) all originating from Egypt. Ironically, those papyri are given European names but not Egyptian or African names to show how European scientists and historians are good at copying without offering any attribution to the original authors of the volumes. Patil (*Ibid.*) notes that behind those stunning discoveries there was one of African famous scientists and administrator, polymath Imhotep whom Osler cited in Faraday (2013) refers to as "first figure of a physician to stand out clearly from the mists of antiquity" (p. 132). Here I am talking about Imhotep, a scientist. There are famous writers who helped Romans to conquer the world such as Quintus Septimius Florens Tertullianus, St. Augustine of Hippo (*jus bellum iustum*), among several. Arguably, Western countries did not only copy from Africa and other ancients civilisations that predate Western one but robbed them as Bidgood (2001) argues that "these artefacts and products are ow deposited in the Economic Botany Collections of the Royal Botanic Gardens, Kew, UK together with plant-based handiwork from all over the world" (p. 311).

Another evidence to substantiate that Africa was not impotent and backward as the current dominant grand narrative has maintained through its toxic and colonial education is the fact that when invaders arrived in Africa and other places of the world they claimed to conquer, they found that these societies were organised, and partly in some places, advanced empires, states and institutions which fiercely resisted the occupation. This is why colonial powers had to depend on weapons, lies, pitting people against others to succeed. Education was for practical purposes based on the environment one faced in his or her day-to-day life. Education was for self-reliance and self-actualisation as a person and society without endangering other people or societies. This is why it was easy for European colonial powers to be welcomed with the thought that they were as civilised as their hosts were which turned out not to be. Indeed, this type of education was more helpful, multipurpose in nature and approach, and more practical than colonial one. Africans used to learn about their environment; and the way they could utilise it well and peacefully and function well as they did before the coming of colonial powers. This is evident in the fact that there is no recorded history of dependency in Africa before the coming of colonial powers. Practically, Africans were educated, and their education enabled them to function without depending on other countries like it is currently due to the introduction of toxic Western education aimed at subduing and exploiting them. For example, Western writers do not credit the Swahili coast for being the harbingers of house hospitality and use of stones to build cities which were scattered on the East African coast (Wynne-Jones, 2016). Didn't the Swahili Coast contribution namely, the concept of hospitality which is the precursor of hotels the world is proud of today? Who talks about medieval coins and artifacts colonial Europe robbed and stashed in its museums? What evidence will one need that is more accurate and real than this to substantiate that assertion that Africa was uncivilised, underdeveloped and backward? Going on with such insults will create more conflicts. Assertion that Africa was backward and uncivilised was a malicious hoax aimed at undermining it so that Africa could lack self-confidence, and thus, submit itself before Western exploitation as the current grand narrative maliciously and wrongly espouses through Eurocentric education.

Before the coming of European invasion and occupation, African societies were divided in administrative strata wherein every member of the society had the role to play in the society and his or her contribution was vitally appreciated. There was no chaos or vacuum at all save the existence of normal competitions among states and societies. Again, whenever conflicts occurred, African societies had their conflict resolution mechanisms they use either to contain, manager or resolve such conflicts. For instance, in Asante, Buganda, Mwenemtapa and elsewhere, some well advanced and strong empires were in existence; and their interests, basically were to equally trade with the foreigners thanks to having many resources such as timber, minerals and animal products. You cannot call such people or societies backward or underdeveloped. If these empires were underdeveloped or backward–as Western historians and thinkers like to wrongly assume–then there would not have been anything whatsoever for Western invaders to benefit from or do with such societies. When they came to Africa–for example–Western invaders found that some skills and institutions such as iron smelting, salt making, knitting, and bargaining had already taken shapes for many decades if not centuries. How were Africans–for example–able to trade with India, China and the Middle East if they were such underdeveloped and backward if we face it?

This link hereunder is rich and gives more descriptions on the nature of what African education and civilisation produced. *https://www.youtube.com/watch?v=9VtIk1masqU*. This link is about the documentary about the Great Zimbabwe, one of the lost and old civilisations; and the way white intruders wanted to purposely mislead whom it belongs to alleging that it either belonged to the Queen of

Sheba or King Solomon to match their biblical assertion. Additionally, the documentary tells how white invaders maliciously ravage and vandalised the Great Zimbabwe ruins as the means of concealing and destroying African history.

However *primitive*–as are always referred to–such education systems enabled Africans to live without depending on handouts and loans from the so-called developed countries whose development is the result of exploiting and plundering Africa wantonly for many decades. Arguably, uncontaminated and self-reliant Africa as it was–at this time–was better than the ever-dependent African of today. The major questions one can ask are: How much wealth did colonial thieves plunder from Africa for all decades they colonised it? How much land did settlers grab from Africans under settler economy? How many innocent people–who opposed the whole project–were killed and displaced; and how much would they have contributed to the wellbeing and development of their people and the world in general? How much energy was sapped from colonised people so as to make colonial powers colossally rich? How many Africans were enslaved and used to develop Europe and the Americas? Again, one may wonder. What does this have to do with decolonisation of education? If we critically explore the milieu of conflicts resulting from poverty and institutional destruction Africa faces today, we will agree that most of them are about the control, distribution, and possibly, redistribution of resources. If the current education were rooted in solving Africa's problems, it, obviously would have addressed this problem instead of exacerbating it as it currently is whereby local elites have conspired with foreign ones to rob Africa wantonly. Many African countries found themselves facing ethnic wars based on the distribution of resources as it currently is in the Democratic Republic of Congo (DRC) where many violations of human rights have been ongoing for a long time while the West that has always fueled such wars kept quiet as it went on trading in illegal resources extracted from the DRC and other countries. Though passive as it may seem or kept under the carpet, all the same, many conflicts existing currently in many African countries resulted from greed, ignorance and power hunger aimed at controlling and trading such resources with the West. This is why the SSA, since gaining independence, is the most affected area in the world (O'hare & Southall, 2007) which has greatly contributed to insecurity and poverty in Africa.

The invasion of the DRC by Burundi, Rwanda and Uganda (Williams, 2013) can show us how Africa is prone to conflict resulting from the drive by some opportunists to control its resources. Sutherland (2011) observes that Rwanda and Uganda were controlling Congolese coltan mines "and the Congolese Ministry of Mines reported zero production of tantalum both in 1998 and 1999, and only 550 metric tons of tantalum in 2000" (p. 15). While such criminality has been ongoing, the West has kept quiet as if this is not a crime. Ironically, when Iraq invaded Kuwait on 2nd August 1990, the West did not stay aside and look. Iraq was repelled quickly due to the fact that, if this invasion was left to go on, the West would lose oil supply. So, here the crime was not the invasion but interfering in the supply of oil. Butt (2014) observes that within a short time span, the Security Council adopted Resolution 660, the first of many resolutions to condemn Iraq's actions; and demanded Iraq to withdrawal from Kuwait. Again, how many UN resolutions have ever been adopted on the DRC? Maybe, if Iraq had promised the supply of oil to the West, it would still be in Kuwait robbing as pleased as it has been the case of Rwanda and Uganda in the DRC. The case for Africa particularly is clear that the distribution of resources has become a very good source of conflict in Africa. This becomes a case because most of local elite groups that colonial education produced and put in power have either embarked on toxic ethnicity, corruption and unfair distribution of resources or kept supervising the interests of colonial masters in their countries. Berman (1998) cited in Martins (2015) argues that:

> The accumulating weight of evidence shows that African ethnicity and its relationship to politics is new, not old: a response to capitalist modernity shaped by similar forces to those related to the development of ethnic nationalism in Europe since the late nineteenth century, but encountered in distinct African and colonial circumstances (p. 7).

Practically, colonialism introduced the 'politics of the belly' (Williams, 2011) whereby ethnicity was socially constructed to suit the division of Africans so that they could be used by the colonisers easily without spending much money on armies or security apparatuses. This culminated in the introduction of 'divide and rule' championed by Lugard in modern Nigeria as it hinged on and gyrated around toxic ethnicity or whatever misunderstandings or weaknesses existed among Africans. Lugard (2013) notes that "the chiefs are keenly appreciative of our policy of indirect rule, and of the full powers they retain under their native institutions" (p. 5). One would ask: Why African accepted this rule if they were united? No society is made of angels or devils. Africa, at that time, had its own baggage resulting from normal day-to-day relationship based on competition. Given that Africans had never been threatened by any outside forces, it was hard for them to foresee what would happen after the arrival of European colonial powers whom they wrongly thought were as civilised as Africans were at the time. They thought the coming of Europeans meant business between them.

In actual fact, the drive and urge for commerce had a lot to do with the easy colonisation of many places almost all over the world. The situation was the same in the Americas even Asia. Peoples wanted new items such as guns and other belongings they deemed fit for their consumption. So, when the British and other colonialists came to Africa, they exploited this weakness the same way they did wherever they colonised.

Truly, before the coming full-fledged colonial governments, missionaries, explorers and traders had already spied the continent so as to put it under the influence of their home or mother governments that paid for all expeditions and explorations paving the way for full-fledged colonisation. By paving the way, colonial agents also made it easy for their mother countries to divide and partition Africa prior. Consequently, it must be understood. Africa and other countries that were colonised were colonised not just because they were naïve or disorganised. It was because of competition that existed among empires and societies in the precolonial African states which is normal. First of all, when colonisers invaded the places that later became their colonies, Aboriginal people trusted them thinking they were well intended the same way the host communities were. Therefore, they generously and humanely welcomed everybody who happened to visit them hoping that their guests would reciprocate equally and humanely. Sadly though, the people the hosts thought would be like them ended up being totally different as far as reciprocity is concerned. Apart from betraying their trust, the newcomers abused, misused, and violated the generosity and goodwill that the host communities extended to them. Funny enough, this abuse of generosity based on a *holier-than-thou* mind-set has been ongoing during and after colonialism. Indeed, Indigenous societies did not practice any form of racism save for those who seemed to go against the norms of the society whom the society reprimanded and regarded as an anomaly. This is why when the cunning and evil colonialists, missionaries, merchants and explorers came to those areas were accorded a warm welcome thinking they were like their hosts. Hence, Aboriginal people extended their warmly welcome to their guests hoping that they would do business and establish strong ties for mutual benefits of both parties. Just like modern governments like to invite investors, African states of that time did the same as Kelsall (2008) maintains that "before the arrival of Europeans the African continent was home to a rich diversity of political formations, out of which, with some caveats, a broad evolutionary pattern of increasing complexity and scale can be discerned" (p. 225).

Oddly, up until now, whenever a foreigner arrives in Africa, is more welcome than an African going to foreign countries. When I look at how Africans and other immigrants risking their lives to reach Europe that exploited them so as to become rich, I re-conceptualise how the situation was when colonial agents arrived in Africa. I see an antithesis to Africa's and other Aboriginal people's true generosity and upholding of human rights and equality. Kelsall (*Ibid.*) makes a strong case to prove that Africa was organised in complex empires that knew the concept of commerce and international relations.

There is evidence to attest to the fact that African empires or administrational institutions those empires had functioned well. For example, Buganda and Kitara kingdoms (as they were then known) were highly advanced compared to some European fragmented territories. Johannessen (2006) notes that:

> At the time the first Europeans arrived in East-Africa, the Buganda kingdom had a well-developed government. Not only did this create a strong attachment between the king and his people, but the Buganda kingdom also maintained a strong position towards the other regional kingdoms in the area (p. 2).

The above quotation speaks volume *vis-à-vis* the *backwardness* of Africa and all other garbage thrown at it. The kingdoms of Africa, as Johannssen (*Ibid.*) argues, were mature and advanced enough so as to have all institutions we see today and think were brought by colonisers. They had their high courts, parliaments, armies, ministries of various affairs, and, above all, awareness of the existence of other kingdoms they traded and cooperated with. Bourdillon (1991, p. 13) cited in Nhemachena (2014) discloses why such kingdoms were successful because "scholars writing about Africa have argued that a picture of the pre-colonial period as feuding chaos is incorrect as there were networks of trading links which could only have been possible in a situation of some stability" (p. 19). Nhemachena (*Ibid.*) shows how African kingdoms resolved conflicts. If they were uncivilised and disorganised as colonial powers alleged, there was no way invaders would have functions amidst chaos and disorganisation. When the first missionaries arrived in Uganda, were mesmerised by the orderliness and advancement of the kingdom so as to equate the king of Baganda (Kabaka) with their godly Adam as Green (2010) notes:

> Especially since the 1760s, when the then Kabaka created a new initiation rite brought Kintu more prominence, Kintu has held a prominent place among the Baganda as both the mythical first man—early missionaries had no problem equating him with Adam of the Genesis story—and as the first Muganda (p. 5).

How can a sane and a well-intentioned person call such a kingdom uncouth or underdeveloped? You cannot call such a person who boggled the minds of missionaries savage otherwise you must include other white savages who equated this king with their Adam. What difference is there as far as the concept of kinghood is concerned between Buganda and Great Britain whose first rulers (The house of Stuart) came to power in 1707-1714? Here I am talking about Buganda. Apart from Buganda, Franz Boaz cited in Du Bois & Akyeampong (2014) notes that Africans had already invented how to smelter and use iron at the time Europe was still satisfied with rude stone tools. Why then were they surpassed by Europe? This is a common phenomenon. Who would think that China that invented gun power would be conquered by Europe that learned the technology from China?

More evidence that proves the existence of organised states with their machinery is the fact that many African countries were colonised after signing agreements. There is no way one can sign an agreement without having representatives or knowledge to understand, at least, the process regardless whether it was right or wrong. The detriment of this action was the fact that written agreements was a foreign thing to Africans who were used to agreeing by vowing. This is why, in the field of conflict resolution, prescribing signing the agreement after mediation can sound colonial to some communities, especially whose freedom was robbed by colonialism. Signing agreements re-traumatises those whose lands were taken through written agreements. They are always suspicious of them. Colonialism is profoundly a falsehearted and violent project that would not honour its pledges. It repressed where it should have fostered, tamed instead of inspiring and enervating rather than strengthened. It succeeded in making slaves of its victims, to the extent that they no longer realise they are slaves, with some even seeing their chains of victimhood as ornamental and the best recognition possible (Nyamnjoh, 2012). Apart from being a violent project, colonialism was an exploitative and degrading project that superimposed its ego, altered some realities and fabricated some information to suit its heinous agendas. In fact, colonialism is a crime next to robbery or piracy. For, colonial governments used weapons to rob Aboriginal or Indigenous people in which process many were killed or injured and those killing them were not persecuted. This is why Europe's wealth was made illegally; and has always had blood on it. Colonial powers robbed everything for many years wantonly. They robbed the colonised almost everything including their story and history.

Along with provision of toxic education that helped the colonisers to leave their stooges in power, the West has used its fickle education system, media savviness and dominance to pedagogically and informationally colonise such countries. One of the tricks colonial education uses is to portray the West as the best while the rest are inferior comparably even if it is not true. If there is a very powerful weapon–more powerful than bombs even guns–is none other than education and media. This type of weapon needs to be reckoned with, especially where there is a simmering conflict. Politicians and protagonists in conflict know full well the power of the media. They therefore use it to their advantages. In many societies, media command a very high level of respect and academics are not only trusted but also revered. The two can, thus hugely influence and sway things the way they like all depending on the level of reception in the particular society or country. This is why media have always been in the center stage in every aspect of life of many societies under the current grand narrative. In every modern society, the media has an important and unique role to play in day-to-day life. It is used by those in power to cling on power almost everywhere in the world.

Although the media is referred to as the fourth estate and the voice of the voiceless, looking at its setting and the way it works in modern world, the truth looks otherwise. Conflict Resolution field knows well the role the media plays in conflict. If anything, the media is a double-edged sword in that it can exacerbate or manage the conflict. All depends on the angle the media take in reporting, evaluating and interpreting the situations around conflicts. In the Kosovo's conflict, Slobodan Milosevic, the then president of Serbia, among others, used the media to fuel the conflict (Bose, 2007; and Carter, Irani & Volkan, 2009). The same happened in Rwanda the same happened when Radio *Milles Colignes* instigated Hutu militias to massacre Tutsis and moderate Hutus (Thompson, 2007). Some authors who wrote about the role of media in the two cases of

Rwanda and Kosovo agree that the media played an important role–be it positive or negative–during the conflict. Academics too had the role to play in mobilising their forces. Generally speaking, the media have a very powerful and important role to play when conflict starts. It can tilt the balance either way depending on who is using it how and why.

Bombarding Africa with their versions of news written from their angles of looking and reporting things has been the tactical method the West has always preferably applied along with toxic education. Therefore, decolonising colonial and toxic education will not only do so to education but also to the media that is also colonised and toxic by the way they functions. Paik (1999) cited in Golan (2008) observes that "discussion on the lack of balance in both the flow and coverage of world affairs by western media is best exemplified by the limited coverage of the African continent by the news media" (p. 43). This has been ongoing for a long time and no media have ever been reprimanded let alone being held accountable for their mess. Poncian (2014) posits that the beliefs and mindsets of Western people are much preoccupied by the misconceptions, misrepresentations and negative images of Africa their media feed them without bothering to balance the stories on Africa. I think this is because of colonial mentality as espoused by the dominant Western grand narrative. True, many such media houses and outlets are owned and ran by the so-called professionals in the field whose education does not enable them to see the injustices they commit resulting from their propaganda, misinformation, biasness, and, above all, malice. Is there any difference between what the Western media are currently doing with colonialism? Cavalieri (2013) cited in Mhango (*forthcoming*) notes that there was an assumption in colonial Europe that Africans were either sub-humans or beasts in the jungle. Gruen & Weil (2012) note that from Aristotle to colonial Europe, "women and "inferior races" have been linked to animals and nature and "othered" in relation to "Man" and "culture""(p. 480). This speaks as to how Western minds and mindsets were and still are corrupted.

Are such media houses and media outlets that portray Africa negatively not similar to colonialism? Doesn't the education that produces such professionals toxic and colonial, especially if we consider the fact that they are behaving exactly the same manner analogous to racist thinkers such as Aristotle whom Hanke (1959); and Bracken (1979) cited in Ramose (2001) note that his definition of "man" as a rational animal, constituted the philosophical basis for racism in the West due to the fact that this definition did not include Africans? Moreover, Ramose observes that "instead, the posterity of the colonised continues to live under the burden of the conviction that the notion of "man being a rational animal" excluded African. Further, there is evidence presupposing that Africans were deemed nonhuman is the exclusion of Africa in the declaration of Universal Declaration of Human Rights (UDHR, 1948). For, it failed to categorise colonialism as the gross abuse of human rights. This is because, in the eyes of the West, blacks were not as humans as whites were. Puzzlingly, while European definition of man excluded Africans, African jurisdiction accommodated all human being regardless of race or any difference that it viewed as trivial and immaterial. This beats even missionaries who purported to teach morality to Africans while they actually were ahead of Europe in this matter. Mhango (2015) poses a good question asking if colonialism and slavery were civilisation while they were exploitative and inhumane. Further, Mhango maintains that—under Ubuntu and other Africa legal definition encompass all human beings—taught Europeans humanity practically, especially by sustaining and trusting them thinking they understood the same when they came to end up colonising Africa. Despite all such historical proofs that Africa was civilised so as to teach those purporting to bring civilisation to Africa, ironically, Western media still labour under such ignorance and malice revolving around holier than thou mentality. Interestingly, while European colonial agents commit such buffoonery-cum-crime, their countries that portray themselves as the champions of democracy and human rights do not see this; and if and when they do, it does not matter. Interestingly, what they are doing becomes a crime when other non-Western countries commit it. What a double standard!

3

Division as the Carryover of Toxic Education

Figure 3 photo; courtesy of edustank.blogspot.com

In this chapter, I explore how colonialism used education racially for the purpose of dividing, ruling and exploiting its victims perpetually. To this day, imperialism has built in this tendency so as to keep on dividing the world among worlds namely, the First World, the Second and the Third World unnecessarily. This division based on geography and economics has always exhibited a racist nature. Before proceeding, let us shed light on division as a concept. Peter Singer cited in Schmid (1996) defines racism to simply mean "the failure to give equal consideration, based on the fact of race alone" (p. 11). So, three things stand out here namely, 1) failure; 2) consideration; and 3) race. To make this argument strong, it makes more sense to define race. Race is a socially constructed way of differentiating humans based on their artificial and trivial external-biological differences such as colour, culture, history, and membership of the group. Clifford Geertz cited in Smith (2007) notes that "there is no such as thing as

59

a human nature independent of culture" (p. 35). However, still some anthropologists and biologists have vehemently refuted such characterisation of differentiation since there are no scientific molecular and other aspects that support the concept of race. So, in trying to see if racial differences exist among humans so as to busy them, we must consider the blood which is like the oil that runs our body. There is not difference with regards to blood groups among the races that were socially constructed. Even if we look at human beings biologically and morphologically, among others, they have the same numbers and types of organs, chromosomes, blood groups and needs among others. I think this is what should concern decolonised academics. You can further see this in the current organ business, colour or race does not hamper those receiving organs from receiving organ parts across race. A kidney is a kidney regardless to whether is donated by white or black. There are so many factors. You can go further in interrogating if medicinal prescription or attacks by diseases primarily and scientifically revolve around race. If this becomes scientifically hard to pursue, you can look at human needs that are identical all over the globe.

Again, the entire colonial period-cum-project in some countries evidenced illegal introduction of artificial people in the populations of the colonies. In East and South Africa, for example, Indians were brought purposely to sabotage Africans–under the ruse of division along race–these imported agents of colonialism were made to believe that they were better than Africans based on their race. So, exploiting or discriminating against them was fair game. This was purely racism against Africans even Indians themselves; however they did not see it this way. Hoyt Jr (2012) defines racism as:

> The belief that all members of a purported race possess
> characteristics, abilities, or qualities specific to that race, especially so as
> to distinguish it as inferior or superior to another race or other races.
> Racism is a particular form of prejudice defined by preconceived
> erroneous beliefs about race and members of racial groups (p. 225).

Racism, if anything, is among the biggest problems that are disturbing the world today as they revolve around colonial-enacted divisions all over the world. It has reached at a point at which people of the same race discriminate against each other as I will show later. Basically, racism occurs between a person and a person and among groups or countries even organisations and others. Even we revisit slavery and colonialism, they, indeed, were the projects of racism. Similarly, inequality between the Global North and the Global South is purely racism based on division as perpetrated by the dominant grand narrative that uses colonial and toxic education. Such racism has recently mutated from economic one to environmental one. Hale (2008) argues that environmental racism covers and spans other human areas nationally and internationally as it gyrates around, *inter alia*, income, geography and international geopolitics that seem to divide the world between who-haves and who-have-nots. Environmental racism is evident today when global warming is threatening the lives of poor people in poor countries in the South. The irony is that rich countries tend to forget that there is only one earth. Therefore, shall anything sinister resulting from environmental harms occur, we all will lose it. Again, if you ask who caused this phenomenon? The lead will point at the same North (West) that invented racism as we will see later. Racism spearheaded by the West, led by Britain, can be seen in British racist tendency as it is known all over the world. Hurlbert (2011) observes that "the assimilation non-European [in Canada] immigrants were considered a much greater problem because they were deemed to be racially inferior to White people" (p. 101). Hurlbert argues that racism still exists in Canada; and those suffering are Aboriginal people and immigrants. Again, who sowed this seed of racism? The answer is simple, British colonial government did. Linking this to Indians in East Africa, British racist regimes made them middlemen in almost everything as Burton (2013) observes that "[f]or Africans, Indians were the shopkeepers on the other side of the counter who bought low and sold high, extracting African wealth between the margins" (p. 6). So, you can see how division, based on race, helped British government to fool itself and those it exploited by dividing them.

Many years since British colonisers left Africa, the Indians–they illegally brought to be used to exploit Africans–are still stranded in Africa where they are neither Indians nor Africans. Again, the *middlemanship* mentioned here–as it was heinously introduced by Britain–is not the normal one we all know. It is a superimposed role aimed of exploiting one community as it is carried on by another community to benefit both colonial economies and its agents. British colonial governments brought Indians to East Africa purposely to exploit and discriminate against Africans. Brennan (2012) maintains that in:

> East African Indians appear to be a privileged community that, by and large, had profited from their participation in systems of colonial rule. Wealthy and endogamous, Indians appeared, to many Africans, as a privileged insular merchant minority who generally refused to participate in a new postcolonial nation" (p. 3).

Here we can trace the origin of the coming of Indian immigrants to Tanganyika (thereafter referred to as the United Republic of Tanzania (URT) after union of Tanganyika and Zanzibar in 1964), Kenya and Uganda. Despite being brought to carry on economic sabotage against Africans–as it was in other African countries including South Africa–Indians went on staying in the countries after acquiring their independence in 60s. The new governments generously and humanly accepted them as citizens. However, the same Indians, the colonial government brought to sabotage Africans, still maintained cultural; and colour exclusionary tactics and seclusion altogether. In other words, they still believe and think they are more Indians than Africans even though when they go to India they are identified by their African nationalities. Yes, they carry passports whenever they go to India.

In essence, British project of exporting people to other countries was not only practiced in Africa. In India subcontinent, Tamils were exported to modern Sri Lanka which evidenced many decades of ethnic wars between the Tamils and the Sinhalese who regard themselves as the rightful owners of the country. So, it can be said that the exportation of populations during British colonial era has, apart from maintaining division along pedigree, has created many conflict up until now. Therefore, what can we do to address this situation? I think we need to encourage the differing sides to integrate and regard others like human being like themselves admitting that what makes them fight is not their fault but that of the colonisers, especially through toxic education. Again, such integration and peaceful and equal coexistence cannot be achieved without decolonising the minds of the population through decolonising education. To go on discriminating against, segregating and fighting one another is, in itself, a colonial legacy-cum-mentality the victims are supposed to fight fiercely at all times and all costs. It is only through a decolonised education for both parties that will enable them to view each other as equal humans and partners instead of, for some, feeling they are superior while others are inferior. It is only through decolonising such minds through education that the parties may be able to see the dangerous future their currently relationship has created. It is through decolonised education that such people can be freed from racial entrapment they are in pointlessly.

Even after African countries acquired independence, there has been existing tensions between these newcomers brought by colonial powers in many African countries. Since they were brought—in most cases of caste system—Indians have lived a secluded life as it was started by their masters. To make matters worse, such *foreigners* still discriminate against their *hosts;* and they are—up until now—regarded by those they discriminate against as the most racist people on earth, even more their masters due to tracing their racist habits from their caste system that goes back thousands of years. I am not trying to be a racist. It is easy—for instance—in Dar es Salaam, the biggest and multicultural city of Tanzania, to see African and European couples but not a single Indian and African couple despite the fact that Indians are many more than Europeans not to mention the fact that Indians have been living in Tanzania for many generations. Brennan (*Ibid.*) notes that "colonial rulers oversaw urban segregation; they reserved for themselves the best housing and services; they instituted inferior and racially segregated systems of education and government employment for Indians and Africans" (p. 1). Thanks to colonial exclusionary and racist policies Brennan, further, notes that the Indians arc almost endogamous in everything such as marriage, religion, domestic space, dress, and even music and food which basically signify social hierarchy and racial exclusion wherein, for example, a non-Ismail can be anybody except an African. Is it the same mentality of avoiding Africans for fear of diluting Indian purity? For, even the situation in South Africa has been the same ever since prominent people like Nelson Mandela who stood against Apartheid system and defended all South Africans including Indians who were brought by British colonial government in 1860. Further, Brennan *(op.cit.)* observes that despite that, Indians are tightfisted and self-denying and forged present satisfaction for future-oriented accumulation whereby Africans, by contrast, understood wealth as a means to the social end of mobilising supporters and clients who, caricatured by Indians, have never underscored the importance of future investments as it revolves around past colonial favouritism and racism.

To know how the relationship based on colour *purity* assumption is in East Africa, and possibly, Africa as a whole looks like currently; Krishna (2013) notes that if a postcolonial Tanzanian government wanted to throw Indians out like in its neighbouring Uganda under Idi Amin which would have been the same case in Madagascar and South Africa. Although Krishna's observation can be taken lightly even ignored, it still tells that something is not well whether we like or not. In other words, Krishna avoids living in a state of denial; instead, he faces it so that we can appreciate the fact that there is a conflict resulting from racism and exclusion that needs us to take some measures to manage it. Without decolonising the type of education Africa offers its citizens, chances of future clashes are high, chiefly at this time resources are becoming scarce due to the booming population in the world. It has already started in South Africa where every foreigner is seen as danger to South Africans. If anything, such conflicts–however they may currently be ignored–are likely to cause problems in the future. As professionals and academics, it is easy to state categorically that we need to address the issue of racism, specifically through decolonising current educations systems that colonial powers left behind for the purpose of continuing to control and exploiting us indirectly. Such racist relationship, seen above, is likely to be a good source of conflict, particularly in poor countries were those unprivileged will take on those privileged as it once happened in Uganda when Idi Amin expelled Indians in 1972 as the then disgruntled Ugandans cheered him despite his act being inhumane and the replication of racism.

Really, Amin exploited the weakness of racism and already pent-up hatred against Indians to expel them. In 1990s, in neighbouring Tanzania there arose a politician, Christopher Mtikila, who instigated Africans to kill Indians if Britain and India would not take them so that their blood would reach India and awaken their colleagues. Mtikila referred to Indians as *gabacholi* or thieves (the same pejorative word Indians use against Africans) and the enemies of the nation (Orr, 2016). Up until now, ruling the elites have always tried to avert addressing this burning issue, especially when they underscore the fact that most of minority foreigners have always been used to do corrupt elites' dirty linens in the country. It is conceivably right to maintain that such elites did not receive the right type of education that would have enabled them to function harmoniously in their environment. The dichotomy found in between the current colonised education and African education is obvious. The former, basically revolves around individualism whereas the latter revolves around collectivism. We need to mend this gap shall we aspire to have a very peaceful society. You can see this in African current politics that revolves around tribalism, cronyism and other anomalies. Are such elites truly educated really? What if they were exposed to decolonised education? I think they would have enacted laws that would have stopped racism by integrating the two societies after educating them about the danger[s] racism poses for both. Certainly, British colonial regimes created racism in Tanzania soon after it took the country as a protectorate. It favoured Indians it used in exploiting Africans whom it discriminated against as well (Brennan, 2011). There is no way the British government can deny its role in sowing the seeds of racism which, at any time, may result into conflict in many African countries where Indians still discriminate against their hosts. However, as the time went by, in Tanzania, slowly, this move Mtikila initiated went under. Again, what is an upshot of this? In the near future, far-right parties will win many elections in Africa just as anti-immigration and ultranationalist parties are doing in Europe currently. The difference is that in Africa chaos will be inevitable thanks to tribalism, ethnicity and all sorts of divisions that the colonial powers introduced. So, as professionals and academics, it is everybody's responsibility to warn both groups of the danger such a division, resulting from colonialism, poses for peace regionally or globally. If anything, continuing to condone race blindness or whatever pretexts is like ignoring embers that will gnash the entire house the two protagonists share.

Interestingly, Africans in India are openly and chronically discriminated against while Indians have lived in Africa for generations without being maltreated in spite of their systematic discrimination against their hosts as indicated above. What transpired on 31 January, 2016, in Bangalore, speaks volumes as far as maltreatments to Africa is concerned despite their generosity back home. Lakshmi (2016) poses a question: "Are Indians racists?" The question appeared to dominate social media and prime-time TV shows in the country on Wednesday after a disturbing incident earlier this week." In spite of all such criminality and disrespect directed towards Africans, they still go to India for educational or medical purposes instead of boycotting them. This, once again, shows how ignorant and unable the victims and perpetrators are due to receiving colonised education that makes them dependent and less creative while perpetrators fail to understand that the same Africans they are discriminating against, killing and calling names contribute a lot to the economy of India. One would think that being discriminated against, and being referred to as monkeys and chimpanzees would piss Africans off so as to find another alternative instead of continuing to take their children or sick people to India to be tortured and discriminated against. Besides, one would think that Indians in India would underscore the fact that their brethren are scattered in many countries in Africa doing the same though covertly.

Suppose Africans wise up and decide to reciprocate exactly the same their brethren are treated in India. What do they expect, especially if they consider the fact that many Indian were exported to Africa in order to help colonial master exploit Africans while these Africans–they are now discriminating against–are in India to seek education or medical services, and thereby contribute to the economy of India. Suppose African countries gang up and boycott everything Indian. Does India think its economy would perform miraculously as it has been thanks to many resources fished out of Africa by its citizens the colonial powers brought. India is currently suffering from Afro-phobia something that can lead to indo-phobia in Africa.

Furthermore, Lakshmi discloses that "a 21-year old Tanzanian student in the city of Bangalore in southern India told the police that a mob pulled her out of her car before setting it ablaze on Sunday night. She said the mob then beat her up, molested and stripped her, and paraded her naked." The hell broke loose after a Sudanese student knocked down an Indian woman. Thereafter, any Africa was fair game. Mobbing an African was the only right thing for any Indian onlookers to do. Interestingly, despite such brutality, there was no call in Tanzania to reciprocate by attacking Indians. One can guess what would happen had the situation been vice versa. Strangely, when the said girl was and beaten up, maltreated and molested, reports had it that, ironically police officers were just watching without taking any action. Majani (2016) quotes Dawson Kimenya who attended his tertiary education in India saying that racist Indians call Africans *kalu* or monkeys or *absiii* or chimps; and even when the victims reported to the police, nothing was done to show how discrimination against Africa is endemic and systemic. To see how accepted, blessed, condoned and internalised racism is in Indian society, please click on this link *https://www.youtube.com/watch?v=OCcgx16e8DQ*. Another student who attended university in India said that, in many areas, Indians do not like sharing houses with Africans. Further, the other alleged that some Indians scratch Africans' skins to see if they can produce colours.

Another example, we currently are evidencing the section of population in Western countries aligning with terror and fundamentalist groups after either being discriminated against or marginalised due to living in, and receiving colonised education. This cannot go on without educationalists doing something. From this tenet, I postulate that we should embark on starting programs, principally designed to cover and tackle racism in order to avoid conflicts resulting from this crime of racism. This can be achieved through decolonising education only. So, for educationists, practitioners and stakeholders, addressing such colonial settings may help in reducing tensions as a way of averting future conflict based on race or ethnicity. This can only be done through decolonising the education regime we currently have all over the world that has always sought to nourish and support the colonial *status quo sui generis*. We need to avoid special treatments to one group as opposed to others.

The other day I was reading about the role of civil society as a Western concept that was exported to Africa. I found that the history of civil society is hand in hand with the "modernization of economy" (Paffenholz, 2010, p. 4) which is lacking in Africa. So, too, I noticed that traditional African civil societies that used to carry out the same role of taking on the corrupt high and the mighty were excluded in the Western definition of the civil society. Again, in addressing Asia *vis-à-vis* the same concept, Paffenholz (*Ibid.*) observes that "Asian values are unique, thereby making Western concept of civil society less applicable in Asia" (p. 13). Asian values are unique to what? Aren't African values unique too? Is this why, for instance, British colonialists brought Indians to Africa because they were special as they still think and feel they are in some countries? Further, Paffenholz notes that "under colonial regimes, civil society organised mostly along lines of ethnicity and religion—thus the philanthropic engagement by Buddhist groups in Myanmar, Christian groups in the Philippines, and Muslim groups in Indonesia and Malaysia" (pp. 13-14). Is African civil society excluded because of being African or what, if at all, almost all African civil society was organised around ethnicity? Is Africa excluded because it lacks the element of being an "appointed one" or neo-religions? The same treatments can be seen on the way the West deals with dictators in Asia and the Middle East compared to Africa. Dictatorship becomes an issue in Africa but not in China, or in the Middle East. Why? Isn't this racism done systematically in the international community? Again, if Africa does not protest against this racism, who else will do? The decolonisation of education espoused here seeks to fully and trustworthily address such anomalies in order to avoid avoidable conflicts in the world. Isn't this systemic and structural violence in the international superstructure?

Evidently, colonial education imposed what Plato would call "ill-structured nature of teaching" (Koehler & Mishra, 2009) (which, basically inflicted an inexplicable disability in the heads of its recipients). Under "social cubism" which offers a mental frame for multi-dimensional analysis of conflict; and allows analysts to develop an informed theory of change (Matyok, Mendoza, Schmitz, Matyók, Mendoza & Schmitz, 2014), colonialism, hugely and negatively altered the lives of the people in colonies demographically, economically, politically, religiously, historically and psycho-culturally. In doing so, colonial education system represented Aboriginal people as hallow and inept. Before the eyes of colonial education, those colonised had, and still have nothing whatsoever to offer except their labour and resources. The role of the colonised was only to sheepishly receive whatever colonial education system offered without even questioning however bad it was. This reminds me of how Aboriginal people and their ways were referred to as barbaric and pagan. It reached the point at which people were afraid and ashamed of using their names, vernacular languages and mores altogether which signified the loss or alteration of their identity and who they actually are. Some were denied the right to use their languages. Their ways of life were abused; and their land and sacred places were desecrated on not to mention land grabbing that followed thereof and thereafter. Sadly though, such anomalies went on conceivably unabated for many years so as to leave behind irreparable and disastrous effects on Aboriginal people, especially in Canada and Australia. In destroying the wellbeing of Aboriginal people in these two countries, colonial education made sure that everything Aboriginal was altered, doctored and misrepresented. The populations of Aboriginal people were decimated next to extinction which was regarded by colonisers as a decree by God or nature (Power, 2008) in Australia. As if this was not enough, Australian Aboriginal people were not included in human census in the country simply because, like Africans, were not viewed as humans. All this can be attributed to European assumption that black people either were not full humans or were cursed from their creation. Whitford (2009) discloses that "Noah cursed his son Ham to perpetual slavery. Ham, according to Genesis 10, was the founding father of Africa. Thus, Africans are an accursed race predestined by God to inferiority and slavery" (p. 2). With such garbage I wonder; how could such people who prided themselves to be civilised would fail to underscore a simple fact that those they were decimating were just created the same way they were. Ironically, such foulmouthed people prided themselves to be religious! Again, when you examine the type of education and grand narrative that guided them, you discover where the problem, up until now, is. Had the current Western education been free of toxicity and naivety, such literatures would be expunged. Religious bodies whose books propagated such stinking racism would be banned, fined and shamed. Viriri & Mungwini (2010) note that "Ham's spiritual curse was also used to convince Africans that the position they were occupying was not out of anybody's malice but it was basically their ultimate destiny divinely put in place because of their ancestor's lack of respect" (p. 37). Is there any different from Indian caste system in which blackness is curse as well? Yet, due to the toxicity of its education, the West still refers to India as the largest democracy! Is it profanity to categorise foreign racist religions as satanic ones? The curse of Ham does not appear in Christianity only but also in Islam. Clarence-Smith (2006) maintains that "slavery has always been a part and parcel of the basic core and a central tenet of Islam." The author relies on various scholarly sources, including the Qur'an and the hadiths…" (p. 119). Historically, the curse of Ham is not confined to history and mythical past. It still goes on even in Africa itself wherein some African still discriminate against their colleagues as Hall (2011) notes that the situation is still persistent in Sudan and Mauritania wherein the racial categories deployed in contemporary conflicts often hunker back to old history wherein blackness symbolises slavery and non-blackness predatory and uncivilised banditry. Further, in tying Christianity and Islam to the invention of Ham's curse, Fredrickson (2015) notes that:

> Historians Bernard Lewis and William McKee Evans have presented much evidence to support the view that the Islamic world preceded the Christian in representing sub-Saharan Africans as descendants of Ham, who were cursed and condemned to perpetual bondage because of their ancestor's mistreatment of his father, Noah, as described in an obscure passage in Genesis (p. 29).

In simple terms, all human beings, as the grand narrative defines them, are under its control consciously and unconsciously, willingly and cogently and morally and immorally. The social cubism, touched upon above, shows how the grand narrative encompasses all six factors of the theory by dictating demographics, economics, history, politics, psychoculture, religion and whatnots as far as colonised society is concerned. Using its contemporary imperialistic tools such as the World Bank (WB) and the International Monetary Fund (IMF), the United Nations (UN) and vetoes, the dominant grand narrative regulates how the world should be ran. It appoints God's *chosen ones* and God's *forgotten ones* on earth. It goes further prescribing how Africa's politics and economies should be ran and conducted and so on. It defines democracy, human rights, international order and whatnots. Essentially, if we use a social cubism theory, the dominant grand narrative fits in it well. Again, is it fair for academics to keep quiet while other cultures are sidelined and humiliated something that leads to conflict?

Furthermore, the economies of Aboriginal people were invaded and toppled while their political institutions were banned, illegalised or replaced by colonial ones. Their natural and true religions were replaced by Christianity and Islam which, negatively and hugely destroyed their ways of life. Their names were abolished through baptismal or conversion which, created new and fake identities that have caused a lot of perpetual schisms and misunderstandings among their followers that is currently affecting them even more ferociously than ever. As if this was not enough, their history was rewritten to favour the narrative of colonisers which was, and still is, full of lies and fabrications. If we look at some Aboriginals such as Africans, we found that they were not supposed to be part of foreign religions. Barkun (1990) observes that "blacks, according to Wesley Swift, were part of Lucifer's rebellion against God, serving as troops transported to earth" from other planets in the Milky Way" (p. 124). Ironically, the same dominant grand narrative propagating such toxic things is the one that came out saying that it civilised those it abused and robbed. Had all Africans read such a doctrine, it becomes difficult to know how they would react. These are the things decolonised education needs to attend to and explain. For any history written by a victor will, of course, demonise or demean the losers it is written about. This is how the history of Aboriginal People all over the world was misrepresented in order to suit the needs of the victor. In so doing, colonial powers and other invaders such as religions made sure that they destroy everything worthwhile that their victims had so as to keep on exploiting and abusing them. Concerning psycho-cultural wellbeing of Aboriginal peoples, colonial powers made sure that they rob everything that gave them an identity and sense of uniqueness. They changed the names of their hallmarks such as lakes, mountains and rivers. They also changed their names through Christianisation of Islamisation. They banned them from using their names, their languages and, sometimes, their land in some places where land was grabbed so as to turn Africans into landless as it currently is in countries like Kenya, Namibia, South Africa and Zimbabwe among others. Colonial powers saw to it that the true identity of Aboriginal people is lost so as to carry artificial and colonial one. It was a disaster so to speak. By changing their identity, Aboriginal people ended up with a pseudo identity that would not help them in identifying themselves as they did before. Instead of identifying themselves as who they truly were, they started identifying themselves as Christians, Muslims, British, French, Portuguese and Spanish; all depending on who colonised them politically or religiously. Other colonial powers went as far as dictating to their victims who their siblings were; and whom they should associate with. Others went a mile ahead teaching their victims even the words they must speak when they go to washrooms or to bed as if before their arrival people did not go to these places. Strangely, when I remember how many times I heard the word Paris in Congolese music, I know how they sing many more times about Paris than the villages or towns they were born in. This is why, today in Africa, for example, there have been scuffles between Muslims and Christians who are naturally brothers and sisters under their African identity.

To see how Africa was deviously divided, in many conferences of the African Unity (AU), Africans are divided along their colonial powers. Those who speak French feel they must be treated differently from those who speak either English or Portuguese and vice versa. Whenever they need to do something, or appoint an official for certain role, they find themselves divided along colonial lines namely, Anglophone or Francophone, *Portugophone* lines. They subscribe to artificial and new colonial identities so as to end up hating one another wantonly and pointlessly. Such hatred and confusion are causing a lot of unnecessary conflicts between the two. This volume is aimed at instigating Africans to ask themselves essential questions such as: Why didn't colonisers see us as brothers and sisters when they bought and sold us to slavery or colonised us? Why are we equal today after they have exploited, sold, abused and misused us? Furthermore, currently, there is another danger emanating from religious background whereby Christians and Muslims compete, based on sectarianism, in some African countries. Colonial toxicity resulting from colonial education such people received can be seen almost in everything former colonies did and still do. To them, better education for them and their offspring is in their colonial masters' but not theirs that they were taught to abhor and feel ashamed of. Recently, even African terrorist groups pledged their allegiances to Arab terrorist groups but not vice versa! Africans carry Arab or European names but not vice versa why? Arabs, Europeans and Indians are highly respected in Africa but not Africans in the trio as I have indicated above in racism scandals in India not to mention the Middle East even Europe. If such people suffering from mental colonialism had received a decolonised type of epistemes, they would question their moves before making them. This problem is a double-edged sword in that it includes the perpetrators and victims in the same basket in that they all need true education that will free them from their ignorance and madness based on blind egoism and self-aggrandisement. Concerning the victims, this volume urges them to stand up and reclaim their lost glory (Mhango, 2016).

I evidenced cultural rot resulting from the introduction of divisive foreign religions when Kenya was writing its new constitution in 2010. Muslims wanted Kadhi Courts (Islamic courts) to be enshrined in the constitution while Christians opposed them. The situation is the same in neighbouring Tanzania which during writing its constitution that ended up being shelved after corrupt rulers feared that it would put them in trouble if it were ratified. In all these two scenarios, nowhere the citizenry were agitating for something with roots in African traditions. Instead, they were all defending their colonial powers' identity as they consciously or unconsciously divorced theirs in such an important and pivotal document that would rein over them and their coming generations. This is because they have already lost their true identities thanks to colonialism be it political or religious. They see one another as an obstacle that needs to be either eradicated or vanquished. They have created what Oppenheimer (2006) refer to as "enemy images" which serve as the impetuses for more enmity and division among colonised societies wantonly for their perilous end. Instead of becoming a "community of fate" (Omarova, 2011) they end up becoming "enemies of fate". Instead of fighting for better constitutions, the citizenry, in the countries above, end up haggle over things that would not address their true identities, aspirations and needs. Sometimes, such confusion ends up producing radicals from both sides. Northern Ireland ultra-Catholics and ultra-protestants divides provide an ideal example of how colonial-sired hatred would be entrenched in the society so deeper that the protagonists think about destroying one another instead of reconciling their differences so as to move forward just like they did for many years since time immemorial before the coming of colonial powers that divided and duped them for their peril. Try to imagine. If Catholics and Protestants, that are all Christians, would hate one another this way, what do you expect of Christians and Muslims whose doctrines are always in a collision course? Again, aren't they all Africans or Irish, and sometimes, from the same communities in the same country or countries? Much time and money are spent on unnecessary differences instead of working together to address other issues that impact on them equally such as socio-political needs of their societies. On their part, misguided and skinny politicians seize this opportunity to do more harm through planting more seeds of destruction, division and hatred among their people. Kenya evidenced such a sharp and dangerous division that culminated in the 2007/08 chaos that left hundreds dead. On 3rd April, 2015, al-Shabaab terrorist group attacked Garissa University and held over 700 people hostage wherein about 148 Christian students were separated from their colleague Muslims; and thereby shot at point blank simple because they were Christians; not to mention 79 people who were wounded (Odula, Muhumuza & Senosi, 2015 cited in Cannon, 2016).

Actually, when sectarian chaos erupts, apart from tarnishing the image of the country in question, it destabilises its economy as well. Again, when this happens, the same colonisers–who wickedly sowed the seed of destruction through divisions and mistrust–either come in as mediators or just laugh at them so as to come and teach them what to do as if they do not have brains.

What's more, even with regards to helping such countries from self-inflicted wounds resulting from colonised education, the international community, systematically and visibly discriminates against them. This can be seen on how quickly or sluggishly they act or how much they offer compared to other countries affected by the same problems out of Africa. Refer to a recent conflict in Syria. Many Western countries offered to help Syrian refuges while they turned a blind eye on refugees from the CAR, the DRC and South Sudan.

The major question that needs an answer to chime with the decolonisation of toxic education is: How long will Aboriginal people languish in ill-structured teaching situation even after the world declared to have entered in the age of civilisation and advancement? Such a question seeks an answer that will address the anomalies in Australia, Canada and US and other Western nations and in their colonies. Despite the world's grandiose declaration of human rights, Aboriginal people in the countries above, as the victims of colonial epistemes and dominant grand narrative, are still suffering from archaic and rudimentary treatments by the so-called civilised and advanced nations. One may argue that the lives of colonised people in the aforementioned countries have been improved due to living in economically-advanced countries. They are provided with social assistance and other minimal emoluments. Is that all they need? Grieves (2007) argues that such people desire to be freed from "government's stronghold on Aboriginal people" (p. 4). Again, is that all that they need for their wellbeing in their countries? Yes, currently, despite living in poverty, some of Aboriginals in Australia, Canada and the US own cars and houses compared to their colleagues in the third world. Despite that, they still live in the third world in the first world. For, if we ask them; is what they need? Owning a car or a house without having the right or access to one's natural foods, shrines and sacred places and land, that make them who they are, is wanting. Importantly, instead of allowing the colonisers and occupiers to discretionary determine and dictate what is good for such a people, it must be they who should decide what they need and want; and what they are satisfied with. For, the way people interpret things differ according to the cultural lenses we use to view them. Therefore, what we may think is a good thing for some people may end up being quite the opposite as far as their needs, aspirations and understanding are concerned.

Since the coming of settlers to occupied lands, Aboriginal people in the Americas and Australia have been subjected to many evils such as alcoholism, introduction of new diseases and different life style from the one they were used to not to mention harassments resulting from bad and foreign policies of integration such as residential school in Canada. Almost in all occupied countries, Aboriginal people were denied of the voice and right to decide how they would like to live. Up until now, they are totally left out in their countries; and they just depend on the mercy of their colonial governments. This needs to change through decolonising education so that we can have the education that gives the oppressed people their voices back. We need the type of education that recognises the existence and vibrancy of the oppressed all over the world. We need the type of education that will free bother victims and perpetrators. And, if anything, without changing the *status quo*, conflicts resulting from lack of voice, identity and other rights will become rampant as it currently is in the Americas and Australia however passive these conflicts may be. Under the current dominant grand narrative and its education system, Aboriginal people are lost and ignored and nobody sees it this way. Why? Because the current education system makes people selfish and blind so as not to see wanton suffering other people are in. Forsey & Low (2014) argue that Eurocentric education views Aboriginal people as static and "frozen in time" as opposed to European progressive as far as knowledge is concerned. Such cannot be emancipatory and true education that the Europeans such as Plato died for in seeking truth.

Let me draw an example from East Africa. In Tanzania and Kenya, Masai were the only people left out in the Western capitalist market due to adhering to their ways of life which were viewed as static and frozen in time. Despite such assumption, Masai lived and thrived without any assistance from outside. One of their legacies is the ability to prevent colonial administrators from colonising them. When missionaries tried to enter Masailand, failed. As Andrews (2010) notes, the Masai did not see anything new. For, "they had their own systems of thought and religion that satisfied their needs. Many saw no reason to change them" (p. 11). This was the same situation almost everywhere in Africa before manipulations were applied. But recently, the Masai were decoyed out of their world in the name of modernisation which seems to impact on them negatively. Munishi (2013) notes that Masai stated to migrate to cities after they lost their land, livestock and became poor after facing unemployment not to mention climatic changes and conflict resulting from resource control. Instead of looking after their animals as they used to do from time immemorial, they were made to believe that urban life is a sign of development that would accommodate them. Thus, many Masai youths left their natural life of looking after their animals as they started adopting personality disorder in "modern life" (Millon, Millon, Meagher, Grossman & Ramnath, 2012). Now, Masai, as a people, are a leading community in guarding shops and houses something that degrades them and sabotages them culturally and economically. Apart from being the new way of life to the Masai, it does not pay them well compared to how their animals used to. Masai have subscribed to the current dominant grand narrative so as to lose their culture and wealth based on pastoralism.

Further, the Masai were the only people that used to attract many tourists from the West due to preserving their culture. The mistake Masai and their countries made is thinking that those *tourists* liked Masai culture. Basically, one may argue that 'tourists' love for Masai culture was the means of spying on it and later destroying it. Sometimes in Kenya, there was a tug of war between Masai women and white women whom the former accused of snatching their husbands. As I am writing, the pride and uniqueness of Masai have become history. They no longer eat their foods that enabled them to run tens of miles looking after their cattle in the wideness of East Africa as it used to be before they were subsumed in the modern capitalist culture. O'conor (2010) deposits that "nearly all of the Maasai who come to Dar find work as security guards; their reputation for both bravery as warriors and honesty, coupled with a lack of formal education that would qualify them for more professional jobs, means that security is one of the few areas in which people will employ them." Had education system been decolonised, would have had a room for addressing this loss that the Masai are now facing. Such education would understand and find a solution to the problem that caused their animals to be "depleted by disease' instead of staying aside and watch as if the Masai are not the citizens of the country that need their property, culture, ways of life and their livelihood protected by the government.

As if it is not enough, after losing their ways of life based on their culture and environment, Masai are now in correctional facilities in these countries due to trying to reverse the situation by involving themselves (*though not all*) in crimes so as to generate capital and go back home to buy some cows. Currently, there is a conflict between Masai and town dwellers in many places in Kenya and Tanzania. The trust the society used to place on Masai is virtually long gone; and the situation of the former is worsening day by day. What was thought to be either a passing fad or cloud has come to stay as Masai lose more and more of their identity. Prins (1992) notes that Masai's "'prestige overstocking' is not the case anymore." Masai are not alone. They are many more Indigenous community that are losing almost everything from their land to their identity all over the globe (Nichols, Boulinier, Hines, Pollock & Sauer, 1992). Arguably, this phenomenon is going to cause a lot of problems. However, nobody can stand in the way of changes if the dominant grand narrative, with its hegemonic education, is not going to be deconstructed, decolonised and detoxified altogether. Again, such changes should be constructive as far as decolonised education is concerned. One important question one may ask is: Why has this phenomenon happened?

Actually, Masai have been robbed of their lives and culture so as to be exploited by the capitalist market that seeks to exploit everybody all over the world through consumerism and pop culture exported by Western media. Unfortunately, this identity theft has been presided over by the so-called elites who run their countries. Modernity seen in Masai and other vulnerable people, that are becoming a prey to Western consumerism, is nothing but perilous encounter. It is like dancing with the devil so to speak. If something is not done to decolonise the current way of doing things as it revolves around colonised education which produced colonised leaders; some people facing Armageddon, conflicts and mendacity resulting from such a situation will never be avoided. This is one example of the many of the people who were forced to abandon their ways of life so as to end up becoming losers as a people and society altogether. A few academics see this as it is so as to agitate that such people should not be disturbed or being forced to abandon their ways of life that have kept them intact and flourishing for many years. Although we may single Masai out, there are many societies that are now losing bigger to the dominant grand narrative. This is where Africa needs to do its homework carefully and urgently to see to it that its people are not perishing wantonly. Suffering from what Kraidy (2017) calls education as cultural imperialism, many academics see and know everything about this danger but lacks the guts to take on their masters. Masai and the likes are suffering from capitalistic and imperialistic drive aimed at controlling the whole world for its benefit as championed by the US. Vandenberghe (2008) calls this "commodification of culture which colonises the leisure time for all people worldwide" (p. 877). Under pop culture, the world is now bombarded with all types of garbage in the name of modernity. A human has been turned into an object for money, a consuming cyborg. For, example, some human parts, mainly female's, have been commercialised under the guise of individualism. One would think that modernity would revolve around cultural parity based on reciprocity as the means of benefiting from; and appreciating one another as the member of one family of humanity. No, it does not work this way. Under capitalism and imperialism, either the winner takes it all or it is the survival for the fittest. To make sure that one survives and wins, manipulations, based on demonising or suffocating other cultures, are used. This is contrary to the other grand narratives, particularly the collectivistic in which a human is a communal but not private agent.

Moreover, behind this cultural imperialism, as one evils of toxic education as it is spearheaded by African regimes in conjunction with their Western masters, *inter alia,* is supposed to get the right answers from decolonised education. If possible, in the course of trying to usher peace in the world by addressing power-crazy conflicts and imperialistic urge to subdue others that are going on in various places of the world, Africa must replace the current colonised education. You can easily and expeditiously prove this occurrence by looking at how Africa and other colonised societies still ape whatever their former colonisers offer. All *power-crazy* we see in many parts of the world are meant by individuals aiming at putting hands on resources that the West, and, now China and India, badly want. They strive to supply these countries with resources so as to become rich. By having control of these resources, these power ogres will be able to enter in a marriage of a venal consumers and suppliers even if it means to be done through shedding the blood of their innocent brothers and sisters as it has been going on in the DRC. This is what neoliberalism advocates using its intellectuals, and pundits in economics and other fields, espouses and uses. Strangely, such educated people do not have the tools to enable them see the sin they are committing against others. Any person can question their moral authority, particularly when some of the countries pretend to be the guardians of human rights in the world. This is why this volume categorises such education toxic and colonised in that it does not bother to serve the humanity as a whole.

If anything, decolonised education—as an impetus needed to turn the situation around—must endeavored in order to manage, transform, stop or reduce conflicts and violence all over the world. So, whatever that causes violence, it obviously stands on the way of decolonised education. This is why the decolonisation of toxic education is extremely important, especially for the victims. Being a violent project the world evidenced, all signs and vestiges of colonialism, and colonialism itself, need to be eradicated wherever they are. If this is achieved, either through individual or structural deconstruction, peace is likely to be more realised than it is currently. When Nyamnjoh (2012) postulates that colonialism is a violent project, he encompasses everything that colonialism brought to ex-colonies. This becomes mainly because colonialism did not come into being to benefit anybody except colonisers at the detriment of the colonised. Even within the colonisers' circles some members of the society were exploited. For example, women were left out. They were colonised in their own countries just the same way as men and women in colonies were brutalised and colonised not to mention being exploited and degraded. The violence of colonialism bears the hallmarks of greed and ignorance of the rights of others provided they are not part and parcel of the project. Again, how come some colonial carryovers are still living on even after colonialism was abolished? Are white women as equal as their counterpart men? Whether colonialism was abolished or not is subject to dialogue. As far as decolonised education is concerned–thanks to its multidisciplinary nature and approach–it allows dialogue almost at all levels and all times during conflict. Decolonised education is something dynamic that allows intervention of any kind at any time.

Further, Nyamnjoh (*Ibid.*) argues that colonial education turned those who received it into shadows of themselves, more of zombies, especially, those who, and their communities, did not benefit from it as a society. If there is anything they knew it was nothing but to strive to become like their masters. You can see this on their manners of doing things such as dress code, and the way some colonised speak and where they want to go. In Africa, for example, those whom Britain colonised like to go to London, those colonised by France make Paris their Mecca. It goes on for those whom the Portuguese colonised. They all adore and revere the capitals of their colonial powers. They go for their tertiary education there. Even the rulers hide their looted monies there too; and ironically, the champions of rule of law, good governance and human rights do not refuse to keep such dirty monies stolen from poor people. You can see how many colonised elites became zombies. p'Bitek (1984) notes that "…and they dress up like white men, as if they are in the white man country" (p. 45). To sum up this face of colonialism, we must ask a question:

How does decolonised education come into this? Decolonised education comes into this scenario because what colonialism produced; and left behind are good sources of conflict and violence globally. And where there is conflict or violence, only decolonised education will always venture in under its arm of Conflict Resolution Field among others.

Colonialism and its appendages had no boundary from thuggery and robbery. They destroyed many lives, cultures and civilisations. To them, words such as coexistence, interconnectedness and oneness did not exist. It is only recently colonialism and its lean-tos realised the mistake they committed so as to look back and talk about the interconnectedness of the world as one family and capricious globalisation. Even though, whenever colonial powers talk about interconnectedness based on globalisation, a major purpose is for them to benefit more than others. Globalisation can be seen as a good if it is not done in a wrong way by having classes and one dominant grand narrative to rule others as it has always been. However, Western society–with its individuality that has always forced onto others from collectivistic societies–still dictates whatever the world undertakes under the pretext of globalism or universalism. We need a community more than an individual; however everybody is an individual. Africa, and many other Aboriginal people, got their power and energy from their interdependence as opposed to individuality. This does not mean that Aboriginal people did not have difference or conflict. Again, the scale of their differences and conflict did not lead to mass murder as it was in the WWI and the WWII or other colonial and capitalist related wars the world evidenced in past decades. Africans were able to live for many generations without enacting any big-scale wars. For, for them, the sacrosanctity of human life is nonnegotiable.

Although the colonisers have maintained silence, lies and denial with respect to the dubious history of the colonised they authored and misrepresented, they destroyed the world due to their greed and myopia. You can see this in the fact that after enacting slavery, colonialism and imperialism, the same people discovered how weak and inhumane these mechanisms were. Today, when the world is changing economically, the same people are trying to befriend those leading in this wave of social and economic changes. For example, they once ruled China and India. Today, when these two humongous nations are acting as the engines of world economy, without forgetting Africa that supplies almost everything, the same folks are changing tacks by becoming more humanistic than colonial and imperialistic as they have always been. They know full well that if those nations follow their example of colonising others, they will not survive due to lack financial clout to compete with them. Again, to avoid going back to using financial and scientific muscles to colonise others, we all need to speak the language of interconnectedness and interdependence. Even the most powerful country on earth today, the US, does not want to travel the way European colonial masters did. For, Mearsheimer (2014) underscores it that "America is likely to behave toward China much the way it behaved toward the Soviet Union during cold war" (p. 161). This means that the current dominant grand narrative will seek more legality and tenacity to survive by belittling and demonising others.

I do not want to become devil's advocate. However, when one looks at how the US tries to intimidate China with its human-carbuncular drive, one wonders if the same US has ever afforded Afro-Americans the same rights it pretends to agitate for Chinese to exercise. The same applies to Australia and Canada that have refused to afford the same human rights to Aboriginal and Indigenous people in these two countries. I sometimes wonder to find that the same countries are reproaching other states such as Afghanistan *vis-à-vis* human rights while sitting on the same messes. Why? Human rights need to be applied equally and equitably globally. Through decolonised education, the colonised, apart from being decolonised, they will have the guts to ask such bitter and provocative questions fearlessly and tirelessly. The current situation under colonised education cannot be left to continue if we learned a lesson from cold war era that put the whole world in the way of harm wantonly.

Educationists and other mavens need to reign in to tell those who still labour under colonialism that applying human rights selectively that going on doing this is unfeasible and counterproductive. The solution to this power tragedy lies on cooperation rather than competition wherein all humans will treat each other practically equally. To reign well and understandably, we need to equip ourselves with a new type of decolonised education that seeks to equally and equitably accommodate all grand narratives of the world with the aim of bringing their potentials together. We need to negotiate the world's future in a peaceful and constructive manner if the aspiration is to have a peaceful and developed world. So, decolonising of the way we think, and think about one another will not only help the current dominant grand narrative, but will also help the whole world from unnecessary conflicts and antagonisms.

In essence, how we view one another depends on the lenses we use all made by the type of education we receive. Equipped with colonial education, many actors in many countries suffering from violence tend to see things differently. For example, corrupt rulers and *hoity toity* see their interests while the *hoi polloi* see a different thing so as to create a conflict. Domestic elites spend public money on personal matters as it was for DRC's dictator Mobutu who bought many villas and mansions in Belgium, the US, France, Switzerland and Argentina, to mention but a few, while his people were dying in abject poverty. Again, those beneficiaries of looted money–despite some of them being the champions of human rights and good governance–did not raise their voices let alone doing anything or something about this crime. All the same, the victims of this theft did not challenge the silence of those countries which pretend to care about the rights of others while they actually are the movers and shakers as far as plundering the DRC is concerned.

I fully understand and admit that conflict is always about the relationship and the interconnectedness, interdependence and proximity of mankind; and it is inevitable in human life. So, always conflict is there save that what we try to do is manage or transform it in the attempts of resolving it. For, dealing with conflict is like peeling an onion which has many layers of different sizes. Importantly, what encourages us to keep up is the fact that, through training in concert with other aspects such as research, practices and theories, we are able to deal with the conflict constructively and productively. Importantly, in so doing, we need a very right, and good type of education which, in this case, is the decolonised education that is supposed to equally empower everybody all over the world.

Also, given the fact that conflict is inevitable, dealing with it is also inevitably important. Therefore, when we decolonised education we try to harmonise relationship based on interconnectedness and interdependency as human beings. Furthermore, we need to underscore the fact that our livelihood is connected to other things such as environment. This is why making peace with each other and environment is essential. Interestingly, this interconnectedness and dependence do not only end with friends but it also ends with enemies. It also calls upon us to treat other non-human things such as vegetation, animals, water bodies and the atmosphere the same way we treat ourselves given that our lives depend on them although some do not necessarily depend on us. This means. In seeking peace or enhancing security for mankind, nobody can avoid enemies. So important is the whole issue of living ecologically positively by seeing to it that we do not cause any imbalance in the universe. With toxic and colonised education that revolves around individuality, one needs to gain where another must lose. This is called a zero-sum game. Why can it we think about a gain-sum game in which all gain? All of the above components of harmonious life are fundamentally *sine qua non*. They are inevitably players in the quest for peace. There cannot be any peace without food production that depends on sound weather we are now disturbing due to climate change and global warming resulting from greed and self-service as espoused by colonised education. Currently, rich countries are plundering resources in poor countries without underscoring the fact that the earth is one. Chinese and Indian companies are now extracting resources from Africa and South America without any regard to environment for the world peril the same the West did for many decades.

Sometimes, I laugh when I see how the world is grappling with plastic materials that pose a huge danger to the world simply because of greed, ignorance and toxicity of colonial education. There are so many examples to prove how toxic colonial education is in respect to environmental death-traps. If we can intensely and continuously apply decolonised type of education on toxic education that is based on collective undertakings, companies, their countries and their hosts are supposed to underscore the dangers that their individuality-geared actions cause to the entire globe. This is the rarely thought about strategy. With the right type of education, such dangers it becomes easy to conceptualise and take on due to knowing the price we are to pay as a human family. To the contrary though, with blinding colonised education, it becomes difficult to see and address such dangers.

Every so often, it is easy to see everything under whatever education. Again, due to the s blindness and covetousness colonised education has afflicted in many of its victims, mainly our pampered princes in power and their academic cronies, they tend to ignore even obvious things simply because they believe in their own survival which is impossible and meaningless without the existence of others. Do you think that all corrupt and thievish dictators are sustained by God or the West and the academics that have willingly decided to be enslaved for the sake of leftovers? To me, this is a medieval trait that is, through thick and thin, exhibited in the 21st century even if it is committed by those who think they are more advanced than others. What makes it a medieval thing is the fact that those maintaining it are preaching equality and human rights while they have a lot to hide thanks to their dirty past that came to light after some of them declassified their dark secret documents.

Why has the current education failed? It has failed to ask and answer questions such as equality or human rights which they chant every day. Why is it okay for rich countries to have discretionary powers in deciding how much greenhouse gases one has to emit? Why, for example, poor countries, which bear the brunt of climate change and global warming, have no say in decisionmaking on the issue? There is a universal assumption that all human beings are born equal. Then, I wonder; why this equality is amiss in addressing such important issues as family of nations? The UDHR (1948) cited in Shimron (2018) expressly provides that "all human beings are born free and equal in dignity and rights. They are endowed with reason and conscience and should act towards one another in a spirit of brotherhood" (p. 7). The preamble of the UDHR–which in law is not a law, or it cannot be applied before the court of law–makes a bold statement, which makes sense hypothetically and rhetorically.

As a professional, I question the rationale behind declaring all human beings, all over the world, to be equal while, practically the situation is different? For the oppressed people the article was supposed to read "all oppressors are the same and equal and have usurped the right to decide who is equal and who is not who and deserve dignity and who does not. Or put it this way: All oppressed people are equal in that they are oppressed except when some become oppressors themselves. When an oppressed person becomes an oppressor, he or she ceases to be equal with the oppressed. Pregnant with toxic education, how can we formulate such an argument that opposes the *status quo* we are part of? Again, it should be appreciated that, despite all these anomalies in enjoying human rights, there are some Western thinkers who saw the fallacies of the system so as to take on them. One of these thinkers is John Locke who is credited to be among the harbinger of the concepts of human rights. However when Locke espoused human rights, his world was limited to European men but not all humans. Thankfully, from his views, some progressive thinkers expanded the concept trying to theoretically cover all humans.

More or less, looking at how controversial and impractical some concepts are, one forms a different and opposing opinion. If human rights cannot be enjoyed equally all over the world, their existence is as good as nothing. This is why we need decolonised the education in order to create a level field which is quintessential to all human beings. This is because we all share the same planet; and hence the same destiny and needs. It has become obvious, especially after the coming of globalisation. Despite its shortfalls, it has made the world a small village with unequal population of rich and poor, informed and uninformed, included and excluded, developed and underdeveloped, civilised and uncivilised, advanced and retarded and whatnots. The village intended here, is crying for justice, peace, harmony, understanding, sustainability and predictability. The only way to get these essentials above is through decolonising the current education and its systems globally. Again, historically, it seems that this village came into being through evolution however controversial this theory might sound. I mean by evolving slowly. Evolution here is not necessarily the one in *On the Origin of Species* that Darwin espoused to favour the West, which is subject or might be the product of colonised education that has all truths even if the said truths are controversial and illogical.

Moreover, given that education takes multidisciplinary approach, I have the liberty to draw from all sciences and social sciences to back my arguments. In a word, the argument I want to make here is represented by the questions: Why were we able to come side by side along the entire long period and journey peacefully so as to reach at what seems to be our premature zenith of destruction resulting from complicity and duplicity? Will this speed of self-destruction enable us to achieve what intelligent creatures like us would be expected of? I love *The Moral Imagination* by Lederach (2005) that tasks us to ask ourselves what we have done to make the world peaceful and safe. The same question can be turned around and ask: What are we doing to cause violence wherever we are at whatever level and capacity? It is the same drive and the danger we are now facing that force me to conceive the idea of looking into education generally and particularly in my field of CRS in order either to ignite the dialogue or contribute to it. This is the primary role of any academic which is to think and contribute to the dialogue in his or her field or discipline. An academic is like a tree full of fruits. Edible and sweet as those fruits might be, need to be reproduced in order to feed others. An academic who does not reproduce knowledge is like a tree without fruits. We, therefore, as academics, especially in our fields, need to ask as many questions as we strive to get as many answers to these questions. Swahili sage has it that to be educated is like to become a torchbearer for others whom the torchbearer must lead and show the way. Again, can colonial education produced safe fruits or lead others to safety or vend them if not killing them due to its passion and poison? These are the questions, among others; this volume makes and seeks to answer based on praxis, theories.

4

Toxic Education as an Offshoot of the Dominant Grand Narrative

Figure 4 photo: courtesy of theblogofprogress.com

Regarding racism which is another anathema the world is currently facing, nobody is spared. Whoever that subscribes to toxic education either became a perpetrator or a victim. Even those you could not think they would be racists, are suffering from this sort of disease. Again, we need to ask: How can educated people become stinking racists? Are they conscious or unconscious of this sin? Why do they do what they do as far as bigotry is concerned? Why is racism prevalent even in international laws? I will venture into Gandhi's racist slurs in South Africa to show how endemic racism is. I present this person who is thought to be instrumental and eminent as far as struggles for equality and justice is concerned. Fundamentally, I will do so in order to draw the attention of the readers to seriously consider racism so as to know its scope and how to deal with it. In so doing, at an individual level and at collective level, humans will be able to embark on soul-searching without camouflaging in hypocrisy and denial in addressing this endemic racism. Although racism exists everywhere, many countries deny; or hardly talk about it. Gilmore (2015) observes:

> The racial mess in the United States looks pretty grim and is painful to watch. We can be forgiven for being quietly thankful for Canada's more inclusive society, which has avoided dramas like that in Ferguson, Mo. We are not the only ones to think this. In the recently released Social Progress Index, Canada is ranked second amongst all nations for its tolerance and inclusion. Unfortunately, the truth is we have a far worse race problem than the United States. We just can't see it very easily.

If you look at Canadian society superficially–especially if one doing so is a foreigner–you may agree with the introduction of the paragraph above. And, unfortunately, this is what has always happen for outsiders who do not know the skeletons that Canada has in its closet resulting from its gruesome past of colonialism. But when you clinically look at the same, you, too, will agree with the last part of the paragraph. Again, I do not want to single out Canada as a leading country as far as racism is concerned. As we will see, racism exists even in the countries thought to be discriminated against. Refer to the oft-resurgence of xenophobic attacks in South Africa not to mention Ethiopia where some Ethiopians reached the stage of recanting their roots so as to become *black Jews* to end up being discriminated against by those they joined thinking they share pedigree in Israel. Frantzman (2015) maintains that "about 1,000 Israeli Ethiopian Jews have held a rally in Tel Aviv to protest against institutional racism in Israeli society." As it was for Kenya with regards to PEV, Canada and Israel are highly educated countries on earth. Yet, the same still face the sin of racism. What good has education brought to these countries if this is the real situation?

This volume explores racism with another angle *vis-à-vis* conflict that has always been a good source of racism as the pretext exploiting and deeming others inferior thereby mistreating them. Many conflicts occur resulting from how we view one another. The lenses we use to view one another, and other things surrounding us, make us see things differently from different angles and biases. Such biases and lenses are the results of racism that makes one people treat others as inferior based on their races or ancestry. Racism can be expressed based on biological features such as colour of the skin, length of the nose and colour of the hair or culture and history whereby one culture looks at others as inferior to it as it has always been for Western culture in [mis]treating other cultures. Again, when did racism start given that it is not a natural but socially constructed anomaly? Popkin (1980) cited in Uzgalis (2002) notes that modern racism began in Spain in 1492; and that the characteristic feature of modern racism seeks to show that one group of people is rendered permanently inferior to some another group by biologising and climatising it, among others (Hall, 1992 cited in Soudien, 2010). This speaks to how racism started in Europe; and thereafter was exported–through colonialism after institutionalising it–to other places under the current dominant grand narrative that invented people in this racist manner. And this has gone on up until now when Western countries are richer than their victims due to looking at them as inferior so as to enslave and colonise them for many years.

Again, why did European did what they did inhumanely? It is simple. When you view another human being as being less human, you will maltreat them more barbaric than you treat your animals. You can see this on how people treat their pets humanely than those they discriminate against. Sometimes, some humans, particularly, those who want to colonise others, hide themselves behind colour, religions even schools of thoughts. We have reached the point at which we complicate life so as to favour animals, and ironically, ignore, kill and irk other human beings by discriminate against them. Does it mean the colours of animals are not a problem to us? Don't we see them or we see them save that we do not fear them; thus, their colours are immaterial to us? This tells us that the problem is not the colour but something else which we need to know and unveil so as to get the solution to race-related conflicts. It can be a disease, ignorance, bigotry or just mere fear. When I arrived in North

America to live not just to visit and go back home, I discovered things I did not know but which helped me to rethink about racism. This may sound naïve. Although Africans are discriminated against in the West, they see this phenomenon when they get out of the continent as a problem. This does not mean that Africa is free from racism at home. There are a few or some people who discriminate against Africa using exclusionary tactics such as religion race, and some adherence to cultures. As aforementioned, some Indians in East Africa, for example, use their inward looking to get away with murder. I shall discuss this later. Sometimes, I tend to regard racists as ignorant and insane people given that the ways and forms in which we were biologically created are beyond our control, correction or deconstruction. Being a man or a woman, black or white is beyond our volition. If there can come, at least, one person who wrote a letter asking to be created as he or she is, at least, my belief that racists, apart from being insane, are sick and ignorant would escape me. Ask racists, sexists, misogynists, and whatnots; if they can prove their contribution to making their colours or whatever they have and deem to be better than others. If they can provide any logical argument or evidence, it will be nothing but fabrications and utter nonsenses as it was for the eugenics and other stinking racists the world has ever had. Eduardo Galeano (2000, p. 56) cited in Bonilla-Silva (2009) notes that "the Americas are sick with racism, blind in both eyes from North to South" (p. 1071) which indicates that there is a state of blind spot resulting to denialism of the existence of racism in the US and the world in general. I partly concur with this. For, I may argue that somewhat, racists are unconscious of what they do.

However disputable this can because racists discriminate against others so as to please, protect themselves or show their ignorance and malice, there must be some awareness of what they are doing given that they, sometimes, do it covertly or overtly by creating some pretexts in order to hide their guilt-ridden mind. Every now and then, racists look exactly the same like the persons they discriminate against save that they use different lenses and mentality in looking at others. You can trace this blindness in Darwinism and eugenics. Interestingly, when Darwin provided a tool for racists arguing that some of the human are primitive, thus, they could not assimilate in complex white civilisation which is not true, he did not know that Chinese at one time were more advanced and complicated than whites Darwin espoused. Also, the term complex is relative by nature; complex to who and how? Evidence is all over the place today. If Darwin could come today and meet former US president Barack Obama, maybe, he would admit how wrong and gullible he was. Again, thanks to colonial-cum-toxic education, Darwin's claptraps have been held high as an academic breakthrough simply because they supported white race in exploiting others under the current dominant grand narrative.

We need to explore racism even deeper. This is why, in the foregoing chapters, we I address racism from a different angle. I know its gargantuan size and effects. As argued prior, interestingly and ironic, regarding racism, we discriminate against human beings but not animals. I honestly wonder how one would fight for animal rights while the same ignores the rights of his or her colleagues, humans, based on how she or he sees their colour. Is the colour really a problem or something big that needs to over-occupy us or there is something else? In the 60s, the US experienced violent and nonviolent confrontations resulting from policies which segregated Afro-Americans in spite of their huge contribution to the economy of this great country. Afro-Americans, just like their cousins in South Africa under Apartheid, were treated in more repugnant ways than animals. They were denied all human rights just because they were black. To emancipate themselves, Afro-Americans decided to fight non-violently until they won the battle and got their human rights. However, racism has never been totally eradicated in the US just like in South Africa thanks to the tentacles of toxic education espoused by the dominant grand narrative. Due to the toxicity and *holier-than-thou* mentality espoused by and entrenched in colonial education, the US became a reference point as far as racism is concerned.

I wonder how such an advanced nation like the US can commit such a sacrilege to its own people. If anything, the maltreatments Afro-Americans still face in the US result from the current dominant grand narrative that views people differently. This is why it was easy and legal in the eyes of colonisers to colonise, rob, enslave and occupy other countries without any regard to human rights due to the fact that, for the case of America and Africa, these rights were proclaimed in 1948. To the colonisers, human rights meant their rights but not the rights of others. Even the definition of a human in their eyes meant a white but not non-white even though the term white has a lot of controversies as we will see hereunder. To the racists, equal and universal rights were counterproductive. In other words, non-Westerners were not regarded as human beings so as to deserve human rights. Otherwise, racists would not have acted the way they did even after the UDHR-1948. Sadly however, the same mentality has gone on, especially, in the immoral *realpolitik* of the world today which serves the interests of the West at the expenses of others. You can see this on the veto rights that a handful of countries have while the majority of others do not have. You can see it almost on all decisions made under the umbrella of internationality.

Again, where does systemic racism come from apart from its Spanish root I have touched on above? Accidentally though, the US and South Africa mentioned above have a great connection with Britain which may be regarded as the father of the current dominant grand narrative. Certainly, those who created the United States of America, most of them are British descendants who have perpetuated racism nationally and internationally even more ferociously than Spain where racism was born. Truly, slavery and colonialism were carried out, and sustained by racism that the colonisers applied on those they colonised. However, the case is different in South Africa where those who enacted Apartheid are the Dutch. Then again, the US used to support the Apartheid regime just as Britain did when Indigenous South Africans were discriminated against, tortured and killed just because they welcomed those they thought were civilised like they were. Therefore, if you cannot connect racists by blood, you can do so by broods arguably. In connecting racism with Britain, mainly in the 21st century, Hall (1996) cited in Cattani (2015) observes that:

> [...] marginalization of the black experience in British culture; not fortuitously occurring at the margins, but placed, positioned at the margins, as the consequence of a set of quite specific political and

cultural practices which regulated, governed and 'normalized' the representational and discursive spaces of English society (p. 15).

Hall's observation is important. For, it deals with the current situation not the past. Further, he helps us avoid being convinced by mealy-mouthed defence that then was then not now. Even if–for the sake of argument, we buy in the "that-was-that theory–what the US displayed just 50 years ago as far as racism is concerned will still act as a beacon as it beckons and bemoans us to ask such tough questions on British racism; because there are many victims of it around the globe. British racism in not only in politics or former colonies but also in its veins and arteries as Sashidharan (2001) observes that "although the debate about psychiatry is as old as psychiatry itself, it is only in the past three decades that the psychiatric institutions and practices in this country (*Britain*) have come under critical scrutiny for their racial bias" (p. 244). Further, he notes the whole profession admitted that there was racism in psychiatry in Britain. Such admission proves how racism is something systemic and cultural in Britain as Hall notes above. Those complaining about racism are British citizens among who are the ones British colonial rule exported to Africa. Health and education are important areas for the wellbeing of any person or country. So, once one fiddles with the duo, she or he means nothing but the desire to destroy the victims.

We can now move to another area to substantiate our claim. This is none other than education. Gillborn, Rollock, Warmington & Demack (2016) adduce evidence in Britain implying systemic racism in which, for example, black students have been overrepresented in permanent exclusion after data was broken down by ethnicity in which Afro-Caribbean students accounted for 14% of London school children but made up more than 30% of all exclusion in the capital leading to production and reproduction of power and social inequality. To prove even more, I will seek assistance from English language. Basically, language is one of important components of our culture that makes us unique from others apart from being the vehicle by which to deliver and impart knowledge. Through using language we create things, chiefly abstract ones that, sometimes, Boers in South Africa alleged black could not grasp (Robert Mugabe's speech at South African Fort Hare University centenary, 20th May, 2016). Therefore, I will examine how racist English, as a language is, especially *vis-a-vis* the concept of blackness. By all standards, English is the biggest language. No doubt, English is a global language today (Crystal, 2012; and Ricento, 2012), thus the language of the current dominant grand narrative. However there are other Western languages such as French, Spanish and Portuguese (former colonial powers), English is the most spoken language globally. Poignantly, the same *language of the world* is among the most racist languages according to what I am going to present hereunder. If you look at how blackness is treated and the meanings it is given, you will understand how the dominant grand narrative goes deeper than in academics. This is why my appeal to the victims of this racism is based on the urge to deconstruct, reconstruct, reclaim, restore and reconceptualise everything. The situation is the same in the US. Gaertner & Davidio (2014) in their Ingroup Identity Model came to the conclusion that there is what one can call racial bias by way of feelings or symbolism in all cases they upon which they conducted research. In their study they concluded that "negative feelings toward Blacks, which Whites acquire early in life, are relatively stable across the life span and thus persist into adulthood" (p. 3).

There has been racist language going on almost in all academic fields. There is a language with full of myths and controversies *vis-a-vis* the meaning of some terms–for example–if we face it, who is white, and who is black? Such a question is very vital in the world of today and in our discourse pertaining to conflicts resulting from cultural imperialism. Let us be fair. If Caucasians and all those who wrongly perceive themselves as white–including brown ones–then what is the colour of milk or snow? We are living in systematic racism embedded in the dominant grand narrative. If we had received decolonised education, we would have been able to question a simple thing like colours that are however complicated they may seem under social construction in order to make some people look superior and others inferior. We tend to condemn racists and pretend that we do not discriminate against others either intentionally or otherwise thanks to our ignorance. Again, unconsciously or consciously we commit the same sin. Why Obama is an African-American president of the United States but not George Bush Euro-American president of the same? I think referring people according to perceived and socially constructed *colourbarism* is itself racism. You read that

Michelle Jean was the first Caribbean (black)-Canadian Governor General. Well, what of her successor David Johnson. Why his origin is not an issue in writing or reporting about him. I would suggest that we use our nationality or continents instead of racial tags which conceive fake colours when we refer to people. For example, to avoid the feelings of racism or subscribing to it consciously or otherwise, I would prefer to hear somebody calling me an Africa rather than a black because in some languages such as English–as I will prove shortly–blackness means evil or negative connotation.

Fundamentally, if we consider the truth meaning of black, I see no way Africans can be referred to as black the same the blackboard or darkness is. Even the degree of *blackness* among the so-called blacks does differ the same way the degree of *whiteness* differs among those who call themselves whites. Again, in all these three cases, it is obvious that whoever is perceived not be white or white enough, his or her origin is made clear under the current dominant grand narrative in order to avoid contaminating white race. This is racism even if the term white is disputable and controversial. For example, despite being a very a successful nation, the US still suffers from identity problems resulting from the invasion of true Americans namely, the First Nations (Lepore, 2009). Instead of being Americans just like Tanzanians, Kenyans, Cameroonians and whatnots, Americans are afro-, Latino-, Aboriginal, Arab-and whatever-Americans except Caucasians. Americans are Americans. Now, let us look at grandparents of white Americans, the British. Ask good English speakers. Many things with adjective black seem to be bad, evil, inferior or negative. To the contrary, those with adjective white seem to be holier and good. Take black Friday, Black Death even black suit that is, in Western culture worn during the funeral; then compare to white such white dresses associated with angels and cleanliness. Puzzlingly, even black people seem to have adopted this Western stereotype and insults on blackness. If they had received decolonised education, maybe, they would have been able to question such artificiality and fickleness in this racism arrangement.

Regarding how racist English language is, the Merriam online dictionary may give us a bigger picture. It defines white, *inter alia*, as 1) having the color of fresh snow or milk 2) not having anything written or printed on it (US), arguably uncontaminated. Further, take another thing idiomatic i.e. great white hope which means: Something or someone that is expected to succeed. For example, Mark is the great white hope of the international division. This expression dates back from the early 1900s, when heavyweight boxing champion Jack Johnson, who was black, seemed *invincible* and the term was used for any white opponent who might defeat him. It gained prominence as the title of a Broadway play, and later (1970) a film. By then, it had been transferred to anyone of whom much was expected. You can go as far as *white collar* which implies a good job or *white hat* that means a good guy. Compare those meaning above with *black day, black book* where someone sins or unpardonable errors are kept, *blacklist, black sheep* of the family, and many more.

Furthermore, he Merriam Webster online Dictionary defines what black is, apart from other meanings, it gives such explanations 1) In the U.S., the term African-American is often preferred over black when referring to Americans of African descent 2) literary: evil or wicked, a black deed 3) very sad or hopeless: The outlook was black 4) When they heard the terrible news, they were filled with black despair 5) very tragic or unhappy 6) That was a black day in our country's history. There also is a black mood. To be able to get the sense of how being black is perceived and how anything or anybody associated with blackness is demonised, de Paor (1971) cited in McVeigh (2014) notes that "in Northern Ireland Catholics are Blacks who happen to have white skins" (p. 183). McVeigh as well as I wonder how Northern Ireland Catholics can be perceived as black while they are not on tropic, and does not have non-white population whatsoever. These are white Caucasians who are deemed black simply because they are unacceptable despite sharing everything with those blatantly disowning and demonising them. If such racists can openly disown and misrepresent ones of their own, how will they treat others? Such a tendency shows how ignorant some of the so-called advanced, civilised and educated societies and people can be.

When I was doing my research on this volume, I came across some clarifications I used to take for granted just like any other people may do. I started questioning even simple past experiences. One of those experiences is the instance that occurred when I was in the store shopping in my Canadian hometown. On that material day, one Caucasian little boy accompanied by his mother, spotted me. He honestly told his mother that "that guy is black." The boy's mother felt terribly horrible as she tried to shush the boy as if what he as saying was a dirty or an insult to me. To show how clear the message was to me, I told the boy. "Yes, I am black in your eyes. Do you think you are white dear little one?" The boy just stared at me blankly. To hit where it hurts most, I then added. "Dear, if you think, you are white, what of snow and milk? Why don't you think and talk about the colours of flowers and fruits instead of colouring people?" I said as I smiled at the boy whose mother was shrinking back as she tried hard to ask her son to leave the scene. Sensing the type of response I offered, the mother pulled her boy's hand; and excused herself before leaving in shame. There they vanished! How do you call this; if we truly face it? Isn't this racism? If what I encountered were not racism, why did the mother want to shush the boy; and why did she pull him and vanished? I think the boy used to hear his parents or those around him saying bad thing about people perceived to be black; or his mother knew those meaning offered above. How many have come across such racist treatments in our streets? How many use the words above unconsciously or out of ignorance or malice and bigotry? Isn't this the evidence that racism is there although we pretend to use the wisdom of the wise monkey which sees nothing hears nothing and says nothing? Again, should we blame those embarking on racist behaviour or teach them by showing them how bad their behaviours are? We need to negotiate what to do about racism instead of blaming or passing judgment wholesomely. For, it will not solve the problem. I believe that if we show those who act in racist manners how it feels, maybe, they will see a big picture; and thereby change even if not abruptly. At least, we will be sending a message that what they are doing is unfair and racist. Again, this depends on the type of education were offering to our people. Decolonised education will show us who we actually are like human beings regardless our income, creed, colour and whatnots. This is where the centrality of incorporating all grand narrative is central.

The controversy of colour–especially the greatness of whiteness compared to black worthlessness–does not end up with this boy and his mother only. It goes far since the dominant grand narrative invented and propagated inequality so as to variably affect many more people within and without its own jurisdiction. You can see this anomaly in other *brown* or whatever societies. Some Asians call themselves *white* when they are with Africans, and yet, they are all put in the same basket of the people of colour when they are in Western countries. Sometimes I wonder why non-whites are called people of colour as if whites do not have colour. Arguably, there is something amiss in this colour tagging which is purely the product of the dominant grand narrative and its education. This reminds me of the story of a South African doctor of Asian/Sri Lanka descent. Despite being a doctor of medicine, thanks to toxic education, when I used to visit her for checkups, she used to openly show how she could not free herself from racism. I remember one racist incident that has stuck in my mind. It was the time one of our boys was born. When this female doctor was joking with a newly born baby, she told him that he is black while she is brown. But looking at the two namely, the baby and the doctor, one could see a different picture. Normally, babies are born a little bit brighter than adults who have already suffered some burns from the Sun. Even by blind standards, being of Sri Lankan or Bangladesh pedigree, the doctor was darker than all of us. Yet, because of her ancestry, she believed she was browner than us. Again, looking at the history of the doctor and the way British colonial powers divided the then Ceylon now Sri Lanka, I forgave her. I remembered Carter, Irani & Volkan (2009) words saying that, for example, "Buddhist revivalists strongly repudiated this view asserting their Aryan roots, claiming lighter skin and a Sinhalese /Buddhist culture to be superior to the Hindu Tamils of darker Dravidian origin" (p. 165). If people of the same ancestry can discriminate against one another, who were we?

Historically, before the coming of British discriminatory colonial powers, Sinhalese lived together as any other societies. But when divide-and-rule then divide-and-depart colonial strategy was introduced, here there are butchering one another under the slogans of chosen ones Buddhaputra and Bhumiputra namely, son of Buddha and son of soil, (Carter, Irani & Volkan *Ibid.*). Where is the daughter of the soil? Teo (2010) examines racism by observing violence so as to come up with the conclusion that racism goes hand in hand with sexism. Under feminine lenses, whatever is socially constructed as weak is treated as female. For, Sinhalese if you are not a Buddhist you do not exist and if you do, you do not have rights just like they have. This racism goes deeper and deeper even within a family or a country. Goeka (2005) maintains that "Sammodamānā—all the time there is compassion, love, happiness, and cordiality. That is the quality of a Buddha putra or a Buddha putri, or a son or daughter of the Buddha. Avivadamānā—they don't quarrel. If they quarrel then they are not fit sons and fit daughters" (page is not provided).

The major question we can ask ourselves in the case of Sri Lanka, for example, is: where did the compassion go? Why Buddhaputra and Buddhaputri did start hating others based on their history and identity? Carter, Irani & Volkan (*op.cit.*) indicate that before the coming of British rule with its divide-and-rule strategy, Sinhalese and Tamils lived harmoniously along with each other with normal misunderstandings that did not lead to such hatred and destruction. Maybe, we should find a chief suspect, especially considering that Sri Lankan first Prime Minister Solomon Bandaranaike, just like Gandhi, was a British trained person who introduced what was known as "detamoulisation" (Carter, Irani, & Volkan *op.cit*, p. 159) that culminated in the destruction of Sri Lanka after facing a three-decade war spearheaded by the Liberation Tigers of Tamil Eelam (LTTE). For, such a highly trained person discriminating his own people shows how the type of education he received was wrong and wanting. If those we think are educated are but colonial brains, what should we expect? Again, why did peaceful Buddhists become violent in this ethnopolitical conflict? Maybe, we can point a finger at toxic education as espoused by the dominant Western grand narrative that made these wonderful people blind so as to hate their brethren the British rule used to pity against each other. So, you can easily see the blindness toxic education causes to society. The people who are supposed to be the eyes of the society due to being educated, sometimes, end up becoming as good as blind one. Despite being highly educated, my doctor would not escape the blindness of racism even when she meant a joke! Interestingly, when things went wrong in Sri Lanka, the same Britain distanced itself from the mess as if it was not the one that created it.

Furthermore, regarding racism, sometimes, one can agree with me that it is a disease that is torturing many regardless their differences, similarities, sameness, and whatnots. For, even among Africans themselves, thanks to the demonisation and exclusion of their grand narrative, the blindness around racism can be easily seen as it is among whites wherein person with blonde hair feels to be better than those who do not have the same blonde hair since blonde is associated with goodness (Swami & Barrett, 2011) or the apogee of beauty (Deliovsky, 2008). Other communities use organs such as height (Masai); nose (Tutsis) and other parts of the body all depending on the lenses a particular-affected society uses. In some African societies, those with brown tinge are referred to as white even though they well-nigh are not. This makes racism even more complicated than anybody can imagine. For the person referred to as white in Africa may be referred as black in Western countries as in the case of Asians above.

In East Africa, for example, many Indians, Arabs and other Asians like to refer to themselves as white while in the West they are all black indiscriminately. To make matters worse, some Indigenous Africans refer to themselves as Arabs in some African countries such as North Sudan and in the Maghreb simply because Arabic is dominant and they were brainwashed and deculturalised that they are not Africans while they actually are. Further, this blind categorisation started long time ago. For example, French colonialists introduced artificial racism wherein Africa was divided into two distinct halves namely; black Africa (Sub-Sahara Africa) and white Africa (Maghreb). Africans categorising some of Africans as white is neither new nor an anomaly despite the fact that it, ironically is not viewed as racism.

Moreover, racism sometimes cuts across races. I have mentioned in beginning this chapter that I would present Gandhi's side of racism. Even the famous *Mahatma* Ghandi in South Africa fought for the rights of Indians to be treated like whites but not just like human beings, Indians or Africans he used to call kaffirs following Boers calling them so. So, for Gandhi, as an Indian, and his colleagues, the right they deserved not to be treated like who they actually are, humans, but like whites in order to differentiate themselves from African. Thus, for them, equality was not the rights for all including blacks as Gandhi cited in Czekalska & Klosowicz (2016) maintains that:

> Ours is a continual struggle against a degradation sought to be inflicted upon us by the Europeans, who desire to degrade us to the level of the raw Kaffir whose occupation is hunting, and whose sole ambition is to collect a certain number of cattle to buy a wife with and, then, pass his life in indolence and nakedness (p. 39).

Due to the above assumption, I may argue that this is why the Indian Congress organised educational youth clubs for children of indentured Indians, and fighting for the general rights of all Indians but not the rights of all people including Indigenous South Africans or Kaffirs as Boers and Gandhi liked to refer to them. Although South Africa under Apartheid was then organised along colour lines, a visionary leader who saw the future, just like Nelson Mandela did, would not self-stonewall behind a tribal cocoon just like Gandhi did behind the cocoon of colour and pedigree. This shows how dangerously blinding toxic education can be. I am a fan of Gandhi. Again, looking how mortal humans are, I can see the other side of Gandhi everybody would abhor or fail to underscore just because of fanaticism and love. I know Gandhi has many fans and sympathisers globally.

Again, if we face things with critical thinking and suspicious eye, everything needs to be analysed and presented as it is so that we can generate dialogue based on correcting its anomalies or weakness. Gandhi–a lawyer, an activist and a beacon–was educated in London though the education blinded him so as to see only Indians in fighting and negotiating for human rights instead of seeing equal human beings. Remember. Gandhi was a human being just like anybody. As Mandela would put it that he was not an angel but a struggling or trying sinner, the same applies to Gandhi. Again, how could Gandhi escape his world that he, thereafter, shed such a myopic, racist and humiliating image after denouncing caste system in India? No doubt. Gandhi was an upright man who was corrupted by the situation of the day in South Africa where he purposely and blindly turned his Indian Congress into the watchdog for Indian interests but not human interests! Circumstantially, the Indian Congress sought to minimise the danger Africans posed towards it because of the wealth Indians made by exploiting Africans after being brought by British colonial authorities. To mitigate the danger and hide this racist behaviour, the Congress invented a duping strategy of giving African education scholarships which has been ongoing in many African countries where Indians make a bomb on the expenses of Indigenous people. As far as Gandhi is concerned, he would not overcome the setups of the dominant grand narrative. In one of the many submissions Gandhi made before the court representing Indians' interests as he was quoted as saying:

> Your Lordship's petitioners have noticed with shame and sorrow the zealous attempts made to compare your Petitioners with the natives of South Africa [and] beg to draw your Lordship's attention to the anomaly that the [Franchise Amendment Bill] would rank the Indian lower than the rawest native (1, pp. 122 and 124)" (Stone 1990, p. 724).

Such words come from the lips of a stinking racist however mightier he might be regarded. Further, Stone (*Ibid.*) cites Gandhi saying that:

> It was this experience for which we were perhaps all unprepared. We had fondly [sic] imagined that we would have suitable quarters apart from the Natives ... I felt that passive resistance had not been undertaken too soon by the Indian community. Degradation underlay the classing of the Indians with the Natives (VIII, p. 119)" (p. 731).

Stone brings even more inculpatory evidence quoting Gandhi's words of October 1908 when Gandhi was jailed again, in Volksrus where Gandhi says that "in this gaol, Indian and Kaffir prisoners were always lodged separately" (p. 732). He adds "we may entertain no aversion to Kaffirs, but we cannot ignore the fact that there is no common ground" (p. 732). How hypocritical Gandhi was to say that they did not entertain aversion to Kaffirs as if they actually loved them. How could Gandhi discriminate against people and say that he does not entertain aversion he had already entertained through actions and words? To show how Gandhi, ironically "entertained aversion to Kaffirs" he notes "we could understand not being classed with the whites but to be placed on the same level with the Natives seemed too much to put up with" (p. 734). Gandhi purposely uses the term Kaffir while–as a lawyer and an educated person–he knew how abhorrent and offensive the term is.

Importantly, Baderoon (2012) helps us to provide the meaning of the term kaffir when he notes that:

> As the Dictionary of South African English on Historical Principles (henceforth DSAE) conveys, 'kaffir' is a comprehensively abusive word used to denote Black people in South Africa, exemplary of the violent disavowal of Black people's humanity during apartheid. Offensive to the extent of being unspeakable today (in fact, its use constitutes a hate crime in South Africa), 3 entries in the DSAE show that even during the colonial period there was an awareness of resistance to the use of the term (1b and 2a: 342) (page not provided).

Arguably, for victims of colonialism, racism and the toxicity of colonial education, it needs the courage of the mad to keep holding such a person with respect or keeping on referring to him as a moral compass while he actually was the opposite. Even his colleagues Indians knew how racist Gandhi was. Bhana & Vahed cited in Kaiwar (2007) maintain that "undoubtedly the most tragic legacy of Gandhi's time in South Africa was his attitude towards Africans. Gandhi sought, at least, national equality for Indians and Europeans, but felt no compulsion to demand the same for Africans" (p. 113). Further, Bhana & Keiwar argue that Gandhi, even when he started Satyagraha in South Africa, he did not invite Africans. He believed that Africans had not reached a religious level of understanding Satyagraha. They accuse him of failing even to mention a single name of an African leader in his autobiography, *Satyagraha in South Africa* published as a book in 1928. Nhlanla Nholangwane (2003) cited in Ramsamy (n.d.) posits that Gandhi was a racist who did not view Africans as human beings; and he supported apartheid's racist and separatist policies. He wonders why Gandhi could not see such a majority to which he turned a blind eye despite his people benefitting from them not to mention accepting them even though the discriminated against and were brought purposely to exploit them. Further, Leishman (2017) cites South African academics, Ashwin Desai and Goolam Vahed who notes that "Gandhi was, like Columbus, a racist. Desai said Gandhi believed in the Aryan brotherhood. This involved whites and Indians higher up than Africans on the civilized scale" (p. 5). To that extent, he was a racist. Again, Nauriya (2006) concurs with Bhana & Keiwar citing (CW, Vol 62: 199) as he notes that "in 1936 Gandhi was asked by an African-American delegation to India: "Did the South African Negro take any part in your movement?" Gandhi replied: "No, I purposely did not invite them" (p. 19). Nauriya posits that Gandhi did not invite Africans simply because doing so would endanger their cause. He did not explain why and how while they all were facing the same enemy. Such a statement seems more abusive and provocative, especially when it comes from the lips of the so-called mahatma. Again, Gandhi looked at Indigenous South Africans negatively thinking, maybe, they were too naïve and inept of embarking on nonviolence struggles. He forgot one nothing that the same naïve natives or kaffirs–as he liked to refer to Africans–were the ones who accepted Indians that British colonial rules heinously brought to exploit them. But due to Ubuntu, they did not demand that Indians be returned to India before and after becoming independent. Gandhi's racist behaviour was known for a long time save that, thanks to international conspiracy and discrimination against Africa, they were ignored. Sometimes, it becomes difficult to differentiate Gandhi from ultra-racists such as Rider Haggard or Rudyard Kipling (2015) who wrote the white man's burden whereas the truth was to the contrary.

Profoundly, I see no difference between Gandhi and Kipling who was acting as the mouthpiece of colonialism by glorifying missionaries who paved the way for colonialism. He in his book *White Man's Burden* writes: "these innocent young missionaries had taken on their shoulders the "white man's burden" (p. 181) which practically was to the contrary; because they enhanced colonialism that became a burden on the shoulders of African so referred to as a burden. Were missionaries truly innocent while they are responsible for destroying African culture and livelihood by paving the way for the full-brown colonialism in Africa? I do not know if the horse is a burden to a human whom it carries with all of his burdens. The horse will never ever be a burden to the jokey (the burden) who rides it.

As argued above, racism is like sickness which is exacerbated by toxic education. I do not think in the normal sanity that missionaries were more innocent than those whose countries they helped to be colonised. Mhango (2016) refers to the missionaries as mere criminals along with the so-called explorers, merchants and other colonial agent that paved a way for the colonisation of Africa at all times. Again, how could Kipling care about *savages* that needed *civilisation* that turned out to be nothing but being sold into slavery and being colonised thereafter? If anything, this is the blindness toxic education causes after turning a person into a bigotry garden if not a tool for malice revolving around narcissism and supremacism. If we face it, what is regarded as a white man's burden turns out to be the burden of the colonised people but not of the colonisers. Or call it a black man's perpetual burden. Maybe, when Kipling (2007) cited in Streck & Wasserman (2016) writes that "the Lair of the Wolf is his refuge and where he has made him his home" (p. 241), he is lampooning himself. Is it a liar or lair? What a lie if at all what is known as a white man's burden is a black man's burden? A hyena in a lair will always be a hyena. Importantly, when we deal with racism, we need to carefully underscore the fact that it is not as simple as we might think.

Apart from subsuming white thinkers, racism did the same to even those you would not expect. Being a monster that has eaten many, it still has many victims such as Gandhi who was influenced– and thus, worked–under the influence of the already-lied-down pattern of racism. Furthermore, Gandhi's racism emanated from his Indian caste system; and was topped up with pure British racism emanating from colonial mentality and colonial arrogance and criminality based on toxic education that he received in Britain and India. This is the type of education this volume seeks to deconstruct and decolonise for the betterment of a human family. Generally speaking, Indians in South Africa felt that they were superior to

Africans. When talking about Indians in the apartheid South Africa Robert Sobukwe cited in Soske (2009) notes that:

> This class identifies itself by and large with the oppressor but, significantly, this is the group which provides the political leadership of the Indian people of South Africa. And all that the politics of this class have meant until now is the preservation and defense of the sectional interests of the merchant class. If we consider where Gandhi came from, we can know why he was naturally a racist that the world did know because he was able to hide everything after going back to India where his so-called nonviolence struggle eclipsed everything. Even if you look at some of his acts such as denying his wife sex are not nonviolent but purely violent (p. 257).

Racism is in Gandhi's blood, faith and psyche. Gandhi has telling many racist stories. Power (1969) cited in George-Williams (2006) quotes Gandhi who maintains that "even the half-castes and kaffirs, who are less advanced than we, have resisted the government. They pass law applies to them as well, but they do not take out passes" (p. 29). For the person who was supposed to unequivocally fight Apartheid in order to achieve equality, Gandhi would have refrained from using such a pejorative language whose meaning he knew full well like we all do. By calling Africans kaffirs, Gandhi, purposely subscribes to the language of the oppressor that he uses to insult Africans. And this—for Gandhi who many call mahatma—was a just and normal thing to do. If Gandhi truly fought for the rights of all oppressed people in South Africa regardless the complexion of the skin of their colour or pedigree non-violently, why did he then use the violent language of the oppressor and fall short of becoming one? It is from this milieu, therefore one can arguably put Gandhi in the same basket with the oppressors whose tool of sustenance was nothing but segregation and discrimination all revolving around brutality and violence. Again, as a true crusader for justice for all—had Gandhi been one—he was not supposed to subvert or supplant anything as far as oppressors are concerned. If more investigation is embarked upon Gandhi unknown deeds, maybe, many horrible things will be exhumed as far as Gandhi's character *vis-à-vis* racism is concerned.

As an activist, naturally and obligatorily, fighting for equality and equal treatments for all oppressed people regardless their creed, race, ideology and whatnots therefore falls on Gandhi's shoulders. Similarly, one would think that Gandhi's organic response would be compatible with equality and fairness he was fighting for, however only for Indians, but not for all people in South Africa. Try to imagine a god who orders a person to wear a cloth of a corpse as it is in Hinduism or the person who dies for his god who—we are told is immortal. This is done willy-nilly against the equality and sacredness of all human beings. Why a mortal die for an immortal if the immortal should not protect them simply because it is immortal? I wonder how people, especially the international community, have been duped to make do with Indian cancerous system aka caste system. Basically, caste is racism enshrined in religion just like any other foreign religions that sanctify racism under the pretext of creation and religion. Annamalai (2005) argues that "caste system is not just Racism, but it is much more Vicious, Venomous, Evil and Cruel; Caste System is Racism, Fascism and Nazism." *http://www.ambedkar.org/News/Cssacndzsm.htm*

This makes me worry and wonder even more when I consider some concepts such as holiness and sinfulness. Consider how the world holy is abused and misused in describing such racist faiths. Due to the toxicity our colonial education, the whole world still refers to India as the world's biggest democracy. Thanks to this ignorance resulting from the toxicity of colonial education, the whole world has rewarded endemic and systemic racism that has left millions of innocent people discriminated against, exploited and violated. What a conspiracy against such a people? Morey (n.d.) observes that:

> The inherent racism of historic Hinduism is thus blatant. You were judged by the color of your skin, not the content of your character, skills or talents. The darker your skin, the lower your caste and rank in Hindu society. The whiter your skin is, the higher your caste and rank (p. 1).

Morey assumption is highly entrenched in Indian culture despite the fact that when the same Indians go to Western countries are deemed to be black or people of colour. Despite this, Morey notes that "the terrible caste system was invented in order to protect the white Brahmins from polluting their sacred whiteness with black blood" (p. 2).

Isn't this pure Apartheid that the world has tolerated simply because it does not touch on the interests of the high and the mighty of this world regulated by the dominant grand narrative? This is purely stinking racism regardless whoever is behind even if it called the biggest or whatever democracy.

Although there is a lot of obnoxious whiff out there regarding racist remarks Mahatma Gandhi made, the evidence adduced is satisfactory to hold him as a stinking racist. Again, for those interested in looking into Gandhi's racist behaviour and psyche, they can follow this link *http://originalpeople.org/mahatma-gandhi-racist-quotes/*

Racism is a universal phenomenon however hidden and deceptive it can be. Although we tend to ignore or deny its existence–in many societies for fear of being branded racists while we actually are–racism is there; and it causes a lot of hatred, mistrusts and suspicions which are good grounds for conflicts be they identity based or human right based. Racism is always there since the neo-and-non-native-grand narratives, socially constructed it to serve them under the expenses and peril of others. There is even racism that can be displayed by many at country level such as the *Newsweek* (1984, p. 37) cited in Washington (1990) notes that "several years ago, in Egypt, for instance, a scheduled telecast of an American movie dramatization of Anwar Sadat's life was cancelled because a public outcry arose when it was learned that the slain Egyptian leader would be portrayed by a black American actor" (p. 209). A public wanted Sadat–who was relatively black–acted by a white man! Who are this public if not the majority of the citizens in such a case? Isn't this national discrimination that Egypt displayed against their colleague Africans? Paradoxically, Sadat himself was black and not Arab. Furthermore, Egyptian official was quoted referring to the SSA as "Saharan Africa as "dogs and slaves" (Gaffey, 2016).

Crucially, apart from Egypt and Egyptians been in Africa, they discriminate against their cousins Africans in the south where their livelihood that depends on the river Nile emanates. What do you call this if not a national blindness and ignorance displayed by its racist madness? As if it is not enough, even Nubian Egyptians are segregated living in their own villages forgotten and treated like second-class citizens in their own country. Here comes another type of education that is not European but Middle Eastern based on religious colonialism. Equally, this sort of education needs to be decolonised given that it has engulfed many parts of the world particularly Africa by way of religion. This is called brown racism. Adinarayan (1964) cited in Washington (1990) observes that, in India, there is widespread prejudices exhibited against dark skinned Indians, and discrimination against African students that face ostracisation by being treated as a pariah group. He goes on noting that Indians in the US, England, Canada, France, and other Western countries avoid being associated with Africans. Again, once the same are targeted by racist Africans–which we do not condone–like Idi Amin (Former Ugandan Dictator who expelled Indians from Uganda in 1972), due to their association with British colonial rule and being a little bit brown, it becomes an international outcry. A racist is a racist despite what. So, we, sometimes, consciously or unconsciously enact racism. In some communities, for example, in Tanzania, a perceived white woman who–principally is of the same community–seeks many cows with regards to paying her dowry. Once again, you can see how racism is crossing borders of colours and origins so as to signify something good, beauty, goodness, value etc. on one the hand while the same signifies the opposite on the other hand.

In sum, we are aware of the truth about the stinking factor that racism does exist even among people of the same race. You can see this every day in some places if not everywhere. As indicated above, people with blonde air among the so-called white are highly regarded while brownish among Asians and Africans are as well regarded to be superior to the dark ones which in both cases is wrong. So, too we have seen how some people go to the extremes considering simple and unreasonable things such as nose, height even the colour of eyes. All in all, I can conclude this chapter arguing that, under the current dominant grand narrative whose media bomb the whole world with their own standards of beauty based on size and colour–which actually favour Caucasians, if things are not changed–conflicts resulting from racism will always emanate from such angles. You can see how the current dominant grand narrative espouses and uses racism in African pageantry. Most of the winners if not all must look like Caucasian women by hair, look, size even their catwalks on the stage. This means that those girls are discriminating against themselves unconsciously or out of ignorance or colonial mentality if not the influence of toxic education that failed to make them self-conscious not to mention the systems running everything. The person who is not conscious of herself or himself is as good as walking copse. Even the governments that allow such abuses to take place under the pretext of respecting human rights such as freedom of choice are dead mentally and consciously so to speak. Primarily, the type of education we receive has a lot to do with our colonisation something that needs to be replaced by decolonised education which will address some endemic problems, *inter alia*, racism that this chapter has profoundly been discussed.

5

Achieving Decolonised Education, the Need for Integrated Knowledge

Figure 5 photo courtesy of ei-ie.org

"We've had a highly Anglo-Saxon view of higher education for many years, and that can't be sustained for much longer," Paul Blackmore, a professor of high education at King's College London said when explaining why Asian university gain recognition in ratings internationally." He goes on that *"the release that Asia's improvement can be attributed to "undoubted growth" in the region's university systems as well as an increase in global recognition" https://ca.finance.yahoo.com/blogs/insight/three-canadian-universities-among-top-50-in-the-world--survey-155226920.html*

According to Blackmore with respect to who makes it to such high score in international education ratings, among other things, the issue is nothing but to have recognition, or call it a nod, from the leaders of the world almost in everything, the West. Again, who gave Western countries the power to decide who qualifies and who does not? The answer is simple that they are able to put some conditions and qualifications in place that everybody who wants to make it to their lists of academic excellence must have and meet. This is what hegemony is all about. This is why almost everything good is in Western countries as far as development is concerned. They define what development is and who is to be termed as developed or not. Another important thing to underscore is why "Anglo-Saxon views" but not the views of other civilisations? This means that if Anglo-Saxons do not favour you, you cannot make it to the list of prestigious universities' status. In a nutshell, the fact is that Anglo-Saxons have hegemony over many things on earth because it is an Anglo-Saxon's dominant grand narrative based on Judeo-Christianity that defines and controls everything. This is why it was able for Judeo-Israel to be remedied when it was wronged by being persecuted by Nazis as opposed to Africans who were enslaved by European countries for many years. Arguably, the issue here was who was wronged but not the magnitude of the crime or the number of victims. For, if we consider the numbers of the victims of slavery and the span of time such brutality the victims suffered, Africans, if they were part of this dominant grand narrative, would have been redressed a long time ago. For, the atrocities against them were committed many years before holocaust was committed. This is why Israel has always enjoyed support and aid from the West even when they know what their support and aid do to innocent Palestinians facing Apartheid-like situation in their own country.

To achieve fully decolonisation of education, we need to have more integrated knowledge that Druckman cited in Cheldelin, Druckman & Fast (2003) defines to mean "to form into a whole; to unite or become united so as to form a complete or perfect whole; unify" (p. 395). Can this "complete and perfect whole" in education be formed without decolonising it by incorporating other views, theories, and practices from other cultures and grand narratives? Does the current colonised education entertain or have this way of thinking? Is it ready to welcome the decolonised education without allowing the colonised education to be decolonised? Given that the current education was born in the West—and it is now hugely globalised—there is an urgent need for decolonising education so that it can accommodate; and promote all grand narratives of the world through equitable and agreed upon globalisation. Paczyska in Cheldelin, Druckman & Fast (*Ibid.*) notes that "globalization processes, by challenging the local cultural, religious, and moral codes, and imposing Western, secular, and materialist values, alien to Indigenous ways of organising social life, are contributing to the emergency of cultural, and religious conflicts" (p. 222) not to mention cultural colonialism espoused by colonised education the current dominant grand narrative espouses.

Again, as Lederach (2005) cited in Anderson (2008) argues that, in dealing with conflict, we need to imagine ourselves in a web of relationships wherein all are included, including the enemies. What a powerful statement if seriously and realistically worked on! All those we brand to be inferior or whatever tags have the right to be consulted and listened to given that this is an intellectual dialogue to which everybody can contribute given that what is brought is discussed, assessed, analysed and accepted or rejected based on consensus and well informed decision. Why doesn't the right to be held before being convicted apply to those we presume to be inferior while it is declared that it applies to all human beings equally? We all live in this only planet. The difference between being an animal and being human is being intellectual; minus this we are all but animals. We, thus, have to listen to what those we perceive to be terrorists, for example, say about those calling them so. So, too, we need to listen to those we view as enemies; and the ways we can put our heads together to go about this dichotomous problem. We all need this world and peace equally despite our differences, cultures and aspirations. We need to be true to ourselves shall we aspire to live together or, as Martin Luther would put it "we must learn live together as brothers or die together as fools" (King cited in Tewkesbury, 2011, p. 619). Indeed, we need to learn to live together as humanity but not humans labouring under animosity and triviality mainly revolving around colonialism and racism. If needs be, we must die for the world instead of killing it for individual gratifications and gains. It does not work. You can see the logic such a statement frankly has on climate change and global warming. We need to consult all cultures to see and find how they may be used to conserve mother earth that is now destroyed by capitalistic desire to profit without seeing how we are all going to lose because of arrogance, greed and ignorance. Capitalism mode of production based on profits and consumerism has totally failed. I am not trying to be a parsimonious doomsayer, but soon this system will collapse. Nothing is forever, especially that is made or created by human beings. If humans are not forever how can their systems be forever?

Strictly speaking, we need free and real education that colonial regime did not want to offer to whoever it colonised for the fear of being toppled. Again, if one critically and unbiasedly looks at what is going on and the way the West fuels conflict in the world, one will find that it has the hallmarks of Western traditions that propound the so-called "problem-solving approach" which has not solved human problems but instead exacerbated them under the current Eurocentric education. I do not know if such an approach as it is espoused by the current education has solved the problems in countries facing conflicts from controlling resources so that they can sell to the West. So, by decolonising education, we are challenging Western traditions that are embedded in it by accepting the fact that even non-Western thoughts, values, civilisations and whatnots are real and equal; and thus, must equally be applied and respected.

In many colonised countries, famously known as colonies as then they were, Western education was offered in colonial tongues such as French, English, Portuguese, Spanish, Germany and others. Missionaries were charged with the provision of education before the colonial governments took over or went ahead working with them for the whole periods they ruled these countries. In effect, missionaries' work was to "soften" potential subjects ready for colonisation. Dubious and evil manoeuvres such as penitence or penetration were used to spy on the colonised people so as to easily know how to treat them after establishing full-blown colonisation. In a simple parlance, the type of education that was offered was more of anesthetic agent than awakening which is the true aim of education as Plato started it aimed at enabling the plebcists to stand for their rights. This means, the type of education people in the colonies were given was not well-intentioned; and would not enable them to solve their pending problems then and thereafter. Instead, it was hypnotising them so that they can be cheaply and easily ruled for good as it turned to be. If there is anything that this colonised education did was nothing but to just enable its victims to change the nature of colonisation without eradicating it as it happened in many, if not, all ex-colonies that have since been perpetually colonised in a different style sometime by their the oppressed who became oppressors. However, colonialism is colonialism. Many colonies acquired independence that ended up furthering dependence on the same masters and the same system so as to force me question the logic of gaining independence that did not free their people. If anything, the type of education offered may tell us why, for example, former colonies face more conflicts, specifically ethnic ones than their former colonial masters. Furthermore, the type of education people in the colonies received had a lot to do with current conflicts in various countries. Most of the conflicts are more ethnic than political ones. Nevertheless, in the end, such conflicts tend to metamorphoses themselves to becoming ethnopolitical conflicts. This is why I want this type of education decolonised. I maintain that it is because of this toxic education, colonisers were able to keep their rule intact by using their victims after pitying them on against another. The essence of all this was for the colonial government to run the colonies at low cost even if this meant to destroy the lives of the victims. Mozaffar (2007) notes:

> Colonial rulers' reliance on local agents to cope with the dilemma of maintaining control at low cost encouraged these agents to differentiate their groups from those not so privileged by colonial authority either by recombining and redefining existing objective markers of ethnicity or by accentuating previously minor group differences (p. 9).

The effects and patterns of ethnoconflict do not only end in the formation of ethnic or ethnopolitical groups. They go far and wide influencing and dictating the voting system and distribution of resources in the many former colonies depending on who is in power. Despite being referred as a country with relatively high educated middle class in Africa, Kenya cascaded into ethnic cleansing in the 2007 elections. Those who do know the true history of ethnic conflict in Africa were quick to blame everybody except themselves. Ironically, some of those who blamed Kenyans are the same colonisers who sowed this seed of destruction that has haunted Kenya ever since. And this has been their chronic predisposition. When chips are down, these *creators* of ethnicity in Africa become the first to blame the victims of their brutality and criminality. When Kenya cascaded into abyss and chaos, it became difficult to mediate the conflict up until the International Criminal Court (ICC) reined in after Kenyans failed to put their house in order. Why? It can be argued that toxic education void of practical skills in one's environment had a lot to do with the chaos in Kenya. All those who butchered one another based on ethnic animosities lacked the knowhow of who they actually are. Again, Kenya is still regarded as a highly educated in Africa which is an irony to what transpired in Kenya during the PEV. Is it belittling Kenya to doubt and interrogate the type of education its people receive? Doesn't Kenya's education need to be decolonised? I have used Kenya just as an example. It does not mean that Kenya is alone and is the one to blame alone. For, there are many, if not all, countries in Africa with the same type of education that cannot address their needs; and thus solve their problems. Such educational deficit in education is experienced all over Africa. This is why Africa has always lagged behind as far as taking the rightful stand before the international community is concerned. So, too, this is why Africa has always been at home with begging and wanton dependency while it sits on vast reserves of resources of all kinds. Decolonise now. Start with education; and you will see changes in the lives of our people. While Africa is chronic in begging, it does not want to venture outside of the box and ask a very provocative question as to why and for how long we will keep on begging. While all this degradation–that some presidents take pride in–is going on, Africa has never asked itself how it can turn things around. The first and most credible way of getting out of this appalling and degrading situation is to examine Africans and the way they are affected by colonial way of thinking that encourages them to become selfish and blind and careless about others. President Mojica once said "so we lay down red carpets, the kind of things used by kings. I don't like those things" because is the abuse of the majority by the minority in power. If Africa wants to move forward, it should look at how it begs and spends. Simple, a begging president does not deserve a red or black carpet, which, apart from wasting money, is a colonial carryover. Where does such a president get luxury and moral authority to abuse money obtained by means of begging or borrowing while her or his people die of poverty? Doesn't Africa have such leaders wrongly and sadly citizenry still trust that they can deliver them while, at heart, they want to live posh lives even if citizenry die of miseries of their own creation? Tell them that what they are doing is bad and wrong, they will detain you simply because they are the only ones with the rights to decide how things should be done even if it is wrong and worse. Yet, such blind and myopia rulers–due to such toxicity colonised education instilled in them–will go around thumbs up self-cheating, cheating others and priding themselves that they are democrats while they actually are demonic as far as love of others is concerned. Many like to defend and promote their own rights on the expenses of others. And, fundamentally, this is what colonialism, whether it is local, or foreign, is all about. Why can't we live equally, especially like those we pretend to represent or rule? Without decolonising education, the situation is likely to be worse than it currently is. All these unimportant things evidenced colonial rulers and people ape from the West, have to do with the lack of emancipatory and decolonised education. In sum, this education has hardwired its victims to just destroy themselves even where they know the root causes of their manmade quandaries. This volume seeks the feat of seeing Africans and other victims of colonisation and toxic education embark on an ambitious mission of making their case to at least, show the world the anomalies of the said education. As oft-argued, this symbolises a move forward not for the victims but also for the perpetrators of all heinous crimes recorded in history.

What is Neocolonialism?

Intrusion of foreign economic domination, as well as military and political intervention, in states that have already achieved independence from colonial rule

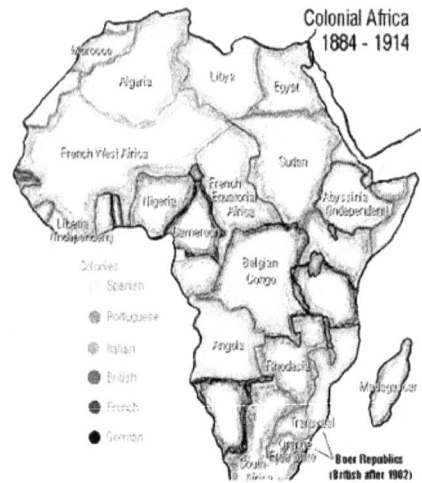

Figure 6 photo courtesy of what-is-this.net

We can sum it up in one sentence: the civilization of the machine has just achieved its ultimate degree of savagery. A choice is going to have to be made in the fairly near future between collective suicide and the intelligent utilization of scientific discoveries. . . . Albert Camus.

Camus, in essence, talks about a self-destructive drive originating from the tendency of one civilisation subduing others as it goes without being unrestrained. If anything, this is where the importance of challenging the current dominant grand narrative, through and by decolonising its type of education, emanates. Striving to avoid self-destruction conceived by greed, egoism and *holier than thou,* we need to decolonise our education systems as well. How we massively consume and abuse resources while others are suffering may tell us that something is wrong. This situation begets many unnecessary conflicts resulting from unfair distribution of wealth and enjoyment of riches the world is endowed with. You can trace this madness on the way Western countries consume without looking at the countries that colonialism starved and goes on starving.

To the contrary, in Western countries, people are dying of overfeeding while in the so-called third world people are dying of starvation, malnutrition due to the fact that they are unnecessarily and purposely underfed. Sometimes, animals are better than humans in that when they starve, they do so together; and when they get plenty they all eat together. More so, currently, animals have many defenders who do not want to see them extinct for the fear that their grandchildren will never know them. Such defenders care a lot about their unborn generations as they ignore living victims in the places those animals are found thanks to the toxicity and loss of sight colonial education has caused. Who currently thinks this way today in the world, where the winner takes it all, even if he wins chauvinistically by robbing the losers? This can vividly be seen on how the rich waste food while the poor are dying of and suffering from hunger. The *US EPA* (2002) cited in Zhang, El-Mashad, Hartman, Wang, Liu, Choate & Gamble (2007) notes that "food waste is the single-largest component of the waste stream by weight in the United States–Americans throws away about 43.6 million tons of food each year" (p. 929). Interestingly, this food waste is supported by academics who espouse food chain in supply and demand based on exploitative neoliberal policies. Are such academics truly educated for the interests of all people on earth? Again, while the US is wasting food, the victims of its bad policies in many African and Asian countries are dying of hunger. While the same is throwing food to the drain, poor and small farmers are committing suicide in India after Western business interfered with their food chain. If anything, this is but an absolute deprivation in which one seeks to suffocate others to death even if helping them would not cost him anything. The FAO cited in Oyefara (2007) notes that in 2002, around the world, 842 million people did not have enough of the food they needed to live an active, healthy life whereby 553 million people facing hunger lived in Asia and the Pacific in which Indonesia and the Philippines have a big share of them while another 227 million people live in Sub-Saharan Africa, particularly in arid countries like

Ethiopia, Niger and Mali. And 47 million people in Latin America in countries such as Guatemala and Haiti. Sometimes, I wonder to find that food is turned into gas for cars (biofuels) while humans are suffering needlessly. Again, under liberal and neoliberal policies, this is the right thing to do, mainly when we consider the fact that such policies sanctify inhumane competition even when it means one person to exploit or kill another provided there is dollar to be made.

While the victims of colonialism are suffering and dying, those who enacted it are investing heavily on the destructive powers such as nuclear, producing energy using food such as ethanol and other products that affect the food chain globally. Their security–even when it means the insecurity and dangers of others–does matter a lot. To amass power for rich countries has become an obsession next to religion. Again, this is another type of terrorism if we consider the fact that hunger terrorises and tortures more harshly even than other types of terrorism that kill a creature quickly.

Another agent of human inhalation-cum-suffering is none other than arms race. Due to toxic education, those in arms race do not see the danger they are causing the way their victims see it. Sometimes, I wonder. What good can come from nuclear weapons which have already proved to be hugely lethal? Refer to what happened to Japan when they were first used on 6th August, 1945; not to mention the just recent nuclear disaster in Fukushima on 11 March, 2011, wherein over 100,000 people were, affected (Holt, Campbell & Nikitin, 2012). Again, have we easily forgotten nuclear menace? I think Japanese know more about the danger[s] of nuclear weapons than Americans who used them against them do. As if nuclear weapons were not enough, ironically, despite knowing the danger that nuclear installations and nuclear weapons pose to those owning them and the world, they still cling to them thanks to toxic education sought to be decolonised. Who wants to let go the nukes that he or she uses to intimidate others? Actually, countries that own nuclear weapons do not love them save that they use to them intimidate and threat others. Therefore, due to the fear of the unknown that colonialism has inculcated in many people in the world, everybody, particularly imperialists would like to have a slice of nukes.

As if nuclear danger-cum-proliferation is not enough, the same so-called advanced countries also compete on making and owning chemical and biological weaponry. Why don't they see the danger? The answer is the same that the type of education offered in Western countries has failed and it does not allow someone to look out of the box as far as egoism is concerned. It has failed to address even the fear of the unknown that has always looms in the minds of the leaders of the so-called advanced and developed countries. If there is another reason apart from this, I would like to know it and study it well so that I can stop my urge for the decolonisation of education which has been given the burden of dealing with the results of such destructive education. The world is suffering wantonly simply because colonial authorities decided to purposely create shortage of almost everything so as to create fertile grounds for conflicts that will keep the victims busy so as to become dependent on those who authored these conflicts under their regime of conflicts. I am saying their conflicts purposely because the power imbalance they have always espoused is another good source of conflicts almost everywhere in the world. One can call this natural trend of Western civilisation in that there must be one superpower nation. Again, why don't we want to do things differently by trying peaceful means instead of always banking on violence and see how we will fare?

The world needs to change the way it thinks views things, specifically, the victims. Victims need creativity and courage to make a claim that they are victims of the current dominant grand narrative. Thorough the right form of thinking, understanding and reasoning victims will be able to showcase the courage and knowledge and make an argument. I remember some of black thinkers who started bugging the colonial powers till they gave in. W.B. Dubois and others had to think differently after decolonising their minds. We need to ask new sets of questions about the plight and fate of the victims of toxic education all over the world. I said it from the beginning that much concentration will be on Africa; however, I will still talk about the same situation all victims of the current grand narrative face globally if need be. We need to think cleverly and differently in order to encourage negotiation and dialogue aimed at removing the barriers on our way. For example, African countries have depended on their colonial powers for over 50 year whereby the colonial powers respond by giving them some handouts they call aid. Time to think about independence in all spheres must start now. For, if we question the history, we will have evidence to adduce and make our argument even stronger. We now know that colonial powers created shaky and weak states after dividing them so that they could continue servicing their economies (Battersby & Siracusa, 2009). We now know why Africa is far shy economically. So, too, we know among us who is in bed with our tormentors and exploiters, we almost know everything. Even our colonial powers know everything. It is upon us to seek to change the order of things in order to prove our words and theirs that we are equal and partners as they like calling us when they give us handouts. Without decolonising education that impacts our minds and understanding, we will still depend on handouts pointlessly.

We now know that political freedom without economic and social freedom is nothing but self-deception to whoever offers or receives it; and takes it to be true. We cannot eat our flags–that have always been used by corrupt rulers who in bed the oppressors–in duping keeping victims down hijacked for the benefits of our oppressors. We need to make radical change through decolonisation of our knowledge–otherwise conflicts we now evidence resulting from extracting resources in Africa–will double instead of going down. The war ahead of the victims of colonialism and imperialism does not need military strategies and weapons anymore. It only needs ideas and readiness to pursue the course of decolonisation patiently and persistently. Victims can change things themselves instead of waiting for someone else to do so.

Looking at the population of countries excluded in the current dominant grand narrative–shall they truly and seriously come together, and fight together–indeed, they are but unstoppable. The current arrangement and order of things need to be changed drastically and urgently. And you cannot expect the urgency and agent of change to come from those enjoying the system and order of the current unequal international arrangement. By negotiating changes, the world is likely to avoid conflicts resulting from colonial and imperialistic settings that are aimed at exploiting others as it has been going on since political decolonisation that failed to deliver its people economically. Through dialogues we can contextualise and effectuate change based on creating a peaceful, and of course, world full of justice and cooperation as a human family. This is where interdependence and interconnectedness play a very important role. If anything, the approach of seeking a peaceful and justice world together is a less travelled road that we seriously and transparently need to think about taking now if we seriously need peace all over the world. We need to seek a collective and creative way of getting out of the current impasse created by the grand narrative that bundled us together and exploited us together ever since. We need to do this safely and soundly if we really seek and need true and sustainable peace of the world. Using a decolonised education, we can alter all disciplines and fields so as to use these fields to help us in generating many ways on how we can achieve our goals together and equally. But this cannot become a reality without decolonising education so as to accommodate other views and schools of thoughts based on their grand narratives, civilisations and cultures.

We, indeed, need to have a decolonised and a true multicultural education to be able to achieve true and pragmatic emancipation of all humans in all aspects of life globally. I like repeating Dr. King Jr's (*supra*) quote that we need to stand together as humans or die together as fools. We are not fools. And we cannot easily accept to be fools. We are humans; however, being humans does not stop us from doing things others can regard as foolish among which is allowing the world to keep on going on unequal foundations of doing things. As we seek to decolonise the way things are and seek consensus aimed at having a peaceful and prosperous world, we need to think beyond our noses and today's interests. The world is changing rapidly. Thus, the fear of change or masters is immaterial and perilous for those who will cling to it be they powerful or weak. Who knew that China would shake the world as it is currently doing?

Furthermore, if we remember and compare the fear white Americans or South Africans had before dismantling their Apartheid systems, we can see how fear has no basis but ignorance. Where are America and South Africa after dismantling their Apartheid systems? They have more sense of security, oneness, and peace than at the times they practiced Apartheid however much is still there to be seen in some areas but not at national level where Apartheid used to be the policy of the country. Colonial authorities were afraid of letting their colonies go for fear of economic hardships. Although they kept on exploiting the same, such a practice is not permanently feasible given that it has caused a lot of expensive and violent conflicts in terms of human lives and material which have also caused a lot of loss of lives and property for the world in general. You can see this in the Middle East and Afghanistan today. How much money have the rich already burnt in the wars in these areas that would have alleviated poverty if not to stamp it out from these areas? I think; a peaceful world based on equality and justice, can become more prosperous than exploitative and violent one. For, looking at how heavily we spend on weapons and wars compared to what such money can do in peaceful times, I am convinced that a peaceful world is more prosperous than a chaotic and violent one arguably. We need to aim at serendipity of the world which needs, as Lederach (2005) argues that "pushes us to think about attitude and humility, the nature of developing theories of social change, and the building of adaptive processes that can sustain change" (p. 114) that will serve us all equally and harmoniously. He adds that if change is taken, seriously, it can increase our capacity to "be responsive"–and of course– responsible for the real world. What are we supposed to do; and how are we supposed to it? It is only through the proclivity of decolonisation of education that will later lead to decolonising everything and being ready to do things differently. However, thinking about a peaceful world or justice might be seen as utopia or naïve, if you do not like it. Again, there must be people to initiate things that others think are impossible. This is the beauty of academia. It enables to you to think out of the box, and, sometimes, allows you to take a less travelled road provided that you must be ready to substantiate your arguments and be challenged. More often than not, we need to be naïve to dare and think about what others think is utopian while it actually is not. In discussing how he contributed a lot to peace, intentionally, Lederach (2008) argues that innocence is bold in regards to the assumption of being perceived as stupid thanks to the boldness in raising important questions not to mention having optimism when everything seems impossible *vis-à-vis* common sense realism. Arguably, we need to attempt to decolonise education before discouraging ourselves, or accepting being discouraged. We do not need to be our own sources of despair or discouragement. Let others contribute to our dialogue so that our arguments can be worked or experimented on. Experimented ideas are better than those kept in the mind of the thinker[s]. Doing so is like detaining a person then hope that such a person can work well while he or she is behind bars. That person will be busy thinking and planning how to get out of the hell.

Among people who travelled a less travelled road is none other than retired South African Anglican Archbishop Desmond Mpilo Tutu. During the logjam that the talks for peace in South Africa faced during the Apartheid regime, Tutu came up with a very creative way of humanising the enemies which turned upside down the whole concept of *Othering* (Jensen, 2011). Tutu did not mean to look a coward or a faker but a serious person in the business of seeking peace where others had seemed to fail or completely failed. Tutu changed his way of thinking and doing things, in particular after being under Apartheid almost for the entire period of his life. Tutu understood the adage that insanity is doing the same thing over and over again expecting different results. He, therefore, decided to creatively and seriously change his way of doing things; which also changed his enemies' way of doing things by looking at the conflict differently and creatively. This is what reciprocity is all about.

Humans are social animals subject to changes now and then. And nobody is immune to change however slightly it might be. We are all subject to change consciously and unconsciously. Through showing how he regarded his nemesis, the then South African Prime Minister, PW. Botha, Tutu was able to move him to the extent that made it possible to open up the channels of communication between the two that resulted into what later was known as the 'dialogue of the deaf' (Landsberg, 2006) before mutating to what came to be democratic South Africa we have now as a point of reference. To some degrees, Tutu's strategy paid by easing up the situation so as to replace "the dialogue of the deaf" with "the dialogue of equals." His strategy of humanising the enemy lit the heart of his enemy so as to erode the fears and mistrusts that existed between the two. Tutu says "it is difficult for me as a church leader to say, 'Go to hell', to say God's grace cannot operate on P.W. Botha" (Tutu & Tutu, 2006, p. 49). How many people, today, are ready to bless their enemies or tell them that they love and care about them despite their differences or enmity? How many are ready to wish their enemies well despite the fact that some of their religions have such provisions or stories showing their leaders or prophets blessing enemies? How many still love their neighbours including their enemies the way they love themselves? How many know even who their neighbours are? As indicated above, we have reached at the stage of loving animals more humanely than humans! Aren't we becoming so judgmental so much that we create more conflicts unnecessarily? Swahili sage has it that: "Those who fight are the ones that reconcile." Isn't this an olive branch when we are facing the vacuum that needs the decolonisation of the current colonial and toxic education? Can't such wisdom enrich decolonised education to make it care and embark on learning how other non-Westerners used their education to live peacefully so as to accommodate foreigners who ended up colonising them? Methinks it pays to humanise enemies if we understand that conflict is inevitable; and it occurs between and among people.

Like Tutu above, we need to convince those who have always used the dominance of their dominant grand narrative to exploit others that their victims are not any threat to their life styles or economies but, instead, are real human beings like them. Thus, we need to treat each other with decorum and with justice based on mutual reciprocity, humanity and practicality. If we were able to sustain their economies under exploitation and violence, we can still sustain each other in peace and cooperation. This become evident specifically when we consider that the globe now has come quite closer than at any time in history. This is what globalisation is supposed to be. Humans share almost everything.

The humanisation of enemies needs decolonised education which–provided that it is done in a good way–is likely to create cooperation and harmony aimed at dealing with whatever differences or conflicts conflicants face constructively. For Tutu to say such words about his enemy, some would think he was a fraidy-cat. Again, it needed the courage of the mad and true conviction, trust and love, for Tutu, to utter such words precisely in front of angry victims of Apartheid in the then South Africa. Further, Tutu in Sparks & Tutu (2011) notes "whether I like it or not, whether he likes it or not, P.W Botha is my brother, and I must desire and pray for the best of him" (p. 117). Arguably, I may say that the words "you are my brother and we all sons of God" softened the heart of Tutu's enemy so as to open up letter communication that, *inter alia*, culminated in the birth of free South Africa. Tutu went through degrading situation as an African in his own country. His country was invaded; and thereby occupied by Boers for many years. Africans were segregated almost in everything. Everything African was segregated and disrespected except their foods, land, labour, resources and toil. It reached a time at which a dog in South Africa was freer than a human being.

While Africans lived in segregated areas, there were no segregated areas for animals. This can show us how blind and worse colonial education is. It blinds and turns people into zombies. What a failure for the world that failed to see the injustices that culminated in violence and pointless killings? Ironically, while Apartheid was blossoming, the so-called advanced and civilised countries supported it by all means. They did not see the big picture any truly educated people would have seen. This can nicely show how toxic education affects both oppressors and the oppressed. Ironically, Apartheid, just like any other form of colonialisms, was conceived and executed by people who were regarded as educated and morally upright. On their part, Boers thought that what they were doing was right despite its ugly face. Doesn't the education that produced such people wicked and dangerous need to be decolonised? What of the so-called *advanced, civilised* and *developed* countries such as the UK, the US, Canada and Australia, *inter alia*, that openly supported Apartheid in South Africa? While Apartheid throve in South Africa and other places that still had racist systems hidden under the carpet, there was the Universal Declaration of Human Rights (UDHR), the United Nations (UN) and other phoney and funny organisations in place pretending to spearhead human rights. Were Indigenous South Africans, by then, regarded as humans? Were they part of the UDHR or the UN?

Are Aboriginal people in Australia, Canada and the US regarded as humans today really when they are systematically discriminated against and oppressed in their countries? Provocative as it is, such a question needs to be asked and answered shall we aspire to have peace all over the world. Such a question and many–if answered correctly–are likely to guide and remind us about what to do rightly and timely. We cannot go on with such hidden *caste system* amidst the so-called democracy and advancement; and be truly peaceful and safer as a people. Interestingly, while all these types of human wrongs and abuses are going on in the above mentioned countries where Aboriginals are treated just like second class citizens, the UDHR is there doing nothing. Sometimes, I tend to agree with the view of Jeremy Bentham, who despite having his racist hidden agenda, calls human rights "nonsense on stilts" (Goodhart, 2013, p. 108) due to the fact that they lack equitable and equal practicability and enforceability. For oppressed people, the UDHR is immaterial and a white elephant racists and former colonial powers use to dupe them. They need to see their human rights wherever they are and in whatever they are doing today. The Human Rights that cannot be achieved are as good as non-existent. I do not know if human rights do exist for poor farmers in Africa who are exploited wantonly and pointlessly to support extended colonial system. Poor people in the Great Lake region, particularly the DRC–whose minerals have surely brought calamities to them–see no human rights; and know no human rights whatsoever. If human rights are there, they are for their tormentors who act with impunity but not for them. For victims in the mentioned places, human rights are there to enable their tormentors destroy them without being brought to book. How can they feel protected by the UDHR while rape, thuggery and other crimes against humanity are the only things they have ironically known in the 21st century? Even if we revisit where human rights were born such as Britain, France and later in the US, we will still wonder how could such countries invade and colonise others while they were the very champions of human rights. This tells us that the so-called human rights were meant for some human beings but not all human beings. Maybe, before the eyes of these demigods, humans were them alone but not others who did not share either pedigree or scheme with them. Arguably, those that they colonised or their governments overthrew were not human beings in the eyes of these colonisers.

Once again, European colonisers' education, grand narrative, civilisation and whatnots failed to open their brains and eyes up to see such simple truth. Therefore, Bentham seems to be right however diminutive and narrow. For, his scope of who was a human being was fickle and racist given that his constituency, just like any other European thinkers of his time, was only Europe. If those human or natural rights could not be enforced or enjoyed under the law or being enjoyed universally, they were not real but mere utopia and utter nonsense on the stilt as they still are today before the eyes of the oppressed people all over the world. Those suffering from some or all sorts of injustices conceived and espoused by neoliberalism and imperialism either are not human beings in the eyes of oppressors or are human beings who have no human rights. So, such a nature of racist human rights in practise deprives the UDHR universality it purportedly provides it has. Again, colonised education still holds human rights as real without underscoring the fact that there are people living in horrible conditions despite the existence of the rhetoric of human rights for all human beings simply because their grand narratives were either ignored or sabotaged so as not to be incorporated in the dominant grand narrative of today. What is going on is just like what George Orwell (2010) said in his book, *Animal Farm*, wherein all animals are equal however other animals are more equal than others. Sometimes, frustrations from miseries committed to the section of people in the world may force them to believe in assertions and beliefs that see Human Rights as fictional rights.

Another concept that needs scrutiny, based on the attempts to decolonise education, is the whole issue of human security as a new concept created by Western countries to show that they theoretically care about others while, practically it is the whole new game. I found that some countries sponsored motions on, for instance, freedom from fear. Again, if you try to make sense of it, you find that all such braggadocios are nothing but attempt by Western countries to further their hidden agenda as opposed to non-Western countries. Western countries always want to look good as the way of duping others they have always duped for generations through colonialism, neocolonialism and imperialism. If the current global education were decolonised, it is obvious that the first question it was to ask is: who is included and who is excluded; and why all policies have always been knitted in the West for others to execute and follow. Logically, no way can one, in the West, talk about freedom from fear while the same countries are still selling weapons to many poor countries whose governments inculcate the same fears–sought to fight. Does it mean that such countries don't see the fear some countries impart in their people through creating imaginative enemies? No way can freedom from fear make any sense to the people facing wars fuelled by the West as it aims at extracting resources such as in the case of the DRC we have already discoursed above. Canada, for instance, sponsored the motion on freedom from fear without addressing the fears Canadians, particularly Aboriginal people of Canada face and suffers from every day from systemic Apartheid they have gone through for many decades. When we talk about freedom from fear, for example, we need to ask from what and by whom. We can deceive ourselves by looking at wars and, sometimes, forget environment, the so-called modern science and other threats resulting from neoliberal policies of suffocating others.

How do you free people from fear while they are underrepresented in their own countries as it is in Australia, Canada and the US among others? Essentially, misperception, be it, of facts or people, creates a very fertile ground for conflicts. Once people perceive others differently from whom and what they actually are, chances of fueling conflicts are high. By revisiting the current way some people are misrepresented or underrepresented, this volume seeks to represent them truthfully and the way they would like to be represented. This helps to avoid conflicts in that; addressing what cause conflicts by looking for what brings us together as equal and worthy human beings. Misrepresenting somebody, be he or she an individual or a group, means altering his or her identity which have always created liminality and vulnerability for such a victim of misrepresentation not to mention perpetual fear and frustrations. Identity conflicts tend to be complicated and ferocious by nature. For, there are fears and mistrusts behind them.

Therefore, to avoid ignoring or mishandling such conflicts resulting from fear is to seek the right representation based on truth and reality. One Sudanese who received toxic education that made him regard himself as an Arab but not an African happened to work in the Middle East where laws prohibit women to expose their bodies. He wondered when he was alone at the pharmacy at which he worked. When Arab women frequented the said pharmacy, they used to expose themselves in front of him without any fear contrary to how they did when Arab males were present with him. Baffled as he was, he asked his colleagues the cause of such misbehaviours. Guess what. When his colleagues dropped the bombshell that, for Arab women, he was not a man they could fear; because he was black; and thus, he could not think about even approaching them. This answer, apart from changing his self-perception, forced him to hate his job and the country wherein he was working. He left for the US he was taught in school that was an infidel country. All this is the result of toxic education that needs to be decolonised regardless who is offering or receiving it. Such a Sudanese brother unfortunately, grew up believing he was Arab but not an African. Before getting this provocative and naked truth, this poor and ignorant Sudanese brother used to regard himself an Arab simply because he spoke Arabic; and he was brought up under Arabic-cum-Islamic cultures. This shows how he was misrepresented in both cases. He was made to wrongly believe that he was an Arab while he actually is an Africa. The type of education he received was colonised and fake so as to need a decolonised one due to the fact that it deceived and enslaved him pointlessly. Ironically, this brother went to school so as to wrongly be perceived as educated while he actually was not. How can a truly educated person fail to understand who he or she actually is? Aren't such things going on whereby Africans are discriminated against; and treated like half beings? Secondly, this Sudanese brother was treated as a non-Arab which he was but was not aware of. To help such a person and the likes, is let him know his true identity instead of cheating him that he is an Arab while he actually is an African; and being an Africa has nothing wrong if we underscore the fact that we are all equally humans despite the pigments of our skins.

This poem written by the late commander, teacher and politician, Yousif Kuwa Mekki (1945–2001) (Ayittey, 2016), one of top-rank officials of the Sudan People's Liberation Army (SPLA), may help us to see through the brain of the person who suffered from identity crisis. Mekki wrote:

With Thousands of my apologies forgive me!
Forgive me for frankness and my courage!
Let me tell you.
Despite all the talk about my Arabism,
My religion, and my culture,
I am Nuba.
I am black.
I am an African.
Africaness is my identity.
It is entrenched in my appearance;
It is engraved in my lips and manifested in my skin.
My africaness is in the sound of my footsteps,
It is my bewildered past and in the depths of my laughter.
Brothers, with Thousands of my apologies forgive me!
Forgive me for my frankness and courage!
Despite my grandfather's humiliation,
Despite my grandmother's sale into slavery,
Despite my ignorance, my backwardness and my naivety,
My tomorrow will come.
I will crown your dignity with knowledge.
I shall light my candle. In its light I Shall build my civilization.
At that time I shall extend my hand. I shall forgive.
Those who tried two destroyers my identity,
Because love and peace is my aspirations,
https://en.wikipedia.org/wiki/Yousif_Kuwa

If anything, the misrepresentation of others, which Said (*Ibid.*) calls *othering*, is among the reasons that led to the split of Sudan in 2011 after the referendum wherein South Sudan overwhelmingly voted for separation, is the major driving force for division and enmity among and within nations in Africa. Before separation, South

Sudanese were treated like second-class citizens in their country simply because they were darker than northerners. Also, because southerners were Christians, as opposed to northerners who are Muslims, who up until now, still call themselves Arabs, were rightfully, in the eyes of northerners, to be treated like second-class citizens. Is this any different from Apartheid? Ironically, when North Sudanese go to Arab countries–as indicated above–are referred to as Africans; which they actually are. Others go to the extreme by referring to them as slaves or abid (Poggo, 2009). This has been ongoing for many years. El Hamel (2008) maintains that "these enslaved groups were usually called either "Abid' or 'Sudan'" (p. 248). Again, despite knowing this stark reality, the victims of this identity crisis have always lived in the state of denial due to receiving colonial and toxic education.

Kuwa's admission above can help a reader to know how decolonisation of education can help the victims of identity convulsion that has been going in many African countries for many years. Such people need a decolonised education so that they can know who they actually are. In my culture, for example, there is a standard that has been used for generations. It says that if you want to know who somebody is, take him or her to those he or she thinks look like or belong to him or her. In other words, if you do not know the difference between goats and sheep just take them to respective groups. You will know who they actually are. Goats know goats and sheep know sheep as it was in the case of Arabs in the above incident. Being denied by those you think you are related to, does prove how you are not related to them. Even goats and other animals know that. The squirrel knows its relatives even distant ones. Again, all this confusion has the root in colonialism be it European or Middle-Eastern whose dominant grand narratives and education have ruined the victims of their colonialism. This is why there comes time when I think that colonised countries need to seek redress from their colonisers in order to cure such scars that have caused a lot of bloodbaths and conflicts in many countries.

Africa and other colonised countries have a good case for their redress due to the ills they suffered from colonialism. All too often, the statistics or numbers of people, goods, minerals and whatnot stolen from them are available. To put it in the perspective anecdotally, ask yourself. How come a tiny country without resources such as Belgium is richer than the giant of the world in resources, the DRC? The answer is simple. Belgium and other European colonial powers robbed the DRC as they still do even today so as to become richer and richer while their victims became poorer and poorer. How much minerals are stolen from Africa currently so as to cause wars of controlling them? These are the questions decolonised the education needs to ask and truly answer. Again, equipped with and affected by colonised education, we do not wonder or ask why such anomalies exist despite knowing the true history of how Belgium authorities under King Leopold destroyed and plundered the DRC just the same way Africa is plundered and destroyed currently even under black and so-called educated leaders who cannot see the truth. What is their education for if they cannot see such a real and simple thing? Furthermore, colonialism, through using its toxic education, committed all sorts of crimes from theft; murder to genocide in some places such as the DRC under king Leopold, the first 21st century genocide in the world that was committed by Germans in Namibia; and later Rwanda where the seeds they left behind under colonialism–though toxic education espoused by colonialism–led to the 1994 genocide. If one can summarise colonialism, I think colonialism is supposed to be referred to as a crime against humanity. So, too, colonialism may be referred to as a crime against environment due to the fact that it contributed a lot in destroying traditional ways of preserving environment by introducing environmental-degrading systems based on mass consumption and uses of toxic chemicals we currently are facing globally. Through its toxic education, colonialism is the causal root of many conflicts the world evidences currently in former colonies. It created a turmoil which ended in a quagmire whose prolongation is, basically conflict-laden world we are currently evidencing in many former colonies. You can see this in Rwanda after genocide. Many Western countries among them which sowed the seeds of destruction or those who supported those who sowed the seeds of destruction, or those who ignored genocide, all come offering aid and other forms of assistance which ended up misdirecting the victims from pursuing the real causal system. On the same note, we can draw another example from Rwanda soon after Genocide whereby Germany and Belgium stayed aside and look as if they were not behind this crime against humanity.

Regarding toxic education, you can see how it worked in destroying Africa; Rwanda provides another ideal example apart from the DRC. The impacts and effects of colonialism culminated in the 1994 genocide. Carter, Irani & Volkan (2009) observe that colonial administrators in Rwanda "offered administration, justice, and access to education exclusively to Tutsi elites" (p. 131). The question we need to ask here is: What type of education was given to Tutsi and Hutu elites; and how much it thereby contributed into creating enmity that culminated in genocide? Has ever there been any detoxification process to correct this type of education? Whenever education acts as a tool for discrimination, such episteme becomes dangerous and wanting; and it must not be referred to as education but toxic education.

In dealing with the needs for decolonising education, I will go back and forth and revisit various victims in the world. For instance, if we face it, how much did Britain steal from Africa for the whole decades it invaded and colonised it? However, n way one can put a value or quantify humans, what Britain did to Africa is inexplicably horrible. Is it wrong for Africa whose people are leaving for greener pastures abroad to seek remedy for the crimes and cruelties against humanity committed to it? Nkrumah (1961) cited in Haller (2014) notes that for many centuries of Europe's domination of Africa made the whites to arrogate to themselves the right to rule and be obeyed by non-white by claiming that their mission was to civilise Africa, while in actuality, their aim was to rob Africans and enrich themselves as they left Africans suffering and wallowing in in abject poverty.

I think; Africans, however poor they might seem, need the right treatment just like others. This can be done through forcing those who robbed them to pay back through redressing them as a way of resolving the conflict and doing justice to both sides. There is no way Africans, for example, can feel to be equal with their former colonisers without being redressed for the suffering they went, and they are still going through currently due to colonialism and its legacies. How will they feel equal without eradicating historical incongruities and lies that the colonisers created; and spread all over the world? Is it wrong, for example, for the DRC, to seek redress for the occupation by Belgium? Is it wrong for the entire Africa to seek redress from Europe and the US that perpetrated and benefitted from slave trade? Shall things remain unabated as they are currently, will there peace in the future? Will the mantra of universal human rights or equality of all human beings tenably make sense? Whatever type of civilisation we may claim to have currently, is nothing without addressing these injustices. I know as everybody does that these are not new issues. What is new is the lack of educationists, especially from colonised countries to stand and make a case for these victims through agitating that the current education and the dominant grand narrative must be decolonised or unseated. Why should they do or support that? True, there cannot be sustainable peace in the world without addressing these anomalies and injustices in the world today among which are the ones toxic education has committed to various people in various countries.

To leave such education with its coloniality and toxicity, if anything, is like to keep a ticking bomb under the bed. It will explode and claim lives.

The reason why the education needs to have colonial poison pumped out of it is, basically the number of *zombies* it created and still does. Such zombies would be seen in dictators such as Joseph Desire Mobutu (DRC), and Jean-Bedel Bokassa (CAR) whose countries are now gripped by civil wars due to the mess they left behind. The duo is just the representative of many of this kind that took over the reins of power in Africa after independence. Where did they leave their countries after plundering them? Both two countries are in chaos and those responsible for supporting and maintaining such venal rules are not forced to redress them or face criminal liability thereof. Many innocent people were killed and properties destroyed in the above countries, among other, for many years of infighting resulting from the vacuum the left after mismanaging their countries. Why they did what they did and became what they became? p'Bitek (1984) answers two questions above in his satire "Amen! The black bishop at the altar is blessing the people in Latin. Do you see his golden crown and scarlet robe?" (p. 149). p'Bitek talks about religious leaders who like to use foreign languages even if they are not understood by those they preach. This has been a norm in Africa whereby Latin and Arabic are regarded as holy languages while they are colonial languages. We can add political bishops who essentially were in the same bed doing the same thing in Africa either speaking the language of democracy of taking over to stop corruption to end up replicating it a million folds.

If anything, most of independent African rulers did what this author calls "monkey see, monkey do" which led to violence and chaos either because of receiving too many orders from their masters; or making many orders to their people which culminated in long time exploitation in some countries. Those who refused to be tamed by colonial Europe were killed prominent one being Patrice Lumumba, the first DRC's Prime Minister who was killed by Mobutu in conjunction with CIA and the Belgium government. Bustin (2002) observes that "in his times, Lumumba was considered a Communist, with so many deaths on his conscience that a consensus to eliminate was developed in the West" (p. 539). Through one-sided education devoid of critical thinking, the West did not see the other side of Lumumba who wanted to liberate his people based on international rule and cooperation. This being said, it is important to decolonise education so that it can help us teach such things in order to enable students to know what is behind the miseries they are now facing. It makes more sense; mainly for students from North America and Europe that do not have many African affairs in their syllabuses. Learning about, say the DRC is not enough. We need to ask Congolese how they feel about the death of their leader so as to do restoration justice to them based on what they will contribute as the way forward. Do we do that or just sit in Washington, New York, London and Paris then prescribe how to go about the conflict and what should be done? Knowing the feelings of the victims is a key tool by which to unraveling how they would like their case closed. Why is it eminent and urgent to decolonise education; and thereafter other specialised fields? Education is always used as controlling tool wherein some standards such as abnormality, deviation and normality are constructed in order to identify the objects and make them identify themselves in order to be easily governed (Rajchman, 1991 cited in Tremain, 2015).

Again, who wants the subjects that need to be identified and identify themselves in order to be governable? The answer is simple; a white man who represents all men even without consulting and agreeing with them. What if the said education enhances the embellishment and survival of one person on the expenses of others? Let us look at another nugget of how wisdom must be. In discussing the essence of true education, Fielding & Moss (2010) argue that it is "a long-established concept…that understands… fostering and supporting the general well-being and development of children and young people, and their ability to interact effectively with their environment and to live a good life" (p. 19). Given that the decolonisation of education is not aimed at Africa only, we must venture out of it to incorporate other victims. A suitable question we can ask is: Did the education that was provided, for example, in Residential Schools in Canada offer capability to its recipients to interrelate effectively with Aboriginal kids with their environment? If we compare the two types of education namely, Aboriginal and colonial education, which one meets the definition of education provided above? Ironically, the one that fits the definition is not regarded as education while the one that does not fit the definition is regarded as education; and it has been in place for many decades destroying the lives of its victims. What a monster that this education has produced! Are Aboriginal people of Canada–who painstakingly went through residential schools–living good lives as they would if their education system been applied in their lives? Are they still connected to their environment as they used and/or supposed to be under their organic episteme? What of Africans whose freedom was stolen to end up becoming poor for many decades? Refer to how Africa is the richest continent in natural resources but the poorest in human development. These are the questions we need to answer in our quest to decolonise and reconstituting our episteme. After answering these questions, we will be able to trace the cause of conflicts, miseries, exploitation and other vices which cause violence, and thus, the lack of peace. Apart from aspiring to resolve or manage the said situations, through decolonising education, the world will be unequivocally, unabashedly and intentionally contributing to the overall and true emancipation of Aboriginal people whose life was annihilated and overturned by the same deceptive colonial education. Decolonising education, as the means of emancipating the victims, falls into the aspect of making this process beneficial not only to the victims but also to the perpetrators. This is how emancipatory, filling and full this attempt is. And this is why I think that the whole world needs to support and work on the idea for its own benefits. Essentially, this is why I can call my attempt to decolonise education a tune out.

I, thus, urge all players to embark on decolonising education wherever they are in order to reconcile the offended people and their offenders for the very purpose of forging ahead with a new and robust episteme truly addresses the needs of all equally. Suffice it to say that "reconciliation is an indispensable process that gives society new life and new hope" (Carter, Irani & Volkan, 2009. p. 250) mainly if it is rooted on the right and decolonised education. Let us work together to see to it that we walk hand in hand in one spirit of realising our dream of making the world a peaceful place to live for us and the coming generations. Additionally, Carter, Irani & Volkan posit that reconciliation "must ascertain the truth and take stand on the historical injustices at issue," (*Ibid.*). Truly, this is the way forward in decolonising education. How can we ascertain the truth; and thereby take stand on the historical injustices without decolonising the education that engineered and sustained them?

This volume presents Aboriginal people in Australia, the US and Canada. However, Africa takes a lion share of the same sin however no residential schools were introduced in Africa. Again, the division colonialism created that gave birth to toxic ethnicity can be attributed to the violence and miseries in Africa. Statistically even in layman language, Africa currently outdoes other continents with respect to the rampancy of violent conflicts and other miseries due to divisions that colonial administration created. Research shows that Africa is lagging behind as far as peace in the world is concerned. The situation is gloomy because Africa outdoes other continents as far as rampancy of conflict is concerned. According to *Index* (2015), nine countries performed poor globally as far as peace is concerned. These countries were Syria, Iraq, Afghanistan, South Sudan, Central African Republic, Somalia, Sudan, Democratic Republic of the Congo and Pakistan; of which five are African. Additionally, Kingma (2016) notes that "over the last decade, there have been at least 30 major conflicts in Sub-Saharan Africa causing an estimate of seven million human lives (p. 35).

Furthermore, according to the GPI, violence cost 13.4% of World GDP. This is not a good thing or a good record or accolade. I, thus, thereafter asked myself if there is an infrastructure to deal with the conflicts. My first question was: How much Africa loses to conflicts? In whatever project one has to embark on, cost is the first thing to consider. For–in the modern world–money plays an important role almost in everything we undertake. So, the cost is inevitable; especially with respect to African affairs be they person or public. There is no way one can embark on a project without doing cost analysis to gauge the feasibility of the project. We need to decolonise our education so that it enables us to invest in peace instead of going on investing in wars as it has been for many years in the postcolonial era. Apart from conflicts, there is another face *vis-à-vis* how Africa loses a lot of money based on the cost of whatever it does. The question of cost brought me to other questions: How many African academics–particularly those who acquired their tertiary education in Africa and abroad under government sponsorship–does the Western world use? How much did Africa spend on educating them even if the type of education they got is wanting in regards to solving their home problems? For, this type of education has failed to enable them move Africa forward so as to remain poor and unnecessarily dependent of the West. One of the decolonisation of the current toxic education is being able to address this anomaly so as to equip and motivate African academics and politicians to ponder on their plight and that of their continent.

6

Peace with Environment and Human Coexistence Based on Decolonised Education

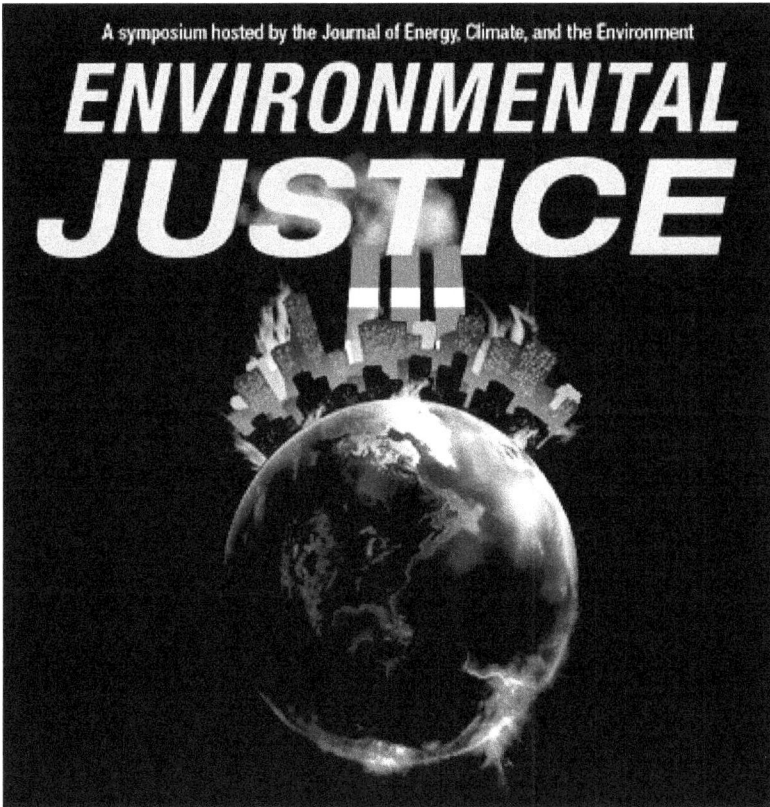

Figure 7 courtesy of news.blogs.wlu.edu

For the world to enjoy feasible, permanent and sustainable peace, needs to have sustainable and all-inclusive episteme; not just episteme but decolonised and detoxified one. Without all-inclusive episteme, conflicts and violence will still be in the corner beckoning at us. With the right and quintessential type of episteme, the citizens of the world will be able to trace their problems and find solutions for them. The current situation whereby poor countries wait for the West to come and solve their problems cannot go on without causing more conflicts. This is why, decolonised episteme is imperative. For, once episteme is decolonised, it will enable the victims of colonial education to advocate the changes in all of its fields. If those whose grand narratives are not accommodated in the current academic regime get decolonised education based on their episteme, values and narratives, they will undoubtedly prove, as a few has been trying to prove and improve the way education should be and offered, has already indicated. The failure of the current episteme based on Western intellectualism and monopolism must act as a wake-up call for Africa, in particular and the world in general, to rethink about education among which is peace education which is very important, mostly at this time the world is witnessing many conflicts.

The Charter of the United Nations (1945) cited in Freeman (2017) defines peace education as the one that strives to "save succeeding generations from the scourge of war, to reaffirm faith in the ... dignity and worth of the human person [and] in the equal rights of men and women" (p. 276). Ironically, despite the definition being crystal clear, American, Australian, Canadian and South African educated whites did not know of it. And if they did, they did not understand it. And if they understood it, they decided to ignore or sabotage it for the peril of the entire humanity thanks to the evils they have been committing. Yes, they kept on using obnoxious systems to terrorise innocent people whose institutions, land and rights they grabbed and abused wantonly. Such people and countries need to be helped out of the impasse they are in by introducing decolonised education. Additionally, when it comes to filling in the gap for Aboriginal people by introducing decolonised education as far as education is concerned, Nyerere (1967) cited in Lema, Mbilinyi & Rajan (2004) poses a crucial question asking: "'What kind of education?'... Rejected simplistic imitation of Western forms and levels of education, on the grounds of both limited economic resources and the different political economic contexts in which children were growing up" (xi).

Where do we get this kind education Nyerere espouses? The answer is obvious that many Aboriginal people had this type of knowledge. For instance, in Canada, Aboriginal women and men were equal before the introduction of Western patriarchal system that ended up creating discrimination between men and women. Why did this educated whites introduce was unpalatable to Aboriginal people? It is because it created schisms which resulted to Western systemic discrimination based on sex and colour. In a Western society–women despite being white–were still under the behest of sexual exploitation resulting from sexual segregation.

Essentially, Western system was blind *vis-à-vis* the injustices against women and non-white. Therefore, discriminating against innocent Aboriginal people in the Americas was a normal thing under such brutal system which did not make any sense to Aboriginal episteme. For, Aboriginal's felled education was supported by the body of literature that substantiates its validity and authenticity. We need to excavate this type of education in order to enrich the decolonised education this volume entails and envisages. With respect to the status of Aboriginal peoples, Smith (2013) argues that colonial education embarked on "research through imperial eyes?" which saw white people only to be superior as the same viewed the non-white as inferior. In this discourse, Smith raises an important question *vis-à-vis* the authenticity and academicism of the stories explorers, missionaries, merchants and colonial administrators told about others through what Said (*Ibid.*) calls "othering others" that aimed at discriminating them and make them look inferior to their assailants and exploiters. Smith (*Ibid.*) underscores this anomaly maintaining that "representations (formal and informal) of indigenous peoples were encoded as the authoritative representation of the Other, thereby framing the wider discourse and attitudes towards indigenous peoples." Sadly though, the view that was superimposed on many Aboriginal peoples in various places in the world is what the imperialists called primitive, naïve and uncivilised. Imperialists did this purposely aimed at distorting the truth in order to get the opportunity of reinventing their preys which they skillfully did. Ironically though, the *advancement and civilisation* of colonial thinkers deprived them the ability to see the truth that is staring directly right in their eyes today. Any academic who fails to see and realises the equality of human kind, makes her or his education toxic and dangerous so as to need a help by decolonising and sanitising her or his brain. If the so-called Aboriginal people's primitiveness, naivety and uncivility not to mention being perceived as backwardness enhanced them to live peacefully for many centuries without destroying the world, it is better than what we have today that seems to near us to ending this wonderful planet. I do not know who is smart between the one who makes weapons to murder others and the one who did not have any weapons but lived comfortably and harmoniously with others. This is where peace education, conflict prevention and conflict management should and will lead us to. This is a self-fulfilling prophecy. Don't some of us spend money from weapon producers to research about peace? With a decolonised education, answers to this controversy must be found. It will help us to look down at and shun serving two masters at a go which is academic and ethical prostitution.

Many Aboriginal peoples all over the world have something that the so-called modern civilisation did not have. They experienced the nature directly and intimately as opposed to *a posteriori*. They honestly and harmoniously lived with nature knowingly that they inevitably need and depend on each other. Under the Optimality Theory, Łubowicz (2002) equates the harmony between environment and humans with palatalisation and spirantisation in phonology whereby the harmony of the two enables us to communicate understandable sounds. Furthermore, Wong, Boon-Itt & Wong (2011) apply this harmony in the demand-and-supply chain as far as environment is concerned. This is what peace between human and environment draws its importance from so as to need to be entrenched and embedded in decolonised education seeking to empower people in their environment in their quest to address their problems and needs. There was mutual respect built on relationship whereby and wherein every part of this equation and setting played its part in the ecological music.

Again, after the greed and madness espoused and used by capitalism set in, the nature–not only of the Aboriginal peoples, but also of the whole planet–is facing a dangerously big challenge since creation. Climate change and Global warming are no longer a myth but a vivid reality although those who caused, and are still causing it, are reluctant to accept it and realistically deal with it due to their ignorance of the nature and the way the planet earth works. In one of graduate programs I came across an awkward course, if I may say. It was about Human Security. I could not believe those derogatory terms such as third world, developing, southern, northern, eastern and Western countries are still in the books. Don't we know that colonialists used these terms to discriminate against others? Don't we know that such discriminatory terms were coined purposely to discourage some communities while uplifting others? Isn't the application of such derogatory terms traumatising to those whose grand narratives are not accommodated in the current dominant grand narrative? Ironically, our so-called modern education has never underscored such anomalies. Instead, it has perpetuated them wantonly. African sage has it that when you want to kill a dog you just give it a bad name. So, too, for the colonial powers to exploit and subdue the victims they "other" had to call them names. Colonial powers invaded other countries. They changed their names even the names of places, British were horrible at this. You can see the rationale of pejorative names when thorny issues such as climate change and global warming are discussed. Nobody is listening to the so-called third world countries. Nobody is fully embracing and entertaining TEK to the roundtable where such matters are discussed by those who pretend to know everything while they have proved to know nothing but destruction of the world.

How much has the world detoxified its episteme by removing bigotries and lies that still exist in the current colonised education under the current dominant Western grand narrative? One may argue that due to *imperial ignorance*, lies were made science and true science was made lies. I, thus, argue that we should not look at social sciences only. We need to go further and look at all types of sciences the current colonised episteme espouses so that other grand narratives can contribute in improving the current regime of sciences in place globally.

For example, I lived in Kenya for three years. During this time, I lived with Kikuyu, the biggest community, from whom I grasped one scientific concept that can be productive to the environment currently if entertained and studied. I found that Kikuyu invented their own eco-deep freezer that does not need electricity or any form of energy. They called this deep freezer Ndigithu. Kikuyu used to put honey in a big pot and put meat which would stay fresh for years, Charles Kinyua who taught me Kikuyu language and some practices, defined this Kikuyu freezer as "that container is called "Ndigithu." It's the earth ware just like a pot but with a long neck normally shaped like a guard." Isn't this science that would have saved us the costs of depending on energy that affects us economically and ecologically? So, too, it would get rid us of cancerous preservatives we gulp everyday due to our ignorance of making experimental science ultimate. Who is researching, seeking or talking about such a science espoused by ignored grand narratives? After being told about this tool, I had to travel to Githakwa village in Nyeri to meet the man who was still using Ndigithu. I found that mzee Ndamu the grandfather to Kinyua in his 102 could talk logically not to mention walking and working around and doing some daily chores. When I asked him about the Ndigithu, he laughed and asked me why I was asking about unacceptable science. I told him everything; and he was happy to show me this tool which was real. So, too, there are still many Kikuyu elders who can make Ndigithu which is simple to make. The upshot is that Africa did not need freezers at the scale of today because they ate fresh foods; and not many people needed any freezers because apart from knowing deep freezers such as the Ndigithu, whatever they wanted was available in their gardens or bans. Therefore, you cannot say that Africa or other Aboriginal peoples were not advanced or developed simply because they did not have gadgets such as fridges or deep freezers even telephones while their needs would be catered for without any need of any long distance supply. Here we are talking about one tool. How many unexplored tools are out there in Africa and other places that need to be revisited in this dialogue of saving our world from environmental self-inflicted destruction?

Arguably, our environment has a lot when it comes to who we are and how we behave. This is why Africa did not even invent motorcar. Even today, if you look at the nature of North America *vis-à-vis* Canada and the US, the need for aeroplanes is higher than Africa due to the weather, and/or the size of these countries. You do not need a train or plane to travel within Benin, Burundi, Canary Islands, Lesotho, Rwanda, Togo, Sao Tome and Principe, Sierra Leone,

Swaziland and Zanzibar. So, the folks using planes to travel in their countries like in Canada or Russia cannot laugh at their colleagues from tiny countries for not using planes as they do. The same applies to weather-related cultures such as invention of warming systems or air conditioners. Such inventories were necessitated by environment but not the smartness of the person behind them. You can see this on we socially deal with weather.

In Africa, people do not talk about weather. Instead, they talk about events due to the fact that this type of communication enabled them to swiftly communicate within their environment. Who would be bothered with temperature, for example, that has never changed much since his or her birth? To the contrary, what is the situation in Western countries where weather dictates everything humans and animals do? Before coming to North America, I had never thought about the weather the way I do today. Even when I arrived to find that people talk about weather even before greetings, I was baffled. I thought that something was amiss without knowing that I was the one who was missing in the big picture. Slowly–and within a short time–here I was talking about weather even more than my hosts! Surprise, surprise! I talk about the weather many more time more than my hosts! I talked a lot about *weather viruses* in my other book: *Africa Reunite or Perish*. Again, I cannot view myself as an advanced person who knows what will happen during the day or week as far as weather is concerned. A healthy person does not need a doctor.

Going back to peace development, basically they go hand in hand with justice. Education that can support injustice is feeble and fickle. Such an education needs to be decolonised so as to advocate for and seek justice for all humans. You can see how destructive injustice caused by toxic education is. For example, before the introduction of guns and Western civilisation, African countries had never registered any loss of life and property resulting from violence, war and conflict in general compared to European who killed thousands of people in WWI and WWII. This shows the peacefulness of Africans. On their side, Arabs–for example–conquered many countries Europe included. Indians did colonise each other so as to introduce a very notorious Apartheid known as caste system that has eluded the so-called civilised world under the current dominant grand narrative simply because it does not negatively affects it or touch on its interests.

To the contrary, Africans and the Aboriginal peoples of the Americas did not colonise anybody save for having small-scale conflicts based on conquering and sharing thereafter. I think this is because of their true and equitable collectivistic nature whereby everybody needs everybody. This behaviour which, is different from Western and Indian societies–wherein everybody is for herself or himself,–had a lot to do with precolonial Africa's peaceability and justice. Collectivism is about caring for one another while individualism means something totally different. If a person cannot care about or for another, how can such a person care about environment? To make peace with people and with environment, we need decolonised education that is crucial in moving forward as we do away with prejudices, injustices and artificial antipathies as colonial systems enacted them to perpetually keep victims under their control for perpetual exploitation. Practically, the education espoused must be decolonised and detoxified so as to help in addressing and solving the problems. The current unequal relationship under the current dominant Western grand narrative needs to be detoxified through accommodating other grand narratives based on decolonised episteme that will cater for the whole world for the benefits of all of its residents.

From peace education, we can jump onto peace with environment which, too, needs the type of education that considers the interests of all humans equally and equitable based on justice and mutual reciprocity, interdependence and interconnectedness. When it comes to interact harmoniously with environment for the bright future of our earth, no doubt; it is logical that environmental ills have now become an in-thing almost in all disciplines. Many scientists, politicians and activists have stood up to face this phenomenon depending on which side one stands and what gears one to do what one is doing or is not doing.

However, to the contrary, there are still academics, activists and politicians who still deny that environmental crisis is real, especially climate change and global warming. Their interests have blinded them so as to act as if they do not have brains or eyes. While others are whitewashing, the so-called poorest president on earth, Jose Mojica, former president of Uruguay, once posed a question that can help us to solve environmental calamities. He once asked why science does not tell us that the culture of consumerism, particularly over consumption is an evil number one that begets climate change, global warming and other environmental evils such as deforestation, desertification, extinction of some species and many more. He once said that if everybody on earth would like to consume just like the citizens of the US do, we will need three planets. Mujica cited in Hernandez (2010) worries about what would happen to this planet if Indians would have the same proportion of cars per household than Germans. How much oxygen would we have left? However, Mojica said he does not hate consumption; instead, he hates waste or what I can call *extravagant, greedy and irresponsible consumption.*

Peace with environment is important. There have evolved conflicts between humans and wildlife in many parts of the world. Due to world's consumerism and mass production, many animal locales are encroached on so as to create conflict between animals and humans. Dr. Michael Hutchins cited in Schaul (2013) notes that "a conflict may arise when the interests of humans and wildlife—real or perceived—do not coincide." Again, this human-wildlife conflict is a new phenomenon in many places in Africa wherein–in a precolonial time–animals and humans used to harmoniously interact and live side by side without any problems due to the knowledge Africans had that was later felled by colonial governments. Post-colonial governments sadly, did not revert to the traditional ways of living with animals. Instead, they applied colonial education to cause more harm to the wildlife which has recently become another problems in many areas. This means, that our current education systems have failed to understand this phenomenon so as to find answers and solutions to it. We may deny–for example–that global warming is real. We may apply all types of sciences to justify our assertions we know to be hypocritical and sham. Again, when we look outside of our rooms, houses and countries, the situation tells a very different story. To some peoples, climate change and global warming are to their advantage while to others it is otherwise. Some talks about human sufferings while other talk about animal sufferings

151

without underscoring that the duo depend on each other and the *a priori* does not need the *a posteriori*.

The other day I was laughing at the findings that the numbers of polar bears were decreasing before satellites said otherwise. Who is telling the truth and lies; and why? Who knows? It depends on someone's priority. Let us face it. Climate change and Global warming are the result of disharmony between humans and environment. Some humans–not all though–have overexploited the planet pointlessly due to greed, ignorance and selfishness. All over again, rich and the so-called advanced countries are leading in this self-destruction whose consequences though are indiscriminately affecting the whole globe. This is where this volume challenges the type of education such countries have been using. Why did it not help them to see the danger[s]? We need to reconsider the ways we have been living with our environment before the introduction of this megalomaniac life style of consuming without thinking about resuming what we consume. The writing is on the wall for us to read. There are lots of stories to warn us so that we can rethink our take on our relationships with environment. For example, in Tanzania, the Masai people lived with wild animals since time immemorial without creating any disharmony with it. Brosius (1997); and Agrawal & Gibson (2001) cited in Goldman (2007) argue that traditional communities are close to environment and should be celebrated instead of being seen as villains. Despite this truth though, after Tanzania acquired its independence in 1961, established national parks in the Masailand without allowing them to be part of the control and management of the parks in their areas. Soon after the government took over the parks, the number of animals started to dwindle thanks to poaching. The environmental science that Masai (Goldman *Ibid.*) used to harmoniously live with animals was not accommodated. In 1967, Tanzanian government introduced *Ujamaa* policy (Lynn, 2010) which razed down many Masai residences so as to completely alter their way of life. Such a move, negatively affected the Masai who were uprooted from their natural habitat. Arguably, such a move partly saved animals because nobody was allowed to become rich without showing how one made such wealth. *Ujamaa* egalitarian policies discouraged individuals from becoming rich without showing how they got their wealth. Such measures brought ephemeral reprieve though. The number of animals remained constant until 1990s when liberalism kicked and everything was free under free market. People started becoming rich overnight and without being legally required to show how they made their wealth; and the number of animals, typically elephants and rhinos dwindled dramatically. Now, these animals are in the verge of becoming extinct (Kideghesho, 2009; and Masanja, 2014). To know what is causing poaching does not require anybody to have a degree in wildlife or environmental sciences. It is simple that after Tanzania subscribed to neoliberal policies that encourage consumerism and unregulated mass production on top of corruption in the country that significantly encouraged many people started finding money by all means. More on the Masai, they were at peace with the wildlife; and one of the causes is the high production of beef that made them less dependent on wild meat. This is logical due to the fact that wild animals were beneficial to them since time immemorial; and this is why there was a harmonious coexistence between the Masai and wild animals. People in their environment used to experiment and learn various techniques of survival which is fundamentally, the essence of education and knowledge. Chinn (2007) observes that:

> Hawaii's students have a unique natural laboratory to explore fundamental biological questions involving evolution, adaptation, and interactions of humans and the environment on isolated island systems. But most learn classroom and text-based science, perhaps becoming literate in school science but not issues relevant to their own lives and communities (p. 1248).

How many countries have embarked on a Hawaii-like way of teaching environmental education, specifically to their young ones? We need to teach our people relevant things based on the experience of the whole world. This reminds me how the so-called Traditional knowledge is belittle, and sometimes, ignored. Even if you look at the terminology used to refer to it, you find that it has never been well accepted or appreciated. Traditional Environmental Knowledge (TEK) is a buzzword in research and environmental literature. Again, is this traditional knowledge which sets it away from modernity and conventionality or TEK was formulated based on toxic education that places itself higher, above and ahead of other types of education. If we could face it, what is discovered or incorporated today is newer and more modern than the one discovered or incorporated yesterday. The argument is: Why call Indigenous Knowledge traditional as if Western knowledge does not have traditions in Europe? If anything, this is systemic discrimination resulting from bigotry of the current dominant grand narrative that seeks to differentiate and distance itself from other forms of knowledge, science and understanding in order to be viewed as the one that is more advanced than others.

To know how there is nothing new in the so-called modern knowledge as opposed to traditional knowledge, refer to how many of what the so-called advanced episteme uses to define others were dubiously stolen from those the current grand narrative despises and exploits. There are many literatures on how explores discovered other people in Africa, the Americas and elsewhere. There are questions we can pose about this matter had our education been decolonised. For example, if explorers came and discovered–let say– the Americas Indigenous habitats, why then was it difficult for Indigenous people to do the same namely, to discover foreigner lost in their terrains? There is laughter in Tanzania. When a Germany explore Johannes Lebmann asserted that he discovered Mt. Kilimanjaro, people asked: Where were those people who lived around this tallest mountain in Africa even before he was born. His *Wikipedia* reads that "news of Lebmann's discovery was published in the Church Missionary Intelligencer in May 1849." What are the implications of such barbaric assertion? It means that those who used to live around this mountain–who, essentially are the ones who taught Lebmann everything about their mountain he dubiously asserted to have "discovered"–were not human beings; and if they were, they were tabula rasa or just beasts in the African jungle. Do you attribute anything to the donkey when it provides you transport to wherever you go for some missions such as archaeology? This is exactly how Lebmann and other Eurocentric thinkers regarded their teachers who helped them to "discover" Mt. Kilimanjaro. It is sad to note that our current colonised education has never seen such blatant lies which openly show how the Western so-called missionaries who in reality were but colonial agents that used religion to easily penetrate and spy on Africa, treated the no-Westerners they purport to have discovered.

Another example comes from the Aboriginal peoples of Canada who, like the Masai, are credited for coexisting with wildlife sustainably and harmoniously for thousands of years. This harmonious coexistence was not just an accidental exploit. Again, when European settlers came to trade in fur, they almost learn everything from them before turning tides against them claiming to be the owners and inventors of everything including the knowledge they acquired from Aboriginal peoples of the Americas. This has been the habit and practices of colonial and toxic education. The situation was the same in Mexico and South America. After messing with Americas' ecosystem, now the same colonisers, copiers and invaders are crying. They are now seeking the knowledge of the same Aboriginal peoples the felled. This is evident that there must be some mechanisms and rules Aboriginal peoples applied to coexist harmoniously with wildlife, not to mention environment in general that the current toxic education does not know of.

For example, it is argued that wildlife such as bison were synonymous with the Aboriginal peoples. Taylor (2011) notes that "the newcomers were unanimous in their appraisal of buffalo as "innumerable" or "countless" and the country was famously described as "one black robe" of buffalo" (p. 6). Where are these magnificent animals in the Americas today? They were decimated thanks to greed and ignorance. Further, Taylor (*Ibid.*) notes that a very positive story of wildlife success that, later, is turned to its head because of lack of expertise by invaders and their greed for *making ease and quick bucks* out of these animals. Taylor concludes by showing who to blame as far as North America's environmental crimes are concerned. He notes that "in the 1870s, America was a large resource exporter with little or no environmental regulation while Europe was a high income consumer of U.S. resource products apparently indifferent to the impact their consumption had on America's natural resources" (p. 47). To add salt to injury, the same US is among leading polluters in the world today; and nobody is imposing any fines on it for such a crime against humanity based on environmental abuses geared by greed and myopia. If, as professionals, we are going to critically look at how history contributes to conflicts and underdevelopment, we are likely to concur with the theory of redress this volume hereby espouses particularly, for beneficiaries that are well to do such as Canada, the US and others. If these environmental criminals cannot be made accountable to their actions in any international body, they must, at least, redress the Aboriginal peoples whose lives they destroyed through their greed and ignorance.

Given that many findings such as Taylor's above indicate that settlers caused the extinction of bison in North America, it is time for practitioners and professionals in various fields to revisit the knowledge that the Aboriginal peoples used to conserve these animals and their habitats so that it can be used to save the world today when it is at its dying bed after being butchered by toxic education. The decimation of bison is a single example among many *vis-a-vis* wildlife milieu. How many natural, medicinal and sacred trees did invaders destroy all over the world? Cameroon provides an ideal example where Prunus Africana, a medicinal tree that was traditionally used to cure diseases such fevers, malaria, wound dressing, arrow poison, stomach pain, purgative, kidney disease, appetite stimulant, gonorrhoea, and insanity has been destroyed after the rise in demand in Western markets. Ndenecho (2011) discloses that uncontrolled exploitation is blamed on massively reducing the wild populations of most reproductively mature Prunus Africana trees in the West and North West Provinces, Cameroon. Unfortunately, colonial education does not want to admit that it has failed so as to become destructive after denying the existence of the knowledge of other civilisations. Can the future of the world be realistic without taming such destructive way of doing things based on the current dominant grand narrative?

I have touched on Canada and the US *vis-à-vis* the destruction of environment. These countries are touched negatively in many incidents of environmental degradation through extraction of resources, particularly mining in many countries all over the world. For example, Canada is known all over the world for its dominance in mining industry. At home, the government in Ottawa has always defended tar oil in Alberta despite the fact that it is more of an environmental-ticking bomb than an economic boom if we consider its effects to the Aboriginal peoples of Canada whose habitats it has destroyed.

Undoubtedly, mining, apart from polluting the world; and resulting into many diseases, has, for decades, been a good source of misunderstandings among the communities either between those benefitting from the projects and between government or between government and the affected communities almost everywhere such extraction has been ongoing. Interestingly, conflicts over resource control are now prevalent especially in Africa (Alao, 2007). The DRC provides an ideal example wherein one country can become a failed state after other countries either invade it or send their agents to ferment and fund violent conflicts revolving around resource control for supplying the dominant grand narrative (Lalji, 2007). We, thus, need to push the envelope further to make sure that mechanisms—that will be incorporated into the international laws—are in place to deal with the redress of the victims, imposing heavy fines, and stopping detrimental, hegemonic and toxic practices that are currently ongoing globally. We may get good insights and how to address this anomaly through asking the victims and the way they used to coexist with resources without any conflict, decimating them or devastating the planet as it currently is.

Learning is a dynamic process. Therefore, it is important to emphasise the dissemination of information and knowledge that will attract us to go back to Indigenous salient means of conflict resolution in dealing with current conflicts resulting from ignoring traditional mechanisms of conflict resolution. Regarding environmental issues and peace, it is obvious that the effects, for example, of global warming, apart from causing many conflicts, will have some domino effects on our planet though in different magnitudes and times. Rich countries will be able to slow it down while poor countries will bear the brunt unnecessarily; because they did not contribute to this phenomenon at the same magnitude as it is for rich countries. This is self-evident currently whereas some islands are facing extinction (Malcolm, Liu, Neilson, Hansen & Hannah, 2006; and Carpenter, Abrar, Aeby, Aronson, Banks,

Bruckner, Chiriboga, Cortés, Delbeek, DeVantier & Edgar, 2008). In the same vein, Humphreys (2005) predicts that the next big-scale wars will be fought over resources we take for granted such as water which is dwindling due to overpopulation and global warming. Thanks to *holier than thou* mentality and wealth the dominant grand narrative has, it will never bother about those it has destroyed and exploited for many decades. What transpired on the Marshall Islands speaks volumes as to how deadly and toxic education can be. Who would believe that the US would dump its toxic nuclear materials knowing the dangers they pose? If such a sophisticated nation could commit this, what does being educated mean for such a nation that is ready to ignorantly and greedily destroy the world? Gerrard (2015) notes that:

> During the Cold War the United States detonated sixty-seven nuclear weapons over the atolls of Bikini and Enewetak in the Marshall Islands. In the late 1970s the United States addressed the massive amount of residual contamination by abandoning Bikini as permanently uninhabitable and pushing much of the waste at Enewetak into the open lagoon. Much of the plutonium was dumped into the crater that had been left by an atomic bomb explosion, and then covered with a thin shell of cement. The resultant "Runit dome" sits unmarked and unguarded in a small island and one day will be submerged by the rising waters of the Pacific Ocean, unless it is first torn apart by typhoons. Radiation from the Marshall Islands has already been detected in the South China Sea. Using the experience of the Marshall Islands as a case study, this article seeks to shed light on the environmental and security challenges of nuclear waste disposal in the Pacific and beyond (p. 87).

Many powerful and rich nations turned a blind eye on this Marshallian problem simply because they myopically and wrongly thought that it was an individual problem. Now, that it is clear that the Marshall Island can be a bomb waiting to destroy the wold, what is the world doing to address it? Instead of looking at things the way we are used to while the situation is getting worse and worse, we need to incorporate traditional knowledge, experiences and sciences from all societies aiming at garnering and harnessing them in our quest of comparting the phenomenon. Many non-Western societies have a lot to offer given that they have already been tested due to historical facts that many Indigenous communities lived harmoniously with environment for thousands of years something that the current dominant grand narrative has overexploited so as to degrade or ignored the environment. We must decolonise our minds then deconstruct and reconstruct our episteme by making sure that it accommodates other ways of thinking and doing things. As indicated earlier, madness is doing the same thing over and over again expecting different results. We cannot go on using the current formulas the colonised education has always applied to many problems without getting expected answers. We need to reconstitute our bank of knowledge and become bold, courageous and honesty enough in taking this U-turn we are not used to. I know; it is going to be hard due to the fact that current Western education was primarily envisaged to save the interests of the West as opposed to the interests of non-Western societies. Being in the game for many years, the proponents of Western education will never throw towel in easily. They will not go down without a fight, especially if we consider the fact that they are the beneficiaries of the whole chicanery. Therefore, one of many things decolonised episteme and techne must produce is the courage and arguments to counter whatever resistance that will happen. I would like to base my argument on Orr (1991) who holds as thus "our education up until now has in some ways created a monster" (p. 1) in the form of colonial, exploitative and toxic education which the current dominant grand narrative espouses and uses as its means of the exploitation of one person by another.

Furthermore, this googly monster is not ambiguous to know or recognise here though. Neither is it difficult to trace it. The current regime of education based on colonialism, capitalism and neoliberalism, all built on *holier-than-thou* mentality, has completely failed. Further, Orr notes that "the advance of knowledge always carries with it the advance of some form of ignorance" (p. 2). It is this ignorance those espousing it used to commit environmental crimes and other forms of injustices all over the world due to their selfishness, greed and ignorance of others' ways of doing things.

Ironically, as it was in many callous treatments under many colonial projects such as slavery, colonialism and wars, the same crimes have gone on up until now. Currently, some animals are declared as endangered while others have become extinct. While this is ongoing, the international community is haggling and politicking about such sensitive issues whose continuation may change the landscape of human existence. Why? The answer still lies—to be specific and honesty—on the type of education and episteme we are now applying in environmental sciences as well as conflict resolution *vis-à-vis* such crimes. Such scenarios remind me of the idea of writing the book titled *Education for Ignorance* that I have not written yet though.

Before the coming of European model of destruction and extraction, African animals, chiefly elephants and rhinos were unperturbedly undisturbed. Where is the world now? Western science and environmental-disastrous policies and their results such as GM products, toxic fertilisers, consumerism, wasting resources i.e. food, water and energy in Western countries, global warming are blamed on global warming and the current colonial education does not do anything to put an end to such detrimental practices. Essentially, the role of the so-called Western civilisation is creating future conflicts. And this is why decolonising education is one of the best ways of helping the current colonial education to clean its mess. I strongly argue that other grand narratives must be accommodated and consulted in solving the current problems resulting from colonial education even if it means to create a new joint grand narrative born out of other negotiated grand narratives of the world. For, some of ways of life of many sidelined grand narratives were totally destroyed and purposely misrepresented. If they had no sound system, how were they able to live peacefully and trustfully without invading others for many hundreds of years? There must be a rich culture of peace that we need to trace and use to solve our current problems. The story of an old hoe which fed the village so as to discover oxen that increased agricultural outputs is very important. The so-called underdeveloped or the third world countries contributed; and still contribute immensely to the development and opulence of developed and rich countries. At least, such a contribution must be appreciated. Do we ignore the science that discovered this hoe that gave birth to a more advanced way of farming? Do we ignore ancient ways Africa and other civilisations of the world used to make peace and live peacefully not only with themselves but also with other societies and environment? Do we ignore our ancestors even if we view them as primitive?

For example, Nubians who are believed to build Egyptian pyramids (Shaltout & Belmonte, 2005) which are believed to have the technology that would have averted or lessen global warming as observed. Evidentially, Nubian craftsmen were masters at constructing domed and vaulted roofs of mud brick which they also used for the walls. Zami & Lee (2007) observe that:

> The structures were cheap; the walls were cool in the summer and were heat-retaining in winter. While implementing the Nubian building techniques, he aimed to train Egyptian craftsmen to build their houses using mud brick or Adobe, which was ideally suited to the local conditions of Upper Egypt and at a fraction of the cost" (p. 368).

This shows that there are cultures and civilisations that were able to harmoniously cope with weather without consuming a lot of energy or endangering the world as it currently is. Nubian, for example, did not use many trees to erect their pyramids. Given that the current regime of energy–despite all chest beatings and thumbs up–has totally failed. Why can't we try already proved types of sciences, knowledge and practices such as the Nubian technology of construction? We need to take such ideas and improve them in our attempts to reduced environmental degradation carelessly and needlessly.

Without harmony with nature, conflicts resulting from scarcity, environmental degradation and misuses (such as endangering sacred places for Indigenous peoples) will become chronic so as to generate unnecessary violence. This has already happened in some parts of the world though. Gilbert (2013); and Kloor (2014) unearth the scandal in which Indian farmers committed suicide after the government allowed Monsanto, an American multinational company specialised in genetic manipulation of plants, to flood its market with Genetically Modified rice which is cheaper than locally produced one. This move destroyed the market poor farmers used enjoy so as to consequently find themselves in debts which forced them to commit suicide. If we step in the shoes of those left behind by their parents and the loved ones who committed suicide because of debts, chances of hating Monsanto are higher than one can imagine. Do we know how they can hit back, especially at this very time terrorist groups attract all types of people with broken hearts or feeling that they are treated unjustly or left out of the system?

Many people in India have already lost their lives due to this crime committed by the high and the mighty. In Andhra Pradesh India, for example, Levin (2012) notes that:

> During the summer of 2010, a number of Indians committed suicide after defaulting on their microloans. International media immediately focused on Andhra Pradesh because the state represented a large portion of India's microfinance industry, and found that most of the suicide victims in Andhra Pradesh were rural farmers (p. 112).

The story is the same that after capitalism, with its ruthless face of course, went to India, under the veil of globalisation wherein some poor farmers could not sell their produces and pay their loans. On top of that, many farmers committed suicide by drinking chemicals they used as insecticide which ended degrading their soil so as to harvest less than they used to. What a double-faced sword this is! There is a reprieve however in countering this calamity resulting from the resilience and application of decolonised education. According to *Al Jazeera TV* (26 January, 2015) in its *Earthrise programme* says that over a million farmers have gone back to natural farming which does not need or use insecticides or chemical fertilisers. In the same light, in concurring with the report, Ranga Rao, Sahrawat, Rao, Das, Reddy, Bharath, Murthy & Wani (2009) observe that "the world Health Organization and UN Environment Programme estimate that each year, 3 million farm workers in the developing world experience severe pesticide poisoning" (p. 21). What happened in Indian brings us to the question: Why did the government of India accept chemicals knowingly that they would destroy the land and the livelihoods of its population? There can be many reasons such as corruption, fear, bad policies etc.

Under Western mass media, many people in countries that colonialism pauperised are made to believe that their population is their enemy number one shall they not apply Western-prescribed methods in farming. Such a take instils superfluous fear on such a people. After fear is instilled in them, on top of having blind and corrupt governments, Indigenous peoples end up becoming fair game and prey for predatory dealings–geared by capitalistic *leitmotif* of greed–kicks in and thereby destroys their lives. First of all, Western companies want to sell their products even if/when these products destroy people's lives. Secondly, they predatory businesses purposely destroy the soil of the host countries. After the soil has been ruined, Western firms such as Monsanto are sure of winning the market. And thus, make big bucks out of the miseries they make for others in the name of business. Thirdly, this has always been the way Western firms have traded with the so-called underdeveloped countries. Fourthly, Western firms do not care whether people are suffering or dying given that they are able to fill their vaults with made out of destroying others. Here is where the philosophy of othering others (Gordon, 2015) kicks in well to show how humanity as barriers in the eyes of Western institutions. The conflict that results from such trades is immense and protracted so much that, if we do not alleviate and arrest the situation, the world is going to face a lot of tensions wherein one part will be fighting a die-or-live war while the others will not have any logic whatsoever to stand by what it is doing as far as environment and human lives in affected countries are concerned. This results in agro-terrorism or "intentional introduction of a plant pathogen, virus or another biological agent to kill crops or animals (Stack, Suffert & Gullino, 2010; Monke, 2004; Foxell, 2003 cited in Caldas & Perz, 2013). Tolerating such practices is a type of modern-times terrorism which contaminates land.

Moreover, the contamination of land in various countries the multinationals cause is not only pernicious but also racism in itself. Despite the dire nature of the situation, home governments just turn a blind eye to this problem that seems to put the lives of poor peoples at risk as the days go by. Hundreds of millions of people will never die without trying to find a solution however violent it might be. After all, those poor peoples affected by Western industries in many poor countries have nothing to lose except their chains of neoliberal exploitative policies. Kenyan Mau Mau leader Dedan Kimathi used to say that it is better to die standing than to live on knees (Mose, 2014). These hundreds of millions will not die on their knees.

Once again, terrorists and their predatory ideologies will move in–to fill the vacuum left by governments and sanity–by assuring the victims that they have the solutions to their problems which is to topple Western hegemonic grand narrative by imposing another heavenly one which also seems to be the same even more barbaric and brutal. We have already evidenced this in many places where terrorists have gone as far as declaring caliphates all aimed at assuring the trodden hearts that there is an alternative to catch upon and latch on which is basically nothing but chaos and violence. Sadly however, when such groups declare their existence–in either avoiding the problem or simplifying it–some quarters, especially Western countries come with the semantics of saying that they cannot negotiate or deal with faceless entities as if these terrorist groups do not exist or pose any danger to humanity as a whole. When they provide such shaky explanations, they forget that whatever they decide does not only affect them alone but the entire humanity that is excluded in such a dialogue about what stand to take. Are terrorist groups really faceless or we are trying to deny and simplify complex issues like this by burying our heads in the sand pretending that we do not know; or if we know, we do not know the truth? How can a group or groups wreaking havoc be faceless? They have faces save that we do not know them or how they operate. But saying that such groups are faceless does not solve the problem. It rather exacerbates it by informing those groups how ignorant about them or incapable of taking on them those portraying them as a world are. Such a message is detrimental to the peaceful world and a gain for those opposing the peace of the world.

This volume has touched on many aspects above as far as harmony with environment is concerned. It imperative here to specifically address global warming that receives mixed reactions. Many reputable scientists and environmentalists have warned that global warming is real; and it is threatening our very existence on this planet. Again, many, especially big polluters and contaminators–for the defence of their economic interests–are always in the state of denial wrongly thinking the phenomenon will go away by itself. This cannot be left to go on while we pride ourselves that our education system helps us to address some global problem thanks to its unfair treatment of others. I do not want to sound as an alarmist. Again, global warming resulting from such practices is a real threat to humankind; whether we like it or hate it. Environmental campaigners, scientists and all those who care about human wellbeing have already made a very convincingly strong case that future generations of conflicts will dwell more on environmental issues than commerce or politics. The world, collectively, therefore, needs to overhaul the way we look at conflicts and their causes.

Furthermore, we need to overhaul even change the economies that depend on polluting or on contaminating the world. All this cannot be achieved or done without decolonising our education so that it can accommodate other grand narratives that have already proved to be in harmony with the environment as indicated in some societies above. A multi-narrative education is need in order to help us to tweak our epistemes and techne based on the interests and needs of all people globally. Our planet is like a boat on which we all travel even if we are in different classes. Those suffering in poor and unfurnished classes chocking and puking are likely to follow us in our first classes or puncture the boat thereby causing a dent that will see us all sinking and perishing because of our ignorance and indifferences. Things cannot go on unabated under the current toxic education that colonial powers conceived and spread all over the globe for their selfish interests. Even in dialoguing about the looming danger of global warming, colonial sentiments and settings are hampering others from reaching the solution. Power is divided along wrong alignments. For example, countries with veto powers which are most of the major polluters use their power to block whatever argument[s] or decision[s] they view as an obstacle to their greedy economic interests. Some enter "an unholy alliance with big business

165

and influential opinion-makers on the extreme right of the U.S. political spectrum (Oreskes & Conway, 2011) and other powerful countries. When they apply their colonial power resulting from greedy and myopic arrangements, they forget that we all have the right to live as dignified human beings. We equally deserve this right including all those who have used the current toxic education to make things harder pointlessly due to their ignorance, racism and selfishness. So, the reconfiguration of the current education system based on decolonising it is inevitably important.

We need to remove the toxins in global education so as to be bold and courageous enough to propose that clean air, safe water, natural soil and natural foods are human rights for all. This is why our contribution should aim at strengthening environmental laws that will deal fully with environmental crimes that currently, the high and the mighty commit against paupers all over the world. We need not to be fooled by the current "negative peace" as (Galtung & Fischer, 2013) would put it. There is turmoil underneath this setting that benefits Western countries at the detriment of poor countries. This cannot go on unabatedly. It needs to be stopped shall global development, peace and wellbeing be our major targets and goals as human beings gifted with big brains.

Even at a country level, there cannot be development, peace and wellbeing in the country filled with people who see injustices committed without governments taking any actions. An empty stomach is always violent; and the one with it is but a time bomb that can explode any time. Importantly, we need to underscore the fact that peoples in poor countries–that are now committing suicide like we have seen above in India–have only one powerful weapon, their population. Refer to what is currently happening in Europe where economic and illegal immigrants are invading many countries almost every day. What will Europe do with such influxes of destitute people on its shores? Ironically, when Europeans went to Africa to invade it without passports, they thought it was an end of the story. Now that the same immigrants searching for greener pastures after colonialism ruined their countries have turned the tables on Europe seeking better conditions of living that colonialism denied them pointlessly.

Ironically, when the same European countries invaded Africa, the Americas and Asia, nobody complained as Europe is currently doing. Will complaining or ignoring the problem solve the problem without addressing its root causes which, in a word, are nothing but colonialism and the way it superimposed its way of doing things almost everywhere in the world? Again, Europe has embarked on the same fruitless measures to address the problem without addressing its root causes. Boswell (2003) maintains that "measures to restrict illegal entry and stay have driven migrants and refugees to use more dangerous routes to enter Europe, forcing many to employ the services of smuggling or trafficking networks" (p. 619). This is exactly what colonial education is good at. It seeks short-time solutions by ignoring long-time consequences. Boswell doubts about the way Europe is trying to curb and frustrate immigrants who seem hell bent to keep on coming so as to put Europe's infrastructures to test. How will unrequired people stop from coming while the situation back home is alarming? I do not think immigrants are as dangerous as colonialism, neoliberal policies, toxic education and global warming are.

Thanks to such fire-brigade-like efforts, the world currently evidences the surge of racism in Europe resulting from the increase of immigrants. Leftist parties are snatching power from liberal governments and parties in some countries in Europe. This is not a good sign. Neither is it a solution to the very problem. To do away with the current anathema, European countries need to get to the root causes of problem instead of dealing with its offshoots. What should the world expect thereafter if not violence and chaos in such countries where supremacists and racists are swept into power by disgruntled racist voters? Essentially, Europe is reaping what it sowed under colonialism not to mention slavery and other criminal projects. History is repeating itself; and nobody can stop it from doing so. Had the West introduced the type of functioning education in its colonies, maybe this "scourge" of illegal and economic immigrants would be avoided. Once again, this sends us back to our metaphor of the boat we are all travelling on. African sage has it that when you leave a thorn in the farm, it shall injure you in the future. If anything, the thorns that Europe left in the colonies are now stabbing it ruthlessly and in a multiple ways.

Genocide as the Legacy of Colonial Education: Two Case Studies

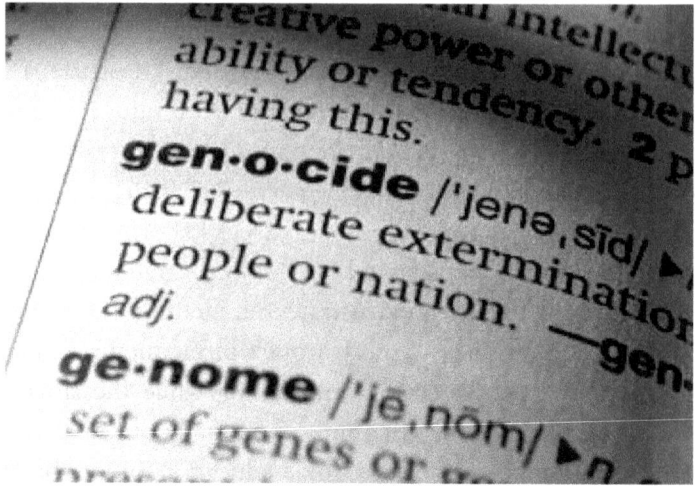

Figure 1; photo courtesy of www.tiki-toki.com

Given that we are looking for doable ways and means to get Africa and the likes rid of miseries, there is no way we can do so without keeping on touching on conflicts of which is genocide that the world recently evidenced in Rwanda. In addressing genocide, this volume presents two case studies from two different countries namely, Rwanda and Canada. The two are found in two different continents and two different societies with almost different everything. Rwanda represents Africa, collectivistic societies and poor countries while Canada represents individualistic and rich West countries. However, the two countries share the nexus in that they are all the victims of colonialism and its toxic education. Again, in both cases, the victims are treated equally. The difference is however, that the former hit many headlines when it occurred within a hundred days while the latter did not attract any international media; and it has been ongoing for over a hundred years. The number of victims in the former is known while in the latter numbers of victims will never be known. While the former has used traditional methods to deal with

168

the problem, the latter has always used the so-called modern (Western) methods to perpetuate the crime. Importantly, these two case studies will show the reader how a liability colonial education has become so as to need its decolonisation, particularly for the victims whose victimhood can be used productively to usher some changes in globally. One of the major causes of conflicts in Africa is said to be ethnicity. Azam (2001) notes that "the reference to ethnicity is used as a ready-made explanation for the eruption of civil wars, especially in the mass media, while a closer look at the facts suggests that it falls short of providing even the beginning of an explanation" (p. 429).

If there is anything indelible that colonial education enacted and left behind is nothing but genocide which, in African, is the product of divide-and-rule strategies that colonial Europe used to weaken Africans so as to rule and exploit them perpetually. Khosroeva (2013) defines genocide arguing that "the word "genocide" originally comes from the combination of the ancient Greek word "genos", meaning people or folk, and the Latin word "caedere", meaning slaughtering or destroying." (p. 1). Therefore, the author argues that genocide means killing the nation, race or tribe of a certain people. Again, genocide is committed as the means of eradicating the *genos* in order to let other *genos* occupy their place or take their privileges. The 1994 Rwandan genocide provides an ideal example of what genocide is; and what humans with toxic education can enact. The Rwandan genocide left approximately one million people dead within the span of a hundred days. This volume will touch on this genocide in details hereunder along with the one in Canada.

Raphael Lemkin cited in Woolford (2009) concurs with Khosroeva by defining genocide as thus: "the term "genocide," a combination of Greek Genos ("race", "tribe") and Latin cide (from cidere, "to kill"), to provoke the world to take seriously this crime that had heretofore gone "without a name" (p. 86). Woolford's definition fits in the definition of genocide that always aims at forcing the "enemy" group into extinction so that it's the perpetrators could eliminate and thereby replace their victims. However, Khosroeva's definition is a little bit broad for involving the term "nation" which is missing in Lemkin's definition.

I). Rwandan Genocide: How Colonial Legacies Created It

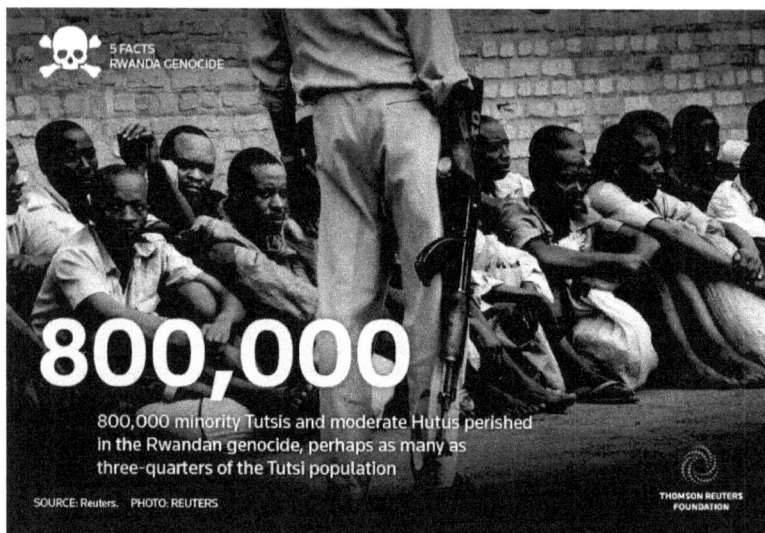

Figure 9; photo courtesy of Reuters

Toxic education has cost Africa and other colonised countries a lot. As indicated, heretofore chapters, *vis-à-vis* enmity and divisions in Sri Lanka where toxic education contributed immensely in fueling ethnic conflicts as it still does hamper the development of many countries. In Africa, the 1994 Rwandan genocide has telling effects. This volume uses Rwanda as a micro variable as far as the needs of decolonising education in the victimised countries is concerned. Since, genocide occurred in Rwanda, how much detoxification of colonial episteme in Rwanda has been put in place as opposed to how the situation was since independence? Or put it this way, how much *academic- vacuum cleaning* has occurred in Rwanda after genocide? Did Rwandan society change the way it perceives things mainly itself? To answer this question accurately, we need to look into the root causes of hatred and genocidal behaviours in Rwanda. Basically, the chief suspect is the type of episteme that was offered before genocide was committed in Rwanda. I can argue that colonial education that–by commission, extension, omission or vicarious means–went on to be offered even after independence created enclaves among Rwandans by dividing them in two artificial entities of superior Tutsis and

170

inferior Hutus. Actually, if you look at the number of elites that participated in instigating killings, you will vividly notice this anomaly. However, new authorities in Rwanda seem to have tried to address the legacy of colonial education as Samuelson & Freedman (2010) note that "Belgian colonial powers who began the school system, would no longer be a medium of instruction in the schools and universities, nor would it serve any longer as an official language in public affairs" (p. 192). On the face of it, Rwanda shifted from French to English however they are all colonial languages as the media of instruction. Again, changing the language from French to English with the same colonial setting of education does not address the root causes. Again, was there any way Rwanda would divorce all colonial languages and survive in international politics of the day? Yes, Hutus and Tutsis both speak Kinyarwanda. As it is in Tanzania, Rwanda would have empowered Kinyarwanda. Colonial education created a few select and privileged group of people known as elites or *electissimus* which means a small special group of people with high power or superior intellectual. After colonial powers created this group, they indoctrinated it to make sure that, when they left colonies, it should indirectly rule on their behalf and behest whether willingly or *ab invito*, consciously or unconsciously based on the superstructure the colonial power created and left behind when they offered independence to their colonies.

Apart from the elites, colonial powers used the media as well as the military and the entire political machinery of the day under the former regime to safeguard their interests at the detriment of the citizens of their former colonies. Samuelson and Freedman (*Ibid.*) make a good point observing that Policy-makers in Rwanda regard the new language policy as a major factor in the success of Rwanda's post-genocide reforms. Is it? Time will accurately tell. Along with education is the issue of the media based on historical realities of the particular society. The media cannot operate in the vacuum as far as the realities surrounding it are concerned; and whenever there is conflict, the victims need to collectively and judiciously address corrective actions such as those that resulted to fear and mayhem culminating in genocide (Freedman, Weinstein, Murphy & Longman (2008). Historically, Rwanda was a divided country in all aspects of life. Politics was revolving around tribalism; so were economic opportunities. It was the "time to eat with my people" for whoever got to power. In this frenzy of eating the national cake, those whose tribe was perceived as an enemy or a threat were excluded. Again, even those who were in power did not eat alone. They had their former colonial masters to serve as Metz (1994) notes that "the Tutsi-Hutu conflict was not a typical African struggle" (p. 8) but the result of colonial machinations that created division and hatred among Rwandans.

Arguably, under such a situation, political power becomes a social capital and tool for those owning power at the times. To get public support, they invite their tribesmen to eat with them, especially when they are from the majority tribe as it was in Rwanda before genocide. Hutus in Rwanda were sidelined and discriminated against under colonialism while Tutsis were favoured. This created hatred that boiled down to genocide. It depends on how one looks at this conundrum. For, Hutus, being in power was the results of their struggle and victory while, for Tutsis, to lose power was unacceptable due to the fact that, when the colonial monsters left, they left the country in their *safe* hands. In conflict resolution studies, the Tutsis would perceive themselves as the "chosen but sieged ones." In such a setting, the groups that are excluded tend to feel like orphaned so as to fight back whenever opportunity avails. If anything, this is what happened in Rwanda before even after genocide which is blamed on Rwandans pointlessly without looking at the type of education Rwandans of both sides received. Essentially, we should not blame anybody. Instead, we must either blame the entire system that failed Rwanda in hour of its need as we think to decolonise it. I may argue that permanent solution for Rwandan conflict will come through rejigging education system, specifically for the new generation so that they can start thinking differently and positively. This can only be achieved through decolonising episteme. Overhauling Rwanda's education system or *vacuum cleaning* it, may yield fruits by getting the world rid of what Byrne in Carter, Irani & Volkan (2009) refers to as the "besieged mentality" (p. 212) wherein two parties to conflict feel beleaguered so as to force the groups to look for enclaves that they normally use as their cocoons of security. In such an enigma, the ruling group deprives its enemy group of all amenities and rights that are all citizenry of the said community or country have to enjoy equally. Once enemies are, essentially relegated to the second class citizenry status, are likely to hit back. This is a human nature. Under the relative deprivation theory, Gurr (2015) notes that relative deprivation is the basic instigating factor for collective violence due to the fact that some people feel excluded. If anything, this is what was ongoing in Rwanda for many years before the 1994 genocide. In effect, the discontentment about the same things–felt by two different and divergent groups differently–normally results from the lenses they use to look at things. Education is one of the tools that enable humans to see things differently and critically. Freire (2000) cited in Yang (2011) argues that "every human being, no matter how "ignorant" or submerged in a "culture of silence" he or she may be, is capable of looking critically at the world in a dialogical encounter with others" (p. 212). Again, this is possible only when the person looking at things has received non-toxic education. So, by embarking on decolonising education, Rwanda will give its people a true tool with which to see things in a Rwandan way but not a colonial one as it has been before. With decolonised education, Rwandans are able to deconstruct everything that has held them captives for many years. Rwandans need to decolonise (Giblin, 2012) their colonised history so as to "construct new academically and politically sound, positive, usable pasts that decolonize the African past and African Archaeology" (p. 127). In decolonising colonial minds, we need to embark on what Brown (2014) refers to as a "problem-posing" strategy which enables one to become aesthetically conscious of who he or she is; and those surrounding her or him. Such understanding is likely to help those entrapped in a logjam colonial episteme enacted in order to act as equal members of a "joint and responsible process" aimed at addressing their problems and needs. At such a juncture, conflicants need to look for; and thereby see what they have in common instead of concentrating on their differences. Further, they need to find what unite them as they discard what divide them. In this case, most of things that cause conflict might be artificial as it is the case in many societies facing tribal animosities. Again, without a decolonised type of education, it becomes harder for such people to see things in this light. For, they need to embark on what Schaap (2006) refers to as agonism or contention for a prize wherein the conflict is faced with positive aspects in the quest of dealing with it positively. Additionally, in addressing the conflict constructively and positively, the parties to conflict need to do it cohesively united in the aim so as to move to the right direction by making sure that they avoid the polarisation of the society engulfed in an embarrassingly *fatal embrace* (Braverman, 2010). This is exactly what was going on in Rwanda before the 1994 genocide. There must be some mechanisms in place that are aimed at overhauling such a situation to see to it that the two parties to conflict are coming together to suggest the solutions to their problems instead of avoiding each other and run away from the problems. Arguably, by overhauling the education system in Rwanda, the dynamics of power will change and shift in the near future if Rwandans are ready to do so as one people and one nation facing identical problems. To do this, young people need to be taught to coexist as brethren or perish as fool as Martin Luther would put it. They need to retell their stories in their own environment shaped by homegrown episteme that seriously and truly aims at readjusting and reorienting the new generation to face the future together. Through decolonised episteme, Rwandans can tell their stories in a constructive manner geared by the desire and commitment to address their differences that were invented by colonial powers. As Kirsch & Rohan (2008) note that, when two stories collide, catch fire as an analogy of how conflict gyrates around such stories that need to be told and heard; and thereby reconciled in order to bring the two to agreed-upon ways of addressing the problem.

Furthermore, through overhauling and decolonising toxic education, Rwanda will be able to find its true identity which, in turn, will remove the artificial ones the colonial powers created; and thereby imposed on Rwandans so as to be a good source a self-destructive intra-conflict. The very questions Rwandans need to ask themselves are: How was Rwanda before the coming of colonialism? How did Rwandans identify themselves as a nation? What can be done to reclaim this lost identity? What stories do they need to tell after the ones concocted by colonial powers led them to abyss of cataclysm? What story don't they want to tell and why? How can they close the dichotomous and antagonistic past they have been in since colonial times which, essentially is based on wrong history? How practicable are the solutions they envisage as a nation? What local mechanisms are in place for decolonisation of education? Again, if there is a huge stone around Rwanda's neck is none other than embarking on redressing itself through new educational approach based on erasing all historical lies and anomalies that led to the 1994 genocide aimed at retracing and retrieving its true history. And this is only possible when and if Rwanda embarks on the detoxification and decolonisation of its episteme at all levels.

Swahili sage has it that the fool is the one bitten twice in the same hole. "*Nunca Mais*" or "Never Again" should be the slogan for Rwanda to envision and pursue its future based on new way of looking at themselves as an interdependent and interconnected family of fate. Fool me once, shame on you. Fool me twice, shame on me the goes the saying. Swahili sage has it that you can choose a friend but not a neighbour or siblings. Through new decolonised education, Rwanda will be able to nourish the minds and altitudes of its people based on the vision of embracing their differences as they stand together to face the future of their own making as opposed to the futile one they had before turning against each other. Rwandans need to get out of fatal embrace to a *vital embrace*. It is only through creating a shared narrative that Rwanda can forge ahead peacefully and unitedly. All the more so, Rwanda needs the transformation of conflict based on constructed nature of narratives without discounting their legitimacy. In so doing, a new sort of relationship will be built. Essentially, creating a shared narrative needs sense of, and readiness to embark on true cooperation, interdependence, interconnectedness, consultations and–above all–consensus. For Rwandans to move ahead, they needed to listen and hear each other's story and evaluate it as if it were theirs. I call this exchanging ears and eyes in order to hear and see what the two parties could not hear and see before and after the conflict occurred. Doing so helps the parties to conflict to be able to learn from their narrative to appreciating and understanding the narratives of others and their situations all aimed at healing and ushering social justice in. This is very true and logical.

If you do not want to understand me, how can I understand you? Basically, this, apart from being the transformation of a conflict, it is the negotiation of meanings based on our understanding, views even visions all regulated and enhanced by decolonised education. Understanding one another is the act of balancing power; and it shows the appreciation of one another. For a people of the same country and origin, negotiating their differences based on decolonised education makes more sense; because such people only have one country they call home equally and legally. They found themselves in that country even if they do not agree or like each other. To deconstruct this tug of war once and for good, Mhango (2015) proposes total unification of Africa so that the larger Africa can subsume such enmities emanating from small groups or small countries. Africa's unification will do away with siege mentality and the "Us" versus "Them" (Muller, 2008; Cikara, Bruneau & Saxe, 2011; and Anderson, 2013) stalemate by creating "*weness*" that has always missed in Rwanda's composition which has always been dominated *holier than thou*. This is the only right way to go not only for Rwanda but for many African countries.

In regards to accepting one another as an equal brother and sisters, this buys in my general view of countering racism. Nobody created him or herself or presented any application letter to be created as he or she is. We are the co-national, brothers, sisters, family members, animals, insects or members of community of fate. Consequently, when it comes to negotiating the future together, nobody should be left out; or nobody should be neglected or ignored. We need to treat one another decently and equally due to the fact that under the basic human needs theory (Adie, Duda & Ntoumanis, 2008) or hierarchy of needs (Cherry, 2014), we need to we avoid the deprivation or sidelining each other. We all have the same needs as human beings in spite of our differences, aspirations, views and whatnots. Therefore, subjecting one another or the section of the society to relative deprivation goes against human needs and human rights. We need one another dearly be it in triumphalism or defeat. Although Rwanda is given as an example, Rwandans will always stand together despite what happened between themselves. And this will become a lesson to others facing similar circumstances and enigmas.

The whole world will look at them and judge them as Rwandans but not as Hutus or Tutsis. Such an understanding is possible through decolonised version of education aimed at resolving the conflict Rwanda has faced for generations. Again, it should be noted that this is no easy task given that the legacy of toxic education is still eminently rampant and presently dominant in Rwanda. Arguably, conflict cannot be resolved overnight. Importantly, Rwandans needs to get ready to deal with their conflict constructively and cooperatively all envisioning the bright future drawing from the past mistakes as were caused by divisive policies as were entrenched in colonial education. In so doing, mistake can be committed. Even if this happens, it should not be allowed to hamper the process; given that humans are not perfect. We, sometimes, learn through our mistakes if we approach such mistakes with a constructive approach and drive.

Importantly, we should strive for perfection and success even if we err here and there. We, occasionally, learn through mistakes and trial and errors. Decolonised education seeks to empower Rwandans and those who received it without benefiting their societies. It seeks to give the victims of colonised education the opportunities and clouts to face their history; and seek some opportunities from it. For Rwanda, specifically decolonised education aims at decriminalising them so that they can see their mistakes and learn from them. Such a move will avert the judgemental danger of seeing each other as criminals, perpetrators, victims and chosen ones. Instead, they will view each other as human beings facing the same dangers and problems they need to solve together for their benefits as a people. Essentially, shall this happen, new decolonised education will enable Rwandans, for the first time, to see the other side of their societies that they did not see before. It will equip them with the tools of finding all elements that unite them as they dispel all those elements that set them apart. Equipped with a decolonised version of education, victims will be able to reinvent themselves so as to bury the hatchet based on artificial entities colonialists imposed on them. Time for teaching victims about themselves is now; and this is only possible through decolonised education. Such an undertaking is aimed at enabling the victims of colonial episteme to know who they actually are. What is wrong today, for example, for French African former colonies to start teaching their people who they are instead of going on teaching them that they are French? Allegations that Africans were taught to be like their colonial dupers is not farfetched. For example, France, among other European colonisers was more assimilationist (Castles, 2009) than others; and its poison went on affecting and destroying its former colonies. The situation was the same in almost all colonies. Portuguese taught their subjects to become good Portuguese while Spanish and British did the same to their subjects as well. Unfortunately–for many countries–after acquiring their independence, did not tweak or overhaul their epistemes. This is why–essentially–Africa's freedom has remained imperfect based on flags which cannot be eaten or used to self-invent. In the case of *francaisesation* of Africans, Castles argues that the emphasis was put on teaching language but not skills or critical thinking due to the fact that language is the manifestation of how we think. Again, colonial powers would not defeat their hidden agendas by teaching critical thinking for fear of becoming counterproductive to their project of exploiting their dupes. This is why colonialism and imperialism have succeeded to continue exploiting former colonies using colonised and toxic education–that needs to be decolonised and detoxified–due to the lack of critical thinking and other academic impetus that would have enabled them to see their problems in true light. This has always been so due to the fact that the type of education ex-colonies have always inculcated in their people is void and toxic.

More on Rwanda, conflict Resolution professionals agree that sometimes, when a conflict is dealt with constructively, it can usher in something usable and important (Fisher, Ury & Patton, 2011). Despite the tragedy that befell Rwanda in 1994 when it faced one hundred days of horrible massacres, the government that stopped genocide and took over came up with creative way of delivering justice based on Rwandan conflict resolution methods colonial education likes to call traditional. Had it expanded on so as to encompass the episteme in totality, such an experiment would have helped other countries facing the same quandaries. After facing huge backlogs of people in correctional facilities, Rwanda came up creatively with its traditional mechanisms of dealing with the situation. Gacaca courts were introduced after the failure of Western legal mechanisms. Wierzynski (2004) defines gacaca thus:

> Gacaca courts or Gacaca (pronounced Ga-cha-cha). Gacaca is a traditional, community-based restorative justice institution that recently has been co-opted by the government to unburden the national justice system from the massive number of genocide detainees who have been awaiting trial, some since 1994 (p. 1939).

Brouneus (2010) brings in the role of truth telling and the way it can arguably help in reaching true reconciliation in Post-genocide Rwanda. Again, to fully embark on detoxification of epistemes, Rwanda can be viewed as one way of reconciling two societies however; partly this process may be deemed narrow due to the fact that Gacaca courts do not address other social issues except restorative and transitional justice.

According to one of the victims of Rwandan genocide who lost many members of his family, remembering and telling the truth are however not ease things as they may seem, particularly where people were killed like houseflies. Consequently, the same victim says that telling truth will free all Hutus and Tutsi altogether despite having two different views of each other. The victim's truthfulness, courage, bravery and daring behaviour in facing the reality attracted and convinced me that Rwandans can do something to address their past in order to venture in the future based on their readiness and commitment to do so based on international *ordunung*. I could not imagine; how it would feel for me to lose the whole family just overnight; and yet, stand facing the reality with forgiveness with such a big heart.

Indeed, there are some unsung heroes; and it becomes difficult to trace them all so that we can hear their stories however traumatising they are. The said victim told the story his father once told him which says that he who does not speak with his father does not know what his grandfather left. The victim went on, as tears started gushing in his eyes, saying that he did not say what he said because he was a coward. He wanted to forgive and forge ahead. He added that he lost his father and mother and siblings from the family of 19 of which only three members survived. This particular anonymous victim wanted both sides to put their acts together by taking their responsibility in genocide so as to move forward together as a closure of this traumatic incident. For, this victim who experienced genocide firsthand, genocide was not a one-ethny show; but it involved all Rwandans Hutus and Tutsi though in different magnitudes and reasons. But, for this victim, putting the past behind and forging ahead as a nation without gravitating to hatred, fear and anguish are more important than revisiting the past as it was created by colonialists without using it to disentangle themselves from its trap. Such a statement is very strong by all standards. This means, if we truly and trustworthily search our souls as a people, we still have people in Africa who can embark on their cultural practises to settle disputes even if they are about the deaths of their loved ones. If anything, this is the way Africans used to resolve conflicts.

Before the coming of neo-religions and colonialists, Africans did not have eye-for-eye or ear-for-ear justices as their mechanisms of conflict resolution. Again, they were not angles save that by trusting colonialists; Africans became the captives and preys of hatred, division and monstrosity. By telling his story–personal story of course–the victim was inviting the other side to feel what he feels and think the way he thinks about the future of his country. What a powerful message if it is well and deeply understood so as to be taken serious and is worked on! Again, how constructive or destructive the victim's message can be understood and applied depends on the lenses Rwandans will apply. This is why decolonising education becomes vital and *sine qua non*.

Although what transpired in Rwanda in 1994 was horrible by all standards, we can still say that the government used the conflict constructively by bring Gacaca to the map of the world. Apart from the introduction of Gacaca, Rwanda is currently embarked on deconstruction of the *caste system* which culminated in genocide that Germans and Belgians imposed on it. To do away with such gory past, National IDs no longer bear the origin of a bearer based on his or her community or tribe. However, much need to be done to change education system to see to it that all garbage colonial dupers left behind are removed from the heads of Rwandans. More importantly, Rwandans young and old should be made to know that colonial conmen maliciously and artificially reinvented them so as to divide and rule them.

Actually, Germany, Belgians and French respectively created a new type of people who could easily doubt, suspect, and hate one other just because of being redefined by invaders. The so-called *Tutsi superiority* or *Hutu inferiority* were hoaxes socially constructed to dupe and weaken Rwandans so much that they could easily be stymied and ruled; and thereby easily and perpetually exploited. What made such a crime dangerously looming is the fact that there was international conspiracy stemming from colonialism behind it. You can see this at the time genocide occurred for a hundred days without any international community even the UN interfering to stop it.

News and stories about this genocide were all over the place; but nobody bothered to step in and stop the carnage! Who would have bothered with such a small country without oil and minerals? If what happened in Rwanda would have occurred in the Middle East where there is gas, no doubt, the big brothers of the world would not be caught in a slumber as it happened in the case of Rwanda. Again, why did the same international community intervene in Kosovo timely and quickly four years after Rwandan genocide but not doing the same in Darfur? Why did African leaders allow genocide to occur others under their noses? Were they waiting for Western countries to decide or interfere or give orders to even save their brothers and sisters? One would argue that Africa's dependency is one of the reasons that enabled genocide to occur due to the fact that Africa countries even the African Union (AU) were all waiting for orders to come from the West. Is it because of toxic education that some African leaders were given so as to fail to understand the magnitude of the crime in the making? Is this the story of blue eyed boy and a black sheep? Decide by yourself. I do not want to be judgemental.

I have given Rwanda as an example of toxic education not to shame or single it out. What befell Rwanda speaks volumes; and it will always bemoan at us collectively as a human family. If anybody can contribute to resolving this conflict, she or he will have contributed a lot even if he or she is not necessarily Rwandan. Also, it should be noted that since genocide occurred in 1994, Rwanda has become a referent point as far as how to deal with such calamities is concerned. I am not trying to be too optimistic or too parsimonious. I think–if we all throw our weight behind the conflict however light or heavy it is–we can motivate Rwandans to reconcile and move forward as a united nation ready to live harmoniously and interdependently as it did before colonial administrators poisoned the relationship of its people. I therefore believe that those Rwandans– be they academics or laypeople who will read this volume–will feel challenged to make up their differences. Again, how will they deal with their differences without decolonising and detoxifying one of the pillars that governs their daily lives namely, education? This is not the recipe for Rwanda only but for the whole world that failed one family of its own at the hour of need. Rwandans are not the first ones, and–too, were not the last ones–as far as conflict is concerned.

Furthermore, it happened in South Africa and elsewhere where conflicts threated the existence of other human beings. We are a globalised world that is interconnected and interdependent. Rwanda's peace is our peace and our contributions are their contributions. Our contributions are the challenge to them. The question they will ask themselves is, if non-Rwandans are so much concerned, what of them? Methinks by addressing Rwandan genocide, and Canadian as we will see later, we are rescinding the refusal and double standard that the international community showed during the commission of genocide. We are all guilt-ridden; and therefore, we are all duty-bound to help wherever we can.

Suffices it to say, despite what happened in Rwanda in 1994 that is obvious undesirable and unacceptable, we, as academics still can build on what came out of the process of delivering justice however imperfect it might be regarded. All human systems are experimental by nature. This is why they are always dynamic and need adjustments and changes here and there. If we can experiment, let say Frankfurt school's philosophy on dealing with conflict, why should we not apply the same zeal to Gacaca that has proved to be effective within a short time? The role of Gacaca courts in post-genocidal Rwanda was great; although no justice system is perfect. Gacaca reduced the logjams in a fragile and infant Rwanda judicial system. It created alternative mechanisms which set the precedent that if we appreciate other cultures and support them to solve the problems toxic education created, we can move forward as it is the case in Rwanda even South Africa.

To do away with the mess just like the one we evidenced in Rwanda, our education systems should enable us to be creative so as to come up with other new formulas and methods of dealing with conflicts chiefly at this time the *status quo* has totally failed due to having a bigger hand in creating and fueling conflicts in many places. We need new formulas for new problems. We cannot go on using old formulas to deal with new problems. And verily, decolonised education is the answer to such a challenge. The decolonised education is supposed to help us devise such methods based on our, *inter alia,* aspirations, circumstances, environment and needs. In effect, the world needs to embark on Gacaca-like traditional mechanisms of dealing with conflicts and other problems. I am sure there are many mechanisms that have not been explored out there. Logically, if the views of the victims of colonialism and its toxic education were to be accommodated, it is obvious that one of the mechanisms they would propose is the imposition of heavy fine on the countries that sowed the seed of destruction in their ex-colonies.

Additionally, as it was practiced in many African societies, the imposition of heavy fines on whoever breaks peace would be preferred to war as espoused by the West. For example, if Germany was able to redress Jews, why can't Germany, Belgium and France do the same to Rwanda, Burundi and others wherein the *genocidal caste system* they created has always curtailed peace and development in these countries for decades apart from claiming many lives? There is empirical evidence to prove that genocide in Rwanda was created by Belgium and Germany as Carter, Irani & Volkan (*op.cit.*) note that, like Belgians and English, "Germans found it logical for the Tutsis to rule Hutus…. they decided to administer Rwanda by indirect rule system" (p. 136) which created and provoked lethal enmity that culminated in genocide as the result of what is known as *Tutsification.* Ironically, Rwandan genocide was only blamed on Hutus but not Germans who enacted this system or Tutsis whom Germans used to create hatred between two Rwandan communities. Under divide and rule, colonial powers created "artificial races" which segregated and hated each another. Suffice it to say, the international community needs to decolonise its view of the victims of colonialism, particularly

the offshoots such as genocide, *coup d'états* and assassinations in Africa and other ex-colonies.

Again, what transpired in Rwanda revolves around colonial and toxic education as the sequels of the dominant grand narrative that views other grand narratives as inferior and moribund. The type of education that allowed such atrocities to occur needs to be decolonised shall the world seriously desire and embark on the mission to, *inter alia*, development, justice and peace.

In sum, we have seen how Gacaca courts reduced court backlogs in Rwanda after applying purely Rwandan mechanisms of dealing with Rwandan problems. Despite being urged to use Western mechanisms and methods of conflict resolution, the victims of colonial and toxic education have their own ways and means of making peace shall the poison be removed from their heads and hearts. If the current episteme were decolonised, we would be able, as argued above, to ask: Why don't we have international laws that force colonial powers to redress countries that suffered from their strategies that created artificial races in these countries. Is it because it is Africa whose grand narrative was felled after the coming of colonialism or the blindness and bigotry of the current dominant grand narrative embedded in toxic education? To do justice, and justice to be seen done, the international community needs to come up with some instruments and laws that will force former colonial powers to redress their victims so that the two can be at par as they close the chapter of inequality and exploitation in order to harmoniously move forward together as partners but not slaves and masters or victims and perpetrators. This argument goes as further as demanding the redress of Africa as a whole due to the evils and setbacks it has experienced resulting from slavery, colonialism and imperialism all drawing from the current dominant grand narrative which made most of European countries richer while Africa became poorer and poorer so as to always depend on handouts, be they financial or policies, from the same countries that plundered Africa. Why is this approach important, inevitable and feasible? It is simple. Africa is still ruled and managed by people who received toxic education that made them tools in the hands of others to use, misuse and even abuse wantonly. Then, why don't African leaders agitate for redress?

Former South African president, Nelson Mandela, due to his bravery and vision, tried to address this issue in South Africa. However, he died before achieving the goal he targeted. Africans leaders, thanks to toxicity of the colonial education they received and kept on providing, were made cowards intellectually so as to be afraid of confronting the truth. To avoid the ambiguity, and possibly, the victimisation or abuses of innocent people as it happened in Zimbabwe–which culminated in land grab–Africa needs to think about demanding for its redress as a whole; instead of a few countries, such as South Africa, to do so internally or severally. However, for African countries with land issues resulting from colonial grab still can embark on internal redress as the way of harmonising their economies aimed at creating peaceful environment resulting from equal redistribution of land. I personally understand the situation in Kenya, Namibia, South Africa and Zimbabwe. All over again, South Africa is trying to redress its black-disempowered people by redistributing wealth without facing Britain which ruled it so that it can contribute to this noble process of restoring justice to the victims. Britain must redress South Africa and other countries it colonised. The same should apply to other colonial powers all over the world. I think redressing former colonies is a good mechanism aimed at fair redistribution of wealth in the world today where rich people and countries are becoming richer and richer while poor people or countries are becoming poorer and poorer simply because the former has perpetuated exploitation on the latter. So, too, redressing victims is a reconciliatory way of bringing two sides together so that they can create the future together. By so doing, the world will be able to move at one pace in harmony and high spirit. I think decolonised education will be there to stand and defend the idea[s] of redressing the victims individually and nationally. For, apart from doing social justice to the world, it arguably is a prelude to peace for the world. Going on window-dressing such delinquency and incongruities resulting from colonialism and toxic education, the legacies of colonialism will exacerbate conflicts and inequality in former colonies which will affect the whole globe when it comes to violence.

Arguably, the lack of laws forcing former colonial powers to redress their former colonies has created another loophole whereby the same colonial powers interfere in the affairs of their former colonies aimed at destabilising them as it was in the DRC soon after independence whereby Belgium–in conjunction with the Central Intelligence Agency CIA–killed DRC's first Prime Minister Lumumba simply because he was not ready to be used by colonial forces to rule the DRC by proxy. The CIA is accused of architecting and executing this criminal project. The CIA's participation in the plot, and later its execution, is no longer a classified secret. Why? Because those perpetrators of such heinous act have nothing to worry about given that under the current international laws, they cannot be charged with/for the offence they committed due to the lacunae that has been purposely created to shield them from any criminal liability. Try to imagine; if another country would have assassinated the president of the US. Would such a crime be pushed under the carpet as it was in the case of Lumumba? Again, why didn't Lumumba's death matter, as it has never matter, before the West and the world at large? The answer is simple that Lumumba was not the head of an imperialistic power that the current dominant grand narrative benefits and protects altogether. Lumumba had a laid down his vision for the DRC. He also had indicated that he would ally himself with the East communist camp. And thus, thereby, he would have given the West the back something the West did not want to happen. For, Lumumba's move meant that the West would lose minerals and other resources that it has dominated since the assassination of Lumumba. Gerard & Kuklick (2015) expressly mention Lawrence Devlin, chief of the CIA station in the American embassy in Kinshasa, as the person responsible for the massacre of Lumumba.

And truly, on 17 January, 1961 Lumumba was assassinated along with his trusted ministers; and his government was toppled thereof. Imperialist forces branded Lumumba a militant leader (Nzongola-Ntalaja, 2014) something that aims at belittling, criminalising and diminishing him if not showing him as a violent person that was supposed to be eliminated for peace to prevail in the DRC. This is wrong. This is judgemental behaviour that academics must avoid and fight. Over again, such a view comes from the same school of thoughts that deems non-Westerners, predominantly the victims of its rotten system, inferior, useless and valueless. Villafana (2011) cites Devlin's cable message from the US embassy in Kinshasa sent to the home government describing how murky things were maintains that:

> Embassy and Station believe Congo experiencing classic Communist takeover Government.... Whether or not Lumumba actually Commie or just playing Commie game to assist his solidifying power, anti-west forces rapidly increasing power Congo and there may be little time left in which take action to avoid another Cuba (p. 7).

The narrative is the same. Lumumba was regarded as an enemy of the West whose narrative this volume seeks to debunk, deconstruct and reconstruct and vacuum-clean in order for justice to be done for the victims. Whether this should be under Natural Justice or whatever form of justice, it is important if we aspire to do justice just for both parties namely, offenders and victims. After realising and underscoring the flaws of its past policies, currently, the US declassified some of its classified documents something that gave a window to see and know what it concealed for many decades. This is good evidence shall we decolonise our education and minds so as to embark on sane politics of fairness and justice for all. Nonetheless, much is still unknown *apropos* the toppling of noncompliant African governments. Is it wrong to suggest that the US redresses the DRC for the wronging and destroying DRC's future by killing its leader who promised a lot compared to those that the US installed to mismanage and rob the country? Truly, the US has a lot of money apart from the truth that it made a lot more money by robbing the DRC and other countries whose leaders it disposed. In spite of knowing everything about how the CIA used to hunt some stable African leaders down; some European so-called thinkers were just ridiculing Africa calling African countries sick.

Who is taking Britain to task in order to help it make just by redressing Nigeria today? Everything is blamed on Nigeria; and that is that. Thanks to colonial-toxic education, nobody bothers to dig deeper to see what the root causes of all miseries Nigeria is currently suffering from actually are. US's story of disposing leaders of other countries does not end up in the DRC or Chile. What happened to the first post-colonial government in Ghana under Nkrumah is another naked truth of how the dominant grand narrative negatively affects others whose narratives are not incorporated in the world order. It is important to state that the US was not alone in the game of toppling governments that seemed not to be ready to be used to safeguard the interests of powerful countries. Back to Ghana, after coming with radical ideas about how Africa can depend on itself, Nkrumah was toppled on 24th February, 1966 when he was on an official tour to North Vietnam and China (Mwakikagile, 2015).

If African rulers can get worthy education, they can turn things around. How come that China, Malaysia, Singapore, Japan and South Korea made it out of poverty while Africa cannot? I think, despite their grand narratives being subsumed by the West, they still invest in their own grand narratives locally. You can see this in the languages they use in imparting education in their people. If you consider the fact that those countries have their partly decolonised system of education based on their needs and understanding, you will easily know what I mean here. So, it can be argued that Africa's poverty is in the minds of its people but not anywhere else. Those exploiting Africa would like to see it going on with producing what it cannot eat and eat what it cannot produce like a chicken (Mhango, 2015). Essentially, without decolonising our epistemes, the toxicity of

188

colonial education will go on eating us as we go on becoming a laughingstock for the world. I know. This assertion is provocative before the eyes of Western countries, mostly the beneficiaries of the conspiracy and evils emanating from slavery and colonialism which acted as capital bases for the West for a long time. Again, what can we do if we aspire to live in a very peaceful world? As an academic and a member of human family, I hope my contribution will help a lot in creating conducive environment for preventing conflict resulting from colonial legacy, toxic education, exploitation and unfair distribution of wealth. It is on this basis therefore, we all need to decolonise our education systems so that we can think by ourselves and do things in the manner that will benefit us as well. And I think it is full of this "form of ignorance" that is eating poor countries.

More on pernicious epistemes, their negative and perilous effects can be seen in the case of Rwanda which I have already touched on *vis-à-vis* study cases of genocide as the product of this toxic education. In this section, the volume basically addresses another aspect namely, the alteration and reinvention of victims. For example, we can discern from Hutu-Tutsi relationship that the type of education France, Germany and Belgium offered was utterly destructive to the Rwandans in both communities. A gory story of self-destruction based on forming superficial identity is evident in Rwanda due to what happened before and in 1994. Arguably, the picture is the same all over African countries facing negative ethnicity although at different magnitude. The same toxic education still makes inroads in many countries as far as ethnoconflicts are concerned. For example, derogative terms are still used in many fields such as journalism which portray African countries as backward, diseased and gullible not to mention limited or no coverage of important events resulting from colonialism and unfair international relations that I will address and cover in an independent chapter later.

For example, the Gacaca courts in Rwanda provide an ideal example of how conflict can be managed or being dealt with using traditional models. After Rwanda cascaded into the 1994 genocide, Western courts tried to deal with the conflict to no avail. Essentially, what happened is the surging of case backlogs. When Gacaca courts were established, the backlogs were comparably eased out easily. For example, instead of looking for who did what so as to jail her or him, the courts sought to know the truth so that it can be used as the means of avoiding repeating the same in the future which the Western judicial system does not address as its first priority. While truth is pivotal as far as Gacaca courts are concerned, Brewin (2001); Byrne (2004); de Ridder (1997); Rose, Bisson & Wessely (2003) cited in Brouneus (2010) show doubts if telling truth cannot pose any risk due to the fact that it has never been tested (Hamber (2001); Thoms, Ron & Paris (2008) cited in Brouneus *Ibid.*). However, the major aim of Gacaca courts was reconciliation which Lederach (1999); Tutu (1999); Biggar (2001); Helmick & Petersen (2001) cited in Brounéus (2008) maintain that leads to forgiveness, healing and reconciliation. Here the logic is simple that in a collectivistic society, everybody depends on another while the situation is totally different in an individualistic society. Therefore, when one is wronged, the whole society is. Apart from seeking to reconcile the individuals and the society, the Gacaca court aimed at dealing with homemade problems by amicably applying homemade mechanisms of conflict resolution based on the needs and aspirations of the society. When it comes to how Gacaca courts fit in, Schabas (2005) maintains that the aim and the spirit of the Gacaca courts are to:

> Prove the capacity of the Rwandan society to settle its own problems through a legal system based on Rwandan custom, since, although the cases that the 'gacaca jurisdictions' will have to hear, are different from these that are normally resolved within the Gacaca framework, these jurisdictions fit well into the custom of settling differences by arbitration, even amicable arbitration (p. 14).

Ironically, despite its effectiveness, Gacaca courts, they are still viewed as a Rwandan thing that fits only Rwanda under the current toxic and hegemonic education. While Gacaca courts are viewed narrowly this way, the Nuremberg mode of trials is viewed as an all-encompassing method of dealing with conflicts universally under the current toxic education that glorifies everything Western as it condemns whatever non-Western. Sometimes, I wonder. While the Nuremberg trials are used internationally to deal with genocidal crimes, the same have never applied to Rwanda as far as countries that plotted to commit genocide with the former regime are concerned. Skinner (2008) argues that "the Nuremberg trials have served as a key precedent for theories of complicit liability" (p. 327) in particularly to include the prosecution of corporations that colluded with the regime that committed genocide. Again, who used to supply weapons to the Rwandan former regime which were used to butcher innocent people? Due to the toxicity of colonial education system, such a crucial question has never been asked; and if it was, no right answers have ever been given. I am trying to imagine if genocide were committed in a European country aided by African states what the situation would have been as far as hunting the accomplices is concerned. Methinks the Nuremberg trials would be revisited to deal with even the abettors to the crime. Again, genocide being one type of racism (King cited in Dellinger, 2013) Europe would not helplessly or indifferently fall-back and look while white people are butchered as it did when Rwandans were butchering each other thanks to the poison the current dominant grand narrative injected into them during the colonial era.

However, it is sad that even the Gacaca courts did not seek to unearth the international colluders so that they could be brought before it. Again, if you look at the localised jurisdiction of Gacaca courts, whatever good that came out them cannot be used internationally simply because they do not form part of the international laws. Therefore, they had no international jurisdiction as well. Interestingly, there were no corporations that were charged or tried during the Nuremberg trials. The same way, there were countries that abetted Nazis (Pingel, 2014) to commit holocaust although they are not making a part of Nuremberg trials' precedent. One may argue that countries were not included in this precedent due to the fact that many of European countries treated Jews badly due to "religious difference, which into the early 20th century was a key dimension of disapproval of Jews" (Bergmann, 2008, p. 349) in many European countries wherefore they wanted to avoid criminal liability in the future. Thanks to toxic and hegemonic education, Jews who suffered from persecution in Europe are ironically now replicating the same against Palestinians so as to arouse new wave of antisemitism in modern times. Kaplan & Small (2006) observe that some institutions in Europe such as the Executive Council of the Britain's Association of University Teachers (AUT) reached at the point to vote for shunning some Israel academic institutions such as Bar Ilan and Haifa. The force was exerted to the duo "as a contribution to the struggle to end Israel's occupation, colonization and system of apartheid" (p. 548) that Israel has intermittently applied against Palestinians.

In regards to the reasons why countries that used to treat Jews badly before holocaust (and by extension, after its commission) not did not became a part of the Nuremberg trials' precedent, it is obvious that they wanted to avoid future criminal liability the same way the accomplices in Rwandan genocide purposely did in creating the special tribune for Rwanda. Therefore, such countries did not like to be part of this process–however, they were part of the crime–for fear of being sued or forced to redress Jews in the near future. This *holier than thou* tendency has gone on whereby some rich countries such as China, the United States (US), the United Kingdom (UK), and Russia, did not ratify international instruments such as the International Criminal Court (ICC) for fear of being prosecuted for the atrocities their personnel have always committed in other countries deemed inferior thanks to the rationale of the current dominant grand narrative under the theory of veto that regulates international affairs especially and the UN. Sometimes, it baffles to find that some countries with veto votes did not ratify and sign this instrument. What signals do they send to weaker states? *Holier than thou,* of course, is the name of the game in this face-saving business. Thanks to toxic education, the international community still looks at such legal circumvention as something normal while sanely, it is not, essentially without considering the fact that the same absconders are always in the forefront forcing other culprits from poor countries to be dragged before the same ICC they did not ratify.

Why truth was the Holy Grail that Gacaca courts sought? The logic is simple that they wanted to put a human face on the conflict so as to deal with it humanely based on African philosophy of Ubuntu–as above defined–that revolves around humanity and collective and connected functions of almost everything wherein social aspect of the society that is more connected than the Western one. Why can we not call conflict management conflict humanising based on Ubuntu? This means putting a human value in conflict so that conflicants can feel more of connected humans than enemies so as to address issues like humans but not enemies. The story from Ghana shows. Lederach (2005) quotes one of the conflicants in the above cited conflict as thus: "you are right father we do not have a chief" (p. 9) whereof the boy from the community that offended another was telling the chief of that community when he wondered why they did not have a chief to negotiate with. Again, despite the opposite side having no chief, based on the connectivity and quality of humanity, the two communities were able to negotiate and resolve their conflict based on humanity but not manipulations, confrontation, competition, power and pomp.

II). Canada's Genocide: How Hegemony Maintained It

When it comes to genocide, it did not only occur in Africa only. For, Canada one of the Western advanced countries, has been sitting on genocide. Woolford (2009) argues that "the impact of colonialism on Aboriginal groups in Canada is often described as "cultural genocide" or "Ethnocide" (p. 81). This is another evidence of colonial and toxic episteme that has failed to bring emancipation to the human family. Arguably, genocide can be defined as to massive and systemic extermination of the members of a certain ethnic group in order to make them extinct; or that the system or group kills or disposes the victims in order own their resources as it is the case in Australia, Canada and the US among others. Essentially, genocide can be termed as a struggle or a tactic aimed at enabling one group to control scarce resources through elimination or subjugation.

Although Canadian genocide is defined as cultural genocide, this definition misses one vital point that Aboriginal peoples of Canada did not only lose their cultural identity and rights but also their populations. So, this type of genocide can encompass both culture and population.

Although Canadian genocide has never been documented as many times as Rwandan has been, genocide is genocide. Canada is not a poor country that can allow everybody in to document its history of shame and brutality. This is because Canada, apart from being the part and parcel of the dominant grand narrative, does not depend on donors to run its governments. Therefore, to clinically examine and document Canada's genocide becomes harder than Rwanda's based on the economics and the international system built on colonial and unequitable policies. Equally so, the magnitude of this genocide, despite being slowly and perpetually committed for many generations, is not as seen big as that of Rwanda however the population involved can be bigger than Rwanda's. This is because of the nature of the commission of genocide. Whereas Rwandan genocide was quickly executed, Canadian has been executed gradually. Also, the victims of Canada's genocide have no power whatsoever compared to Rwanda's. A few people know that Canada once committed genocide; and it still goes on doing the same in the twenty first century. Being a wonderful country, Canada has always been bedeviled by this genocide that the European settlers committed. It has always clung on the chests of Canadians both those of European pedigree and those of Aboriginal pedigree. Indeed, it has become the shame of the nation. Due to the nature of the theme of this book, the author decided to use two different genocides from two different countries in order to do justice and show how poor countries are implicated in many evils than rich countries even when such evils are not of their making. We can apply Orr's observation to Residential Schools in Canada whereby Aboriginal peoples were tortured, degraded and their culture butchered after their families were destroyed. Wasn't the introduction of residential schools a monster that devoured many innocent Aboriginal peoples in Canada not to mention the US, other South America and Australia? Has genocide stopped from going on swallowing them so as to decimate or make them become extinct?

Ironically, behind this notorious system, by all standards, there were professors, doctors, educationists, administrators and above all, the governments led by the so-called civilised white folks in committing this sacrilege! Even calling such ridiculous and obnoxious system residential school is an insult to true education. These were prisoners but not schools. Fundamentally, Western so-called civilisation is unrivaled currently in criminality. For, instead of becoming an impetus for peace and good life in the wold; it is becoming itself and danger of everything including itself. Championed by Western civilisation, residential schools were introduced to "civilise" the "uncivilised" natives. Instead of civilising them, it proved how uncivilised this *civilisation* was. How do you deny somebody her or his identity and ways of life and say you are civilising her or him? Mhango (2015) argues that civilisation, *inter alia*, first and foremost must be measured by how it promotes justice, equality and humanity. Ironically, with all of its liberal democracy, science, and technological advancement almost in everything except in truthfulness and humanness, neoliberalism and all foreign isms, the so-called civilised cabal failed to underscore a very simple reality that all human beings are equal; and therefore need to equally be treated as humans but not superior and inferior humans. They all die and need to live. All human want and need to be free, respected, protected and appreciated. Animals are better sometimes than humans. They appreciate each other more intimately and truly than humans whose hypocrisy takes a lead when it comes to treating each other. If our episteme cannot address this dilemma, then we still have a lot to do to see to it that we actualise peace in the world based on decolonisation of the same.

Courageous thinkers have minced no words. Some equates Indian Residential School with genocide. MacDonald & Hudson (2012) hold the federal government of Canada with primary responsibility for adopting and implementing explicitly genocidal policies. We need this courage and trustworthiness to be able to address the problem which stands in the way of peace for Canada even the United States down south as far as the rights of the Aboriginal peoples are concerned. Further, MacDonald & Hudson maintain that what transpired culminated in what he calls genocidal outcomes "in terms of intergenerational trauma and cultural disintegration." It is sad to note that while countries that went through genocide, are addressing the problem decisively despite depending on foreign aid, Canada, despite being rich by all standards, is either window dressing or just sitting on the problem. What is wrong? This is the question decolonised educationists need to ask the authorities in Canada. Ironically, Canada is among the champions of human rights and human security in the world. Oddly, it does so while its own people, the true owner of Kanata, or village from which comes the name Canada, are languishing in the same crime. Under social process theory, we need to underscore social interaction as a source of conflict, and thereby, "conceive conflict resolution as a marked reduction in social conflict" (Macdonald &Hudson, *op.cit*, p. 9) by decolonising the type of education that failed to resist such genocidal drive at national and international levels. We need to ask provocative questions on how to come together and decolonise our minds based on decolonising and detoxifying global episteme. I have incorporated Canada's and Rwandan experiences in order to avoid being biased by only dealing with Africa. For instance, how often

Aboriginal models of conflict resolution are used in Canada just like Gacaca was used in Rwanda?

Despite being the first inhabitants of modern Canada, Aboriginal conflict resolution models, and other types of knowledge are still disregarded or ignored not to mention to be regarded as if they are in their infancy while those of the newcomers (settlers) are viewed as more mature and often used comparably thanks to Western academic hegemony. For decolonised educationists to answer the issue of genocide in Canada, they will not only be fulfilling their responsibility as thinkers. They will also be providing the two-sum impetus of pulling Canada out of the impasse that has been going on due to sheer naivety, fear and ignorance. If we can decolonise our education and emancipate others, what else do we need? By expounding theories on how to do away with racism, consumerism and genocide, *inter alia*, we will be helping both the perpetrators and victims to become free and safer comparably.

Again, academics, teach students about genocide that occurred in Rwanda while, at the same time, turn a blind eye on other genocides. I would urge all professionals to use Canadian or Australian genocide against Aboriginal peoples when teaching or introducing genocide in their classes, seminars and other discourses. When they teach about freedom and lack of it, they should refer to people in zoos in their countries. They must refer to daily discrimination and tortures in the camps known as reserves in the mentioned countries above. I am not being cynical or biased. How can a citizen in her or his so-called free and advanced democracy live where some else has ordered him or her to live. Aren't these Bantustans like those we used to read about in Apartheid South Africa? As to why such reserves were created? Legassick & Wolpe (1976) cited in Neocosmos (2010) maintain that reserves were created in order to create cheap labour from blacks in the country according to the demand of the industry the whites monopolised. Is there any difference between former South African Bantustans and reserves in Canada now? Though Aboriginal peoples are not attractive to the job market in Canada, their land produces a lot of oil, minerals, timbers and other resources. Although some academics have researched on the issue, it seems, nothing was done to inveigle the government of Canada to stop this horrible genocidal policy which seems to be an extension of residential schools that destroyed Aboriginal ways of bringing up their young ones as Blackstock (2007) posits that:

> For thousands of years, First Nations communities in Canada had their own systems of caring for children when their parents were unable or unwilling to do so. Beginning in the 1950s, these systems were forcibly usurped by provincial child welfare laws that emphasized the safety and well-being of the child as the paramount consideration whilst assuming parents could, with available support, ensure the safety of their children (p. 3); also see Kelm (2011); Landertinger (2011); and Mascarenhas (2012).

Although this matter is known in academic circles, it still is new internationally. Western media is not interested in it for fear of putting their dirty linens on the agora. What makes it worse is the fact that its consequences for Aboriginal peoples, as a people, are unbearably inexplicable so to speak. Even after the government admitted to have erred, nothing was done to do away with the practice save to transmute the same into another notorious one, *reservesation* of Aboriginal peoples in their land where their movements are curtailed and monitored. To add salt to injury, Canada introduced the documentation in order to profile and single them out. Why? One would say that the government wants to know them so that it can protect them. It does not make sense. No decolonised thinker can buy into such nonsense. Does it mean other Canadians do not need and deserve this sort of protection? If Canada were run under decolonised education, such fallacy would not have been allowed to become a national policy-cum-shame. As professionals, what have we done to address these crimes against humanity? Furthermore, the Aboriginal peoples of Canada did not only suffer from reserve but they permanently suffered from Residential School that robbed them of their children, family values and connection, networks and ways of life for generations.

Verily, what is referred to as residential school was nothing but illegal and brutal imprisonment of the bodies, minds and hearts of the victims so as to subdue and subsume them altogether. Those who enslaved and tortured those souls were right according to Western way of "thingification" of everything which normally acts on the body, be it human or body politic, in enforcing its machination (Jameson, 2013) in this process of degrading and exterminating others. Whose body is this? This is a crucial question we need to ask and answer, fundamentally if we remind ourselves that capitalism will stop to nothing when it comes to making a buck. This is why the dominant grand narrative, driven by profit-making and accumulation of wealth, commodified culture at the time cultural industry was still conceived as a matter of symbolic superstructure (Monnin, 2009) but not an economic asset.

Those who went through this Apartheid incinerator ended up becoming functionless to themselves, their societies and the country at large. Therefore, when we consider whose body this is, we should situate ourselves in the locus by stepping into the shoes of the victims so that we can vividly experience what they went through even if doing so is for a short time. By locating ourselves and rehearsing the situation, apart from decolonising our understanding of the crime, we will also be able to find the solution[s] to this problem. What would I do or like to be done had I been the one of victims? Swahili sage has the answer saying that a spear is good for a pig but for a human is bitter. How can you call residential school policy that Canada used for many years before abolishing it recently? If it is a policy but not a crime then it is a notorious policy. Calling residential prisoners school is but to ridicule, abuses and misrepresent school and the total meaning and purpose of this institution. The definition of school entails the place or body from which education and skills can be obtained. Looking at what came out of residential school in Canada, you find nothing but the situation wherein the victims lost almost everything. The victims did not gain anything save that they lost everything immaterial and material. Refer to how miseries such as alcoholism, drug abuse, suicide and the disintegration of the families have always haunted the victims and their progenies thereafter even after this pathetic system was abolished by its makers. Again, was residential school imprisonment totally abolished or changed into another way of controlling the same? Try to think of the results of the *reservesation* in Canada today. Despite having niceties

199

in theories such resistance, social, development and everything theories, thanks to its toxicity and tunnel vision, our education has failed to decisively address such problems.

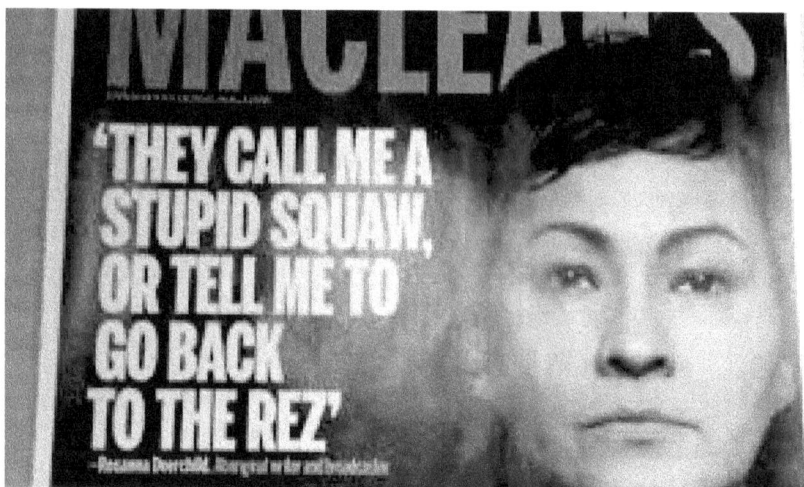

Figure 11; photo courtesy of MacLean January 2015

The picture above is self-explanatory; there is racism in our society. How deeper this vice is, in fact, depends on which side one is. Essentially, racism against Aboriginal peoples of Canada is systemic and endemic due to the fact that it has been in place for over a hundred years and nothing substantially has ever been done to either alleviate or stamping it out. Even a visitant in a Canadian society can notice it easily. Further, the picture and its caption above, apart from exposing flagrant racism, questions the logic, and the legality of confining people in reserves in a free country they call theirs. Have we asked ourselves how much we lost when we espoused one unchallenged education system? Academia basically, is found on dialogues, critiques, challenges and whatnots. How come that the current system goes unchallenged so as to embed, arrogance and ignorance in the advancement of knowledge. All this can be attributed to the toxicity the current colonial education produces as we swallow it hook, line, and sinker as a people and a society simply because, for some, it enables us to exploit others. If we look at how the so-called civilised and advanced countries are producing the Weapons of Mass Destruction (WMD) and yet, the international community keeps quiet as if this is not a looming danger, we can clearly explicably appreciate the fact that our education inevitably and urgently needs to be decolonised.

III). Colonialism, Colonial episteme and Terrorism

Besides genocide under whatever name[s], what is now disturbing, in Africa currently, is the rampancy of violent civil wars which revolve around terrorism. There are violent civil wars in Uganda where the Lord Resistance Army (LRA) has, for over two decades, terrorised people in Northern Uganda. The conflict in the Democratic Republic of Congo (DRC) is on and off not to mention the Central Africa Republic (CAR) where sectarian conflict resulting from old and neo-colonialism based on religion is rife. Cameroon, Chad and Nigeria, as well, are subsumed by the same type of conflict whereby Nigeria-based Boko Haram, a fundamentalist Islamic Group, is causing carnage. We do not know how many more conflicts of this nature are going to break out any time from now due to the toxicity of colonial education based on toxic politics and misguided interpretation of ideology. All over again, if you look at the history of colonialism, you wonder how, for instance, British colonial government was able to abolish kinghood in Africa but maintained it at home. Due to having toxic education devoid of critical thinking and critical questioning, we do not ask them this question however bitter and provocative it may sound. There must be something to do with the type of education we receive, principally the one that missionaries, who paved way for full-blown colonialism, introduced. Who is agitating that the Christianity and Islam responsible for such calamities and mental slavery, whose consequences are felt everywhere in Africa every day, be brought to justice? This should not be taken as the attack on these two institutions. They are the ones which taught their victims that whatever sin one commits, he or she will be punished for it. Equally, they, too, must be rewarded for the sins they committed on its victims. We need to ask ourselves again and again; why we are afraid of asking such important questions. Maybe, it is because the victims of its double standard were taught that religious bodies are holy even

201

when the situation shows otherwise. Decolonised minds will doubt and question any and everything without any fear of going against anybody's belief, *diktat*, or religion.

Actually, colonialists did not have heavy and many armies in their colonies. The armies they used were the colonised people themselves by the way of setting one group or community against one another to end up fighting and hating each other pointlessly. And the very type of bullet they used was none other than toxic education that turned colonised people into intellectual cyborgs. This is the type of the knowledge that challenges us to embark on soul-searching, researching and disseminating information pertaining to colonial education and its consequences in order to realise permanent and sustainable peace in Africa and wherever such a system was introduced. This knowledge, for instance, for the victims of colonial education, is better than Western approach of teaching or coaching the victims about reconciliation or mediation that are not based on their cultures, mechanisms and methods of conflict resolution. This is one area and one field. There are many areas that need to be vacuumed.

Battesby & Siracusa (2009) address the issue at a national level. Academics can address the same at an international level. It is true that we need to renegotiate our relationships, especially in international arena and issues that are unluckily currently dominated and dictated by Western dominant grand narrative. We need to aim at realising the stance whereby we must equally and equitably treat everybody and one another decently and rightly regardless of his or her races, economic, academic status and whatnots. In so doing, we will be able to attenuate conflicts resulting from interpersonal, intercultural as well as international differences. This can only be done and practically achieved through a decolonised episteme, mainly in the world. We need to precisely redefine ideologies such as mission *civilisatrice*, among other imperialistic superimpositions on others, which was, in any sense, racism, and colonialism which are crimes against humanity. If all human beings are equal, all cultures are equal as well. No culture is totally satanic or angelic so as to need to be ignored or silenced. All cultures have good and bad things altogether. We cannot go on with such thoughts as prescribed by

202

colonial drive, and approach towards others and avoid conflicts. Of late, terrorism has become an issue of concern among terrorists, those they target and those they wantonly terrorise just because they do not subscribe to their aspiration, beliefs and world views and of course how we treat, and look at one another.

Currently, many Western-born youths are moving to areas under terrorists to join them after noting some failure in their home systems. This has something to do with toxic and hegemonic education in these countries. We can use this as an eye opener and a lesson for us to think about and embark on paradigm shift as we move from one dominant grand narrative to accommodation of other narratives of the world. In many Western countries, for example, the majority of educated immigrants and refugees do not get jobs that are equivalent to their education levels thanks to racism and stereotype. Once such peoples move in, they end up doing menial jobs which dishearten and frustrate them. As a result of such maltreatments, the victims start to hate their host countries, something which are bad and dangerous. Again, why does this happen? The answer, *inter alia*, is that two societies do not understand each other. Some of the victims of such ignorant-of-each-other situation wrongly think that getting out of such entrapment is by joining enemy groups. As for homegrown youths who surprise many by supporting terrorism, their countries fail to understand that the maltreatments people of their origins face discourage them as well as it acts as a motivation for joining whatever camps that articulates their hatred and aspirations even if this is done wrongly, and with bad intentions as it is in terrorism currently. Also, despite being born in Western countries, immigrants' and refugees' children are still viewed as immigrants and refugees as well, especially based on their pedigree and pigment of their colours which is racism in itself. We need to cross the border of colour identity as we entrench our understanding on nationality free of colours. For example, the son or daughter of a black person however being born in Western countries, will always be asked where she or he is from which is itself racism *per se* and by implications. Again, why don't oppressors and racists see it differently or from the angle of the victims? If the type of education the world is receiving were critical in thinking and application, such would not have become a problem at all.

Truly educated people from the part of victims and oppressors would see it clearly and with the same interpretation and urgency. Again, the type of education we offering and receiving is basically based on a curtain of a *do-not-see-another-part* approach. It is a totally one-tunnelled view sort of education. Again, thanks to toxic and colonised episteme that has always espoused *holier than thou*, these receiving such defective education become so egoistic and myopic that they end up becoming completely blind and unaware of others which endanger their relationships. So, without overhauling the current regime of education to provide impetuses and propensities in order to embark on critical interrogation and critical thinking, terrorisms and other vices will be on the rise pointlessly and unnecessarily. Importantly, if we decide to truthfully negotiate our differences and needs, we still have means of resolving conflicts we are now facing. Out of such a dialogue and negotiation we can create what Battersby & Siracusa (*Ibid.*) refer to as the *communities of fate*. Indeed, it makes more sense to coexist under whatever agreed arrangements rather than destroying one another wantonly as if we are crazy and lazy in using our gift of brains. We need to change the way we do things based on the realities of today but not the interests of yesterday.

Cultural-related conflicts can be seen currently at the very time the world is facing many Islamic fundamentalist groups which see and view Western culture as a threat to their culture, *diktat* and existence as a civilisation based on faith and history which is true the same way they are to the West and others. Notable groups with fundamentalist Islamic background such as al Qaeda, an international network of terrorist groups, al-Shabaab, Somalia-based terrorist group and Boko Haram, a Nigeria-based terrorist group, provide an ideal example of the very problem we the world is collectively facing and supposed to carefully, faithfully and seriously work on. Ironically, when it comes to these groups, they are exerting the same colonial tendencies to others, predominantly in Africa where their menace is vividly felt. By decolonising education, we will be able to come up with ways of addressing the problem scientifically and judiciously.

For example, we need to have thinkers and activists from the so-called terrorist groups which also regard their adversaries as terrorists so that we can engage them and hear their stories; and thereby assess them and ask them what should be done to accommodate their views without hurting others. I know. For such groups, Western superimposition on their ways of life is unacceptable the same way it is for them to superimpose their *diktat* on others. We are all sharing the same one world that begs us to cooperate rather than daydreaming of eliminating one another. It does not work. If we see one another as humans, we will be able to make sense of each other. Again, we verily need the type of education–we are equipping our people with–that addresses the needs of both parties in this conflict based on cultural and hegemonic drives. By so doing, we will be able to let them see the bigger picture instead of being preyed on easily.

More importantly, having a dialogue with those we perceive to be terrorists should not be misconstrued as sanctioning their activities or bowing to their demands. To me, negotiations are better than wagging destructive battles in which all protagonists are losers. Where are we now when air travel that used to be the safest has been turned to its head victimising innocent people that are not part of the conflict? How much money has been lost in serving the fear and insecurity not to mention the lives of people that have already been lost pointlessly? How much money has already lost–after many planes were brought down, building bombed not to mention insecurity globally–due to the terror threat globally? With decolonised education, we will be able to wage our wars on a round table instead of killing innocent people in the battle fields wherein we know there is no straight winner. For, as the look of things is, we are posed to lose all just like fools who refused to coexist and talk to each other. Negotiating our differences indicates the appreciation of one another apart from mitigating the effects of our refusal to face each other and talk. African sage has it that discussing with or talking to your enemy is a step ahead, and it enables you to know what your enemy is planning against you.

Although terrorism has become a hot potato of which many people steer clear, we need to change the narrative by listening to the other side after listening to one for long. Currently, the Western dominant grand narrative dictates the terms of engagement in that nobody should talk to terrorists otherwise that person is the West. This is why it is easy for the West to talk to the Taliban in Afghanistan but the same refuses to do the same to others. In so doing, despite being the Western *diktat*, the entire world is made to believe that this is the take and view of the entire world. If we had decolonised education, such a take would be taken on head on to prove how wanting it may be. This volume touches on the Syrian conflict above wherein two superpowers, the US and Russia are fighting a proxy war. Who is tasking them to put their acts together? Instead, we are all silent which–by implications–means we are supporting this self-destruction. The world is not safe now because of terror attacks. What is the source of the current terrorism if we clinically and carefully examine its genesis from Afghanistan to the Middle East and now Africa? Historically, terrorism has been there however, in different reasons, manners and magnitudes. This volume will not go into the history of terrorism due to the fact that one volume cannot satisfactorily cover it. However, African sage has it that when you want to destroy a tree, you must cut the roots and uproot it completely. Again, we need to address the root causes of terrorism instead of dealing with its offshoots. Again, without free and decolonise education in place, this is impossible. For, we tend to be made to believe that we are fighting terrorism; however if you look at how we do it, you find that something is terribly missing. Up until now, we do not have even a single agreed upon definition of terrorism. Instead, what we have today is the clusters of definitions from which Martin (2015) cited in Mhango (2017) names three common elements that are found in 109 definitions of terrorism which are the "use of violence motivated by religious, political or ideological beliefs to instill fear as means of coercing government or society" (p. 61). What's more, the history of terrorism goes back as year 74 CE when a Christian group known as zealots or Zelos (ardor or strong spirit in Greek) which, according to Martin, committed suicide after being surrounded by the Roman soldiers. Another group was an Islamic group known as assassins that used to kill its opponents or members of its own suspected for betraying it. Thereafter, there came many other terrorist groups in North and

Latin America, Europe, and Asia. Of all continents, it is only Africa that has no any recorded history of terrorism. For example, Europe, the Middle East, North America and South America faced many threats and mission from terrorist groups in the 60s and the 80s.

Currently, the world is grappling with terrorism which, if anything, has changed the shape of the world as far as security is concerned. Sadly though, up to this moment, as noted above, there is no tangible and one–acceptable definition of terrorism. Sometimes, those who coin the definition of terrorism are viewed as the terrorisms themselves by those they call terrorists. Refer to what transpired after 11/9 when the World Trade Centre (WTC) was brought down by the acts of terrorists. We need to define the term and agree upon how to deal with this scourge. We need to consult with those we perceive to be terrorists to hear what they say; and what they can contribute to the dialogue. I am not trying to play devil's advocate.

However I can briefly touch on terrorism for the sake of making a few clarifications. Essentially, there are four types of terrorism. The first category involves terrorist groups mentioned above namely, those fighting losing battle under the cover of religion. These are the highly known ones currently due to the frequencies of their acts of terror. Such groups seek to inflict pains; and thereby create fear as a psychological tool and major weapon based on self-sacrificing which is carried under what is known as "propaganda by deed" (Chaliand & Blin, 2007, p. 116) whereby suicide is used to show how serious the groups are. Apart from propaganda by deed, terrorist groups use whatever means available to make their political statement. It becomes harder to defeat this sort of terrorism due to the fact that most of operatives mingle with the general population; and do not use conventional methods of war such as having a specific and known army or openly declare when they are going to start or end war. They were no uniforms. The second category involves governments. This is known as *state terrorism*. Governments can commit acts of violence either with the aim of suppressing dissent voices or countering terrorism. In both cases, the governments commit violence to send a message to their opponents that they are able to deal with them unsympathetically. In committing terrorism, governments aim at safeguarding their interests locally and internationally. Martin (*Ibid.*) notes that, governments "choose from range of overt and covert options" (p. 76) in carrying out state terrorism within and without their territories. This means; the governments that carry out state terrorism can commit it openly or secretly depending on the enemies they are dealing with; and in doing so, according to Martin (*op.cit.*), "state terrorism has been responsible for many more deaths and much more sufferings than has terrorism originating in small bands of terrorists" (p. 29). Further, governments cause bigger harm; because they have more resources and capabilities under their disposal compared to terrorist groups or their enemies that are normally weaker than the government's agents. The third category involves guerilla movements or "little war" (Martin 2015 cited in Mhango, 2017) which aims at toppling the government in order to bring about change. Such groups existed in the Middle East, Latin America and Europe to mention but a few. Unlike terrorist groups, sometimes, guerrilla movements morph into political parties–particularly, if they win their campaigns–and thereby control the reins of power as it occurred in South Africa where the then declared-terrorist group, the African National Congress (ANC) won elections; and in so doing formed the first democratic and non-racial government after outlawing Apartheid that was ruling the country. However, this phenomenon is rare due to the fact that–sometimes, as opposed to what happened in South Africa where the ANC won–governments defeat them, and brand military groups opposing them terrorist groups aiming at illegitimating them nationally and internationally thanks to the lures and dominance of the Western grand narrative. The fourth category involves citizens either opposed to government policies or other groups. Such citizens can commit act of violence as means of achieving their goals. This category involves vigilantism, civil disobedience and chaos, principally where the government is repressive or irresponsible.

In regards to the causes of terrorism, many terrorist groups use it as a last recourse due to understanding that they do not have possibilities, capabilities, enough power, people, and resources to win the war compared to their enemy who is always stronger than they are. Governments use terrorism as means of suppressing dissent voices or curtailing the power of their enemies if such enemies are other states. Other reasons are: unmet basic human needs such as identity, employment, access to resources and enjoyment of human rights, fanaticism, and above all, radicalism. So, there are many and different reasons why terrorism occurs. Recently, for example, some fundamentalist Islamic groups came up with more demands such as wanting to force the world to follow their old fashion ideologies resulting from radical interpretation and misinterpretation of religions. These are a new type of demands that were not heard of for a long time in the past. Islamic fundamentalist terrorist groups such as Al Shabaab, operating in Somalia, Boko Haram operating from Northern Nigeria, and the Islamic State of Iraq and Levant (ISIL) operating in Iraq and Syria, announced that they want to form Islamic caliphates in already legally established states as opposed the international law. Such groups think that they can change the current world order; and thereby run it under their *diktat* which is itself colonialism regardless whether it is propagated based on religion or whatever motives. All these groups force people to become Muslims; and those who do not buy into their demands are branded enemies whom they, sometimes, kill when they attack them as it happened in Kenya a few years ago as indicated above.

After looking at terrorism in a nutshell, we need to ask a single big question: Why do some governments–under the drive to fight their other enemies–allow other groups or people to alter the identity of others through indoctrination that they finance overtly? I will speak on behalf of Africa. Is it fair for African governments to allow whoever comes in with his ideology to operate freely even if what he preaches is totally against African cultures and ways of life that all foreign religions term and refer to as barbaric, unreligious and ungodly? If we had decolonised education, such a move would not be tolerated; or be allowed to operate at the detriment of our cultures and our ways of life. As argued before, if all human beings are equal; and thus all cultures are equal in that they have some good and bad things regardless whether they are propagated and spread by religion or politics. Decolonised education needs to teach everybody about her or his uniqueness as a human being. Decolonised and teach the importance of multiculturalism based on diversity as the strength that needs to enjoy equal recognition based on equality, equity and reciprocity.

Going back to how to deal with terror threats, we need to appreciate the presence, the ways and feelings of one another regardless of colour, ideology, history, closeness or enmity. In other words, we need to humanise our enemies so that they can reciprocate equally. Although their reciprocation, sometimes, may be different from what expected, at least, doors for negotiations must be opened first. Again, when such an olive branch is broken and set on fire, stern actions can follow. It is unfortunately that Western mechanisms of conflict resolution do not accommodate such a view. We will later see this humanising enemies or humanising conflict in Ubuntu, an African philosophy towards humans that argue that you are because I am.

Significantly, by using purely Western epistemes, theories and prescriptions only is our education-cum-approach still rational and workable in addressing problems such as terrorism? Mhango (2017) answers the question suggesting that the Global War on Terror (GWOT) which–he calls the Global War over Terra Africana (GWOTA)–needs to be deconstructed to see to it that it accommodates all grand narratives for the interests of all but not the interests of the a few self-appointed pontifex maximus. Another example can be derived from defining things such as terrorism and development and many more.

You can see this in terrorism that this volume has explore briefly above. Who is spared now? You can look at how a disease breaks in one place to end up threatening the whole globe. What else do we need to understand that there is no winner who will take it all in the current world? Like genocide, terrorism needs to be blamed on the West as the product of the colonisation and neocolonisation the dominant grand narrative has maintained cultural, economically and politically not to mention toxic education, and religion's colonialism always used as its engines of sabotage and suffocation.

7

Whose Story Should We Buy into or Ignore and Why?

WHAT THE WORLD FAILS TO REALISE IS THAT A VILLAIN IS JUST A VICTIM WHOSE STORY HASN'T BEEN TOLD

- Chris Colfer

LIFE IS SHORT SO SMILE WHILE YOU STILL HAVE TEETH

- Unknown

Figure 12; photo courtesy of likesuccess.com

The volume has touched on the importance of storytelling prior. Essentially, every human being is a story that he or she needs to tell but not others; else that person is dead or deprived of her or his voice. This has always been the plight of Africa and other colonised people. The importance of storytelling or writing one's history is well. Achebe (2000) cited in Gordon (2016) who notes that "hence the

African proverb which states that 'until the lions [prey] produce their own historian, the story of the hunt will glorify only the hunter'" (p. 5). The same goes with colonial education. "The lions"–slept ones, of course–need their mechanisms to be incorporated in the current dominant grand narrative based on the decolonisation and the incorporation of their education. In fact, incorporating other grand narratives' epistemes, mechanisms and narratives will help the victims of the current grand narrative to tell and have their stories told accurately as a way of doing justice to both parties.

Arguably, the significance and meaning of any story depend on who, how, why and when is telling it. When your enemy tells your story, he or she distorts it to misrepresent you the way he or she wants but not the way you want and what you are. If your enemy tells your story, nothing meaningful or real will be found in it. We saw this during the World Wars in Europe whereby Europeans defined others like vampires due to their enmity at the time. If people of the same pedigree can [mal] treat one another this way, what of the oppressed people of the world whose history was told, misconstrued, misrepresented, and above all, doctored? From the eyes of an enemy, the subject has nothing good one can mention or be proud of. Or put it this way. What will you expect shall Israel tell Palestinians' story or vice versa? I used to tease my mentor who is a native of Northern Ireland that there is no danger like allowing somebody to tell your story, especially if and when such a person is your sworn enemy. If anything, this is what happened to Aboriginal peoples all over the world, mainly in Africa and the Americas among others due to hidden motifs and intentions. For example, the history of Africa was told and written by those Robinson (2013) refers to as criminal saying that "David Livingston, Henry Morton, Stanley and Columbus were criminals without conscience and morality" (p. 234). How many academics have such guts to call these criminals who they actually were instead of lionising them the same way colonial education has always done? Robinson refers to Mhango's article in the *African Executive Magazine* (2012) that claimed that some parts of Africa, chiefly the City States such as Kilwa, Sofala, Mogadishu and Lamu– to mention but a few–were more civilised than Europe at certain period of history when Dr. Livingstone arrived in Mozambique to find that metallurgical technology was more advanced than Britain. Notably, when such invaders told such stories of their victims, they concealed many facts to avoid defeating their project of colonialism. Therefore, there is the whole lot of decolonisation to be done to see to it that the true story is told by those it is about.

Ironically, such criminals assertively alleged that there was no even sense of time in Africa at the time they paved the way for colonialism. However, there are some literatures to prove these criminals wrong about what they said. Mbiti (1969) cited in Lederach (2005) observes that the description of African concept of time seems to accord much more with the modern physicist's view of 'spacetime' than does Western usual notion. Mbiti says that that he received inquiries from scientists who were intrigued by the fact that Africa was ahead of them as far as spacetime is concerned. With such assertion can someone courageously and sanely say that Africa was backward as the current dominant grand narrative kept on portraying it? Again, there is nothing new in the concept of time to fight over save that we need to keep on putting records straight.

In principle, wherever there are days and nights there must be mechanism and sense of time for regulating time. For Africans, debate about time is immaterial given that they knew how to use it in their environment. I may argue that the lack of obsession with time helps Africans to be free from unnecessary heart attacks. For, African wisdom dictates that whenever anything happens, it is not the end of the world. It is as simple as that. Try to live it and see. It works very well. I think even materialism and consumerism emanate from this sense of time. Arguably, for some collectivistic societies, having many materials does not concern them a lot. However, nowadays–after they adopted Western standards–people who did not worship materials are falling preys to this self-destructive behaviour, especially when the lust for materials is about unnecessary materials. This is because they are not sure of tomorrow.

Another example is in the fact that nothing good, in news or in the streets, about Africa can be seen or heard, particularly in Western countries. Here you can see Kipling's white man's burden at work. This is what colonised education inculcated in its victims. As indicated above, what is known as white man's burden is nothing but black man's burden if we consider how the so-called whites exploited Africa in all of their colonial and cold-blooded projects. My experience in Canada is that wherever I go from schools, universities, hospitals, thrift stores such as the MCC, and various malls, I see degrading photos of Africans and others who need to be *helped* without telling why. Isn't this the deliberate misinformation, institutionalisation and internalisation of stigma that is passed on to new generations of the so-called *Caucasian* kids to believe that they are always Africa's saviour and other so-called third world countries? Are these things done accidentally or purposely to foster the *holier-than-thou* mentality thanks to toxic and myopic education? What do African and poor countries do to counter such a stereotype? Isn't this systemic discrimination aimed at portraying others like unfit and backward creatures that will always need *white saviours* to emancipate them while the truth is to the contrary shall victims wake up from their slumber?

Moreover, if you look at the messes such people are in, you note that the same *saviours* are the cause of the same miseries. Who needs a double-faced saviour? I think Africa's survivor is within Africa. Shall African academics stand up and reclaim its lost glory; they indeed, will emancipate Africa without necessarily needing any saviour as it has been misconstrued for many years. Even those taking those photos are not intending to help the victims; instead, they use those photos to solicit money to end up swindling it. To know how endemic this type of institutional racism is, you can see it when you meet a person to whom you are new. Many ask about diseases, poverty, wars, and miseries in respect of Africa. For them, Africa is nothing; and has nothing to offer but miseries and negative things. Yes, Africa maybe regarded as the poorest continent according to their exploitative standards that failed to appreciate all tons and tons of minerals Africa is sitting on. Who cause this poverty? Despite advancement intellectually and scientifically, those despising Africa have never underscored the fact that Africans were not used to economic models built and ran on Ponzi schemes whereby a conman goes to the bank poor and comes out filthily rich. Further, they do not get it that under collectivistic economic, there were no jobless, poor or disadvantaged people in African society before the arrival of colonial and criminal rule. In line with the point made prior, when you ask them about the cellphones, computers and planes they use if they know that all these gadgets depend on some minerals from Africa, they end up swallowing their pride. Again, you cannot blame such victims of colonial education. This is the way they were brought up to believe. They were taught to look at people using prejudiced lenses. Can we avoid conflict without changing such undercurrents and malpractices? The only surest way out of such unnecessary conflicts resulting from *stereotypification* is only through decolonising education. We, essentially, need to winnow our education to see to it that all chaff is out.

Again, much of the bulk of Aboriginal stories were told by their tormentors and detractors who paved the way for colonisation and the plundering that culminated in what they from today. Such stories are not but stories of lies and fabrications. Essentially, when we probe the narratives of the so-called explores, missionaries and merchants, we will find that the said narratives are but flaw and full of fraud. These criminals above doctored; and purposely misrepresented the true history of Africa by demonising it so much that they can have a claim on it. Had they told the truth, the need for "pacification" and "civilisation" through religion and toxic education would not have met. This is why words such as savages, pagans, barbarians and uncouth were used many times in stories describing Africans. Even to date, the same trend is still ongoing wherein African history is misrepresented as a continent of miseries that needs to be saved from itself. How could Africa need *saviours* while it has almost everything European countries needed for survival? How could Africa with its kinder weather need *saviour*s compared to warring Europe which enjoys warmth only once a year? Arguably, Africa has saved Europe not once or twice but always. Many European former colonial powers were able to hang on economically and financially thanks to the resources and precious minerals they plundered from Africa. Where are they today when their economies are in the Intensive Care Unit (ICU)? If African rulers were not the victims of toxic colonial education, we would be talking about a different story. Again, it is just the matter of time for Europe to come to its knee thanks to the wave of Africans, Indians and Arabs who enter it in thousands every day running away from the miseries the current grand narrative created without looking at the future that is today. To avoid more breakdowns, we need to dialogue how to equally distribute the resources based on historical wrongs committed on Africa and other victims. Here we are talking about redressing colonies that colonialism exploited and destroyed.

As we will see later in addressing the issue of challenging the grand narrative and the way it reinvented and recreated people under its toxic education, a major question we may pose here is: Whose stories are we telling and who is telling whose story considering the power of storytelling constructive and destructive? Senehi in Carter, Irani & Volkan (2009) observes that:

> Storytelling is language. Encompassing vocabulary, grammar rules, norms of communicative behavior, and narrative forms language is society's most complex symbolic system. As such, language encodes the culture of a particular community, including shared understandings of identity, power, history, values, and utopian visions" (p. 43).

The survey made on the use of the word black above speaks volumes here. I tend to fully concur with Senehi (*Ibid.*) in that our power or weakness or strength and whatnots can be expressed in our words, among others. So, the languages we use and the story we tell can nicely tell who we are. When somebody else tells our story, we become something different from who we actually are. Instead, we become what the storyteller wants us to be. The role of academia is to offer information that is well researched and trusted after being proved. In other words, education is about telling a reliable story of knowledge but not about misconstruing and misrepresenting the said story of others and other facts be in pure or social science. Language is a means through which communities develop and articulate their worldview. Senehi (*op.cit.*) observes that "the knowledge encoded in language and culture facilitates common understandings of experience and forms the naturalised truths for a particular community" (p. 47). Senehi defines knowledge in a clear and simple language. She goes on saying that narratives underpin cultural identity, knowledge, and history in ways that encode the conflict in their identities. You can see how narratives create our world. You can see the role of language in telling a story on how African history was told by racists; and biased so-called thinkers like Thomas Hobbes. Mudimbe (1988) cited in Mudimbe (2010) argues that:

> One might think that this new historical form has meant, from its origins, the negation of two contradictory myths; namely, the "Hobbesian picture of a pre European Africa, in which there was no account of Time; no Arts; no Letters; no Society; and which is worst of all, continued fear, and danger of violent death (p. 55).

Such assertion is absurd and nonsensical as the evidence of great ignorance. Experience shows that every society knows the concept of time. In Africa, even chickens and all birds know this. How small creatures with small brains like these could have the sense of time but not Africans? The sense of time is inborn. This is why a baby is able to wake up in the morning and demand to be fed. Swahili sage has it that he who abuses you does not select an insult. I understand that current defenders of the current dominant grand narrative would argue that that was then when thinkers wrote bad things about Africa, especially calling it a dark continent as Mudimbe (*Ibid.*) rightly postulates. How can–logically and intellectually,–a society exist without sense of time or art? Every society however developed or otherwise it may be presumed, has the sense of time and art, among other things that make a society unique from others. Every society has its grand narrative and intellectual ways of imparting knowledge to its people. Mhango (2016) makes a good argument that those African societies, which are now dependent on rich countries, must revisit their history in order to see how they lived independently of aid for many centuries before the introduction of colonialism to Africa. Again, where will Africans and other victims go for their history if they are not ready to decolonise the kind version of education that has always accommodated the doctored history of victims?

To make matters worse, Africa, according to Hobbes–who is thought to be among great thinkers the West has ever had–did not have even a society. Again, when Hobbes wrote this, he, indeed, seemed to have been suffering from the hangover of what Bose (2007) notes that "a self-congratulatory positive image of the European and "the west" has been constructed" (p. 114) emanating from colonial, egoistic and toxic education that was not aware of the sameness and equality of others. One may argue; such a tendency drawn from toxic education is likely to have affected thinkers such as Hobbes. In a word, writing all such sacrilegious and offensive things about others needed high degree of bigotry, egoism, ignorance, myopia, and self-aggrandisement; and above all, disregard of others. A truly educated person–who is principally the one regarded as a thinker–cannot use his knowledge to erase the existence of others as it is the case of Hobbes and other bigots and xenophobes who wickedly and intentionally denigrated and distorted the history of Africa. Such a people about whom such insults are written were not humans in the eyes of such a *great thinker*. Sadly though, such provocative language and style of referring to others in derogative languages and ways still receive academic leverage; and is being taken to be true while the world became so interconnected that the same people, subscribing to such garbage, went to Africa and find a very different story. Yet again, the so-called *developed and enlightened thinkers* of the West still cling to such nonsensical things like Hobbes' insults! This cannot go on unabated if we decolonise our education as humans and as victims. For, such education will enable us to see what we were not able to see regarding the equality of all human beings.

Actually, colonial education, apart from borrowing some good things and secrets from other grand narratives it used against them, it largely copied from Indigenous Knowledge. The flip side is; after getting what it wanted, the former destroyed latter. Akyeampong (2007) candidly observes that "colonial rule in Africa privileged Western Knowledge Systems and discredited Indigenous Knowledge Systems, and provided the context for the fashioning of 'scientific knowledge' about Africa" (p. 174). This is the same picture one finds everywhere colonialism was introduced. Colonialists did not only steal resources but also destroyed Indigenous Knowledge in order to promote theirs.

How many negative impacts such as problematic, stigmatic, systematic, traumatic, lack of self-respect, provocation, psychological menaces, discrimination and other kinds of humiliations have Africans and other Indigenous of various places suffered for hundreds of years since the inception of colonialism which, in essence, is the architect of such irresponsible, judgemental provocative language and toxic education? Does this need a PhD or title expert to understand and deal with? This challenge reminds me of the discussion I had with an American PhD student who called me aside and asked: Why do you guys like complaining about colonialism while you got your independence a long time ago? To answer her question, I asked her: Why and what did she think caused such a proclivity? Her response abhorred me. For, she seemed not to know anything about the causes of all stigmas, and of course, the miseries that forced some of victims to complain as a way of putting the message across apart from venting which is their right. For a person of such a level of education, it would have made sense even to logically understand that whoever suffers must complain. This is a natural phenomenon of attracting attention and venting so that the solutions can be found to the problems. Again, when bigotry, and sometimes, *holier than thou* mentality kick in, all senses of reasoning escape.

However small our conversation may seem to be, it showed me how toxic education is real; and its dangers are bigger and many more than one can enumerate shall all fields of education be explored. Instead of applying and displaying her empathy and knowledge as a Peace and Conflict PhD student viewed to be highly educated, just showed her naivety and ignorance saying that she thought the victims of colonisation are lazy; and like complaining about the past pointlessly. She forgot that the present is made from the past; likewise the future that is conceived and given birth by the present. For a PhD student, this was something she would have known firsthand even without thinking or reading. Our conversation started in the class. When said student seemed perturbed by what she thought was a complaining syndrome. Ironically, complaining, for her, was her sole right but not others' as well. Sadly, when this student complained openly about our complaining behaviour, the professor seemed to take it as a normal thing. I wondered how the professor who was teaching us made do with and took such derogatory words lightly so as not to reprimand the student or give some elucidations about the real situation. This means, the professor, too, was ignorant of the plight of the victims we were talking about. She actually reinforced the stereotype and blameworthiness to them wantonly and pointlessly. This boiled down to condoning this conspiracy against others. Maybe, the professor did not look at the issue with the same lenses as I did given that she was a privileged white and academic. This is why I cannot blame her for the silence about such a contentious issue she was supposed to know. Again, it depends on how the professor was prepared in school.

Also, this can show the toxicity of the type of education people are offering and receiving. Again, I cannot paint all professors with the same brush. For, some professors were so compassionate about the plight of the victims of the current dominant grand narrative. Again, most of such professors either were from victimised countries or were travelled if not rebels against the colonial epistemes. This is why in my acknowledgements; I applauded Western-made thinkers who do not connive with the toxicity of the colonial education. This is why many of the literature I have researched to support my claims consists of many Western academics who innocently and correctly see the problem; and some take on it in their works.

I exceptionally salute the courage and contribution of my professor Sean Byrne, a native of Northern Ireland. Going through the same plight as other victims, he was always been vocal against injustices colonial project caused others. He used to say that—for example—that divide and rule was experimented in Northern Ireland which is true. So, the incident that left me traumatised and annoyed is a normal thing for many academics that do not bother about the plights of the victims of colonialism. I know such incident may be seen as trivial. Again, we need to ask the question Gladwell (2002 cited in Lederach (2005) asks: "How little things make a difference?" (p. 90). Lederach uses the fission in nuclear science—and the way the reaction of neutrons produces a chain of reaction—to effect social change in a mass movement.

Honestly, like a reaction of one neutron, the accusations by one student at one university geared me to write this volume. I, therefore, believe that—even though this one volume will not address the whole issues exhaustively–it will lay a foundation for others to ask as many questions about the issues it raises as possible *vis-à-vis* the urgency to decolonise the current toxic education and the hegemonic current grand narrative. If anything, as three neurons namely, the student, the professor and I, whom Lederach calls critical yeasts, we will start the chain of reaction whose effects will add something to this academic dialogue on toxic education and the way it affects our daily lives globally as espoused by the current dominant grand narrative. You can see how a simple act can trigger bigger and many reactions. Swahili sage has it that every sum starts with one. To cut a long story short, I told the student in question that I have lived victimhood and it was my right to complain and vent.

Therefore, I know the effects of toxic education firsthand. I wound up our discussion a little bit provocatively and rudely saying "it is sad, and I am sorry that you do not get it despite doing PhD in Peace and Conflict studies. Later, I regretted my reactions. However, I was proud of my honesty and the display of my feelings genuinely. Sometimes, we need to be true to ourselves before we think of being taken seriously. Again, I thank the ignorance of this ignorant student. For, her answers imbued me to do more soul searching and research to come up with this volume. In other words, she forced me to start probing answers of this nature in various classes. The pattern was the same, blaming the victims. If anything, this is the nature of the current dominant grand narrative. Refer to how many countries experienced conflicts resulting from colonialism are now are blamed on those conflicts while those who created, fuelled, funded and benefited from them become the first ones to throw the stones. Finding the same pattern was, in the first instance, disheartening however later it became a motivation that kept me on course in writing this volume.

Often times, I used to ask myself: If, for example, graduate students of CRS do not know the history of the victims of the conflicts they study or deal with, how will they solve these problems? I honestly, therefore, should say that for such education to fail to offer courses about victims of violence and injustices they study in the field can be seen as an anomaly. Is it because of colonised; and toxic education whereby those who caused all miseries are the same who enacted the regime of education in use? To decolonise education–in all fields–we need to teach the real and true histories of the victims to our students so that they know the people or societies they are dealing with. This will help them to make a good judgment apart from contributing more to the dialogue in academia. Regarding the incident of the PhD student who openly showed her sheer ignorance, there are a couple of questions we can ask, 1) Who is to blame?; 2) Should we blame a student or the system that moulded her?; 3) Doesn't her reaction invite us to do something about our education system nourished; and spearheaded by the current dominant grand narrative based on colonial underpinnings?; 4) Is it fair to blame the system without suggesting the solutions?; and 5) How much ignorance of others is embedded in our current education system in general in that education is supposed to be a beacon of knowledge in whatever field or discipline that is offered in our schools and universities? I am asking these questions since many problems–though not all–the world experiences are caused by the way we conceptualise and address them; be they political, social or economic.

I think we need to say that the solutions to such misunderstandings, wrong approaches, methods and practices are basically on the deconstruction; and the overhaul of the current education system so that it can suitably serve us all equally and equitably instead of benefitting a few on the expenses of the many. We need to be courageous and honest enough in addressing this anomaly if we aspire to live in a peaceful and judicious world. Again, such an undertaking needs, the courage of the mad, trustworthiness, steadfastness; and above all, the will to bring about change based on the needs of today for all but not the needs of the dominant ones. Giroux (1997, p. 287) cited in Phillips & Whatman (2007) observes that:

> Cultural/colonial interfaces are mediated by colonial codifications which largely associate Indigenous peoples with 'negative equivalencies' or, in some cases safe spiritual standardisations, serving to deny colonial injustice while affirming what Giroux describes as the

222

'repressed, unspeakable racist unconscious of the dominant White culture (p. 4).

Essentially, Giroux talks about the fallacy of the current dominant grand narrative embedded in high learning institutions all over the world. I think this is why all injustices that were committed to many people have never been addressed and redressed altogether. You wonder, for example, how Europe has managed to ignore the role its slave trade played in dehumanising and pauperising Africans wherever they are not to mention colonialism which has been extended up to the present day. The answer is simple that the type of education the world has received since independence, somewhat, has no difference from the one offered during colonial era all over the world. To forge ahead equally, we need to bring about change by decolonising education so that we can all stand on the same footing.

Nonetheless, if we explore the current generation of thinkers even great politicians such as George W. Bush, the former president of a great nation, the US, which is the sole superpower of the world currently, we will dwarf any views which espouse that such bad things were written in past centuries. Bush (2003) cited in Razack (2004) says that "our security will require transforming the military you will lead–a military that will be ready to strike at a moment's notice in any **dark corner** of the wold" (p. 3). (*I bolded the dark corner of the world to show how the myth of the Dark Continent still goes on even today*). If the president of the nation that poses itself as a high guarantor in many conflicts can use such an offensive language, what else should we expect out of the policies of the country he was leading? Such toxic utterances, apart from being irresponsible and offensive, exacerbate conflicts. This is why, up until now, the international community has failed miserably to address the terror threats due to the bigotry and such a *holier than thou* mentality. Bush shows the type of education he received which he used throughout his stint in power in presiding over world issues based on his hegemonic view of the world.

Again, when Bush used such a derogatory term, those supposed be offended and victimised did not even ask him to retract such annoying words. Further, the victims did not seek any clarifications in order to know what dark meant here. As well, victims did not fear that such reference would guarantee any invasion and occupation as it later happened in Iraq or later in Libya where a long-time, controversial, and erratic dictator, Muamar Gaddafi, was toppled under suspicious and fabricated reasons that he was intending to massacre demonstrators not to mention another tin-pot dictator in Iraq that was pulled down before. The West just alleged that Gaddafi was intending to butcher his people without substantiating their allegations or adducing any evidence to the effect. Even the justification for enacting the war did not meet international standards. Now Libya is in chaos; and nobody is doing anything to pull it out of it. Those of who destroyed Iraq and Libya are now busy in destroying Syria in the proxy war between the US and Russia. Do you erase wrongs by wrongs or follow procedures?

The International Commission on Intervention and State Sovereignty (ICISS) provides the framework in which war aimed at R2P, or the Right to protect under international obligation when one of the states fails to protect its people or kills its people altogether. MacFarlane & Khong (2006) maintain that the ICISS "defined the threshold in terms of "large scale loss of life, actual or apprehended" and or "large scale 'ethnic cleansing,' actual or apprehended. The ICISS also, proposed that a number of precautionary principles needed to be satisfied before an intervention should proceed" (p. 178). Looking at what happened in Libya, for example, none of the criteria were followed. No precautionary measures whatsoever were taken. The size of the loss of lives was not showed. In fact, everything was shallow and wanting save that–given that those behind it were powerful countries–who would stand in their way? The African Union (AU) tried to oppose the move, but due to its negligible position in world *realpolitik*, nobody listened to it.

The AU, thus, decided to keep quiet as one of theirs was toppled captured, and later, summarily executed in front of the media cameras. Refer to how graphic photos of the killing of Gaddafi; and the way the corpses of Gaddafi and his son were displayed and shown all over the world without those tutoring others about human rights saying anything). If anything, this is the nature and behaviour of the current dominant grand narrative that segregates against people due to *holier than thou* mentality. This grand narrative is always controversial even in following its own rules and laws. Because under its laws, everybody is presumed innocent until the court of law proves otherwise.

Again, was Gaddafi tried before the court and got death punishment? Is there any law that can sanction mob justice? Western countries that attacked Gaddafi; and thereby caused his fall from grace might argue that they were not the ones who captured; and killed Gaddafi. However, they knew what would happen after toppling him due to his rapport with his people whom he brutalised for over four decades. After his lifeless body was displayed, why didn't they treat him with dignity just like any human simply because he was a human? I understand. Gaddafi was a stinking, brutal and repressive dictator (Castro, 2011). Again, he still was a human being under the law and by nature. This is why suspects such as Charles Taylor (former Liberian strongman); and Laurent Gbagbo (former Ivorian strongman) are not denied food or legal representation before the court of law.

Essentially, what happened as, it later came to be known, was but settling scores between Gaddafi and the West which was done by deceiving the world so as to get away with murder. The same happened in Iraq where long time American ally in the Middle East Saddam Hussein was toppled, captured and later hanged. Thereafter, leaked information was brought forth stating that, essentially, the allegations that Hussein had the Weapons of Mass Destruction (WMD) were false and a total lie. However, the truth is Gaddafi and Hussein were not good leaders; and the reasons used to justify their toppling were illegal and wrong as well. Arguably, this is how the current dominant grand narrative works for the advantage of its makers as opposed to the detriment of others. Another example, when France and Britain were killing the Aboriginal peoples in the Americas and Australia, nobody intervened to save them. Systemic elimination of the Aboriginal peoples of the Americas has since gone on unabated up until now. Wolfe (2006) summarises it well that:

> As practised by Europeans, both genocide and settler colonialism have typically employed the organizing grammar of race. European xenophobic traditions such as anti-Semitism, Islamophobia, or

Negrophobia are considerably older than race, which, as many have shown, became discursively consolidated fairly late in the eighteenth century (p. 387).

This is the reality of current *realpolitik* of the world whereby the high and the mighty accept whatever the grand narrative offers and get away with murder. Thanks to toxic episteme the same dominant grand narrative espouses, such atrocities are left untouched; and whoever dares to take them on is either ignored or called names in order to belittle her or his claims. Such atrocities are treated just like mere historical happenings while their victims are still suffering even more as the world looks on as if such victims do not have the right to be heard just like other human beings whose rights are provided by the same grand narrative. Why are they always ignored? The answer lies in the power and the mighty lures of the current grand narrative. Bush (2001) cited in Kam & Kinder (2007) puts it that "either you are with us, or you are with terrorists" (p. 321) or the policies of "you're either with us or against us" (Pinter, 2013, p. 18) wherein, if you oppose the current dominant grand narrative, you are punished even if you did nothing wrong. In normal circumstances wherein common senses are used, no war can be fought based on "either or" rationale. But thanks to colonial and toxic education the dominant grand narrative spread all over the world, nobody question such an irrational stance Bush championed. And truly, this is how the "war against terror" was waged up until truth started surfacing that the reasons for enacting this war were based on lies and vengeance. No single WMD was found in Iraq or displayed before the international community to prove US's allegations. Again, due to the blindness and fear the current grand narrative has inculcated in the world, who would dare to shame the US? If other grand narratives were allowed to be heard, it is obvious that the world would have heard the other part of the story in order to pass a judicious verdict. But this did not happen. Even the killings of minority Kurds–that Hussein had committed in the village of Helabja after two youths fired at his motorcade–had backing from the West that provided the napalm that Hussein used to massacre innocent civilians. In this crime, there was more than Hussein as far as the culprits are

226

concerned. Those who supplied him weapons were supposed to be part of the crime had the world used its sense in dealing with this crime. Such an affront is said to have been the reason why on March 16th, 1988 Hussein ordered the bombing of Helabja using chemical weapons the US had provided him when they used him to fight Iranian theocratic rule Ayatollah Khomeini established in 1979 after overthrowing Shah of Iran, a West's stooge. During his trial, Hussein wanted to implicate the US; but the court frustrated him and ignored his appeal to do so. You can see the toxicity of colonial education and the blindness of the current grand narrative. The judge who ignored Hussein is the same who administered an oath for him to tell plain truth while the same judge was doing plain lies by contradicting the oath he had administered to the accused.

After Bush unleashed intimidation to whoever thought differently from him as means of getting support to topple his nemesis, the whole world rallied behind him; and the sequels were catastrophic. For ever since, the world has not remained the same. Ahmed (2004) argues that Bush used war against terror to enact the act of war whose end and–of course–consequences to the whole wold are not easy to predict. Again, who would prevent Bush from doing what he wanted if at all the current dominant grand narrative was there to protect and back his actions against others? I am not trying to play devil's advocate. Up until now, the world has never asked the right question as to who created Hussein or al Qaeda, an international terrorist group. Al Qaeda is known to have originated in the US and the USSR proxy wars over Afghanistan during the cold war. This is the truth. Rollins (2010) maintains that al Qaeda would not become what it became had not for the cold war era wherein the Soviet Union had invaded Afghanistan. In other words, al Qaeda that was contracted by the US to fight the Soviets ended up backfiring so as to hurt those who cloned it. And this is obvious for whoever knows how al Qaeda burst into the scene. Again, who is talking about implicating the US?

Currently, there is a mantra that the US started that there is no way anybody can negotiate with terrorists without giving them legality which is not true and subject to dialogue had we had decolonised education. A major question one may pose is: Why was it possible and legal to cooperate with terrorists during the Cold War but not now and thereafter as we can pinpoint such like states in Africa? Isn't this a double standard that is governing international politics today? Arguably, all this has to do with the toxic education this volume seeks to deconstruct, decolonise and detoxify as a way of helping the world to get out of the impasse is in due to this civilisational and generational anomaly the current dominant grand narrative enacted and spread. It needs the courage of the mad to stand up against such a long-time systemic toxicity that has been turned into science and truth even if it is a lie[s]. History is clear as far as the creation of al Qaeda is concerned. It takes two to tango. Osama bin Laden, the founder of al Qaeda, was contracted to fight communists out of Afghanistan. Once his role was completed, his makers forgot to destroy him. African sage has it: do not teach a dog to eat eggs. Once it cannot hunt, it will turn against your own chickens. Or put it this way. When you keep a dog for hunting, before doing so you should consider what will happen once the forest no longer has animals to hunt. Obviously, the dog will turn against your own chickens, goats, rabbits and whatever it deems fit. For, nature commands that the dog must survive by eating other non-dog animals. This is the natural law. The logic behind this sage is that; it is easier to create a conflict than to resolve or manage it or to get the jinni out of the bottle than to return it back. Laying traps is always easier and quicker than securing them. The good lesson one can get from Bush's move is that his own bullet ricocheted so as to hurt America's economy hugely. Belasco (2009) observes that up to March 2009, the US had already authorised the expenditure of $ 1.08 trillion including $ 709 billion for Iraq and $ 300 Billion for Afghanistan (p. 2). This money is humongous by all standards. If our education were real and decolonised, some questions would have been asked and provided with right answers before burning such relatively humongous money. Had our education been decolonised would have affected how war on terror id supposed to be fought by embarking on principles and demands based on the real situation but not force by politicians. Academics would have played a great role in helping politicians out on how to fight the war. Again, the situation was vice versa. What do you expect out of such chaos? How much poverty would this money alleviate in Pakistan if it were spent on peaceful means of dealing with terrorism? How many jobs would this money create or how many people would this money help to stop producing poppies in Afghanistan? Again, before an egoistic grand narrative, Afghanistan and such thorny issues do not exist except the interests of big guys.

Ironically, Bush easily ordered the army to go into Iraq without underscoring the ramifications such a move would have on the US and the world at large. Getting out after many years and human and material losses was not ease for the most powerful nation on earth. Had it foreknown this, all this would not have happened. So, to avoid making it easy for powerful countries to enact wars or conflicts, as academics we need to take on the current dominant grand narrative that gives leaders like Bush the *carte blanche*, clout and discretionary to act the way they want. This is planet is ours equally. When someone somewhere makes a wrong decision, we end up suffering all indiscriminately as Swahili sage has it that rat's trap catches those intended or targeted and those unintended.

Interestingly, the effects of toxic education–to great extents–are visible almost everywhere and almost in every aspect of life. You can see it on a common person in the street; and on the sophisticated elites in the universities almost everywhere. One friend of mine from Africa reprimanded me when I gave a five dollar bill to an Aboriginal Canadian after parking my car in the street in one city in Canada. After we left the man at the spot where I parked my car where I gave the bill to this poor Aboriginal man, my friend told me. "I don't know why these guys like drinking and abuse substances so as to live depending on begging." He went on "they are lazy and unreasonable." Before saying much, I interposed; and told him to feel pity for himself; and for what he was saying. For, he was becoming unnecessarily judgemental; and he honestly and shamelessly displayed his ignorance. I had to bear the pains of educating him about the situation based on historical accounts of how the Aboriginal peoples of Canada found themselves in a desperately awkward situation they are in today. Ironically, in this instance, this friend of mine–who also was a victim in his own country's internal colonialism–was victimising another victim–in another country that took him after suffering for a long time–simply because he did not bother to know why; and how others were begging whereas they would work in their own country and live a decent life just like any other person.

First of all, my friend failed to appreciate the fact that everybody would like to be somebody. However, somebody or certain situations forced that person to become a laughingstock as it is in this case in point. My friend used a tunnel vision to visualise, analyse and thereby judge that person and all of his people as if he knew how all of them lived. Had he looked at him the same way he would have liked to be looked at, I am sure; such a judgmental tendency would not have been his tool of assessing and defining that person. For, the same friend of mine ran away from his country after his tribe was persecuted by those who thought it was not Arab enough to deserve to live equally along with others in their God-given country known as Sudan then. I, therefore, decided to rejig his knowledge by giving him a historical tour of the Aboriginal peoples of Canada telling him how the current dominant grand narrative reinvented them; and thereby destroyed their rich culture so as to end up becoming second-class citizens in their country. For those who do not bother to learn their history, judging them unfairly is always the case. My short lecture seemed to have worked. He discovered that he was facing the same fate and situation as those Aboriginal peoples he was carelessly despising and pointlessly accusing of being ham-fisted and hopeless; just because he decided to use his ignorance as means of assessing them. He admitted his ignorance openly due to the way he looked at Aboriginal peoples after that lecture. For, he showed openly how remorseful and ignorant he was. I just told him that not knowing is not a sin if one struggles to know instead of using his or her ignorance as a point of reference. I emphasised to him that he should look for opportunities of helping in such a situation instead of pointing a finger at others while the rest four fingers point at him. Sometimes, ignorance gears people to do things that they would not do if they understood the underlying reasons just like in these two cases of the PhD student and my friend. All this is the toxicity of colonial episteme this volume seeks to decolonise and detoxify.

230

In conflict resolution studies, we do not deal with the conflict as we see it outwardly. Instead, we think that what people see on conflict is but the tip of the iceberg. For, there is no way one can see the entire iceberg given that the bigger part is immersed underneath water. For my friend, understanding the true history of the Aboriginal peoples of Canada would act as an interventional means in their situation resulting from the current dominant grand narrative that belittled; and destroyed them and their ways of life the same way it did to other oppressed people all over the world. When we consider this instance, this, indeed, is a long-time conflict that has marred the image of Canada for many years. Despite haunting Canadian society, thanks to colonised education, it has however become difficult to divorce it. So, dealing with the conflict, to borrow the words of my mentor, Professor Scan Byrne, is like peering the onions. It is not an easy task. It needs preparedness, and, above all, readiness to encounter onion's itchy juice. The great lesson one can get from this incident is that we should not judge the book according to its cover. We need to read and understand it before passing our judgement[s]. Doing so will make our judgement fair and helpful for those suffering. Instead of being a problem, we will be a solution.

Back to the humiliation and degradation toxic education produced, and goes on producing, for oppressors and the oppressed, the signs and its effects–the decolonisation of education in general seeks to eradicate–are all over the place in our daily lives in various places. To put it into context–it should be noted. What has been ongoing for hundreds of years speaks volumes. Try to associate what is currently ongoing whereby Western NGOs such as World Vision are degrading poor people in so-called third world by taking their pictures and exposing them in the media without their consents under the pretext of soliciting money for them. Isn't this the traumatisation of victims of colonialism not to mention exploitation? For how long will such organisation use/*fend for* them without addressing the root causes of their predicaments? Arguably, the dents these organisations cause to the people–whose photos they take–are bigger and deeper than the benefits they get if there is any. Try to imagine; if this were done by other people from non-Western countries to poor and disadvantage Westerners in the streets of

Western capital cities. Due to the existing superiority complex, these organisations violate the rights and dignity of their victims. And yet, they go chest beating that they are helping them while they actually are degrading and exploiting them. Why don't their education and advancement, largely in human rights which enshrines the equality of all human beings, help them to see the other side?

Essentially, the fact is that they do not see the other side of the coin. They truly see it. Yet, they do not want to accept the truth that what they are doing is colonialism in itself. Before committing such a crime, one would think that those doing so would ask themselves: What if the pictures we are using to vend these poor souls would have been my relatives'? Again, under egocentricity embedded in neoliberalism that careless about others, such a question is hardly asked or thought about. If it does, it does not get the right answers given that there is no criminal liability behind such criminality. Why should they bother or care about the wellbeing and human dignity of people deprived the light and right of reasoning as some so-called Western thinkers put it as you will see hereunder? Swahili sage has it that spear is good for a hog but not for a human. If they want to help them, why don't they help their governments that have invented this sort of humiliation? One would wonder. Why should, for example, Canadian and American anthropologists love African more than their *homemade-third world* residents in reserves? Aren't most Aboriginal peoples in Australia Canada and the US living worse lives than some residents of poor countries they pretend to love and help? Why doesn't the World Vision, for example, help the penurious people at home first? For, charity begins at home. Why doesn't the World Vision go to the rich Middle East and beg for Aboriginal peoples in their backyard?

Ironically, African activists, politicians and intellectuals who are the victims as well, still stay side and look as if what is being done is really intellectualism or professionalism, which is supposed to be non-bias and all-encompassing. In both cases, there is evidence that the type of education we are providing and receiving is hugely defective and contaminated if at all we cannot see such injustices directed to the whole continent. Without true inclusivity, peace is going to remain a very expensive item in the world. Take, for example, wherein the highly revered Dr. Livingstone referred Africa as the Dark Continent (Miller, Deeter, Trelstad, Hawk, Ingram & Ramirez, 2013). Ironically, some African countries still teach their children and refer to this criminal as an explorer. This criminal is a product of filthy and toxic education based on the current dominant grand narrative that invented colonialism as its means of exploiting and subjugating others (Anderson, 2009; and Memmi, 2013).

However, such misconception of Africa is opposed by Ghanaian philosopher Kwame Gyeke cited in Carter, Irani & Volkan (2009) who wonders how and why Western thinkers do say bad things about Africa as if people had no brains. He says that African philosophic thoughts existed in form of traditions, folksongs, myths, proverbs, and ritual; thus it is reflected in people's altitudes (introduction). Furthermore, Senehi (2009) concurs with Gyeke (1995) cited in Letseka (2000) arguing that Africans are, like any other peoples, endowed with mythopoeic imagination in the continent abounds with myths and tales. Gyeke wonders how Western thinkers would recognise Socratic philosophy, but rejected African episteme, while he did not write but instead he preached. Gyeke says that using the pretext that Africans did not know how to read and write does not mean that they did not think. Even Jesus and Prophet Mohammad did not write anything save only preaching. Their messages were written posthumously; and still the two are famous and trusted thinkers to whom many thinkers run to seek knowledge. Are these two personalities viewed as philosophically educated simply because their teachings benefitted the dominant grand narratives superimposed on other felled grand narratives? Therefore, arguing that the lack of scripts or written work presupposes the lack of knowledge is but garbage and intellectual insolvency. Again, if the state of having thoughts is connected to writing, Africa had its own scripts which still exist up until now even if they were not popularised as Western and Arabic were.

Meshesha & Jawahar (2007) maintain that "however, there are also many languages in Africa with their own Indigenous scripts that vary considerably in shapes. Some of these scripts include Amharic script (Ethiopia), Bassa script (Liberia), Mende script (Sierra Leone), Vai script (West Africa) and Meroitic script (Sudan)" (Page not provided). Again, it is an indubitably understandable that not all Western societies had their own scripts. Even those they boast of having originated from somewhere else, especially if we consider the fact that the art of writing first appeared in Egypt. Fisher (2004) testifies that "Egyptian hieroglyphs–live on, unrecognised, in the Latin alphabets in which English, among hundreds of other languages, is conveyed today" (p. 7). Fisher argues that the letter 'm' we use today was derived from Egyptians' consonantal n-sign.

Again, we cannot ignore other realities such as the mnemonics Peruvian Incas in the Americas produced or the Sumerian scripts that were discovered in Uruk in modern Iraq. It means that evidence is all over the place save that those demonising Africa and other civilisations ignore or maliciously distort it for their hidden agendas. I wonder those calling African an impotent society intellectually if they read or research on it without any malicious intent. Despite Western historians and thinkers writing African history egoistically and maliciously, the truth still surfaces that Africa was as intellectually competent, but not impotent, just like any other societies. So, to avoid unnecessary developmental and intellectual decay, delay and conflicts, we need to address such anomalies in order to forge ahead peacefully as a world family of equals.

Another aspect that shows that Africa was highly developed intellectually can be derived from African languages which are the vehicles of delivering knowledge to humans; and which differentiate them from other animals. Just like any society, ontologically and epistemologically, African languages have all aspects that any language has. Solipsistically, their metaphors, innuendos, proverbs, and grammatical structures, *inter alia*, have all elements other so-called civilised languages have. Essentially, going on referring to, or treating Africa as an anomaly to other parts of the world–thanks to toxic education–is neither fair academically and intellectually nor feasible logically. If there is a lesson we can learn from this is nothing but machinations by Western intellectuals which are maliciously aimed at holding Africa at ransom so as to perpetually and easily bully and exploit it. To do just to Africa, other Indigenous peoples and those who with malice aforethought misconstrue and exploit their wrong history is treat them equally, erase the erroneous history and redress them. This way, justice will not only be done but also will be seen done; and some of the conflicts evidenced in Africa will go down. And thus, Africa will start its journey to normalcy just like any other societies that are now making out of historical conspiracy-cum-injustices. This is very essential move in reducing the cause of conflicts. Importantly, there is no way we can do justice to the victims of colonialism and its toxic education without decolonising and detoxifying it. There is no way we can succeed in this adventure without incorporating their grand narratives to the current dominant grand narrative.

Apart from intellectual and historical racism, Africa is facing conflicts resulting from struggle for extraction and unfair distribution of resources, underdevelopment–as defined by the hegemonic-grand narrative–and bad governance under corrupt rulers the powerful countries support seeking to extract resources in and from Africa. I can, therefore, argue that underdevelopment, poverty and violence in Africa are typically caused by those who distorted, abused, misconstrued and misrepresented its history apart from defined by the current dominant grand narrative based on its own yardstick that excludes some crucial aspects of wealth such untapped resources in its calculation of development. To erase such above indicated anomalies, our decolonised education needs to embark on addressing these cause roots by acknowledging the malicious and fallacy–that need to urgently and systematically be corrected–in presenting and construing the African history. Currently, the world is globalised so as to look like one village. What transpires in one country can have ripple or domino effects to the whole world. Therefore, supporting the recollection and resurrection of African history is not an option but a duty for the whole world. This way, meaningful development and peace for the entire world will be attained largely after creating a peaceful situation based on equality and equity. MacFarlane & Khong (2006) note that the path to peace must be sustainable development to mean that there cannot be any development without peaceful environment as an enhancer of almost everything humans do. To do away with existing unequal and unjust relationship between Africa and other Indigenous communities in the world and the West, we need to appreciate the fact that ignoring their plights and wellbeing is ignoring the future of a peaceful and developed world. If Asian countries such as Asian tigers were supported to get out of stinking poverty, what is wrong with Africa and other underdeveloped parts of the world? With the decolonised education, the fear of losing cheap resources by the West will become immaterial; because Africa has never regarded its resources as solely for its uses. Is it because of their resources or just racism as catapulted by the grand narrative embedded in toxic education that allows inequalities and injustices among the citizens of the world?

To usher sustainable development, sustainable peace and sustainable human security in the world today, we need to address historical evils Indigenous people have suffered all over the world Africa in particular sustainably. Our interconnectedness and interdependence are growing day by day. You can see in the fight against terrorism today. Nobody is safer now. Everybody is exposed and is vulnerable so to speak. Young and desperate people, particularly from disadvantaged and pauperised countries are recruited every day after being promised a good life or an alternative to miserable lives they are living currently after being shut out by neoliberal policies that the current dominant grand narrative espouses based on toxic education. If unequal relationship is not addressed, chances of terrorism becoming another opposing force in the world are high.

Furthermore, toxic education has vacuum-packed the hearts and minds—which takes a centre stage in this volume—so as to ruthlessly and wholesale condemn and refer to the entire continent or a people with the most ancient civilisation as the Dark Continent devoid of "the light of reason." This is but another source of conflict due to the fact that the West-led and dominated world has—for many decades—heinously and purposely—thanks to toxic education, neoliberal and neocolonial drive—ignored or pretended not to see the anomalies and injustices the West has maintained in exploiting others for its future peril shall things not been changed. Where do we put Egyptian civilisation whose monuments and pyramids still fascinate the world thousands of years after they were exceptionally and mystically erected? Aren't the pyramids a miracle to today's advanced science and technology? Aren't they a fable that has cheated many

236

so-called advanced thinkers and intellectuals? How on earth do you call Africa an intellectually impotent continent while it boasts of such magnificent and scientifically-complicated pyramids whose construction and complexity have beaten the so-called advanced science that has never been able to decipher them? Those calling Africa names, failed even to develop a theory of how the pyramids were built without using any visible machines. Is this the intellectual impotence Africa is accused of? Where do we put the oldest stone houses of Zimbabwe which literary means Zimba za Mabwe or stone house? Makoni, Dube & Mashiri (2006) note that "the name Zimbabwe has a number of variants: dzimbabwe; dzimbahwe. Dzimbahwe is a generic term for stone dwellings (pl. madzimbabwe)" (p. 378).

Ironically, despite all lies and malice about and against Africa, we can still use the history Westerners maliciously and erroneously wrote to prove them wrong as far as Africa is concerned. This shows how the true history of Africa and other Indigenous peoples cannot be whisked away easily. Again, we need to appreciate the fact that despite being the force behind everything, the current dominant grand narrative has critics and detractors even from within. Such positive thinkers need to be supported. For, their contributions help victims to reclaim their lost world not to mention making their case against the maltreatments of the current dominant grand narrative as far as oppressed societies, countries and continents are concerned.

Moreover, African civilisation does not only end in pyramids and stone houses of Zimbabwe which pre-existed many years before European civilisation at the time "in Europe, primitive dwellings were constructed of woven wood and clay evolving to unburnt clay" as (Stone, 2004, p. 367) observes. Remember. This Stone (*Ibid.*) is a white man telling the truth that has always surfaced despite efforts to foil it. It goes far back even before Europe knew the existence of others out of Europe. While Europe was not aware of the difference between the Americas and Asia, Africans had already established ties with Asia; and there was nothing new about Asia. Such links prove that Africa was not as empty, intellectually impotent and static as some ignorant and malicious Western writers used to believe. Jinyuan (1984) maintains that "there are indications that indirect exchange of products between China and Africa could go back to two thousand years ago" (p. 242). This means, Africa traded with China even before the Birth of Jesus.

One may argue that Africa was able to reach this pinnacle when it was using its true type of episteme before the introduction of colonial and toxic one. How do you call the entity that fully participated in such a long distance and an international trade at the time the current regime of commerce was not even conceived? Yet, some gullible Western intellectuals kept on referring to such an entity uncivilised and technologically backward? Despite such stark truth, this is Africa those who misconstrued and misrepresented its history did not want to appreciate. Was it really? Even *Periplus*, which is thought to be the foundation of modern navigation science, mentions the coast of East Africa as a trade partner with many outside world at that time (Lytle, 2016). Africa has its own weakness just like any other human society. Again, claiming that Africa had, and still has nothing to deliver, is a wee bit too much. How–for example–the continent that produced great empires apart from being the cradle of human kind can be termed as barren and impotent almost in everything as if such successes are not achievements? We need to do justice a little bit. This corpus presents and revisits these ancient historical hallmarks in order to make the case that historical racism evidenced currently in Africa was purposely and wickedly created by colonialism that is now despising Africa calling it names which result into unnecessary conflicts Africa is now evidencing. Resolving African conflicts needs to be done after and through exploring its true history so as to chart the way in a true and logical direction. This is only possible through decolonising the current toxic and hegemonic education regime.

To show how the fallacies of abusing and misrepresenting Africa are systemic and deliberate, even when you write the term Dark Continent, the dictionary of English in the computer corrects you by capitalising the term to show how it is socially constructed and accepted. Thinkers and everybody uttering such nonsense about Africa cannot be true academics in the real sense and light of reason. Again, Brantlinger (2004) cited in Harris (2015) traces the source of this myth full of bigotry noting that:

Africa grew "dark" as Victorian explorers, missionaries, and scientists flooded it with light, because the light was refracted through an imperialist ideology that urged the Abolition of "savage customs" in the name of civilization. As a product of that ideology, the myth of the Dark Continent developed during the transition from the main British campaign against the slave trade (p. 11).

Ironically, those who created and benefited from the slave trade and colonialism are the same persons who are accusing Africa of these evils as if they did not commit them for many decades! Using toxic, false and hegemonic education, such skinny academics thought they would get away with murder forever. There is a time when Europe was referred to as the Dark Continent, too, due to its gruesome warring nature. Yet, as the time went by, this reference came to an end while–for Africa–it has gone on and on. Why if this is not historical racism embedded in toxic education? Is there any dark continent like Indian subcontinent that invented a racist caste system that has caused a lot of suffering for many people chiefly black ones? Who points a finger at it? Thanks to toxic and biased education, India now is referred to as the biggest democracy on earth while it is the most demonic and racist country as far as human rights is concerned. Is it the biggest democracy or the biggest *demoncracy*? Assertion that African was, and still is the Dark Continent needs to be erased so that we can all work on earth as equal and worthy. History has a very important role to play in conflicts. So, to correct such damning history is important. This is why I have taken my time to research on the subject so that history can have it that something was done to address this anomaly. Moreover, it reminds me of a thinker who has a lot to offer but he is not accepted, the late Professor Mussamali Nangoli who wrote his masterpiece "no more lies about Africa." Nangoli was very provocative with regards to tell Western domination to its face. Full of humour and wits Nangoli (2001) cited in Ndegwah (2007) notes that "once upon a time in Africa, we paid no taxes, there was no crime, there was no police, there was no inflation, there was no unemployment, men did not beat or divorce their wives, then the white men came to improve things" (p. 304). It is unfortunate, very unfortunate, to state that despite telling the truth about Africa, this book has never been incorporated academically even in Africa by being taught in schools. Why? How could it be incorporated while it tells naked truth that leaves some African homemade colonialists dressed down and unhappy? Had it been accepted and welcomed in Europe, African countries would as well have revered and incorporated it in their syllabi.

When I was researching for this volume, I tried to look for Nangoli in Google Scholar which I often times use to access some academic materials to only come across only one work of the professor who authored many books. Apart from fumbling on the above mentioned title, I only came across the obituary in which Mafabi (2001) notes that:

> Chief Musamali Nangoli Nawodya is dead. The scholar-cum-prolific writer of 33 books, including bestsellers, Lords of Slavery, and No more lies about Africa, humorously described by the New York Post as unputdownable, passed on at Eldoret hospital in Kenya when he succumbed to brain tumour on Saturday January 2. A family source said Chief Nangoli had been in and out of hospital for some time.

By the look of the article, this thinker was a force to reckon with save that he hailed from Africa. If anything, this was his sin before racist education system. How can a person write such a huge number of such titles and fail to make it to google scholar? To show more of the man, Mafabi (*Ibid.*) notes that:

> His popular and articulately penned book, No More Lies about Africa, which pokes the nooks of slavery and colonialism in Africa, is humorously described by the New York Post as unputdownable. It is at once exhilarating, well-researched, educative, captivating, controversial, and entertaining. Chief Nangoli's other intellectual output included Preparing Well for and Passing Any Exam; and How to Make Money.

By writing 33 books, on top of being a professor, the man was a highbrow who was supposed to have some academic prominence, mainly in the field of decolonisation if not in the history of Africa or the History of Colonialism. Here we are talking of a self-educated person and Western educated one. What of those traditional gurus such as Shaaban Robert of Tanzania who is equated with Julius Shakespeare? Even when Robert is mentioned, it is just scantly, as it is said; as Achebe (2003) cited in Selasi (2013) maintains that "those who in talking about African literature want to exclude North Africa because it belongs to a different tradition surely do not suggest that black Africa is anything like homogeneous. What does Shabaan S Mongo Beti of Cameroun and Paris with Nzekwu of Nigeria?" (p. 4).

The above quote, however true it maybe, shows how African intellectualism is discriminated against and sabotaged pointlessly to maintain nasty assertion that Africa is intellectually moribund while it is not. Ironically, Shakespeare is known all over Africa. I do not think Robert is as well known in Europe. Whenever Robert is mentioned, he is nobly mentioned by his colleagues, writers and Africans who, unfortunately, happen or happened to be teaching African literature abroad. wa Thiong'o (1994) observes that "to end with Shaaban Robert poem which says '*titi la mama litamu lingawa (ingawa) la mbwa, lingine halishi tamu....watu wasio na lugha ya asili, kadiri walivyo wastaarabu, cheo chao ni cha pili dunia, dunia la che*o" (xii)

Wa Thiong'o quotes from Robert's poems can be translated from Swahili to English as "mother tit is sweet even if it is that of a dog, another is always sweet...people without their original language, however civilised, their position is second, in the world." This can be expanded arguing that people without their traditional education, however civilised they may wrongly think they are, are doomed. This is reason why I have written this volume. The role of Ubuntu which means your humanity depends on my humanity is so great in addressing the sufferings and the indignation Africa has, for a long time, faced and suffered. No human out of recognising the humanity of one another. Mabovula (2011) defines Ubuntu saying that:

> The concept Ubuntu originates from the Xhosa expression 'Umuntu ngumntu ngabanye abantu', which means that each individual's humanity is ideally expressed in relationship with others. Ubuntu consists of the prefix ubu-and the stem ntu-ubu evokes the idea of being in general. Thus, ubu-ntu is the fundamental ontological

and epistemological category in the African thought of the Bantu-speaking people (p. 40).

It is this humanity that makes Africa more civilised than others, especially those who despise it. It is only Africa, and the Americas that did not colonise others. However, Mabovula argues that Ubuntu–apart from having a plethora of definitions–it is hard to define due to the fact that it is more entrenched in African society to mean or/and be used in many situations. Ubuntu can be used to deal with conflict, run the society even teach the society all depending on what one wants to do with Ubuntu. Being a Peace and Conflict Studies scholar, I use conflict in gauging many aspects of the society due to the fact that conflict busies the world more costly than anything. Coming from the concept of u-muntu or, o-muntu, u-munu, u-munthu or a Bantu which actually means a human, Ubuntu can function the same way a human being functions by carrying multiple functions and multiple identities. Therefore, when dealing with Ubuntu, as a philosophy and way of life, we need to underscore its complexity, multipurposity as well as its simplicity based on its applicability and the scope it covers all depending on its spirit and definition and the spirit of using it. Müller (2015) argues that Ubuntu is so complex that it sometimes becomes difficult to understand in Western ways due to the fact that Ubuntu is about generosity, morality, spirituality, hospitality, compassion, caring, sharing as opposed to individuality which leads to loneliness, selfishness and lack of spirituality and immorality. Again, how many Ubuntu-like mechanisms are there all over the world? I argue that if there was no conflict in South Africa whose settlement baffled many people globally, maybe, just maybe, Ubuntu would not been appreciated and celebrated as it currently is. So, as academics, we need to dig deeper and see how many unused indigenous mechanisms are out there. Also, if there was no this concept in Africa as well as South Africa, maybe, the end of Apartheid would have been violent and tragic in regards to the loss of many human lives.

Basically, nobody can comfortably confine Ubuntu in one or two definitions due to its complexity and far-reaching applicability on the lives of Africans and humans in general. For, Africans, Ubuntu was like a religion that affected all aspects of their lives that defined how must treat and live with another in the society. Moreover, Ubuntu, for Africans, is like Judeo-Christianity to the current dominant grand narrative. However, the difference is that Ubuntu did not concoct things or impose some utopian things on a human as the religions do. To show how complex Ubuntu can be, Murithi (2006a) notes that "these mechanisms pre-dated colonialism and continue to exist and function today. Ubuntu societies place a high value on communal life, and maintaining positive relations within the society; is a collective task in which everyone is involved" (p. 29). The scope of Ubuntu was too big for Westerners to understand at the time they arrived in Africa due coming from an individualistic society that puts premium on an individual which is the opposite of Ubuntu. According to Murithi (*Ibid.*), every member of the community is interconnected to others in good and bad or all situations. So, when the conflict arises, the whole community comes into the play to see to it that it is either managed or resolved due to the fact that every member of the society is a stakeholder whom the conflict can affect. This means, under Ubuntu, there is a communal way of dealing with or resolving conflicts.

Furthermore, African society has its unique ways of addressing conflict, miseries, achievements and whatnots pertaining to the society. Instead of prescribing everything, African conflict resolution model encompasses both the offenders and the victims equally to see to it how they can be reconciled and move forward together as a society. To the contrary, Western model of conflict resolution is mainly adversarial while African model of conflict resolution is more collaborative than adversarial. So, we can see that, in Ubuntu, everybody is involved either as a party to conflict or mediator or facilitator.

As argued above *vis-à-vis* Indian caste racism, the so-called Apartheid against Palestinians has been going on for decades; and the so-called civilised world has always supported it without its education system guiding those behind such complicity to see the light and do the right thing. Just like the abnormality of referring to Indian as the world's biggest democracy–which is the mockery to democracy– Israel, just like India, too, is referred to as a democracy. Sometimes, you wonder if those who spread the so-called democracy to the world know what it means; or if they forgot its true meaning. How do you call democracy the state or system that discriminates against and maltreats people based on their history, pedigree or cause? While democracy replaced tyranny, tyrannical practices have been ongoing under democracy without the so-called advance education's radar detecting, or detecting but pretending that it has not detected anything. If Israel is a democracy while it openly, perpetually and conservatively has oppressed Palestinians as the means of frustrating them from claiming their land, China, too, is a democracy that has perpetually intimidated Tibetans from assuming their place in the history and politics of China. While it has become difficult for Tibetans to attain their autonomy simply because they have no strong backers, Hong Kong is able to sustain and attain the same just because the West backs it. Here you can see how half blind the current education system is. It sees one thing and does not see another thing even if it is of the same nature and size. It is able to see all things that benefits the current dominant grand narrative while, to the contrary, it is totally unable to see whatever benefits others that it has for many years excluded and erased. True education must act as a microscope. It must see a thing as it is however ugly or attractive that thing is. Education is more of a reality than conjecture. Education is supposed to be as nonbiased as a gun. When you point your gun at yourself, it will kill you. This is reality. Education needs to bring truth forth as it is without discriminating or favouring as the current toxic education is. The regime of education that begets bigotry and exploitation be they systemic or individual is not truly an education worthy giving people.

This story is about two conflictual tribes in Ghana whereby one had chieftainship while another did not have any. When the two met to deal with the conflict about market squabbles, the tribe that had a chief left the role in the hands of the chief. The tribe without a chief appointed a humble and wise boy to speak on their behalf. When the boy from the opposing side took the podium, he humanised the chief of the opposing party by addressing to and calling him father as the above quoted words indicate. The wise young man ended up softening the heart of the chief so as to change his mind; and make him concede. If anything, in regards to dealing with differences, some societies had their own practical mechanisms of dealing with issues that seemed to be thornily tough and convoluted. Once we superimpose our mechanism[s] on others whose mechanisms we ignore or sabotage, the results are likely to be different. To know how practical Ubuntu is, one can explore what happened during negotiations between the African National Congress (ANC) and the Apartheid regime in South Africa. Despite having backing from international community, the conflict in South Africa was constructively resolved mainly depending on the culture of the country that draws a lot from Ubuntu.

In winding this chapter therefore, the author goes back to where he started; by asking the same question: Whose story should we tell or buy into? Had this story been told by the Boers, before pulling their Apartheid policy down, it would not have the world Ubuntu or humanity. This is the danger of allowing somebody to tell your story. Importantly, humans need to view each other as one but not many and different when it comes to dealing with conflict.

8

Relationship and Peace and Conflict Based on Decolonised Education

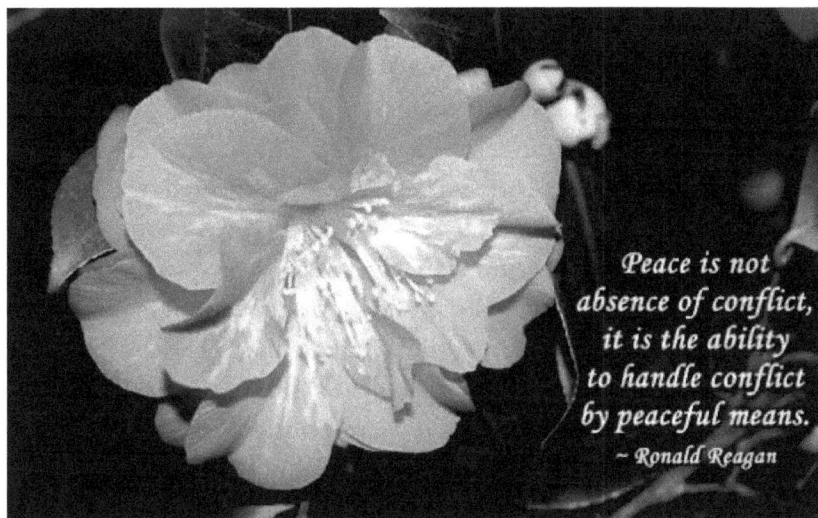

Figure 13; photo courtesy of kuweight64.blogspot.com

This section explores the significance of living with environment harmoniously before delving into whose story should we tell and buy into. Tellingly, let us expand the web by bringing together relationship, peace and conflict all aimed at devising the formula for living harmonious lives with each other, environment; and, above all, as we aspire to minimise or use conflict constructively for the benefits of all stakeholders living and dead. I was looking at a long time conflict in Angola resulting to decades of destruction. This conflict dragged on for a long time as the West–which had its hidden interests in it–tried to *resolve* it to no avail. As far as African mechanisms of conflict resolution apply, the West would not succeed simply because of a couple of reasons.

Firstly, it was the party to conflict but it tried to portray itself as a neutral player while it was not.

Secondly, the West wanted the resolution that enhanced its hidden interests even if that was at the detriment of the other unallied party which in this case was the ruling party, the *Movimento Popular de Libertação de Angola–Partido do Trabalho or* Popular Movement for the Liberation of Angola (MPLA).

Thirdly, the West wanted to use only purely Western mechanisms of conflict resolution by ignoring and sidelining local mechanisms of doing the same.

Fourth, the West was openly biased in this conflict. Fifth, there was another party to conflict who had the same characteristics with the West namely, the former USSR that supported the MPLA. Hegemonic as the two superpowers were in this proxy conflict, every party wanted to make sure that its interests are secured at the detriment of the other side. In this zero-sum game though, there were more than five parties however the two were the only ones that were dealt with. These fives were, firstly, the MPLA against the União *Nacional para a Independência Total de Angola* or the National Union for the Total Independence of Angola (UNITA). The Second were the US against the USSR. Thirdly it was the MPLA and the US on one side against the UNITA and the USSR on the other side. Fourth, this very conflict was between the East and the West.

And fifth, the Conflict was between hegemonic powers on one side and disadvantaged and exploited country of Angola. Le Billon (2001) argues that the double standard in dealing with conflict is behind its failure in Angola whereby the duality of fortune and miseries result from the fact that violent economy rewards political-military rulers as it punishes the majority. The trend is the same almost in all African countries facing violent conflict resulting from struggle for the control of resources these countries are endowed with. One important question arises: Why are these political-military rulers blind so as to become unable to see the miseries they are causing to their people and their countries? Bush & Saltarelli (2000) argue that dominant groups seek education in order to further their privileged positions instead of serving the societies. Therefore, for such groups, the quality of education is immaterial provided that it helps them to rich their goals.

Bad use of education—which is not only colonial but also toxic—informs us how political and military personnel in power seek to education not for the purpose of delivering the societies but use it egoistically instead as it has been in Angola since independence. Without decolonising such education system, many violent conflicts will always be there to stay. If the elites can behave in such a manner, what should we expect of those who are not highly educated who, in a sense, comprise the majority of the population of the country? Is there any difference between having education and not having it in such circumstances? Despite underscoring such an anomaly in the intentions of ruling groups, Western conflict resolution experts proposed what should be done as they miss a point by thinking that the conflict was about politics while it actually had its roots in toxic education. There is no way the ruling party, the MPLA that was formed by Marxists whose education inclination was to view capitalism as an evil everybody had to fight could nicely resolve this conflict. MPLA's nemesis, the UNITA suffers from the same toxic education and tunnel vision in that it was formed by capitalists who viewed Marxism and socialism as a sacrilege everybody had to vigorously fight.

In a simple language, two political parties in Angola were used by two camps not for the benefits or interests of the people of Angola but for their own benefits. What makes the decolonisation of education in this conflict crucial is the fact that the parties to conflict in this conflict are equally blind and so much brainwashed thanks to toxic education elites leading these parties received that made them unable to have any inputs as far as the resolution of the conflict at hand was concerned. You can currently see this in Syria where the Middle East's powerful allies and players, Russia and the US have been dictating what should be done to address the conflict that saw the country become a failed state. So, the dominant grand narratives of the day created two enemies in a distant country who were able to fight a proxy war at the detriment of Angolan people. This enmity benefited the duo namely, the East and the West camps due to the fact that Angola has vast resources they needed. The situation was the same in the DRC under Patrice Lumumba and Joseph Mobutu.

The two camps used toxic education to divide; and thereby exploit the two countries.

Because of colonial and toxic education, many African countries found themselves facing mayhem wantonly simply because the elites in these countries received toxic education something that has been ongoing up until now. Thus, by instigating ideological wars, the two narratives were able to create conducive environment that enabled them to swiftly access resources in Angola; either through the ruling MPLA or a guerrilla group, the UNITA or getting an open market for selling weaponry in exchange with cheap resources (Mac Ginty & Williams, 2009). In this game of deceit, two fighting factions in Angola became victims by all means. They all spent much money buying weapons they used to destroy their country pointlessly.

So, too, in this game, the superpowers gained immensely by selling weapons exorbitantly while they got resource cheaply. Essentially, the war in Angola helped the USSR and the US to get cheap resources either smuggled out by the UNITA or sold at a throwaway price by the government that needed money to finance its war against the UNITA. As well, the UNITA sold resources in order to get the weapons and money to fight the MPLA. For the US and the USSR, the war in Angola was a policy as envisioned by the Nineteenth century German military strategist Karl von Clausewitz cited by Battersby & Siracusa (2009) claiming that war is "an act of policy" and "merely the continuation of policy by other means" (p. 44) which in this case was to plunder Angola by sacrificing justice for Angolans. The real problem was pushed under the carpet as Battersby & Siracusa (*Ibid.*) maintains that "from a normative view, political violence is caused by the absence of economic justice and human rights, while from a materialist view, the nature of the real world works against the realization of ideals" (p. 40). In Angola– during the civil war–justice was sacrificed while the *realpolitik* of the time worked against the realisation of human rights and justice for Angolans–which include economic and political justice. Battersby & Siracusa are trying to pin down the reasons that cause violence, wars and dissatisfaction among the citizens of countries facing civil wars. All such sufferings can be attributed to toxic education that needs to be detoxified due to its nature of serving its grand narrative at the detriment and expenses of others.

Furthermore, the civil war in Angola took a long time to end despite "efforts" by two guarantors who, ironically had vested and hidden interests in the conflict. They mounted all forms of mechanisms to end up the conflict in vain due to the fact that their interests surpassed those of innocent Angolans (Ferreira, 2006). By mounting political and diplomatic pressure to resolve the conflict, whose *diktat* would mediate ended up being pulled in so as to exacerbate the conflict that dragged on for decades pointlessly. If anything, this was a failure of prescriptive conflict resolution model as espoused by colonial education which, in a sense, is one sided. For, the attempts to peacefully resolve the conflict in Angola did not accommodate traditional mechanisms of conflict resolution or the inputs of the victims. In other words, for Western academics and conflict professionals, Angolan people had nothing to offer despite being a party to conflict. What undoubtedly added up to the complexity and stalemate to the conflict is the fact that the two camps had two different approaches and templates that they applied to the resolution of the conflict? Kissinger (1995) cited in Battersby & Siracusa (2009) argues that "nations have pursued self-interest more frequently than high-minded principle, and have competed more than they have cooperated. There is little evidence to suggest that this age-old mode of behavior has changed or that it is likely to change in the decades ahead" (p. 41).

To show how the two camps had what it takes to resolve the conflict but did not opt to, the conflict in Angola came to an end after the fall of the Berlin Wall which signified the hegemonic demise of the USSR; thus, the elimination of one of the two dominant grand narratives. The fall of the Berlin wall assured the US that the MPLA would no longer pose any danger to its interest due to having a unipolar hegemonic power in the world. Therefore, the US let the UNITA die a natural death after its leader Dr. Jonas Savimbi was killed to signify the end of the conflict. This means, the US won; and it still enjoys unbridled power in doing business with Angola while the USSR lost; and it interests in Angola became vulnerable altogether. The war in Angola is one example. Another ideal example

251

can be drawn from the DRC which is bleeding to death due to civil wars whose lifeline is none other than rich countries selling weaponry to both protagonists in order to get the supply of cheap resources. In so doing, rich countries, just as it was in Angola, get away with cheap resources, essentially precious metals and timbers among others. Further, rich countries do not care about the fact that such war is causing injustices, sufferings and gross abuses of human rights such as rampant rape, deaths, starvation, displacement and the instability of the country and the Great Lake region in general. Their self-interests–Kissinger talks about–surpass the interests and rights of the citizenry in the DRC. Ironically, Kissinger seemed to contradict himself by being carried away by the current dominant grand narrative that espouses colonial, toxic and hegemonic education. For, he says that that the United States was dutifully charged with being a moral force for good in the world. Is the US the moral force really? Again, this becomes so in the lenses and eyes of toxic education espoused by the dominant grand narrative. I do not know if victims in Angola, the DRC and other places see the US as a "moral force" rather than amoral, evil and greedy force hell-bent to rob them by all means. Again, this is the weakness of the current dominant grand narrative built on dichotomous foundations full of contradictions to signify the lacunae caused by suffocating other dissent views from other grand narratives it subdued. Interestingly, the same country, the US, ironically, still regards itself as a champion of democracy! As luck would have it, Battersby & Siracusa (*op.cit.*) asset that Kissinger is a war criminal that will never be brought to book thanks to toxic education and the dominance of Western grand narrative.

Due to the one-sidedness of colonial education, Western rulers are beyond reproach even when they commit atrocities as it can be seen the two countries in question. Whatever crime they commit, they do so with impunity knowingly that they are above the law. On their side, academics and rulers from victimised countries such as Angola, the DRC and African in general, due to receiving toxic education, perceive such systemic injustice as a normal thing under international order. Arguably, the type of education that turns its recipients into cyborg-like creatures or machines needs to be deconstructed in order to avoid more dangers in the future. Such an anomaly does not only affect education. Lombardo (2008) notes that negative effects of toxic education existed even in the laws that run the countries such as the US which portrays itself as the moral force of the world. Lombardo refers to eugenics whose decoys affected the US government in Virginia so as to enact the law that forbade intermarriages between the so-called whites and black up until the court in **Loving vs Virginia** invalidated; and thereby struck down the law. Here I espouse the idea of decolonising education, especially based on the s superstructure the current dominant grand narrative created. As social scientists, if we change the social structure which in this case is the way education is organised revolving around hegemonic culture and civilisation based on the dominant grand narrative—which in essence, is dictated by capitalism—we can effect changes aimed at strengthening and overhauling education in all fields.

By so doing, we will be able to come up with the type of education that can and will accommodate academic diversity of the world aimed at strengthening our intellectualism based on our diversity of ideas emanating from all grand narratives of the world. And such education will enrich the whole system; and thus, makes changes to all fields of education so as to trickle down to the whole society. The current dominant episteme as espoused by the dominant grand narrative, just like other systems running the world, was conceived in London, Frankfurt and Washington (Cheldelin, Druckman & Fast, 2003). This shows how Western hegemonic grand narrative has dominated education and other fields of education. This is not right at all. Drawing from my fields of CRS and PACS, I found that ironically, Africa that has many conflicts currently does not have as many universities that deal with conflict studies not to mention having many diseases real and unreal without universities dealing with them as the ones the West have despite not having the said two problem at the same magnitude with Africa.

All over again, why should Africa have many universities dealing with conflicts and health issues while it has been made to wait to be saved by a white man who has become a self-appointed saviour? This is when the myth of *white man's burden* is internalised and reinforced among the victims of the current dominant grand narrative. Basically, academics and politicians are the ones to blame for treating such an anathema as a normal thing. And such intellectual *impotence* has been ongoing for years as it is supported by the dominant Western grand narrative which aims at making everything the West the best for the world. While such relationship and interdependence abhors, the latter is happy with such unofficial role of the saviour who happens to be the same devil that crucified Africa on the cross! Can emancipatory and true education coexist and function with such corrupt and dangerous relationship whose product is nothing but conflict? Even the experiments, theories and practice used in many academic fields are mostly drawn from the West except for a few such as Taoism, Islam, Satyagraha and Ubuntu or humanity from Asia, the Middle East, and Africa respectively in conflict resolution. The irony of having many universities churning professionals in various fields in the West signifies the fact that Africa and other forgotten areas will always depend on the West for everything as if they have no brains or civilisation, culture, history and sources of knowledge of their own. It is like having many sick people in a certain place then you keep doctors hundreds or thousands of kilometers away from such the place. The type of education that enforces, reinforces and normalises such abnormalities is itself wanting and wrong so as to need to be decolonised for the benefit of both parties namely, the perpetrators and the victims.

What should be done to decolonise education in all fields? Arguably, this is possible. We should accommodate other views and practices to suit the needs of all people all over the globe. For example, in regards to conflict, in Western culture, mediation is preferred in order to protect the party. Fisher, Ury & Patton (2011) note that "the best way to protect against being deceived is to seek verification the other side's claims. It may help to ask them for further clarification of a claim or to put the claim in writing" (p. 10). Thanks to the dominance of the Western grand narrative, this is now the norm internationally despite the fact that other narratives such as African had their own ways of securing the security of the contract based on verbal avowals of trust. This volume addresses the fact that African culture, traditionally and historically suffered a lot from written agreements that paved the way to colonialism. Although written agreements are now used in Africa, this is different in some African cultures where an agreement is oral, and no documentation is required. I must clearly state it from the outset that I am not an expert on all African practises nevertheless; most of them share the same experiential nexus as far as colonisation. So, when I say some African societies are not comfortable with written agreements, this should not be taken as to mean all African cultures. Again, if we look at a few of African societies I know, I found that certification of anything does not appeal to many members of these societies. You can see this in marriage certificates issued by, for instance, Catholic churches clearly stating that the marriage so entered is monogamous. Once nuptial ceremonies are over, some Africans go back to their traditional practices devoid of written agreements that they do not honour. For example, some polygamous tribes, in Tanzania, go to the church for marriage. Thereafter, they go back to their traditions by marrying many other wives. They serve two masters. For them, the papers or certificates are procedural things but not an issue that bids or busies them. The manners of entering agreements differ from one society to another. Goodwin & Roach (n.d.) note that:

> Alternatively, early medieval Germans making an agreement could lay the palms of their hands together as they held them over their heads (presumably to maximize visibility). Saxon practice permitted a raising of the hands, with two or four fingers extended, without actual touching. In some African societies, buyer and seller communicate agreement by "waving their right hands up and down and then touching each other's palms with the fingers stretched away [Sic] page not provided).

Many African societies have never understood the importance of marriage certificates among others. Abogunrin (2005) cites an example of Afrel tribe in Nigeria noting that "many African Christians and Muslims even opt for swearing and oath-taking in Afrel when they mean a real business or when they desire a strict compliance to an agreement," (page not provided). Basically, with respect to many African societies, their understanding, according to their traditions, marriage is justified by love but not papers, oaths and religious braggadocios. Despite Christianity and Islam having more than a hundred years in Africa, many traditionalists still view marriage certificates with a suspecting eye. To them, certificates that they view as depending on papers, lack love and sincerity. Another example you can find it in the fact that the so-called modern societies have many more divorces than traditional ones.

Written agreement is a superimposition on non-Western countries even on some Westerners. This is in line with even with some Western thinkers, especially with experience in non-Western countries. For example, some respond to this mentality and understanding of the agreement well. Lederach (2005) poses a question that he later answers asking: "What is the agreement?" one may answer that it is of course the signed document. But even the person in the street in settings of armed conflict will say "no, it is not the paper" (p. 44). Lederach makes a great point. If we consider those who forge, for example, degrees and other certificates to fulfill their ambitions, we will agree with Lederach that those people do not respect those papers. And those papers do not guarantee the fulfillment of the duties of any agreement.

Additionally, we can argue that forgers do not need or like, respect or care about such papers Western grand narrative holds to be binding. Should we blame and fault Aboriginal peoples for not respecting written agreements or those who brought the same to them without underscoring the fact that their civilisation did not have such things? One can comfortably argue that colonisers taught colonised peoples to abhor and hate written agreements due to the fact that colonisers entered dubious agreements which enable them to dubiously and criminally make claims over other territories and countries without binding them to honour what were agreed upon despite being reached according to their terms. Colonialists did not abide by their own rules. How could those to whom such things are impositions honour them? More importantly, colonisers did not only dishonour their terms but also dishonoured the spirit of entering agreement from the beginning when they crafted dubious contracts.

In other words, they turned their written agreements into a sham everybody can dishonour and forge as it currently is when people forge academic certificates not to mention swearing and thereafter tell lies. Colonialists lied right away from the beginning. This is why certificates of any form have never totally convinced those who learned the art of putting vows on papers instead of putting them at hearts. Such a take on agreement reflects well on what many Aboriginal peoples think of written agreements as Western and Arab superimposition on them. Writing an agreement does not make sense if those entering it are not committed to fulfilling obligations and what is stipulated and agreed upon. This takes me back to the times I was in my secondary education. My maternal granddaddy used to teasingly ask me what was wrong with the education I was receiving. By then, I viewed myself as an educated person *per se*; particularly in that part of the world. My grandpa was neither *enlightened* nor *civilised* as the missionaries used to put it to mean that those who lacked the so-called formal education or baptismal were *unenlightened* and *uncivilised*.

Apart from calling them uncivilised, missionaries used to call them sinners who did not accept and receive Jesus as their saviour while Muslims called them *taghut* or Kaffirs or rebels if not idolaters. You wonder how Western education enshrined such abuses. This is where you see the toxicity of the said education openly. Ironically, in regards to righteousness, my grandfather lived in his marriage comfortably without any written documents for over seventy years of successful and peaceful marriage up until he died. Despite being relatively poor by today's standards, my grandfather never bothered about material things that have become another source of divorce and killings among spouses currently whereby cases involving spouses killing their partners or fighting over maternal property are high. My grandfather used to tell me how he wondered about how some women or men could kill their spouses so as to claim their estates. He did not know that such a problem is a capitalistic legacy resulting from division of labour (Parpart & Stichter, 2016). For my grandfather, just like any other elders of his time, fighting over estates was sinful and sacrilegious next to a curse.

So, for some African people, fears of divorce and property disputes have never been the matter that would force them to enter marriage agreements or murder their spouses in order to assure themselves the right to live together. Neither did they result in spouse killing to gain material wealth. They had their ways of settling such disputes based on their environment and laws. My experience of growing in Africa shows that; for the people I know around me at work, home and school, the rate of divorce is high compared to the time traditional African marriages were rampant. The trend is reversing the situation in some societies currently whereby many young people either marry through their traditional ways or just cohabit something that was not used in Africa before the coming of colonialism and Western liberal thoughts. African education and traditions required those entering in matrimonial institutions to seek permit from their parents.

More on my grandfather, despite his *uncivility and ignorance*; he was able to know how things were going. He used to ask me how people could swear by the name of God; and thereafter tell lies. He used to say that in their culture, they used to swear by the Sun, rivers and mountains without going against their oaths. If anything, this is what the so-called "modern" religions, and of course, education brought to "uncivilised" folks in Africa. "These guys cheated us and broke our relationship so to speak," my grandpa would oft-say. Romanticising apart, the introduction of new faiths ended up becoming the end of African solidarity and peacefulness that many African societies used to enjoy for centuries. There are those, like my grandpa, who refused to join the bandwagon of faith. They still see the gods of new religions as the gods of lies as opposed to African images and concepts of truth. Such religions went to the extreme so as to try to teach their victims who their brothers and sisters were while they naturally knew their relatives. Mhango (2015) maintains that even goats, despite having small brains, know their siblings naturally. To me, such animals seem to have decolonised minds due to the fact that animals have always maintained their natural instincts.

Moreover, those who brought foreign religions of "equality" ended up discriminating against those they baptised and put under their submission. If there was a question that used to disturb my grandfather, and possibly other non-believers in neo-beliefs, is none other than saying that some places on earth are holy. My grandfather used to say that if there are holy lands, so, too, there are unholy lands. He used to call the so-called holy lands gory lands. If we face it, what do you call the act of saying that some lands are holy? This means those lands that are not included in this holiness are unholy. Is there any holy or unholy land really? If you look at the so-called holy lands you wonder if the meaning of holy you know is the same one applicable to these so-called holy lands. Try to revisit the story and history of Sumerian people in Iraq the Western myths view as the first civilisation. Despite having all such sweet names and other concomitantly unique titles such as the garden of Aden, sacred places, chosen ones and whatnots, the same are barren; and life there is harder. Ironically, most of what is said to be holy seems to be desert. Jokes aside, the concept of the "holiness" or "sacredness" has already cost the world dearly. Refer to current terrorism. Evidently, September 11th, 2001 when America's World Trade Center (WTC) was flattened, changed the world after al Qaeda revenged because the US has sent its soldiers to occupy the holy land, Saudi Arabia.

You can see the toxicity and lie of the current dominant grand narrative of making whatever the West does to mean the world even in the name of the said center. Instead of being referred to as the American Trade Center (ATC) it is referred to as the WTC as if it belonged to the entire world. Ironically, if the Dubai's Burj Khalifa were in the US or the UK would be referred to as World something. On this material date, two planes hit the then world's tallest twin buildings in downtown New York. These twin towers were regarded as US's symbol of dominance and pride. Therefore, hitting it was but hitting the pride of the sole superpower and the guardian of the current dominant grand narrative. Therefore, its impacts were felt all over the world so as to change it abruptly. In these terrorist attacks, the chief suspect was al Qaeda, a terrorist group formed by those America used to fight Russians in Afghanistan during the cold war. Its founder and leader, Osama bin Laden, was angry with America when it established close ties with Saudi's kingdom so as to be allowed to have its military base in what bin Laden regarded as a *holy land* that should not be trampled on by kaffirs (Americans). To cut a long story short, you can see the effects of calling places holy and sacred while they actually are just like any other places not referred to as that. I can argue that everybody's birth place is holy and sacred to her or him. So, under this presumption, there is a naturally

259

universal set of sacred of holy lands which the current grand narrative does not accommodate or recognise.

The holiness of certain places is the result of missionary teachings. Missionaries and their colleagues taught abuses to those they conscripted to their army of believers who can call their sisters and brothers names such as kaffirs, infidels and pagans wantonly! Actually, missionaries committed a crime against humanity as far as the freedom of culture and beliefs are concerned. For, they badly destroyed the identities of their victims so as to cause the lack self-confidence in themselves and their ways of life. It needs the courage of mad and high degree of ignorance and arrogance to call a person you find believing his way such names.

Additionally, the missionaries and colonialists desecrated the holy places of their victims by calling only colonial places holy while the whole earth is holy due to currently being the only planet with life in it in the entire universe. This cannot go on without being addressed given that sometimes the conflict between neo-faiths and traditional faiths end up causing the killing of many Indigenous people as it is currently going on in, *inter alia,* the Central African Republic (CAR) Mali and Nigeria where Africans turned against one another simply because they believe in different faiths. Basically, all this carnage results from toxic education be it secular or religious that the victims of colonialism received. It does not make any sense say for an Africa to kill another African because of religion. Such a person needs to be re-educated so much that such a person can know where the bond of his *Africanness* is. Sometimes, you do not understand why victims of colonialism and its toxic education did not learn unity and connectedness from the perpetrators. Since introducing colonialism and other crimes against humanity such as slavery, imperialism and neocolonialism, the West has always acted as one solid entity against several entities it created after dividing them. Importantly, you cannot blame the victims for their weakness due to the fact that they received toxic education they still believe is true while it does not address their needs and problems. It is not easy currently to find a white person or an Arab systematically killing another just because of any belief from Africa.

Empirically, it is a normal thing currently to find that Africans in some countries are butchering each other just because of the wrong type of education they were offered by their masters through religions. As academics, especially victims, we need to explore this anathema wherever religious proxy wars are now denying the world the peace we aspire and work for. Such a controversy, normally reminds me of my grandfather who used to ask me why God offered his son to die as a symbol of emancipation while there were other noble means such as sacrificing animals as the Africans used to do whenever they had a problem that needed their God to intercede. Though this was his take on religions, it still provokes many reasonably provocative questions we need to ask and address as we seek the causes and sources of conflict, especially faith-related ones. We need to interrogate the *holier-than-thou* tendency embedded in fake, mythical and factious religion that caused a lot of problems to those who received them wrongly thinking they were more superior and more genuine than their condemned faiths that have proved to have been better than them. This is what Roca (2010) refers to as "moral imagination" as the means of understanding moral conflict emerging from stigmatisation which may help in embarking on the journey of building broken relationship resulting from evils such as colonialism and other isms instead of quantifying unquantifiable things which is defined as the dehumanising process of *thingification* (el-Malik, 2013).

Back to the written agreements, if anything, the current capitalistic and individualistic episteme is to *thingify* almost everything as far as agreement is concerned. Therefore, professionals in the field of Conflict Resolution, we need to deal more with relationship and creating conducive environment for understanding and coexistence among the members of a human family than striving for obtaining written agreements. Agreements must be at heart before being put on writings. In the same breath, we need inclusivity in academic discourse through decolonising episteme so as to accommodate other world's narratives and institutions of knowledge. Instead of using one grand narrative in looking into issues and practises of peacemaking and delivering education, justice, among others, we need to look at how other, choked off, cut off, forgotten, sidelined and unused mechanisms can be replicated and used in addressing the problems. I know. Arguments will be made that traditional methods as they are called are only suitable in non-Western countries. This can be true. If this is the case, how then Western centric mechanisms are applied all over the world without assuming and underscoring such uniqueness and the fact that they are only suitable to Europe as traditional mechanisms are for non-European countries or societies? I vividly remember the story of a priest and an African newly baptised devotee. The priest was teaching him about his God of deliverance. He said that his God was the only God; and all other gods were untrue, and thus, they must to be abandoned and disrespected. The new African believer asked: Why should God be alone as if his parents were mean. The priest replied, "God has neither father nor mother; and he was not born and he can't be born. The convict asked "if he can't be born, how did you know he is not she is?"

The priest replied "he is because of majestic qualification." The convict replied "well done sir, majestic qualification like that of the queen of England who invented colonialism and slavery; and exported them to Africa?"

"No. Majestic qualification is not only assigned to the queen. It can be used even to refer to the king." The priest replied as he smiled bitterly for being challenged by a new soul that traditionally was supposedly duty bound to respect him and believe in whatever nonsense said. This is what believing is.

The newly baptised believer went on asking: "If your god was not born, then how did he come to the existence?" The priest replied "you cannot know. This is why you need to believe." The newly baptised devotee quipped. "If I cannot know, how did you know?" He paused and went on "just like you who don't know however you pretend to know?" The priest replied sarcastically and vividly annoyed "it doesn't mean that I don't know. I know our God; the Lord of the universe cannot be seen. This is why you need to believe." The new believer reciprocated saying "thanks. If you respect the God you cannot see while you abuse those you can see, there must be a problem. Take your knowledge. I will retain my ignorance that has no border with your knowledge." Once more, the priest replied sarcastically though "new soul, remember. I am

262

teaching you what is written and what is written is forever, *Scripta est manent*." The new soul quipped "is it written in stones that refuse us to use our brains?" No reply. Heavy silence then followed.

To cut a long story short, the convict ended up being excommunicated from the church for committing the sin of reasoning instead of blindly believing which is the essence of colonised and toxic education that forced people to believe without doubting and interrogating them. Notably, this story is aimed at proving that the victims of colonisation did not just receive all those lies cowardly, sheepishly and unreasonably. Some tried even harder save that they were overpowered, especially after their secrets were sold to the invaders that used such secrets to finish their victims.

Back to the written agreements, I know many Aboriginal peoples abhor and disregard written agreements knowingly that they are not written in hearts. They are dead right to do so. Written agreements, apart from being foreign to Aboriginal peoples, show how trust is amiss between the parties to the agreement so as to need the force of law to enforce them. This is strange and ridiculous, for example, for Africans and other collectivistic societies whose, lives, prosperity and wellbeing depended on their connectedness and interdependency. So, too, apart from being viewed as an imposition, the victims of written agreements view them as the tools of colonialism dubiously used to claim land in many colonised countries. Such a view is still freshly palpable to the victims. Furthermore, even the stigma of being colonised by the means of written agreements is still there. Therefore, when the proscriptions of written agreements are offered to its victims, apart from opening the wounds, it re-traumatises them wantonly. Arguably, this is why decolonised education proposes that issue of written agreements needs to be addressed in order to find the middle ground. We can fulfill the essence of peace by using the force of law or the force of love as Mandela (1994, p. 54) cited in Nussubaun (2003) would put it saying that "people must learn to hate, and if they can learn to hate, they can be taught to love, for love comes more naturally to the human heart than its opposite" (p. 24). Notably, the disregard for agreement resulting from appending signatures has its origin in the fact that when colonisers went to Africa and other places that they colonised, they used written agreements obtained by means of deceit as tools of legalising their claims that culminated in full-fledged colonisation. You can see this in some language like Swahili whereby Europeans wrongly known as whites are referred to as *wazungu* or those who can change position at any time or the unpredictable and unreliable ones. All this comes from the fact that when *wazungu* or those who cannot be trusted or those that are unpredictable came to Africa, they used bogus and written agreements to secure their unpredictable and unrespectable ways of invading and occupying Africa for years. I think such derogatory way of referring to Europeans either came out anger or the way Africans felt after being betrayed, specifically after trusting them thereby signing the agreements they wrongly thought were genuine, sincere and aimed at fostering good and mutual relationship between the duo. Or maybe, from their grand narrative, Africans were trying to give their betrayers a bad name for future generations to be cautious of if not the self-aggrandisement of their grand narrative. Also, this may be construed as the evidence that shows that the crime that colonial powers committed to Africans has never been forgotten. For, the name speaks volumes that the future users of the same language are likely to inherit this fact through the meanings attached to the name. And thus, become wary of such a people due to the experiences of those who lived before them.

Accordingly, I must state clearly. The aim of taking on written agreements, as agent of colonialism, should not be misconstrued as condemning it entirely. The art of writing should not be regarded as a bad one or the best one. We need to appreciate and apply other means of enhancing peace and understanding among the world family. Importantly, the use of the art of writing needs more scrutiny than just believing in what Latin proverb refers to as *scripta est manent* to mean what is written is permanent or is forever; and thus it is always true even if it has some flaws. Is it forever truly or lie? Is such a take logically helpful in the current environment with many victims of written lies as espoused by colonial and toxic education? If anything, this is where the drive to decolonise education lies. Can truth apply in *scipta est manent* in a given situation in which some *truths*, for instance, about the Weapons of Mass Destruction (WMD) in Iraq, happen to be a hoax? Is this *scripta est manent* understanding permanent *vis-à-vis* the WMD lie really? Should we concern ourselves with the eternity of what is written or its truthfulness or untruthfulness before we believe and uphold or interrogate it? Hence, written agreements are not preferred in many local and rural settings the same way it is appreciated and respected in Western culture. Through those written agreements Africans and others were enslaved and colonised for centuries if not decades.

Why Africans and other Aboriginal peoples abhorred and despised written agreements? Indeed, they had their own practical and reliable ways of entering into agreements and keeping certainty legality and validity of the agreements among agreeing parties. They had their mechanisms of abiding by agreements even if those agreements were not written. Oaths, vows or words of trust (all done orally) used to guarantee the fulfilment of the commitment so entered or agreed upon. This was the case even in Europe. Rutgers (2009) observes that "originally, what we can call, a true oath was required, i.e. a solemn promise involving a reference to a transcendental being (God or gods) as witness and avenger" (p. 5). Which God is this; is the question that we can pose (Milhizer, 2009). You see. Oaths saved the purpose of guaranteeing security, be it under God or god or "natural and universal custom" that has been found virtually everywhere human society exists" (*Ibid*). Again, when manipulative neo-faiths invaded Africa, they dubiously espoused only their gods they called God. For Aboriginal peoples, especially in some parts of Africa, once a king or chief was sworn in, it was not easy for him to go against his oaths. Two things would happen whenever this occurred. Either the king or chief would die or being forced out of power. Failing to honour one's oath in African traditions such those of Igbo in Nigeria is a crime of perjury which seeks capital punishment or miseries as Okafor cited in Oraegbunam (2009) notes that "the perjurer may die as the result or he may suffer grave misfortune or illness" (p. 70). If we apply the same rationale based on the culture of a certain people today: How many presidents and premiers that were sworn in under the Western or Middle Eastern Gods (Bible and Quran) do we have currently that swear to protect their countries and end up vending them?

For many Aboriginal peoples, signing agreements as means of resolving conflict can, as noted above, end up re-traumatising them, especially for those who accurately and truly know their history *vis-à-vis* colonialism and its effects. Agreements that resulted to the colonisation of Africa will be always suspected the same way Residential Schools were in Canadian history whereby the mentioning of Residential School opens a can of worms for Aboriginal peoples who attribute the miseries that befell their families to such arrangements resulting from written agreements. For, they enhanced the invasion and grabbing of their land and country. This is especially true when we consider how Britain became an academic hub of the world during its heydays as Fulford & Kitson (2005) note that "it is often pointed out that the historical moment which saw the emergence of the academic discipline of English also produced a distinct brand of colonialism" (p. 3) that subsumed other civilisations of the world based on its grand narrative that became dominant for many years thereafter. Given that education draws from various disciplines, if we will, chances of decolonising colonial practices are high as indicated in mediation above. Essentially, the dominance of the Western grand narrative in theory and practices is a product of what Said (2012) refers to as grand imperialism revolving around cultural dominance. This is why Western experiments have dominated many fields of science and social science not to mention being applied universally today.

9

Prescriptive Nature of Colonial and Toxic Education: How the Dominant Grand Narrative Monopolised Knowledge

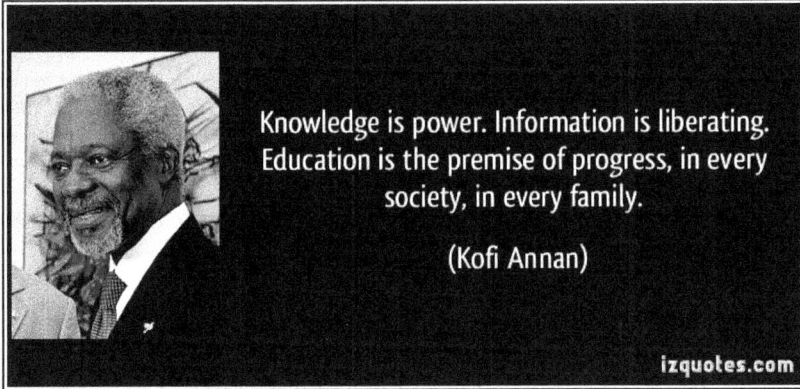

Figure 14; photo courtesy of izquote.com

Although colonialism was abolished, its tentacles and toxicity were left behind under neocolonialism which can be defined as the predatory practise wherein the country so colonised is granted independence with hidden intentions of a colonial state to exploit it (Boshoff, 2009; and Sangmpam, 2012). This is very true up until now. For, former colonies enjoy having their flags but not total independence. If you compare the lives of the people in former colonies to those of the people that colonised these countries, you can vividly notice the difference. The economies of ex-colonies still depend on their former colonisers. Essentially, since independence, clientele relationship has been ongoing between colonial masters and their former colonies from the day African countries gained their political independence. For, most of them are still depending on handouts in materials and policies from their former colonial masters under the sweet name of aid. Mhango (2016) calls such dependence the "second-hand everything" from the West to former colonies the situation he equates to the tendency of chickens that eat what they do not produce and produce what they do not eat.

Furthermore, such dependency brings us to the question: Why don't these victims question the authorities that allow others to decide their fate without consulting with them; and when they do, they overrule their decisions? It needs decolonised education to embark on such undertakings. Basically, the current world system is more prescriptive than creative or elicitive as we will see later. I wonder how people who pretend to be truly educated to go around praise themselves that they are free while what makes them think they are is a mere cloth known as a flag. Hume (1994) makes a very constructive advice as far as total freedom is concerned. He admonishes people to fight for freedom so that they can live as dignified people. He quotes his father who argues that "you can't eat a flag" (p. 1088). Hume maintains that, instead of fighting about and for raising flags, people should fight for the right for human beings to exist or live peacefully, equally and equitably but not otherwise as it currently is whereby the world is divided into exploitative and unfair worlds such as the first world, the second and the third wolds. These are the view of the person who lived under colonisation by his European counterparts firsthand.

Looking at African countries with their flags, I always wonder. Are they truly independent? Whatever the answer, I still wonder why over fifty years down the line, Africa's education has never enabled African countries to take decisive measures to alleviate or arrest the situation they are facing. For, they have always depended on aid from their former colonial powers. And much of the aid either financial or technical that African countries receive always has strings attached on to it. Apart from their economies' dependency on their former colonial powers, Africa's *political health,* too, is determined by Western hegemonic imperialists. Ironically, despite such an awkward situation that has existed for over a half-century, African countries have kept quiet due to receiving toxic education that is full of colonial baggage. With such mindsets, such countries are unsecured. Thus, they need to embark on the decolonisation of their epistemes in order to decolonise their minds and mindsets altogether so that they catch up and compete with their former colonial masters. Doing so will augment them to have the guts and edge that will enable them to rebel against and questioning the dominant grand narrative that has kept them in shackles for many years even after getting their flag independence over a half of a decade ago. Some scholars explore the history of insecurity resulting from clientele relationship–that always causes conflict–in regards to human security. Such scholars argue that the imperialistic West has caused many more deaths and miseries than any other civilisation we know of today. Such death were caused either by fighting among themselves–refer to the WWI and the WWII–or the tendency of sponsoring and supporting proxy wars in other countries not to mention the hardship their economic policies cause to the economies of their former colonies. And this is a historical factor that is entrenched in the dividing; and thereby weakening Africa especially in order to exploit and dominate it indefinitely. The Commission for Africa cited in Battersby & Siracusa (2009) posits that "'the division of Africa into its present countries was the product of Western interests, not African minds" (p. 18). This is an open secret that every African and Western academic knows full well.

Again, if you ask African academics and politicians what they have done for the remedying of this situation in Africa in order to do away with the problems their division has caused, I do not know if you will get right answer. I always wonder. If African leaders know the truth that their countries are weak because they were divided, why don't they work on it to truly liberate their countries and continent by reunifying Africa? The answer lies on the type of education they obtained from their former colonial masters. In the 50s Kwame Nkrumah, Ghanaian first president, wanted to unite Africa. He did not succeed after some countries–either used by their colonial masters or geared by narrow interests–sabotaged the entire project. Worse enough, even today when regional unification is encouraged, the same still happens whenever the interests of former colonial masters are endangered. Mhango discusses this in details in his coming book, *Africa's Best and Worst President: How Neocolonialism and Imperialism Maintained Venal Rules in Africa.*

Another thing apart from the division of Africa that can show how the current education does not work or serve the interests of the world, especially for the victims of colonialism and other neo-isms can be drawn from current practises. For example, when, colonial administration introduced the death sentence to Africa in order to deal with those who opposed it, such a move was not an issue at the time it was introduced. Those fighting for human rights did not see it as a gross violation of and cruelty against human right to life; and if they did, it was not regarded a gross violation of human rights as it currently is viewed. This is because, colonialism wanted to get rid of it opponents who happen to be the victims.

Again, after African countries became independent, most of them kept the death sentence in their statutory books so that African presidents could use it to fix and finish their opponents. Ironically, human rights activists of the time watched without doing anything so as to force us question their sincerity today. All this can be attributed to toxic education that did not see colonialism as a crime against humanity. However, now things have changed dramatically; and the interests of the West are safe. Therefore, the same West that introduced the same penalty is propagating that Africa must abolish death sentence while some countries in the West such as the US still regularly use it (Smith, 2012). Interestingly, no human rights activists are now questioning or taxing the US and the West come clean about death sentence despite its callousness. Paradoxically, when colonial administration introduced the same, it seems; it was *humane* and a right thing to do. Due to the toxicity of the education, therefore, nobody questioned its legality or the rationale of such a double standard. To the contrary, currently, many countries in the world are grappling with death sentence. Sometimes, some countries want to abolish it but people want it to stay; sometimes it is vice versa. Empirical evidence shows that, for example, many African societies did not have death sentence. Among many, Onuoha (2013) notes that in Nigeria, local chiefs and emirs "most traditional societies preferred to employ banishment as an alternative to death penalty" (p. 12). This shows that traditional justice did not have a room for the death sentence except for Buganda and Nigeria (Bernault, 2007). Even currently, Africans are still cagey about death penalty. For example, Metz (2007) cites an example wherein the South African Constitutional Court uniformly judged Ubuntu to be incompatible with the death penalty or any retributive reasoning that could underwrite it. As noted above, before the introduction of colonial rule, many African chiefs and kings did not sentence their subject to death. Instead, when somebody committed murder, he was repatriated with his family so that he could look after it in his maternal place or wherever the society decided or deemed fit for him to go.

In other African societies, when murder occurred, they consulted the oracles by invoking the ancestors to administer justice. Kasomo (2010) observes that "any bad experience such as killing or pouring of kinsman's blood in a conflict would cause anger to the ancestors. Such an action demanded a sacrifice to propitiate the angry ancestors; otherwise a calamity would befall the wrongdoer" (p. 25). This tells and shows how capital punishment is a product-cum-legacy of colonialism. Hynd (2008) maintains that "capital punishment has a long and controversial history in Africa, beginning largely in the colonial period" (p. 403). Again, the question that needs to be asked is: Why now countries are struggling about what to do with murderers while such a good practice of not killing killers is known to have been practised in Africa still lingers? Simple logic dictates that Africans did not practise an eye-for-an-eye justice.

Instead, such justice was brought by some religions. The Bible stipulates: "O Lord, thou God of vengeance, / thou God of vengeance, shine forth" (Ps. 94.1), "for the Lord God of recompenses shall surely requite" (Jer. 51.56) also see Quran (5:32). Some religions went even ahead allowing their followers to kill whoever oppose their god or religion without underscoring the fact that uncontaminated Africans or other Aboriginal peoples could not fall under their jurisdiction while the same religions thrived by abusing, despising and misconstruing and their own religions and ways of life. Although African traditions did not allow death penalty, there was an exception to the general rule. For example, in Buganda, Kabaka ordered the massacres of Christian convicts as Banja (2008) notes that Kabaka (King) Mwanga of Buganda killed his subjects from 1885–887. Again, you can see that such a brutal punishment was introduced after colonial agents started to dupe Africans to join their faiths something that infuriated Kabaka so as to replicate the practice on his own people, especially those who betrayed the society.

Furthermore, death penalty can be traced in the Bible (Matthew 27:32-56) and the Quran (6:151). In these two books of neo-religion, capital punishment is legally administered to those convicted of some crimes according to their interpretations. Therefore, in addressing the problem of capital punishment, Africans, through decolonised education, can go back to their roots to study how such matters were handled without shedding more blood. The past has the keys to the future in this matter. Apart from having somewhere to learn from, namely, African traditional ways of addressing homicide, African cultures have something even more workable and practicable. Killing somebody, be it illegally, or legally, is violence and totally unacceptable regardless who does so. So, if we decolonise toxic education to allow the opportunity to studying African traditional mechanisms of conflict resolution that were used when homicide was committed, surely, such mechanisms can help countries and societies that are now grappling with people sentenced to death. Further, such mechanisms provide an alternative. By having such practices against death penalty, we would be able to see and show them how archaic and brutal the practice is. History has it that capital punishment was brought by colonisers in Africa. As argued above, the purpose of imposing death sentence was to rid the society of those perceived to be a threat to colonial administration or those who opposed their stooges in office in after African countries got independence by imposing capital punishment. Colonial administration caused violence and gross violations of human rights in Africa.

The importation of violence to Africa does not end up with death penalty. Arguably, even corporal punishment as well was introduced by missionaries who were the agents of colonial administration in Africa not to mention the colonialists themselves. For Africans, before the introduction of colonial rule, it was a shame for an adult to be beaten under whatever circumstances.

First of all, in many African societies, delivering justice was the venue for ancestors and oracles but not humans. Furthermore, on corporal punishments, many stories about the corporal punishment, for instance, in Tanzania, show that this punishment was introduced by Germany colonisers. Apart from Germans, Killingray & Plaut (2012) note that British colonial rule in Africa sanctioned corporal punishment they used to refer to as "the rod of the empire" (p. 201). One wonders; how could the so-called enlightened people that invaded to *civilise* Africa could not see such a simple thing that corporal punishment was inhumane as they hypocritically do today. Deconstructed-cum-decolonised epistemes will seek the answers to such questions. Likewise, Durrant (2008) maintains that it is the British Colonial period in Africa that introduced and institutionalised corporal punishment, including whipping, flogging, and caning that was applied to African laborers, soldiers, prisoners, and schoolchildren.

Corporal punishment traces its roots to Europe which exported it to Africa and left it there after handing over freedom to former colonies. In South Africa, for example, corporal punishment was introduced almost at the same time it was carried out in Nigeria. In South Africa corporal punishment was applied on Africans as the tool of dehumanising and harassing them; and there was an assumption that whipping is the only thing that, like horses, Africans understand (Super, 2011). As for corporal punishments in schools and partly homes, it is an extension from colonial rule. African ways of teaching were much more based on relationship (Agbenyega, 2006) and strict codes–wherein young respected the old–were practised without a cane. Essentially, colonial powers and their agents introduced this sort of punishment among others, in order to humiliate and threaten Africans so that they could subjugate them and thereby exploit them.

Ironically, now the same criminals are accusing those to whom they introduced the crime of committing the same crime. There is a lot of evidence to show that **corporal punishment** and other cruel punishments were introduced by colonial rule in many places. For example, Aboriginal peoples in the Americas, just like Africans, did not use corporal punishment. Furniss (1995, p. 49) cited in Pearce, Christian, Patterson, Norris, Moniruzzaman, Craib, Schechter & Spittal, 2008) observe that "in sharp contrast to traditional Aboriginal systems of learning, the missionary-teachers of residential schools

273

utilized "strict discipline, regimented behaviour, submission to authority, and corporal punishment" (p. 2186).

I remember; when I was a child, I used to be threatened with two people when I was crying namely, the policeman and the teacher. You could hear this at school or home where a teacher or parent who used to whack children was known as a German due to the fact that, in this part of the world, it is the Germans who introduced corporal punishment. The evidence to support this argument is still vivid and all over places in Africa. For example, in Tanzania, teachers are more revered, feared and respected somehow than parents simply because they have "the rod of the empire" to use against those who do not respect their commands. Ask any African student or professor or anybody who went through colonial education system in Africa. The answer will be the same that teachers were, and are still feared due to their power to unleash corporal punishment that missionaries and colonial powers introduced.

I remember when I was young. When a child misbehaved, parents would threaten him or her that they would tell his or her teacher. All the same, in Africa, even brutal leaders are still feared because the first colonial rulers were brutal; and would mete out corporal punishment even on adults. My mentor, Sean Byrne is a good witness. For, when I was communicating him via email and the way he replied, I told him that, in Africa of my time, such a thing was unthinkable to happen between a professor and a student. By that time Professors were like gods in Africa. There is now way a student would call his professor by name without adding the title Dr. or Professor. I do not know if this has changed. Police officers are more feared than chief's guards and officers were feared at the time before the introduction of colonial government. Colonial administration was a brutal system or a violent project as noted in the first chapter. So, most of its tools of administration were violent. And this was not accidental. Violence and brutality were purposely used as the means of instilling fear in people so as to control; and force them to carry out orders without questioning. Religious institutions, too, used the same brutality despite preaching love for some. Such brutality oozed down to even individual even after colonies became independent. In a nutshell, this is the genesis of corporal punishment in many Aboriginal societies all over the world.

The System Asks for the Overhaul

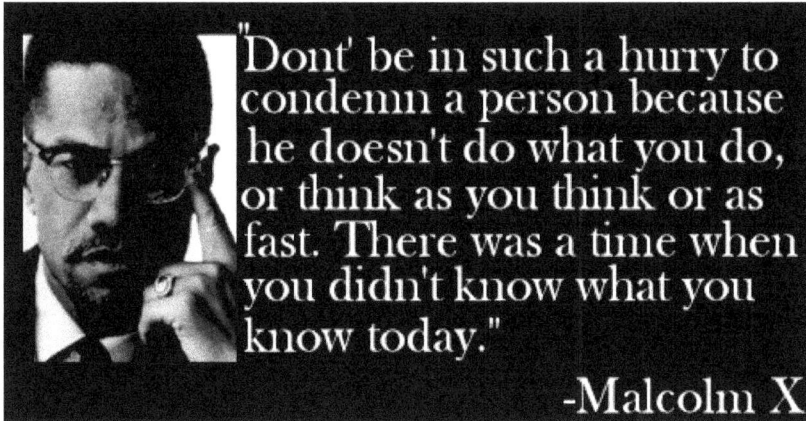

Figure 15 courtesy of solidmars.deviantart.com

Due to the neoliberal style of doing things based on the current dominant grand narrative, the world has evidenced many conflicts resulting from colonial leftovers among which is toxic education this volume seeks to decolonise and detoxify. Although this can sound weird to some quarters that are comfortably in bed with this toxic education, the truth is; we need to overhaul the current system of education by underscoring the agenda behind neoliberal drive that uses market to exploit others as the legacy of toxic education whose results can be easily seen in the above mentioned Africa's dependence on its former colonial masters. Jeong (2005) smidgens it down nicely as he notes that "the notion of "neo-liberal peacebuilding" characterised by establishment of formal democratic processes combined with promotion of market economy has been accepted almost universally in spite of reservations about its application strategies" (pp. 10-11). Here decolonised education will help us to assess if truly neoliberal policies were accepted or superimposed universally. How many times have you heard Western countries emphasise the introduction of its brand of democracy in other countries' epistemes? If anything, the nature of prescription of almost everything draws its powers and ruses from this system. This begs a question by observing two important terms, formal democracy and the promotion of free market which go hand in hand. Whose market and democracy for who and whose interests? Whose democracy and for who? Why only formal not informal if what we need is people to rule themselves as they deem fit as free people?

Essentially, many conflicts the world currently evidences, mainly those resulting from resources, have the root here. For countries that are used as consumers without being allowed to produce for their own consumption, such a neoliberal democracy cannot bring peace to them. And this is where we query the essence of the type of education the leaders of such countries got.

Thus, as academics, we need to underscore this; and address it well. This is why decolonising the education become crucially necessary. When this volume talks about free market, for poor countries, it denotes allowing their markets be flooded with products from rich countries to whose markets they have no ease and free access as a sign of reciprocity. Is this fair? Isn't this a good source of conflict, particularly due to the fact that some rich countries support and sponsor some corrupt governments to rob their people and supply them raw materials? With such an exploitative and unfair relationship, there cannot be stable and sustainable justice and peace in poor countries. This needs to change for the good future of the whole world. And it is only decolonised education that can bring about such changes. Jeong argues that neoliberal democracy stressed formal institutions and political representation through election. Is this feasible or controversial? Poor countries have leaders who rig elections and stay in power against the will of the majority. The same make sure that they go to bed with rich countries so as to remain in power. Such a practice itself has created a lot of conflicts in many countries. So, banking on election does not help anything if the same can be–easily and in most cases it is the case–rigged. For whose interests rigging governments are in power? Another offshoot of such failed and preferential policies is the creation of ethnic conflicts in Africa whereby power in many countries–despite being referred to as democratic–revolves around family, clan and ethnic lines. Equatorial Guinea, Gabon, Togo, and Uganda provide an ideal example. Other dictatorships that are referred to as democracy are run by dictatorial political parties such as those in Mozambique, South Africa, Tanzania, and Zimbabwe.

Traditional mechanisms for the management of ethnic relations and resolution of conflict had some good provisions for good ethnic relationship aiming at enhancing peacefulness, coexistence, cooperation and relative social stability despite the fact that they are not often being totally democratic just like democracy itself. Mitja Zagar in (Byrne & Irvin, 2000) shows how worse the imposition or adoption of prescriptive conflict resolution mechanisms can be. Zagar holds that the former Yugoslavia, among other reasons, collapsed because there were no conflict resolution mechanisms that were put in place to deal with ethnic conflicts at the time of its collapse and thereafter. When such failures occur, Mac Ginty (2008) recommends that there must be the hybridisation, or using mixed forms of conflict resolution mechanism in which Western and the so-called traditional ones should be used to address the conflict.

I can say, therefore, that a big problem was not only the lack of conflict mechanisms but also the lack of traditional conflict resolution mechanisms suitable for Yugoslavian environment. This has been the case in many conflicts whereby Western conflict resolution mechanisms were applied in trying to resolve conflict and failed as indicated in Angola the foregoing chapters. Again, what should we do where there is the lack of conflict resolution mechanisms? For the case of the former Yugoslavia federation, the problem was the lack of mechanisms by which to manage the conflict systemically. To the contrary, at societal level, there were some conflict resolution mechanisms but the government did not want to accommodate or apply them due to not being able to see and value them. All this can be attributed at the type of education that was used in Yugoslavia at the time. Such lacunae contributed more in exacerbating the conflict in the former Yugoslavia federation as it was in many other countries.

Among conflict scholars, John-Paul Lederach is renowned for admitting the weakness of Western mechanisms of conflict resolutions resulting from the dominance of its grand narrative. This does not mean that all Western conflict mechanisms for dealing with conflicts are condemned. What is condemned is Western nature of having answers for all problems and people in all circumstance or prescribing everything as if all societies are Western even where it knows that its answers do not address the problem. Again, in maintaining its hegemony, the West still applies its conflict resolution mechanisms either aiming at maintaining its hegemony or experimenting them. Jeong (2005) notes that "an insistence on too rigid terms for settlement produces a political crisis" (p. 6) in dealing with the settlement of conflicts, especially after violent conflicts have occurred due to the lack of mechanisms that can accommodate all interests of parties to conflict. This has happened in many conflicts such as Burundi, Liberia, DRC, Sudan and elsewhere.

Profoundly, Western model of conflict resolution varies from non-Western ones. For example, as indicated in the foregoing chapters, the signing of agreement is more emphasised than relationship is. In his book *The Moral Imagination*, Lederach devotes the entire chapter discussing serendipity to mean being flexible; and staying put in dealing with conflicts. He argues that mediators need to exhaust all possibilities instead of depending on a linear way of looking at things; which can be detrimental and counterproductive. He calls this move going "sideways" instead of using tunnel vision by offering and thinking about new ways of looking at conflict by emphasising flexibility, serendipity, humility creativity, collectability among other. By humility, Lederach admonishes us to respect the cultures and ways of others while by serendipity Lederach means to make adventure in the quest of resolving a conflict. Lederach cites an example wherein he admits that his university knowledge was not the only thing that helped him to deal with the conflict in Costa Rica. He talks about an incident when Yatama Commandos met in his house. When he was out, his wife came home to find her house full of invaders she did not know. After introducing one another, Lederach's wife asked her guests if she could make a meal for them. They agreed and from that meal, trust was built so as to go ahead with dialogue. What would have happened had the duo met in a formal office? This adds another aspect of space. So, this volume suggests that we go sideways by accommodating other conflict mechanisms from other grand narratives so that we can enrich the ones we already have. We need to let various models of conflict resolution complement each other instead of looking at other as impotent. By accommodating other cultures and their models of conflict resolution, we will dispel suspicion that has been going on for a long time between Western model of conflict resolution and other cultures. We need to build cooperation and trust in making the world peaceful, mainly at this time it is highly globalised.

In many practises and theories, Western episteme is too prescriptive, especially on how to deal with problems almost in all Western and traditional settings. It prescribes the setting of how to deal the problems based on Western solutions even to the problems that do not need such formulas and solutions. Ironically, such a take is seen as empowering to those receiving them. How do you empower people already with power in their collective roles? Although Western culture tends to look at other cultures as unequal, it has never been equal itself. Women in a Western society are still exploited because of their gender. This is different from some non-Western societies. For example, Many Aboriginal peoples have their ways of enhancing equality through obligations and contributions to the society. Murithi (2006b) maintains that "people derive their sense of meaning from their culture. What does it mean to be human?" (p. 26). We need to answer this question. What does it mean to be human? This question may seem to be simple.

Actually, it is very sophisticated due to the way we perceive ourselves and others and the way others perceive us. So, in trying to define what it means to be human two points of views may apply namely, how I view and perceive myself and how others view and perceive me. So, what it means to be human for me is different from others; given that I am unique and the way I perceive myself is different from the way others perceive me. The same applies to how I perceive others. The way they perceive themselves is better than I perceive them. I know myself as a unique entity more than anybody around me. Sometimes, when we think about what is it that I am, I the one who says my name, my soul, my body, my wife or husband, my children, my property and so on. This person is more than the person with the name I carry. It is more than the body the authorities take photo of and issue identity card to. I am more than that. And this idea that owns everything that I claim to own is very complicated.

Thus, I am more who I am. So, too, I more than that entity or person whom people define me to be. This "me" or "I" is the one I am talking of that has suffered from toxic education that colonialism brought to many Indigenous people of the world. To deal with such a rebellious "I", we need to have decolonised education. For, it will enable us to see each other in this equal and hidden personality instead of colour or status. With such education, we will be able to negotiate and dialogue as equals who deserve everything equally due to sharing the same needs and vulnerabilities as humans. This rebelling person that wants education to be decolonised cannot be seen. If you want to see me, you just see what my body displays that is not me entirely. This is why Western hegemonic education has been trying to reinvent and recreate others in a wrong way. It is simply because it is unable to see the real and true them (persona).

For example, many academics use the word animist to refer to people who do not believe in neo-religions without asking them who they are. Such tendency accompanies every tag, animist, feminists, traditionalists etc. This is an insult to such people to prescribe them the name they do not want or even know. Before the term animist was introduced, missionaries used to use a derogatory term pagan which means an irreligious or hedonistic person or an uncivilised or unenlightened person. This is not right. Not believing in neo-religions does not mean that one has no religion. How many conflict resolution professionals and academics are still using such derogative terms? Due to the blindness and toxicity in the current egoistic education system, we tend not to see such insults we heave on others. Conflict resolution professionals, practitioners, students and academics need to avoid using derogatory languages. Religious people–for their vest interests–tend to disparage their opponents so as to weaken them; and therefore, thereafter subsume or subjugate them. Whom are we weakening as professionals or academics? I do not wonder to hear Muslims, for example, calling non-Muslims kaffirs or Christians calling other sinners and other bad names. Based on their duplicity, *modus operandi*, and toxic education, they do these things purposely however detrimental they are. *Holier than thou* tendency is not supposed to apply to education or conflict resolution studies in particular; for academics and whoever have extra skills and knowledge are not better than any. Instead, they have better skills in dealing with some problems for the benefit of the entire human family. This is the difference between academics and laypeople.

Going back to prescriptive episteme the dominant grand narrative espouses, it prescribes how to divide time. It also prescribes some frameworks and timeframes of how to deal with issues using techno nuances and parlance. All this prescription is done without considering other grand narrative, civilisations and cultures as if they have never existed. For example, we need to know if the language we use in addressing a certain problem is understandable and clear for those we sometimes teach either through workshops or seminars how to deal with the problem[s]. Do we ask them to teach us the language they understand so that we can learn and use it to deliver our message? Do we ask them to teach us how they manage or deal with the problem[s] or how they would like to see their problems they face given that, to them, challenges and problems are not a new thing just like the knowledge we bring in from our grand narrative? Coming with our r baggage of prescription is not is not wrong, good or bad. Save that we need to accommodate other mechanisms from other cultures which do not subscribe to prescriptive regime of dealing with challenges and problems.

I am from CRS as I admitted from the outset. Therefore, many of my examples come from my field. For example, in the conflict involving people from other non-Western cultures, prescribing what to do when dealing with conflict without understanding their practices in conflict resolution are arbitrary. So, too, constructing a road or a dam without consulting those you expect to benefit from it is arbitrary and abusing them. For instance, Western mode of conflict resolution prescribes that when dealing with conflict we need to empower the powerless and reduce power from the powerful. This might be right in some instances and wrong in others. In societies were seniority is important, putting people at par might result into failing to understand and appreciating power arrangement and power dynamics thus, fail to resolve the conflict. There is no way you can want me to be at par with my father; and make me happy so as to feel that I am comfortably and truly empowered. The same is different from the person coming from individualistic society where parents are just normal human beings as opposed to some collectivistic, especially African societies where parents are but like gods on earth. To deal with the conflict in such a setting, we need to appreciate and uphold local practices. Although, this can be seen as a weird suggestion or support to inequality, this is not the case. In some cultures weakness can be seen as strength as it was in the case of the tribe without a king in the foregoing chapter, especially if the weak know how to use this weakness also as it was in the case of Liberia long time and bloodletting conflict. When women humbly confronted Charles Taylor, former Liberian warlord who committed grave atrocities against humanity, he did not perceive any threat from them; because he regarded them as weak creatures that could not harm him or snatch his dear power away. In the eyes of Western mode of conflict resolution, what women did in Liberia was degrading, sexual discrimination, more insane and a mere impossible. Again, if you look at how women used their weakness as their strength, you will appreciate the fact that equality sometimes is immaterial in some conflict up until the solution[s] has been found. To cut a long story short, Liberian women were able to soften Taylor who ended up handing power over. Thereafter, it became easy for the international community that had failed for long time to net him to indict him. Using their weakness, against all odds, Liberian women were able to return the jinni in the bottle, and Liberia is now peaceful and a little bit democratic.

Another example comes from African court jesters. However weaker they seemed to be compared to the king; they were able to pacify the king, especially when they thought he was going astray. Such a tradition used to maintain peace by: 1) correcting the king when he was wrong and 2) enabling those who wanted to talk with or see the king to easily access him. And thus rule competently and peacefully. Sometimes, I tend to wonder. How can Western culture sanction the powers of say, president, PM and other political personnel in day-to-day life of a nation but fail to appreciate that there is no way all people can be treated equally, especially during conflict. Why do we prefer prominent people to mediate high profile conflicts more than professionals in the field? The logic is simple that sometimes power imbalance can be an impetus that can help us to solve the problem as we have seen what transpired in Liberia. The success resulting from power imbalance based on the culture can be summed up in the words of Alaga (n.d.) who maintains that:

> Today, the women of Liberia serve as an example to women and communities all around the world. In Liberia, their work in bringing about peace and electing a female president continues to generate positive results for the women and people of Liberia. They have also, to some extent, reversed the common trend that women tend to be "relegated to the background in the aftermath of wars and armed conflicts in spite of their active participation in bringing conflicts to a halt, especially during formal peace negotiations and post-conflict reconstruction processes (p. 4).

Women role in Indigenous conflict resolution does not end up in Liberia. African traditions empowered women as far as peacemaking is concerned. And the logic here was simple that, apart from the concept of equality—which is totally different from Western society—women know the pains of birthing firsthand. In many instances in many African cultures, when a husband fought with his wife, his mother would go and punish her son for that; and this was kept secret in order to avoid spilling the beans which would make her son a laughingstock. Swahili sage has it that *Mke hapigwi kwa ngumi wala mateke bali kwa upande wa khanga* namely, a woman is not punched or kicked but with a piece of cloth. This saying is self-explanatory as far as woman's treatment in conflict is concerned in Swahili culture. However, after the introduction of colonial practices, things changed. Africa has become one of the leading continents in women battering. Despite that, compare to Asia where honour killings and the likes have claimed many live, African traditions still have a vital role to play.

At a societal level, when grandmothers felt that things were not going well, they would issue a warning which was a threat by nature to the authority to rectify things. When it happened that the authority ignored them, they would strike by stripping naked as a last recourse of knocking sense into the authorities. There was a belief, and it still is, that looking at the nudity of senior women is curse. If anything, this sort of weapon was rarely used. It was like a nuclear bomb among Africans. Therefore, using it was not an easy thing to contemplate for both sides; otherwise there were necessity for one party to conflict and rigidity on the other party to conflict. Even when the authority became hard-headed so as to require the use of this weapon, those in power would end up in calamities and shame. As of recently, this intimidatingly powerful-but-rarely-used weapon was used in Kenya when the government wanted to erect a multi-storey building in Uhuru Park in 1980s in Nairobi. The late Professor Wangari Mathai organised senior women who stripped naked after fasting to no avail. Fasting was used as a warning for the government that there could be another way of twisting its arms. Nivola (2008) observes that "one of her most memorable undertakings is when the struggle to save Uhuru Park in 1980s and Karura Forest in 1990s" (p. 5). Indeed, nudity saved Uhuru Park and Karura forest.

In explaining what this weapon of nudity is Turner in Ekine, 2008 cited in Tyler (2013) notes that:

> [T]he [naked] curse is invoked only under the most extreme of circumstances. Before it is even threatened, women usually take a formal vow to honour the enormity of its symbolism. We all come into the world through the vagina. By exposing the vagina, the women are saying: 'We are hereby taking back the life we gave you,' [...] it's about bringing forth life and denying life through social ostracism, which is a kind of social execution. Men who are exposed are viewed as dead (p. 214)

I know. This may sound outlandish for those who do not believe in it. Again, if it works, why should we underestimate it? And of course, it worked in Kenya whereby the government—despite having police force, power, discretion, brutality, guns and all tools of intimidation—was intimidated so as to abandon its project it was hell-bent to fulfill. It is difficult for detractors to find such a belief funny and sometimes laughable. Even though, if people can believe in the God who has never been seen to protect them, why can't they believe in nudity curse? If people can believe that a cow is god or other objects, why not believing in this long time tradition that was used to make things work peaceful where other means or weapons could not work? Indeed, up until now, the curse of nakedness does exist among those who believe. All in all, "the curse of nakedness" shows how powerful women can be, if they well utilise some practices and resources under their disposal. What a cheap and powerful weapon! However, African mechanisms of conflict resolution suggest that during the conflict, we need to empower those thought to be powerless. Under such circumstances women have already empowered by the society by recognising an important role they can play if they apply nudity if need be. It is this belief and readiness to accommodate it that makes the curse of nudity strongly effective.

A woman was, and still is, respected in Indigenous societies. Her body was highly respected so as to treat it in a special way. In Africa, even when, women, stripped naked as an act of making an ultimatum, their demands were heard, met and respected thereof. This does not mean that African bodies were not naked however. There are some societies where people walked half nude. Again, this was not the issue of *thingifying* woman's body as it currently is under beauty for sale and other dubious many enticements. Woman's body was not an item one would display in the agora for whatever purpose except when there was an issue so striking that this action had to be taken. Women were not put on the market as sexual or merchandises as it currently is in the pop culture in Hollywood or anywhere else where women are traded through degradation and exploitation. This explanation is offered to help those who would like to misconstrue normal half nudity that had no curse attached on it. Even in European culture, it is a normal thing to see half naked breasts–so exposed as a fashion thing–without creating any commotion. Expose them and see when the aim is different from business like breastfeeding. Many Indigenous cultures did not objectify or *thingify* the body, or soul of a woman. For, doing so is just immoral, colonising and degrading the said body. You can see this in many Indigenous communities. Women are more mothers than sexual objects. They were sacred and respected by the way of marriage. This is why, for instance, divorces are not a problem in many so-called backward communities compared to Western ones.

285

What's more, I can cite recent examples where women were respected and heard when they exerted pressure on the high and the mighty. Liberian example above provides an ideal example. Liberian women did not need anybody, be he or she, as a mediator or whatever to empower them. They needed and used their womanhood knowingly how African cultures respect and revere it. They needed their bodies. They had their power that needed not to be supplemented. So, in a nutshell, the way individualistic culture looks at power is totally different from collectivistic cultures do. So, too, the locus and power the woman occupies and commands in the society are completely different from these two cultures. This goes as far as to encompass trust. Trust in individualistic culture is guarded by a written agreement while it differently the opposite in many collectivistic cultures.

Another ideal example on how women were respected in Africa can be drawn from Ghanaian proverb that says *Obaa na awoo obarima; Okaa na owoo ohene* [It's a woman who gave birth to a man, it is a woman who gave birth to a chief] Akan proverb. This proverb shows gender equality and interdependence among Akan people which was based on the fact that the Akan were matrilineal (Takyi & Broughton, 2006) and women had high status (Badenhorst, 2010) before being converted to either Christianity or Islam. Gender equality was not only applied in giving birth but even in belonging. Some Africans were matrilineal but became patrilineal after acquiring cattle (Holden & Mace, 2003). This shows how patriarchal system in some place was imported by circumstances or colonisers. Mintah (1996) maintains that "today westernized and Islamised Africans who were traditionally matrilineal are shifting to *patrilinealism* in compliance with either western or Islamic standards" (p. 215). This assertion speaks volumes. Try to imagine. If some societies were able to be at home with matrilineal heritage which seems be an anomaly for Western patriarchal system, how could they torture, segregate or disrespect females? For such societies, equality was above comparison if compared to today's dominant and exploitative patriarchal system. In other words, in those societies, maybe, women were like the men of today in present setting. Osborn (2003) maintains that:

Available studies of Asante's history have provided illuminating insights about Asante's society at different point in time. These snapshots were often taken of a centralized the Asante state in the eighteenth and nineteenth centuries...egalitarian social structure and stratified imperial Asante (p. 481).

According to the political setting of Asante Empire, a typical replica of many African societies, women (grandmothers) were charged with power of checks and balances. They made sure that the king toed the line. Whenever the king failed to meet his obligations, grandmothers would pull their votes out which were represented by sandals they used to place before the king during the legislatorial sessions they fully attended on top of other official functions they assigned to them. Additional, Asante's women had more powers and rights than European women in their empire. There are some similarities in many African empires. There were some mechanisms that enable justice to be delivered equitably based on gender balance. For instance, in many African kingdoms, one of king's obligatory roles was to make sure that his subjects get essentials such as food, security and representation.

Many African Indigenous Conflict Resolution Mechanisms deal with conflicts not only aiming at doing justice to the victim individually, but they also redressing and doing justice to the society due to a cyclic or collectivistic nature of the society. They go further to include even the perpetrators. For instance, while Western model encourages us to separate people from issues, to some many traditional mechanisms or settings, everything is intertwined. For instance, in a cyclical way of interrelating wherein everyone and everything are stakeholders, how do you draw a line between issues and people? To put it clear, cutting trees in an Aboriginal society is as equally bad as killing your brother or sister. In such a setting it is difficult to separate issue and people. The cycle does not end up here–as indicated above–even ancestors, oracles and gods are involved in the process in case of the need of oath; and when things go beyond human control and understanding. For, separating anything in the process disturbs the equilibrium of creation and the process.

However, I do not mean that issues and people should not be separated in dealing with a conflict. The question one may ask is how. Due to African traditional setting, time for separating people, things and issues arrives when an opportune time arrives too. For example, in awarding punishment or rewards, all things are not treated equal. In some cultures when a cow or sheep is slaughtered to signify the end of the conflict, the living ones eat more than the dead. Bonsu & Belk (2003) maintain that they found that bereaved Asante's consumers engage in conspicuous ritual consumption in pursuit of newer social identities for their deceased and, of course, themselves in that, for example, funerals involve a reciprocal and continuing relationship between the living and the dead. Arguably, for the culture wherein everything is interconnected, Western prescriptive education does not work; and if it does, it does not bring desired results. Thus, we need to be aware of the differences between and among civilisations, cultures and grand narratives so as to accommodate them whenever we deal with conflicts. In such a setting and situation, it is better to avoid superimposing Western mechanisms of dealing with conflict. And wherever the two cultures find themselves in conflict, it is better to hybridise or apply both mechanisms of conflict resolution based on consensus reached by parties to conflict.

10

Taking on the Dominant Grand Narrative as the Beneficiary and Creator of Toxic Education

Figure 16; photo courtesy of jadour.wordpress.com

In this last chapter, the author suggests that academics, especially victims, supported by anybody who is not satisfied with how the current dominant grand narrative is terrorising others, must join hands in the quest of decolonising and detoxifying it. Decolonisation, which sets out to change the order of the world by detoxifying and decolonising education as it challenges the dominant grand narrative, is, obviously, a program of a purposeful expedition that is aimed at restoring order. It seeks to clean not wash the brains of those brainwashed and those brainwashing them so that they can both work together equally and equitably.

The author has used the term dominant grand narrative in many sentences in this volume. Now it is the time to fully delve into it so that we can see how it works for or against whose interests. In its approach in trying to define the grand narrative, this volume will go with the definition by Foucault (1979) cited in Irving, Howard & Matteson (2004) who defines grand narrative as "the formation of knowledge and the increase of power" (p. 740) aimed at benefiting from it even if it is by means of hurting others as it has been under the current dominant grand narrative. There is no way we can decolonise education–and if possible–all fields of education without revisiting the history of the current order, and that of the victims of the current dominant grand narrative based on Western culture and philosophy.

Decolonisation, basically, is possible through the hybridisation of our education which will help us to do away with current essentialist regime of doing things. Seehausen (2004) argues that "hybridization is important as a mechanism" (p. 198) that can help to put to different and antagonistic parties together; if it is applied well with well intentions. However, Seehausen speaks in terms of biology; still such rationale can be applied to other fields in education in general. In trying to reconcile conservative and liberal, colonised and decolonised thinkers, Seehausen comes up with the concept that reconciles them by arguing them to accommodate each other in order to generate constructive and positive e dialogue. We need history to help us underscore and address the way we can use it to deconstruct and reconstruct the current disorder in the world dictated by the grand narrative we seek to show how convoluted and flawed it is. Larkin Jr (2000) observes that:

> It is the grand overarching narrative which is regarded as "really true," for it legitimates some knowledge, beliefs, and practices that explain our culture in terms of origin and destiny and the power that sustains us. At the same time it marginalizes other knowledge, beliefs, and practices (p. 406).

As you can see above, the dominant grand narrative almost defines everything *vis-à-vis, inter alia*, origins of things, knowledge, practices, theories and truth; and its *truth* is regarded as the ultimate and the only truth compared to other truths. Such aggrandisement is applied and maintained purposely all aimed at making other grand narratives and civilisations impotent and moribund if not empty and inferior comparably. Furthermore: Jean-François Lyotard (cited in Larkin Jr., *Ibid.*) observes that:

> The modern grand narrative contained the themes: progressive emancipation of reason and freedom; progressive emancipation of labor; improvement of all humanity through progress of capitalist techno-science; and the salvation of humanity through the conversion of souls to the Christian meta-narrative of martyred love (p. 406).

Here is where I trace the origin of the current dominant grand narrative. You can see how corrupt and evil such a narrative is, especially when you delve into its history. To know its fickleness, one needs to examine the tools the dominant grand narrative used in conquering the world. Did Christianity save its victims or rob them? Where is progress if Africa, for instance, has always been made to lag behind and believe that this is normalcy under the current dominant grand narrative? Such are provocative issues and questions decolonised education seeks to ask and provide answers to. Hermaphrodite as it is, the current dominant grand narrative draws its roots from Judeo-Christian tradition (Luke 2005; Navarro, Muntaner, Borrell, Benach, Quiroga, Rodríguez-Sanz, Vergés & Pasarín, 2006; and Vaden & Woolley, 2011) that gave birth to the capitalist or the West grand narrative we have today. Additionally, Wright (2007, p. 17 cited in Wright, 2013) concurs with Larkin Jr. (*op.cit.*) observing that the:

> Mission is, in my view, a major key that unlock[s] the whole grand narrative of the canon of Scripture. The whole story, not as Geschichte (saga, myth, or legend) but Historie (a true account of what actually occurred in time and space), gives a metanarrative provided by the Master storyteller himself (p. 3).

Wright does not tell who this master storyteller is. Is it a person [s] or institutions or both? It depends on which grand narrative you are talking about. For example, the current dominant Western grand narrative, as indicated above, is the product of Judaeo-Christian creation that ended up metamorphosed itself into the current dominant grand narrative.

Furthermore, what is grand narrative or metanarrative? Lyotard (1984) cited in Gilstrap (2007) notes that "metanarrative has classically been defined in literature and philosophy as a 'grand narrative' that attempts to narrow phenomena into a single, structured analysis of "truth" (p. 3). So, you can see that truth is the most important root word to consider when dealing or analysing the grand narrative. Despite being there many truths, the dominant grand narrative wants to have only one truth, the one it creates and propounds based on colonial-cum-toxic education. After defining the grand narrative though in a nutshell, I can now address the reason why it has been mightily there. Mariano (2017) observes that the aim of the grand narratives is "to chart the interdependence of world events, while allowing for the brute fact of Western domination" (p. 6). So, the biases that led to racism, exploitation, toxicity and blindness are the fruits of a dubious but purposeful project that seeks to belittle other grand narratives so that it can dominate; and thereby exploit them as it has been ongoing for many decades now.

The efforts behind taking on the dominant, hegemonic and colonial current grand narrative are the sojourn to find real truth that will be equally appreciated by all humanity after agreeing upon and defining it for the benefit of all parties namely, the human family. This is possible; if we consider some facts such as human shared understanding of some concepts such as death, life and the universe. Therefore, this corpus seeks to accommodate my truth, your truth, her truth, his truth, their truth and our truth based on our informed agreement. I seek to put the truth from one grand narrative to a test after finding that it does not match with the truths of other grand narratives that have been ignored and sidelined. So, we are involved in the *dialogue of truths* in order to get, at least, one acceptable and agreed-upon truth for all of us as human beings. This is why decolonising our grand or metanarrative is very crucial. Gilstrap cites the Oxford Dictionary Oxford English Dictionary arguing that metanarrative "is concerned with the idea of storytelling, specifically one which alludes to other narratives, or refers to itself and to its own artifice." In other words, talking about the grand narrative is talking about how stories are told *vis-à-vis* the essence of things or ideas of our being reflecting one's way of looking at and interpreting things to form his or her truth that can, sometimes, be incompatible with other truths. To get this truth, we need to have unlimited or unrestricted knowledge that decolonised education provides as opposed to the current dominant grand narrative that seeks to impose its *truth*. In other words, we need to think out of the box of the dominant grand narrative. Freire (2000) cited in Ravitch (2014) argues that "knowledge emerges only through invention and re-invention, through the restless, impatient, continuing, hopeful inquiry human beings pursue in the world, with the world, and with each other" (p. 73) without being restricted or dictated by one reality or truth as it currently is.

When I was contemplating about writing this chapter, I conducted many researches about the current dominant grand narrative. I ended up finding nothing save mentioning of it without defining. Among scholars who used the term are Jean-Francois Lyotard (whose works in postmodernism are renowned), Seyla Benhabib (who also covers postmodernism), Nancy Fraser and Linda Nicholson among others. The expressly meaning of grand narrative was hard to get. However, Bueger (2013) simply and summarily defines it as 'a master story' that is viewed and maintained as the true one compared to others thus dominant or an all-encompassing and interpretive lens by and with which past, present, and future events and identities in society and state are analysed, defined, prescribed and proscribed (Adebanwi, 2016). Further, grand narrative may be expanded so as to come up with another name for the grand narrative known as "metanarrative" or dominant ideologies and theories (Lyotard) which can be understood and used interchangeably.

All over again, with toxic education that has been pumped in many heads in the world, the current dominant grand narrative uses to superimpose its truth and interpretation of things to its victims for its advantage and the disadvantage of its victims. There is no way we can find the truth that this grand narrative has concocted, doctored, promoted and propagated to suit its interests without decolonising and deconstructing it. I know; many will wonder why I create doubts about; and declare the current grand narrative and its form of education unfit. The answer is simple; its history shows that it is there to colonise and demonise others. It is only fit for those whose interests it serves. To those whose interests were and are still sabotaged, this grand narrative is not only colonial and hegemonic but also toxic. Refer to slavery, colonialism, imperialism and currently neoliberalism.

When I talk of grand narrative, I mean many things in one. The grand narrative I mean encompasses all spheres of life for all walks of life. It defines physics, science, philosophy, knowledge, intellectualism, and above all, our social, political and economic state of being. Further, the grand narrative defines Truth and truth altogether. It defines almost everything. In other words, the grand narrative is the source and custodian of knowledge and the order of the world however wanting and controversial it is. It is the one that says in its unity and oneness then claim what it says is universal in that what it holds to be true is self-evidently universal even when it is not.

Try to imagine. How–for example–can we enjoy peace while those teaching us about peace and human rights are the same folks creating conflict by pitting one against another so as to sell their weapons or obtain cheap resources? If you interrogate the grand narrative the rationale behind such anomaly, you will find that this is business under capitalism whereby every individual has to mind his or her business as opposed to collectivistic communities in which everybody has to depend on, or fend for another. You can see this individuality even at a national level. For example, under the Westphalian Treaty of Peace which gave birth to the modern nation state and its sovereignty, every country has to enjoy its sovereignty in some matters such as security, defence and politics. To me, the sovereignty that allows the destruction of one another is the source of conflicts. And thus, it cannot be a guarantor when it comes to resolving the said conflict. You can see this in the Middle East conflict where the US acts as a guarantor while at the same time supports one side against another. This is the work of the current dominant grand narrative. It is infallible. Again, if we face it, is it?

Given that the grand narrative is in everything, we need to understand it so as to rebel against it by deconstructing and reconstructing it in order to realise justice and peace for the world. In addressing the controversies of the current dominant grand narrative, I have tried as much as I can to avoid academic jargons. Again, I have also tried to restrict myself from using many scientific figures and definitions altogether. I know full well; many lay people, especially do not like definitions; however, the same concept of defining almost everything according to the angle and desire of the grand narrative have pushed people into believing and serving things they do not agree with or believe in, specifically if we consider the fact that they can actually rebel against the grand narrative if they get a right episteme. Arguably, the grand narrative meant here means the worldview created by the dominant culture or civilisation as it calls itself which supresses others in order to become hegemonic and dominant for the benefit of those whose culture author the said grand narrative.

Regarding to how the world should be ran, for the current world, the dominant grand narrative is like the *Alpha* and the *Omega* or the beginning and the end to borrow the word it invented to justify its dominance and eminence. Again, where did it start? Wright (2013) traces the grand narrative expressly saying that "the Mission of God according to the three foci of Israel's worldview: first God, then his people and last God's earth" (p. 1). If anything, the mother and father of the current grand narrative is nothing but the Bible–also is the creature of the grand narrative–which means the collection of books or library in Greek (Schniedewind, 2005) as it was written by various scholars of the time but not angels "over 1,500 years, from 1,450 BC to 100 AD" (Houghton, 1972, p. 7). To show that there are many doubts about who wrote the Bible as the creator and a creature of the current dominant grand narrative between God and Man, Law (2013) makes a very provocative irony: When God spoke Greek or whatever first language wherein the Bible was written before being translated in many languages? He notes that as of the first Century CE there was no Bible in existence but some Jewish scriptures of which some were excluded in the finalisation of the compilation of the Bible by humans but not God. The Bible and its grand narrative act like yin and yang by nature in that they depend on and reinforce each other. You can see, the Bible was written for a long time of consultations. It is said that during the writing of the Bible many manuscripts were brought but 'a few' were passed by humans who took the role of God whom they ended up creating by giving them another yin and yang role of creating them! When did they meet God or when did God authorise them to do *his* work which is their work? Who knows? Who witnessed this blank authorisation that empowers some Western and Middle Eastern humans to decide and act on behalf of God by exploiting and suppressing others? Suppose I argue that this is not true? Some, for fear of having their cover blown, will persecute those interrogating and opposing the *authenticity* of their claims while others will demonise them in order to get away with it. This is the nativity of the grand narrative that ended up to be challenged and toppled due to its flaws such as postulating that the earth was flat like a table. Refer to the execution of Galileo Galilei (1564–1642) who opposed the view of the grand narrative so as to be convicted to death. This shows the fallacy and fallibility of the grand narrative made by man in the name of God. Why was Galilei convicted and executed? If the grand narrative goes on this way unchallenged and/or being deconstructed, it will ruin the world. For instance, why should we fight one another over God while God is always silent without even bothering to mediate in our conflict? If anything, arguably, this lacuna forces us to intervene as academics to debunk the myths of beliefs, faiths and religions as the colonial tools of the current dominant grand narrative. All civilisations and humans equally have everything the current grand narrative portends to have invented. For example, every human society has its religion and beliefs and the story of creation.

Galilei was able to make observations that demonstrated that the earth and other planets revolve around the Sun; thus confirming the Copernican system of astronomy. Such a system was not in line with the Bible's description and propagation of the origins of the universe under the Western dominant grand narrative. To make it worse, such false knowledge was offered by the first school in Africa that missionaries ran. This shows how the foundations of Western education in Africa was completely false and misleading thanks to the ignorance and arrogance of those who offered it all aimed at softening Africans to be ready for colonisation and exploitation. This

296

proof was a significant challenge to the accepted thinking based on ignorance an lies, particularly in connection with the teachings of the Roman Catholic (Brecht, 2015). Brecht makes a good point saying that Galilei was not the first to allege that the planets revolve around the sun. Actually, Aristotle had made such a crime before but he luckily escaped the hangman's lariat.

By law, in its infancy, the grand narrative was supposed to be believed but not to be questioned or queried. Again, despite this myopia and ignorance, the conflict ensued whereby the opponents of such fallacy and ignorance were persecuted. One would ask: What has this to do with the current regime of education? The answer is simple. Such misunderstandings led to conflicts between the grand narrative and freethinkers who challenged some its truths. Conflict is like an onion. When you peel the onion you need to analyse many layers it has. So, too, looking at current conflict resulting from religion, we need to educate ourselves about these religions so that we can offer good answers to the problems they pose.

Despite applying brutality and intimidation on Galilei, he did not go down without a good fight though. For, Galilei (1957) in telling the high and the mighty of the time maintains that:

> In my Starry Messenger there were revealed many new and marvelous discoveries in the heavens that should have gratified all lovers of true science; yet scarcely had it been printed when men sprang up everywhere who envied the praises belonging to the discoveries there revealed. Some, merely to contradict what I had said, did not scruple to cast doubt upon things they had seen with their own eyes again and again (p. 1).

Galilei was accused of Heliocentrism or the model wherein Earth and planets revolve around the Sun or Galilei's finding which was opposed to Vatican's geocentrism model in which earth is the center of all celestial bodies. The lesson we get from Galilei's defense is that we should be ready to be taxed for what we hold to be true instead of being persecuted. For, Galilei it would have made sense if the church that persecuted him had academically challenged and persecuted his findings instead of persecuting him. In spite of the brutality Galilei faced, he stood his ground with his *eppure si muove* or "(And yet, it still moves" (Culpepper, 2007) testimony to the truth he knew full well. To save his neck, he recanted his discovering due to the lack of academics' support. Like Galilei, don't we see the injustice Aboriginal peoples are facing all over the world all committed by the makers and perpetrators of the toxic education originating from this grand narrative and fail to say *eppure si muove* like Galilei? What are we afraid of if at all our aim is to make the world peaceful including those duping others? Even though Galilei's defense fell on deaf ears, many years thereafter, the church had to make a formal apology to Galilei as Chan, Louis & Jetten (2010) note that "… despite the fact that the Catholic Church's position that the Sun moves around the Earth proved to be untenable, it was only in the 20th century that the Catholic Church apologised for Galilei's persecution" (p. 1103). Although the apology took hundreds of years to come out, Galilei was vindicated; and thus truth however opposite it was to the dominant grand narrative finally came to light. Such a posthumous apology does not make any sense to the victims however. Instead, it makes sense in that it shows us how power can be misused to distort and subvert truth. You can see this in many historical realities such as colonialism, slavery and imperialism among others. We know for sure as Galilei knew full well that everybody will one day die be he or she a persecutor or a persecuted as in Galilei's case. So, we should not fear to reveal the truth because of the threat of death or deprivation.

More on the grand narrative or the "mission of God" (Wright, 2013) perfected by those who prosecuted Galilei for telling truth, can be said to be the beginning of the grand narrative that I am taking on now as it is promoted through toxic education. To make the world understand the *Mission of God*, Christianisation of the world was forcefully conducted all over the world through brutality, deceit and ignorance as it paved a way for colonialism. Protestants, Mennonites (Kopko, 2012), Huguenots and others, for example, were burnt at stake, drowned and butchered just because they opposed the grand narrative of the day before being toppled and commuted to the current one. Sometimes, this is how brutally the grand narrative works. It defies logic and norms in its quest of instilling fear in people so that they can appreciate its rationales of doing things even if they are completely illogical. If anything, this is a good source or causal agent of conflict that we need to deal with watchfully and truthfully. We need to rebel against it as thinkers so that those using it can get the message.

Further, *the mission of God* did not take a long time after another crop of thinkers just like those who authored the Bible surfaced. This time, the banner was not the Bible, but it was enlightenment. Foucault (1984) maintains that there must be a distinguishment between the realm of obedience and the realm of the use of reason. Although this wave of thinking ended up forming a part of the current dominant grand narrative, at least, it became a breath of fresh air whose precedent we can apply today to take on the dominant grand narrative and its toxic education now. True, the enlightenment challenged and changed almost everything regardless of the supremacy and force the grand narrative of the time had. However, such changes were intentionally and only aimed at liberating Europe from such archaic and brutal way of doing things but not the whole world. Appreciating that there must be change helps us to agitate for change for the whole world without fearing the powers, prowess and the propaganda machinery the current grand narrative employs. If Galilei, the 'apostles' of enlightenment, Foucault, and others challenged the grand narrative even if not for the benefit of the entire humanity, why not we?

Essentially, dealing with the current dominant grand narrative is dealing with the story and history of formation of knowledge which is displayed in power according to the *diktat* and interpretation of the dominant grand narrative however fabricated and wrong it might be. This is why we have all reasons and guts to question the current Western history and story of knowledge that have made the West more powerful than others so as to dominate almost everything at the detriment of others whose grand narrative are excluded or demonised. Such demonisation and domination have caused a lot of injustices from slavery, colonialism, imperialism and now terrorism. However biased the history written by the messengers and prophets of the current dominant grand narrative, I still can find some nuggets in it that I can use to back our assertion that the current dominant grand narrative needs to be deconstructed and decolonised in order to secure a place for other narratives to top it up or work with it concurrently after detoxifying it.

Hence, I am advocating the debunking of the current grand narrative based on history that shows its feebleness and nastiness as far as history of others is concerned. This corpus refutes many allegations, so-called truth and facts and whatnot *vis-a-vis* exploiting others and their grand narratives through intentional manipulation and misrepresenting their history. Essentially, this corpus seeks to show how the current grand narrative becomes a good cause and source of conflicts where it was supposed to be a solution. All this is because of imperialistic and colonial mentality based on *holier-than-thou* way of thinking. I faced an uphill task when I was researching the concept of truth so as to define it. My findings are that, truth, real truth, is one of undefinable words. I, therefore, decided to go with James (1975) cited in Molander (2013) who argues that "truth we conceive to mean everywhere, not duplication, but addition; not the constructing of inner copies of already complete realities, but rather the collaborating with realities so as to bring about a clearer result" (p. 8). With respect to what is truth and whose truth and for what, arguably, the current dominant grand narrative is in conflict with other grand narratives that it subdued through colonialism and imperialism. This is why–for example–there has been terror related actions aimed at punishing the West for undermining other narratives. I cannot argue for those behind such never-do-well ideologies and beliefs. Again, this is what they say, as it is for the dominant grand narrative, they think their truth is the one we should subscribe to and accommodate as we divorce others however wrong, colonial, egoistic, toxic and misguided they might be.

Fundamentally, we I circumstantially state that there is a conflict between the West and those using terror to make their case however it is not a good and sound way of dealing with such a conflict resulting from some academics refer to as clash of civilisations (Beale, 2014; Moghaddam, 2010; and Eriksson & Norman, 2011). Again, there are many ways of dealing with a conflict; all depends on the means and mechanisms the parties or one of the parties to conflict use to address the conflict. Some do accommodate, avoid, assert, negotiate or mediate when they feel there is a conflict wherein they are involved. Although this volume has not solely dwelt on the conflict between the West–and say, fundamentalists or terrorists as they are referred to–it seeks to show the chasm resulting from the dominance of one grand narrative that has resulted in conflicts in many places as a way of showing how truth is difficult to find under one grand narrative without agreeing upon it. I have clarified this by delving into some African conflicts.

Arguably, many African countries face civil wars resulting from proxy wars aimed at accessing resources in these countries either by governments or rival groups just for their interests as opposed to the interests of the public that ends up becoming a mere victims of this greed-geared conflict as shown in Angola's case. Other countries are on the verge of collapsing due to endemic corruption, nihilism and lack of vision thanks to be ruled by leaders or rulers who received toxic education. Others are thriving depending on who backs them under the current dominant grand narrative. Circumstantially, when one looks at how some Africans–especially corrupt ones–the West or China sustain corrupt regimes; it becomes obviously clear how the dominant grand narrative works. To understand this, try to think about dictatorial regimes you know that trample on human rights and yet remain in good books of the current dominant grand narrative championed by the West. Why do they remain in power even if their citizenry do not want them? Whose consent is keeping them in power? Who is protecting them and why? Why other like-minded regimes that refuse to be in bed with the West are toppled or forced to embrace neoliberal democracy while others remain immune to it? Such dichotomous existence of some regimes is itself a conflict.

So, to adequately address this conflict, we must explore the grand narrative that back and keeps relatively unwanted regimes in power even if the citizenry oppose them without success thanks to the protection the grand narrative championed by the current dominant Western countries provide them. The controversy of how the grand narrative operates *vis-à-vis* the democratisation of others reminds me of the cartoon which showed two autocratic rulers. One, the king, was in bed with the dominant grand narrative while the other, the president, refused to be in bed with it. Guess what. What happened is that the big folks clobbered the president who refused to be in bed with them; and decided to force democracy down his throat while the king who was in bed with powerful countries was laughing as he watched. Actually, democracy sounds good. Again, is it logical to force democracy on others through undemocratic means?

Naturally and logically, every people, society, and culture has its grand narratives carried forward through cultural, political and economic settings in making sense of things or the way we create and attribute meanings to ideas and things based on our ways of looking at and interpreting them including how to democratically rule themselves. Further, all societies have their stories of creation and how things were formed or *created*. All societies can intellectually tell how things came into being without necessarily referring to neo-religions which superimposed their own grand narratives. All societies have their philosophies and myths revolving around everything they encounter in their day-to day lives. They have their grandeurs and spitefulness, triumphs and defeats and whatnots. Every people have their Truths and truths which need to be shared or incorporated in the current dominant grand narrative. All societies have their stories which are important to them. They have their glories and traumas, memories and golden eras. Those stories presented through their narratives make people who they uniquely are. Ignoring their narratives is tantamount to ignoring their existence too. This is a universal nature of all human beings. All those things their narratives present are dear to them; and they are part of who they actually are. So, no narrative is–or should be regarded as–inferior or superior to others. And thus, no narrative is supposed to dominate others. Instead, the narratives of the world can share dominance; and thereby coexist as means of living harmoniously and productively based on recognising and appreciating each other as humans based on their grand narratives and how they identify themselves. Again, to understand the importance and vitality of equal and equitable narratives, we need to ask the question that Lederach (2005) asks: "What center holds things together?" (p. 75). Some will say that the center that holds things together is the human beings however the same human beings do not act and do things in a similar fashion. Furthermore, human beings are not perceiving and treating each other equally. Some are more of the center while others are more of the periphery. If one narrative can dominate and outsmart others, can we then say it holds things together while it has utterly created total carnage, division and exploitation? Yes, it might in a very wrong way as it currently is.

Again, is everybody satisfied with how the *center* holds things together? Lederach gives us an answer saying that we need to seek to build constructive social changes through invisible web of relationship, which I may argue; should be interrelated and interconnected of relationship; and must accommodate all grand narratives of the world equally and equitably. Lederach (*Ibid.*) equates the centers holding everything to the Sun which supplies energy for it to function equally, interdependently and swiftly. Again, if we look at the current dominant grand narrative, does not act as the Sun does by controlling and serving everything equally? The Sun equally gives the solar system the energy that is needs for the lives of almost everything while our dominant grand narrative sucks energy from others so as to create schism and inequalities pointlessly. If people can live in their land sharing their goodies through the web of business without causing any harm to others, why then should we fear the coexistence of grand narratives of the world? The coexistence and dialogues among grand narratives of the world based on decolonised education add value to our knowledge by creating the culture of dialoguing and broadmindedness. For example, we need to dialogue with those who think their narrative [s] must dominate others just because they are theirs and wrongly perceived to be superior. We need to ask them why and what would be their responses and reaction, if the same could be turned vice versa. This means, those whose faiths, beliefs and cultures want to dominate and consume others instead of subsuming other faiths, beliefs and cultures must be asked if they are ready to serve under those faiths, beliefs and cultures they have for long demonised, disparaged, subsumed and subdued.

The other day I witnessed a heated dialogue between two passengers in the bus we were travelling from Tanzania to Kenya. There were two passengers, a Christian who was defending the dominance of his faith over a Muslim who had an issue about conspiracy against his faith and people. A Muslim was complaining that Western countries are suffocating Islam in Africa while the Christian was complaining that Muslims are converting some of his people. The quibbling was very fierce and long. After noticing that every side was striving to maintain its grand narrative, I asked them if I could chip in. They thankfully allowed me due to the weariness of their dialogue on them.

I told them that I am a traditionalist and a deconstructionist who does not believe in their faiths. I wanted them to tell me where they put me in this conundrum. They were shocked to find that everybody wanted to subsume me in his faith by telling me its beauties without knowing that I had read about the two faiths. I told them that I cannot subscribe to any of their faiths, beliefs or cultures; however I do not oppose their existence. I asked them why it was fair for their faiths to subsume mine but not otherwise. This point seemed to convince them. Then, I asked them why there are many more mosques in Western countries than churches in the Arab or Muslim world? Both of them wondered. For, they did not know that this was the truth.

To cut a long story short, we ended up agreeing that we need one another but in equal and equitable fashion and footing. I drew from the golden rule saying that do unto others the way you would like to be done or treat others the way you would like to be treated. In fact, this was a remedy that brought the dialogue of what seemed to be the *dialogue of the deaf* to a good ending. This rationale can be applied in the quest to decolonise and detoxify education.

To put the golden rule in the context in another way, the other day I read a story of a loving couple who got a baby. After getting the baby, the love they enjoyed started to drift away for two reasons.

First, the husband complained that his wife was concentrating so much on looking after the baby that he felt ignored; and not loved anymore.

Second, the couple quarreled a lot about who should change diapers, especially at night. The couple went to an experienced married couple to seek help. What the couple did was laugh and laugh. Such a move annoyed the couple. They thought their relative would feel for them and offer some support. After laughing for a long time, the relative said: "Golden rule."

Then to the puzzled wife and husband, the relative said: "Do unto others the way you would like to be done." And continued, saying: "There is still love between you, save that it has been moved to the baby. If you both concentrate more on the baby, you will notice that something is amiss." The relative discovered that while the mother concentrated more on the baby, the father did not. So, to balance the equation, the relative advised the couple to try to concentrate on the baby equally.

As for the second problem, the relative asked the man "have you ever imagined how it would be or feel if you were the one to breastfeed the baby and change diapers alone?" He replied "that is not fair." And the relative repeated the same. "That is not fair." The last word from the relative was "Golden rule." He added "whenever you happen to forget or become selfish, try to remember the golden rule." The conflict was thus resolved. Again, if we ask why people from the same culture were fighting over love, we do not get the simple and right answer. Sometimes, it becomes hard to get rid of some of the cultures we are used to. This also is likely to happen for those who used to the culture to exploit and rule others almost in everything by using their grand narrative and toxic education.

I have purposely used the way cultures play in our lives knowing how hard it is to define. Edward Tylor cited in Fieldhouse (2013) defines culture as "that complex whole which included knowledge, beliefs, art, morals, law, customs and any other capabilities acquired by man as a member of society" (p. 2). Many academics have tried to define culture with many difficulties due to the fact that it is a very hard term to define. With regard to the convolution of defining culture, Baldwin, Faulkner, Hecht & Lindsley (2006) cite an example of American anthropologists, Kroeber and Kluckhohonn, who surveyed 300 different definitions of culture; and came up with 164 definitions of it (Katan, 2014). For the purpose of this volume, culture means all and everything that make a certain group of people unique from other groups. So, additional to what we know about it, culture is all those elements, visible and invisible that make us who we are. Some are good and others are bad across all cultures and societies.

I remember when I visited Lushoto district in Tanga Region in Tanzania where my wife hails from; I found it more beautiful than Maswa district in Simiyu region where I was born. Lushoto was mountainous and ever green. It can be cold like Europe minus snow. And this characteristic helps Lushoto to contribute hugely in ecotourism, attracting many tourists from Europe, especially Germany. As for Maswa, it is in the region that produces diamonds and animal products. By comparison, the weather in Lushoto is better than it is in Maswa. Yet, after spending some weeks in Lushoto, I found myself missing Maswa. I missed the dust, the smell of soil, and the songs of the birds, which were different from those of Lushoto. I hankered for the view of the mountains, foods I knew and their tastes, the familiar horizons and many more inexplicable elements of nature found in the place I was born.

When someone wants to know who I am, such tiny and complicated things must be considered. However, the media used to know who I am is what foreign grand narratives fail to capture and appreciate in trying to know who I am. In spite of every people having their grand narratives, one grand narrative seems to rule the world currently. This is an anomaly or a misnomer so to speak. Thus, this chapter introduces the grand narrative and seeks to provide answers that can be used to deconstruct it so as to reconstruct it by discarding all unwanted baggage it has as we accommodate all goodies found in it.

Therefore, the aim of challenging the current dominant grand narrative aims at trying to see how such a move can reduce conflict or create peace in the world that is facing many animosities resulting from history and the interpretation of the dominant narrative as opposed to other grand narratives. Taking on the grand narrative aims at incentivising it and other subjugated narratives to have a dialogue in order to coexist mutually and peacefully after the current relationship has proved to be thorny and unequal. Arguably, the issue we should consider here is how we use our resources–largely our narratives–to create conducive environment for peace which emanates from sound relationship. Contrary to hegemonic drive or victimhood, this volume seeks to unequivocally deal with the issue many like to avoid. So, when I question–for example–if Caucasians are whitish, pinkish or brownish, I should not be branded a racist but the deconstructionists seeking to redefine things, specifically important and sensitive things. I do so either from experience or knowledge acquired both in class and outside of it.

Fundamentally, writing this volume resulted from my personal experiences with regards to the dominant grand narrative, especially its detrimental side as far as things we differ on in understanding are concerned. For example, when somebody says she or he has been discriminated against, it tells us that such a person is in a radicalised setting where colour seems to be a divisive factor. Such an experience cannot be gainsaid or ignored. We need to ask such a person how he or she reached at such a conclusion. We need to question her or his grand narrative that offers her or him the lenses one uses to interpret and view things. Everybody has something to contribute to the dialogue, especially in deconstructing and decolonising colonial episteme whose multidisciplinary nature and inclusivity are great.

However, this volume uses the current dominant grand narrative by touching on it for the purpose of clarity. Again, we can say that grand narrative means the version of things that is regarded to be true, thus a standard for almost everything. There are many grand narratives all over the world; save that one of them is regarded as the best of all so as to dominate others. Such a dominant grand narrative is none other than Western that has become the standard of doing or weighing things. In other words, the dominant civilisation has produced its grand narrative that has overruled and destroyed, if not alienated, other grand narratives of the world. An ideal example is the facsimilia of government, financial institutions the order of the world currently which is ran according to the *diktat* of neoliberalism.

The current grand narrative dominates almost every discourse of world affairs, especially after the demise of communist that had its own counter grand narrative. The primacy and supremacy of the current dominant grand narrative can be seen in the terms we use every now and then universally such as Reaganomics (derived from economic policies based on liberalisation that former US president Ronald Reagan initiated) Victorian (Derived from Queen Victoria era), enlightenment (the wave of liberal change in Europe) and whatnots. One may ask: Why Reaganomics not Nyererenomics (African Social economy that former Tanzania president Julius Nyerere initiated or Buntunomics. There is even Maonomics (Napoleoni, 2011) or the economic policies that Chairman Mao of China initiated. Where is Pan Africanism that awoke Africans to fight for freedom, Ubuntu or humanity, African philosophy based on the interconnection and interdependence of all human beings which was known but not used up until Nelson Mandela, first black president of South Africa, applied and amplified it in the liberation of South Africa which led to the demise of Apartheid system? We do not hear these *a posteriori* terms used in modern leitmotifs or given some economic eponyms compared to the *a priori* due to the fact that the leaders of the said models are not accepted by the current dominant grand narrative that represents capitalism while their policies were against capitalism. Furthermore, the proponents of the current grand narrative did not even bother to give academic or whatsoever term to those terms which are my own in trying to show how the current grand narrative behaves and works.

Arguably, there cannot be any decolonisation of colonial episteme without questioning, and intentionally rebelling against the dominant grand narrative current academia and intellectualism borrow from and/or depend on whether consciously or otherwise. It needs to be–*sui generis*–deconstructed and reconstructed as well in order to suit the aspirations and needs of its adversaries and victims. We need to take all good things it has as discarding all bad things it has. Just like any other culture or civilisation, this chapter has sought to point at weak points of the current dominant grand narrative. It does not mean to condemn the whole thing. Instead, the chapter seeks to show the crust, crux and weakness of the matter so that other thinkers can expand and build on it in advocating and agitating for the decolonisation of the grand narrative itself.

As professionals, academics, practitioners, stakeholders, beneficiaries and victims of the current dominant grand narrative, we need to do our parts in our fields believing that other fields will do the same to see to it that the current grand narrative is saved from itself for the betterment of the world we all desire to live in. As it has been stated from the outset of this volume, the concentration has been put on education simply because it is consisted of many fields and specialties. Thus, it should be underscored that if its decolonisation and detoxification–is well accepted and well undertaken–need to encompass all fields due to the fact that they share the same nexus. They affect the lives of everybody in this planet either directly or indirectly.

Fundamentally, the dominant grand narrative this volume seeks to decolonise and deconstruct controls almost everything under the Sun. It created almost everything that is seen and unseen. It also has the power to turn whatever it creates upside down according to its need based on its needs and set timeframe. Escobar (2008) maintains that "the oppressor, the colonisers, the dominant seek to occupy time and energy of the subaltern to preclude difference from becoming an active social force" (p. 18) in so doing, the current dominant grand narrative seeks to dominate everybody so as to follow its line of thinking (*pensamiento unico* or single thought as Escobar puts it) which will deprive him or her chances of rebelling against it. This reminds me a famous Latin maxim *Roma locuta est, causa finita est* namely, Roma has spoken the cause if finished. This sounds like Bush's assertion–I touched on earlier–who says that if you are not with us you are against us. It means this is the prolongation of the same mindset by the person of high position that toxic education created based on hegemonic grand narrative. In other words, what Bush said is what the *modern-day Roma* had decided; and had no appeal. Moreover, the current dominant grand narrative is, in a sense, so divisive that others cannot use their differences to take on it if they are obsessed with serving the grand narrative as it currently is. The simple example is nobody thinks about changing the neoliberal democracy based on market that benefits rich countries. Oddly, such countries have been using the yardstick of democracy as a cudgel to whack their enemies as it happened to Gaddafi, *idi*, mentioned hereinabove.

Furthermore, the current grand narrative started from faith which is displayed through religions and the *realpolitik* of the world currently after inventing the Bible–as a constitution of a patriarchal system of the world–created, defined everything that was thereafter just fitted in easily and methodically.

So, too, this is the time when and how Adam–the father of patriarchal arrangement–was invented and created to represent man, the ruler over everything under the Sun. Here the concentration was what on Plato refers to as andropoeisis or *fabrication of man* instead of anthropopoiesis or *fabrication of human* and gunaikopoeisis or *fabrication of woman* (Calame, 1999). So, we can arguably see how the whole process was based on fabrication and invention of somebody but not the creation of humanity. After Adam was fabricated and given power, thereafter, Eve–the weaker, criminal, sinner, irrational and emotional–was created, criminalised and condemned to represent weak creatures (females) for men to rule, own, use, and abuse as they deem fit for their benefits and pleasures. After creating such dichotomous existence among genders, the myth-cum-tale of "forbidden fruit" was enacted and started arguing that Eve received the forbidden fruit from the serpent and gave it to Adam. Unfortunately for the dominant grand narrative, it did not define or tell who this serpent was.

Likewise, by creating the serpent with high reasoning and convincing powers, the dominant grand narrative forgot the fact that by doing so, it was portraying its *God Almighty* as an antithesis to the position of knowing all and everything the dominant grand narrative apportioned to him or her or it. Controversial as it has been, the arrogant grand narrative seemed to have lost its brain in that it created visibly contradictory things. For example, under the constitution of the dominant grand narrative, the Bible, the role of a woman was to be under the authority of the man. The man was created as a go-getter and the protector of a woman. Therefore, circumstantially, the man was the hunter and the king of everything including the woman who unfortunately was not made a queen in this utopian kingdom of God of the dominant grand narrative.

Looking at the subservience and controllable role a woman was given, one can ask, her role was to stay indoors and the man outdoors (private and public spheres), how then Eve was able to loiter and meet with the serpent and agree upon harvesting the forbidden fruit? This contradicts the whole chicanery in that Eve was more reasonable and heuristic than Adam who waited at home for Eve to bring him what she gathered. A real and true God cannot be biased or misogynistic as the gods of new religions have always been through demonising women and making them half humans or just commodities in some societies. Refer to the honour killings in some countries or exclusionary policies in many countries–including the so-called developed ones–where women do not partake of politics equally with men. Refer to the US where Hilary Clinton became the first female presidential candidate for a major party in the history of the country. This is after over 200 hundred years of independence.

More on Adam, as a man, if he were more rational than Eve, why did he fail to manage the situation while he was empowered by God? For, he would have stopped Eve from eating the forbidden fruit. But instead, he, as well, ate the fruit while he was aware that it was brought by an irrational creature according to status Eve was relegated to by the Bible. The Bible, Genesis (1:26-27) notes:

> Then God said, "Let us make man in our image, in our likeness, and let them rule over the fish of the sea and the birds of the air, over the livestock, over all the earth, and over all the creatures that move along the ground." So God created man in his own image, in the image of God he created him; male and female he created them.

On its side, the Quran (38:71-72) says "and (remember) when your Lord said to the angels: 'I am going to create a human (Adam) from sounding clay of altered black smooth mud. So when I have fashioned him and breathed into him (his) soul created by Me, then you fall down prostrate to him." If what the two books of the neo-religions say is true, why did Adam accept the forbidden fruit without questioning its legality as his way of proving his rationality and superiority while he knew God had "forbidden" it? Does it mean that Adam did not know how irrational Eve was? The Quran (2:31) seems to dispute and contradict itself noting that "he taught Adam all the names of everything." If this is the case, was Adam taught the name of the fruit and the sin? Doesn't Adam's behaviour prove that, while he was tabula rasa, Eve gained knowledge before he did so as to become his teacher after entering an agreement with a serpent? The Bible does not tell where the serpent or Satan in the Quran got the knowledge from and why; and if it was God who gave this knowledge why giving it to it but not to Adam or Eve if God really loved them? Such questions are not asked to see or find whom to blame. According to these two books, the buck seems to stop with God. All such questions are asked in order to get right answers that can only be provided by the decolonised education that will be unbiased. Further, the aim of these questions is to emancipate the woman, among other victims, from the sin the patriarch system created. For, thenceforward, despite the coming of Jesus to purify the sins of mankind, a woman has never been exonerated. She carries her cross along with Jesus! The woman is more on the cross than Jesus who was put on it just once and saved.

Moreover, the victims of neo-religions have always been on the cross suffering from trauma, shame, exploitation, humiliation, and above all, division and hatred among themselves as it can be seen in many sectarian conflicts. MacFarlane & Khong (2006) précis the fate of women in that they are the last to be educated and employed but the first to be fired due to the fact that their gender attracts abuses from childhood to adulthood under the current dominant grand narrative. This is the plight of women all over the world including the West itself where women are still exploited, used and abused compared to men. I usually tell my wife that if I were a woman, no enemy would par with religion for me. Despite the West preaching equality, just like those they preach it to, it is still doing the same. If you exclude Scandinavian countries wherein females are approaching parity with males, the rest is still patriarchal, especially in politics and financial institutions. The salary between men and women are different. In many countries, women receive less than men with the same level of education and the same job. In the US which has always acted as a champion of human rights, equality and liberties, women are exploited based on their gender. West & Curtis (2006) maintain that "by 2003, women comprised 43 percent of all faculty, 39 percent of full-time and 48 percent of part-time faculty. Women occupied about 9 percent of full professor positions at four-year colleges and universities in 1972 and still only 24 percent of all full professors in 2003" (p. 5).

Once again, such findings and statistics above show how unequal, and of course, unfair the current grand narrative is. The statistics also shows the double standard of the grand narrative in that Western countries are good at tutoring others to fulfill women's rights while they trample on them at home. All these miseries women know of today originate from the creation of Eve. For the sake of argument, let us agree that Eve brought the *forbidden fruits*. Even if it were true that Eve brought the fruit, a sane, considerate and fair God or human would not wholesale condemn all females for all generation *ad infinitum*. If Adam had refused to eat the *forbidden fruit*, maybe, men would have gotten a pretext to condemn all women however unfair and unreasonable it would have been. Again, do you condemn all women born and unborn because of one person, Eve? If it were before reasonable court of law today, Eve and the serpent were the ones to be punished but not all women or mankind all depending on their defense.

Primarily, when Adam agreed to eat the forbidden fruit, in law, he became an accomplice who is treated as equally guilty as the actual doer. By conspiring with Eve, Adam, too, became a culprit but not their progenies. Religions argue that Eve was told that she would deliver with pains. Well, why do female animals–which did not commit this crime–go through the same horrible ordeal while they are innocent? Another weakness of this grand narrative is the continuation of the punishment to women indicated above. For, the Bible says that a woman will bear babies with pangs (Genesis 3: 16), and the snake would crawl and eat dust (Genesis 3: 14) which is the nature of everything. Maybe, the Bible was ignorant of the fact that without labour pains, no expectant mother can naturally deliver a baby. We see this in animals that were not a part of the curse. As argued above, treating labour pains as a punishment is the ignorance of science the same drive that forced the church to punish Galilei for making a scientific statement. This shows how the Bible failed to understand the causes of labour pains which are but the forces that help the baby come out. This is a simple science that even animals know the Bible failed to underscore. After being done with Eve, God then told Adam that he will live by toiling. Again, how come female animals do toil like male ones if God intended to be a fair judge?

Ironically, for the humans that God "loved" so exceptionally so as to send his only *begotten son,* still face the consequences of Adam's and Eve's sins as if they were accomplices. Is this why Jesus said that everybody will carry his cross? Moreover, you can see this fallacy in the belief that the crucifixion of Jesus annulled the sins on earth while the same Jesus clearly stated that everybody will carry his cross. Such myths and lies have persisted for over two thousand years due to the toxicity of colonial education devoid of critical thinking. While free and true African thinkers wonder on the relevance of such myths, European thinkers, too, do the same and they are not ridiculed the way Africans have been ridiculed for many generations. For example Lubbock (1871) cited in Strother (2013) notes that "the negro believes that by means of the fetish he can coerce and control his deity" (p. 16). What difference does it make for the one who uses his fetish to coerce his deity and the one who uses whips to coerce his God like how it was done when Jesus was crucified? Swahili sage has it that the monkey does not see its buttocks. This is why it laughs at the backsides of other monkeys. Giacomo Casanova cited in Lehner (2010) maintains that whoever invokes faith to elucidate or ponder on an event that can be explained by reason is a fool and unworthy of reasonable thought.

Fundamentally, the arguments and questions above aim at showing the flaws of the whole idea of biblical and qur'anic creation as it was invented and executed by the current dominant grand narrative. No human system or ideas are perfect a hundred per cent. The current grand narrative has always mystified its God. Again, God who can carpet bomb everybody with punishment–present and absent–cannot be God of justice and Truth. Such cannot be God at all. To add salt to injury, the proponents of colonial grand narrative assert that their God is love and merciful. Is this love? How if the same God did not apply the same to females? If this God of the current grand narrative were merciful, why didn't he, she or it forgive Adam and Eve? Why did he extend the capital penalty to all creatures as Genesis (2:7) maintains that "but of the tree of the knowledge of good and evil you shall not eat, for in the day that you eat of it you shall surely, die." How ruthless this God is who can condemn a person to death for the first offence that does not involve homicide? What makes this God ruthless and irrational is the fact that he, she or it extended the same brutal punishment the world is seeking to abolish to all living creatures.

Again, did God commit all such fallacy or those who created him did? Furthermore, one may argue that all such fallacies were committed to show how ignorant the authors of the Bible were at the time. If they could not know that the earth was spherical, how would they know death as a natural phenomenon?

No wonder, such flaws have ruled the world for decades. It is simply because toxic education did not equip its recipients with critical thinking so as to question and thwart such fallacies. I think with toxic education it is easy for such things to be rationalised and internalised even if they are nonsensical and full of flaws. The criminalisation of females may be cited as a good source of family violence, sexual abuse, battering and commodification not to mention *thingification* (Lütticken, 2010) or objectification (Gruenfeld, Inesi, Magee & Galinsky, 2008), the vending and commercialisation of human and cultural *femmincidio* or the killing of women by men because they are women (Meyers, 1994 cited in Giomi, 2015) and many more brutalities females face simply because they are females. By addressing the flaws of the grand narrative, among others, patriarchal and misogynistic behaviours, as academics, we will be able to seek to lessen conflict resulting from discrimination or exploitation based on sexual orientation. By identifying the sources of such conflicts, it becomes much easier to address the root causes of the phenomenon and persistence of gender-based violence (GBV). It is important to take on whatever root causes of sexual-based violence regardless of the power or fame the entity or philosophy, faith, belief or system espousing is. This is obvious. For example, when sexual scandal rattled the Catholic Church many were shocked. Slowly, fear has dissipated and victims are coming forth. The same goes with GBV. Professionals and academics need to speak for the voiceless victims of such violence. By researching and exposing flaws in the institution that sanctions systemic sexual abuses based on patriarchal and hegemonic system espoused by some metanarratives be they dominate or not, we will be breaking the ice. And this is only possible through decolonised education. Such a take should benefit all victims of the evils of the current grand narrative equally and sustainably.

Despite long time sufferings women endured under the current dominant grand narrative, one may argue, they took a long time too to take on it, at least, from within. One may wonder why women did not rebel against this supremacist grand narrative. There are many explanations. Firstly, when the grand narrative started to work, it would be sacrilegious for any person to oppose or question it. We have seen how Galilei was intimidated for telling the truth he got after conducting researches. Therefore, in the first phase of the grand narrative, it did not make any sense to question it or rebel against it. First of all, it was risky for one to try to do so. Despeux & Kohn (2017) cite an example of Daoism in China that considered women to be inferior creatures. So, too, as I have indicated above how the Anabaptists and other reformist groups were persecuted in Europe. If cohesive, committed and strong groups such as the Huguenots and Protestants tried and faced indescribable terrors, how could women start the same while they were under the close watch of their beloved ones (husbands) as the conscious or unconscious agents of the dominant grand narrative?

Logically, it was illogical at the time for women to question the grand narrative due to the fact that they were conditioned to see through its lenses the same way some degraded and exploited females in some cultures and religions still see the system that brutally dehumanised and destroy them. More importantly, through the mass media of the time, women were bombarded with the gospel of submission the grand narrative authored so as to be part and parcel of it as it currently is through toxic education whereby victims cannot question the *status quo*. Through such means, women internalised everything without any right to question any fallacies or controversies. As indicated above, one of those controversies is the whole story of creation of a macho man to rule over docile and soft females, animals, plants, birds, lizards and all creatures. In other words, neo-religion made a man to be the *god* of all creatures. This grand narrative gave immense powers to man; and it prescribes the objectification of the females on the one hand while it pretends and refers to the victims as the beloved ones! Ironically, they *love* females so much that they end up objectifying and torturing them! Again, is this a new type of love, if God loved the world so as to poignantly send his only begotten son to die for it? Did he? If he did, was it for the *love* of the world of his self-preservation not to mention father's declaration of his conditional kingdom? Controversy, controversy, controversy *ad infinitum*! You can see these controversies in the story of creating the grand narrative has maintained to be true while it is not.

Almond (2008) explains creational controversy and myth very well arguing:

> This is the book about central myth of Western culture–the story of the creation of Adam and Eve, of the Garden of Eden, of mysterious tree of the knowledge of good and evil, of a talking snake, of temptations, of nakedness of shame and shame clothed, of loss and expulsion. Furthermore, Almond argues that Adam was not a paradisal creature.

Who actually was Adam? Almond goes further arguing that the Hebrew text suggests that Adam was created somewhere else to prove how suspicious this account of creation the grand narrative uses is. Such an argument proves how false and fabricated the whole project is. The Bible seems to concur with such an argument as I will prove hereunder. Again, despite such claim that Adam was the first person to be created according to the Bible and the Quran, there are some controversies of which one can be found in the Bible in the book of Genesis (6:4) which says that "there were giants in the earth in those days; and also after that, when the sons of God came in unto the daughters of men, and they bare [children] to them, the same [became] mighty men which [were] of old, men of renown." This statement tells us that there were two types of hominids at the time namely, Adam's generation and that of giants or otherwise known as Nephilim that seem to predate Adam's generation due to the fact that they had been on earth before Adam was created. Rizvi (n.d.) notes that "as per Hebrew linguistic the noun Nephelim is emerged from primitive root verb Naphal which means "to fall" so the noun "Fallen one" is correct English translation, which means "the defeated one

317

and the extinct one" (p. 2); also see Roberts (2012); and Bosman & Poorthuis (2015). Where did they come from; and where did they go and why? Neither the Bible nor the Quran knows. In other words, Almond (*Ibid.*) testifies to the truth that Adam is but a creature of the grand narrative but not the product of the intentional creation of God. Adam is more a theoretical-cum-philosophical tool than real for the grand narrative to assert the omnipotence-cum-omniscience as opposed to any other logical and antithetic thinking. When it comes to conflict, gender-based conflicts are always tilting the balance of the life between men and women. Sexism, gender violence and sexual degradation, sexual exploitation and sexual segregation originate from this creation of Adam (Genesis 2:15); Eve (Genesis: 22), serpent, tree of knowledge and the Garden of Eden (Genesis 2-3). In other words, the current mantality or masculinising everything powerful (which is superior to females or womantality or feminising everything weaker) was conceived and put in place for the male to dominate everything in the world.

Thenceforth, anything related to man was associated with being competent, kvell or proud, powerful, knowledgeable, privileged and authentic and perfect compared to everything female. Imagine; how we use the word to man to mean furnish with strength or powers of resistance among others. As indicated in the section of racism how black is used, here is where the philosophy of exploitation and inequality espoused by the grand narrative of reinventing everything emanates. A simple example is on how Adam got knowledge. The Bible says that Adam and Eve got knowledge of evil and good after eating the forbidden truth the serpent gave to Eve who also gave to Adam (Genesis 3:5-22). Again, if Adam and Eve obtained their knowledge of good and evil after eating the forbidden fruit, one may argue therefore that the serpent did a good job of equipping humanity with the knowledge we currently boast of having over other beings. For, it is this knowledge of good and evil that differentiates us from other animals. Again, if Adam and Eve did not have knowledge to know good and evil, they were *tabula rasa* even the whole exercise, by the serpent to teach them what to eat and not, is a mere fabrication so to speak. How could people who did not know the difference between bad and evil be taught anything? In law, once a person is mentally incapable just like Adam and Eve were, such a person [s] cannot be held liable for any offence so committed by her or him. If this is the argument, then God created *tabula rasa* creatures; and of all creation, he did not create knowledge. So, the argument that God created everything becomes more suspicious and untenable than anything.

Additionally, you can see this fallacy in the fact Satan was an archangel that rebelled against God. Isaiah (14:12) notes "how art thou fallen from heaven, O Lucifer, son of the morning!" Arguably, the whole concept that Satan was the archangel who rebelled does not make sense if we consider the fact that angels are like robots in that they do not have the will of theirs. So, too, it shows that God does not know everything just as the Bible asserts (Luke 1:37). Had God known that his *archangel* would rebel, he would not have felt bad so as to become angry and thereby curse him so as to become Satan who is as so confusing as the *forbidden fruit*. When I was a kid I asked what type of the tree of knowledge it was so that I could have more knowledge. I did not get the right answer until I grew up. If you read the Bible–among many contradictions–you see the fabrication clearly. Genesis (1:29-30) says:

> Then God said, "I give you every seed-bearing plant on the face of the whole earth and every tree that has fruit with seed in it. They will be yours for food. And to all the beasts of the earth and all the birds in the sky and all the creatures that move along the ground—everything that has the breath of life in it—I give every green plant for food." And it was so.

If God truly allowed Adam and Eve to eat from all trees, then where did this *forbidden fruit* come from? Not only that, even the creation of serpent is controversial given that there is no special mentioning of how it was given more intelligence than humans were given. There are a lot of contradictions so to speak. Again, with toxic education, for many years, people have never questioned the authenticity of the story of creation. They swallowed it as it is as if it is true. And this has been done for many decades without education providing answers. Essentially, the education that supports discrimination, injustice and exploitation is unjust; and such education is as good as ignorance.

Again, when I asked about the forbidden fruit some people misconstrued it as the act of Adam and Eve to have sexual intercourses which means that God did not create sex or sexual desires, if it is true that the serpent is the one who taught them. If this is the line of thinking, without sexual desires how would Adam and Eve multiply so as to fill earth like the sand? Does it mean God did not create humans to multiply while the Bible says they were ordered to go and multiply like the sands of the ocean?

Again, why were all forgiven except the serpent and the woman? Where did serpent's hyper knowledge go if at all the current generation of snakes we have do not have more knowledge than human do? Others say that the snake means the penis. If it is so, why did then God create it or a serpent? It is illogical to say that there can be baby delivering without pangs or without penis being put at work. Naturally, pangs are the forces that enable the baby to get out of the womb. This is a simple science that even goats know. There are many questions about this myth that needs to be demystified so as to liberate females from the so-called natural sin that seems to be a creature of the grand narrative.

Additionally, there are those who assert that whatever appears in the story of creation was the God's plan. If it were God's plan, why did God punish Adam and Eve for fulfilling his plan of starting the multiplication of the world? Had God not conceived this very plan, Adam and Eve would not have fallen in the trap. Such question covers even Jesus' death on the cross. Judas Iscariot, who enhanced his capture so that God's will could be fulfilled, was condemned. Again, why should you condemn the person who made God's "plan" possible? Why condemning the person or force that is fulfilling what is written and desired by the creator? And why did Jesus cry on the cross as if he did not know what was to happen to him given that he said that his father called him and chose him to take the cross which he affirmed? We need to revisit the story of the criminalisation of females that seems to be the creation of patriarchal system. As conflict academics and mere thinkers, we know that many females in various places of the world are tortured even killed simply because they are females. This–apart from being a crime against humanity–is a violent conflict. Violence in families and workplaces resulting from gender discrimination are real.

Once more, where did it start? The answer is that all started with the coinage or invention of the grand narrative we have today; that needs great changes to benefit all members of human family. We read about sad incidents whereby women are killed or they set themselves on fire to free themselves from tortures based on gender discrimination displayed under various pretexts such as honour killings resulting from religion, traditions and whatnots. The suffering does not end up here. Women are owned just like any objects because of their sexual category. When discrimination against females goes on in many places, the very grand narrative comes in advocating for equality of all human beings without erasing historical discrimination based on the narrative of it creation as displayed in religions. To do justice, the same grand narrative should declare null and void all writings, belief and ideologies that assert that God first created a man and the woman came from his ribs, or she was created as a helper to the man. All this needs the decolonisation and detoxification of the current education. There is no way justice can be served or be done to females without banning all literatures that portray them as weak creatures from the day they were created.

Additionally, in some countries, women are offered special seats in the parliament and other decisionmaking bodies. Instead of benefiting them, such seats have acted as means of causing squabbles among women if not acting as a speed governor as Tripp (2005) observes that "in some countries, the introduction of quotas was linked to the attempt to create new state patronage networks" (p. 58) all aimed at keeping the *status quo*. Tripp shows that preferential or special seats were introduced to African countries after the change of international politics. I do not think that women need special seats. Instead, they need special tools of looking at the truth as it is; and this special way is the decolonisation of education.

Many a time, I wonder. I do not hear the story of special seats in the US, Canada and Britain to mention but a few. Why? I think it is because Africa has always been on the receiving end almost for everything as far as *modernity* is concerned thanks to the grand narrative that re-invented it and everything. Sadly though, despite this open political segregation, African countries that have "empowered" African women by increasing the quotas of special seats are going around kvelling for having embarked on true democracy. As mentioned in foregoing chapters, some African empires and Aboriginal peoples of the Americas had a very elaborate-, progressive-, and gender balanced representation in decisionmaking bodies. Tripp makes a good point in her conclusion showing that, sometimes, special seats can be a ploy males use aimed at getting women support the *status quo* during elections. Further, Tripp *(Ibid.)* notes that "in other instances, government leaders may be seeking to create new lines of patronage and to ensure loyal support as old networks become problematic or threatening (Rwanda and Uganda)" (p. 60). Currently Rwanda is praised to have more women representation than any country on earth. Again, how many female presidents or Prime Minister has ever Rwanda or Uganda had? Indeed, for many countries celebrating the *liberation* of women through special seats the situation is the same. For, you will wonder to hear countries termed as authoritarian democracies meet this requirement while the system that led to women exploitation is still the same. Why should women be favoured if we are all equal?

Truly, if we want to do justice for women as far as representation is concerned, we must reform the patriarchal system espoused by the current dominant grand narrative. If we want to do justice for females, we must agree to correct all historical injustices they have suffered under the dictate of the current dominant grand narrative among others. Without addressing these anomalies, gender imbalance, sexual exploitation, battering and many more gender crimes, violence will increase due to being supported by the current dominant grand narrative that pretends to fight against them. In many cases, many people have received threats for opposing certain carbuncular things. Historically, religious violence (Danjibo, 2009) has been the hallmark of neo-religions. Many societies were destroyed and many people, especially females borne the brunt due to being categorised as second-class human beings almost in all religions.

Up until now, despite being discriminated and commodified, females have never been treated equally in the eyes of religions. As to the question why females took a long time to question the grand narrative, I think that it takes time for victims to become aware of their plight and fate. The decolonised education seeks to enable such victims take their destiny in their hands to make sure that all anomalies embedded in the current grand narrative are being dealt with and erased so as to create an equal society of humans. All narratives and beliefs that condemn people based on their gender, history, race and whatnots need to be legally forced to recant such beliefs, canons and *diktats* regardless whether they are from God or man.

Back to the evolution of the grand narrative, as it gained momentum, slowly, God became he, the king and a man-like power that created all things privileging males over females. Subsequently, it created the son; and lastly, the Holy Ghost to make the holy trinity. Jesus, an Arab or Jew was reinvented to become a Caucasian (refer to his modern portrait). His mother, too, was *caucasianised*–and of course–Westernised to look like a Greek or an Italian but not an Arab which she was.

Slowly, Europeanisation of the faith took shape by Europe propagating the same even by committing unspeakable crimes against humanity. Refer to the burning at stake, drowning of Protestants who took a shot on the *chosen faith*. Going against this "sacred and chosen" narrative warranted all types of persecution. Slowly, the faith became the government of the world. Rome became the center of everything before others schemed to come with their versions of grand narrative based on faith. It has reached a point when it has become a god that can challenge even God it invented. The current grand narratives outsized and outthought even God it said it was prophesying! Really, if there is the source of the current look of things *vis-a-vis* Judaeo-Christian grand narrative which is the parent to the current dominant grand narrative, it is nowhere except here where the concept of belief was invented to mean being sure of what you are not sure of as if you are. Are you? Merriam Webster online dictionary defines faith as, 'a feeling of being sure that someone or something exists or that something is true. Does it and is it? Nobody bothers to explain or interrogate! To me, God–if he or she or it ever exists–is too convoluted and large for a human mind to conceive and comprehend. S/he is too wise to be defended by myopic humans who do not even the whole of their bodies. And I think; this is why there are many versions of God and faiths. Anyway, this is my view. However it is not hard to see the controversy and contradictions if one investigate and interrogate the whole shibboleth. Indeed, beliefs have become a very big and multipronged problem to the world today. Beliefs and faiths are used–as they were used before–to create many conflicts wantonly. Everybody stands by his or her faith, which is good.

However, without providing any proofs of what the said faith or beliefs asserts, the world now is caught in between off-guard. Terrorism, self-aggrandisement and monopoly of the beliefs are tearing the world apart. Everybody says her or his faith is the most authentic and superior to others without even scientifically substantiating. Despite such fallacy, neither the governments nor the dominant grand narrative force such a person to prove her or his claims. It is a mere confusion-cum-convolution whereby faiths and beliefs are used as vehicles of achieving other hidden goals and intentions all aimed at dominance of one another wantonly. Faiths and beliefs have stood now to define civilisation and superiority of the world by uplifting and disparaging some civilisations, cultures and parts of the world.

Fundamentally, the grand narrative of any people defines almost everything. For example, the current dominant grand narrative has created too many rules and laws governing everything and everybody in the universe so as to end up contravening itself. It decides as to when we should go to bed or awake depending on what it wants from us. Although is the invention of man, it is here to stay if we do not take on it by radically advocating and agitating for overhauling and decolonising it so that it can serve all humans based on their grand narratives. Along with the current grand narrative, we need to overhaul other grand narratives that are now dividing humans based on faiths whereby some preach brotherhood based more on religion than biological relationship and reality?

The world currently has even misconstrued version of brotherhood that is more built on religious affiliation than biological and human. This is why you see Western folks go to fight along radical groups in some parts of the world as it was in the case of many so-called terrorist groups in the Middle East and now in Africa. Such "brotherhood" becomes even stronger than anything to the extent that such the "brethren" are readily to kill their blood brothers and sisters they grew up with because of this utopian and newly-found brotherhood. As for who my truly brother is, I think; I do not need anybody to teach me who my brother or sister is. Even birds, despite having small brains and crania know who their siblings are. So, trying to reinvent and redefine who is my brother or sibling is nothing abusing my intelligence. The problem of being taught of whom your brother or sister is that when you refuse to buy into such ridiculous chicanery hatred, and intimidation, threats follow as it currently is in areas where terrorists operate. Occasionally, I wonder when I hear some people misconstrue their faiths saying that God orders people say to die for his religion. Why should God who cannot and does not die let mortals fight for his religion while he or she or it cannot die? Is there any truth in such a take? Is it God who orders that or people who use God or create God to justify their buried agenda? Such questions cannot be ignored or pushed under the carpet. Knowing how to go about them arguably create good environment for peace. By allowing dialogue, questions and answers, freethinking and doubts, we will be able to defend what we believe in so as to convince or otherwise our opponents all aimed at seeking understanding. All in all, such a leveled ground cannot be reached without decolonising the current regime of toxic education based on only one grand narrative of the West.

More on who is my brother or sister, ironically, most of those brethren are the victims of the same grand narrative perpetrated by those who want to redefine their identity and relations in order to save their faces or avoid liability in the crimes they committed against their victims under whatever ruse be it political, economic or religious in the past! The victims and perpetrators as well need to question newly-found brotherhood by looking at the history of–for example– colonialism or slave trade. Well, if this drive for brotherhood is true and sincere, then where were such narratives when the same *teachers* of newly-found brotherhood and equality were selling Africans to slavery or colonising them? Controversy!

One of the areas to be revisited and interrogated is the past especially when the current grand narrative stated to dominate the world. For example, during colonialism and slavery, making profits was closer and more important to the preachers of *brotherhood* than the *brotherhood* they are preaching now. To put it in the context, try to imagine if you were an African peasant who was converted to Christianity before your beloved ones were shipped to America. Will you subscribe to such brotherhood those who sold or bought your beloved ones are now preaching without seeking redress from the institutions that offended you? Would you listen to such empty talks without asking for forgiveness and redress first?

Besides, you can see double standards in many things with respect to the current dominant grand narrative. For example, foreign religions assert that committing adultery is a sin which indeed it is even in the so-called African traditional religions. What will be your reaction if your teachers–under whatever religion–told you that adultery that you know is a sin is no longer a sin? Will you just turn and follow such double-faced teachers, doubt them or start rebelling against their teachings? The right thing to do here is obvious. However, sometimes, when you rebel against such double standards and impositions, you are called names. All this happens simply because you have decided to use your will and common sense. Calling names does not end up with rebelling against such lies.

In a nutshell, the current grand narrative is always controversial due to the fact that, sometimes, as the time goes by, it exposes itself through changing goal posts. While all this happens, toxic education embedded in the current grand narrative does not offer right answers to such issues. It was the same as it currently is when the same torturers talk about human rights based on exonerating and protecting themselves. My grandfather used to tell me that the day the elephants become aware of who they are so as to start talking like humans, the humans will preach reconciliation and equality among beasts and humans to avoid being punished by the elephants that humans have brutalised for many years. Try to imagine. If African countries could come together and form cartels (Mhango, 2016) for everything they produce, do you think multinational companies and their mother governments would be attaching strings to whatever deals they do with Africa? Remember; what oil cartels such as the OPEC caused to the consumers who changed tactics so as to embark on overthrowing whatever government that seems to reinvigorate the aims of the OPEC. Remember what befell the Saddam Hussein when he started reawakening Arabs on how to use oil as their weapon against the current dominant grand narrative?

One of the contentious issues resulting from the current dominant grand narrative is the whole concepts of human rights, even human security. Although human rights, as a concept, is a good move that hypothetically aims at realising human rights to all human beings, it makes more sense theoretically than it does practically. The concept has some controversies such as its universality as opposed to selectivity, viability against unviability, applicability against inapplicability, and impracticability against practicability all over the world. Goodhart (2013) observes that "the rhetoric of human rights declares the idea to be universal" (p. 11) which is practically and viably not the case though.

Poignantly, looking at the meaning of rhetoric, I find that from its inception, the UDHRC (1948) was meant to be a more theoretical than a practical tool of realising human rights to all human beings in the world. It was not only practical for the West and a hoax for the rest. Underscoring such flaws, we need to find what should be done to see to it that human rights are attained all over the world. It is only through the decolonisation and detoxification of education that we can achieve this either collectively or severally; however, united we stand and divided we fall. Africa can lead the way by starting to decolonise its episteme and demand its grand narratives be incorporated in the order or the world. To know how rhetoric does not imply the practicability of the action intended, Poulakos (1983) cited in Jafarian, Azizifar, Jamalinesari & Gowhary (2015) defines rhetoric as "… the art which seeks to capture in opportune moments that which is appropriate and attempts to suggest that which is possible" (p. 214). How possible has the realisation of human rights for non-Western been, particularly in Africa? Due to being rhetorical, the said rights have become what Goodhart (*Ibid.*) observes that "have been dogged by philosophical questioning" (p. 13). This "philosophical questioning" (Pennycook, 2006) is obvious due to the fact that since the inception of human rights, they have never been realised in many parts of the world, especially in Africa that went on being under colonialism even after the inception of the concept under the UDHR. Goodhart (*op.cit.*) notes that "Western theories have commonly conceived of human rights as entitlements" (p. 33) but not rights without asking "to and for whom" due to the fact that they were enjoyed by a few as opposed to all. With decolonised episteme, the schism between entitlements or privileges and rights would have been explored. If human rights are entitlements for every human being, how come that African countries did not enjoy and feel them?

Maybe, if entitlements are interpreted as privileges, they become something optional for someone to have or enjoy. In law, when something is an entitlement for all, it becomes legally enforceable for all; and when someone does not get it is offended. Thus, such a person has legal rights to seek remedies before the court of law. To the contrary, when something becomes a privilege, it cannot be deemed legally as an automatic right for everybody to enjoy or get. The question still lingers, did all non-West enjoy the said human rights? The answer is obviously negative, as indicated above, women were excluded. So, as victims, academics and professionals, we should seek to change the current grand narrative so that human rights become equally available to all human beings universally. We cannot preach equality while some of us are more equal than others.

Again, under the current dominant grand narrative, those who own it are more privileged under its prescriptions than others who are excluded not to mention their grand narratives. Through the decolonisation of epistemes, the world will be able to see the weakness of the practicability and applicability of human rights and other so-called entitlements so as to think about redressing those who were denied the very rights after the UDHR. For, it is historically evident that they did not enjoy or get the said rights.

Moreover, human rights being more rhetorical than practical need to be deconstructed, and completely be reconstructed and redefined to suit all human beings universally, and equally. This is essential due to the fact that "the greater part of what we appeal to when we appeal to human rights is controversial and contested" (Goodhart *op.cit.*, p. 23). This controversy can be seen even today in Australia, Canada and the US where Aboriginal peoples are systematically marginalised and maltreated. The evidence to support such claims is not hard to get. There are some reserves that do not have safe water. Boyd (2011) observes that "thousands of First Nations people, living on reserves across Canada, still lack access to running water or flush toilets." If the section of population in such a developed country is going without such an essential need, what of people in developing countries? Correspondingly, such violation of human rights and double standard can be seen in many conflicts today.

Sometimes, it baffles to find that conflict resolution professionals; diplomats and academics are invited to deal with conflicts whereby some powerful countries have interests. They pretend to suggest resolutions while, at the same time, the same countries arm and finance those violating the rights of others wantonly not to mention sidelining ordinary people in the grassroots. Sadly though, not all professionals and academics who tell such countries that there cannot be any solution without telling those powerful countries stop from tampering with the process. As professionals and academics, to prove that we are not subscribing to toxic and colonial education, we need to boycott such processes that we surely know cannot bear any fruits without changing the *status quo* and the way things are done in an *ex parte* way. Participating in such processes we know will fail, apart from degrading us by proving how our toxic education is at work, exacerbates the conflict. Evidently, this proves how we fear those countries so as to condone their dirty deeds. To free ourselves from such controversy, we need to state categorically that level ground is important; shall there be any need for resolving such protracted conflicts. And indeed, through decolonising education by taking on the current dominant grand narrative is the only way we can succeed in this adventure that is aimed at benefitting everybody on earth.

Colonialism, under the dominant grand narrative, uses hegemonic and toxic approaches to intimidate and thus rule over and overrule others. It is duplicitous and full of flaws simply by being colonial and hegemonic. I think and advise everybody, particularly academics, politicians and activists, to use their expertise in their fields to carry out the decolonisation and the detoxification of the current regime of hegemonic and toxic episteme[s] so that every civilisation, culture and grand narrative can equally and fully contribute to the new decolonised regime of education that aims at seeking answers for all human beings without discrimination or exclusion. Should those benefitting from the current dominant grand narrative refuse, victims should come and work together to decolonise all epistemes they inherited from their former colonial masters.

Nothing is impossible if human beings face the reality committedly and honestly for the benefit of our world that we all share. We need to decolonise and overhaul the current system of education that has proved to be a failure for some people on earth, especially when we consider the fact that those who have an upper hand tend to use it to exploit those with no say at all. We need to think about equality and equity in addressing all anomalies and evils mentioned and discussed in this tome. Furthermore, the book has clearly stated that the current dominant episteme is biased; and it has created astounding academic racism and neo-racism (Gupta, 2007) based on double standard and fallacies aimed at and applied on non-Western societies. This is why the decolonisation of this sort of episteme is inevitable and viable as it aims at acting as a catalyst for cultural and academic reconciliation that aims at garnering other nuggets from other civilisations of the world to top up to the current narrative or forming a new grand narrative of the world. The current colonial-cum-toxic education has failed to do justice for other civilisations of the world. Instead, it has been used to exploit and belittle them as if they are not the societies or civilisations of humans. Essentially, the colonised education has totally failed to do justice in that it has totally failed to treat the world fairly and equitably.

Moreover, the current hegemonic and toxic education has caused a lot of suffering for the whole globe especially in environmental, conflict, human rights and legal issues as elaborated above. Therefore, this regime of education needs to urgently be changed so that it can serve and suit all human beings judiciously and equitably in order to alleviate or eradicate conflict in the modern world.

Most importantly, the decolonised episteme[s] must incorporate other grand narratives to top up on whatever good the current dominant grand narrative has. So, too, everything needs to be deconstructed *vis-à-vis* all notable anomalies resulting from colonial desire to perpetually exploiting others. It is evident that, just like any other purely Western-centric systems and fields, the current hegemonic education needs to be deconstructed structurally, and thus decolonised in principles, theories and practices so as to accommodate other cultures and civilisations of the world. This decolonisation can go through various phases such as deconstruction, reconstruction, reconstitution, restoration and then consensus building. Also, the deconstruction must be noted; it is the process that may take many generations. Importantly, we need to leg up for it by making sure that victims do consciously participate in the process in order to bring about desired change in conflict. We can expand on this saying that our consciousness should involve not only conflict social change but change in all fields. We henceforth, as academics and victims of the current toxic education, have to start thinking about taking new steps of decolonising our fields with the aim of doing justice to both sides namely, the perpetrators who benefitted from this sort of education and the victims who suffered under it.

I can wind up this tome with nuggets from Moore & Brugnatelli (2003) who, when faced with reality of America being hated by many people under George W. Bush, in their book *Stupid White Men*, note "friends, when are we going to stop kidding ourselves?" Let us stand together to decolonised and detoxify the current colonial-cum-hegemonic education embedded in the current dominant grand narrative so that we can move forward together as partners and equal human beings.

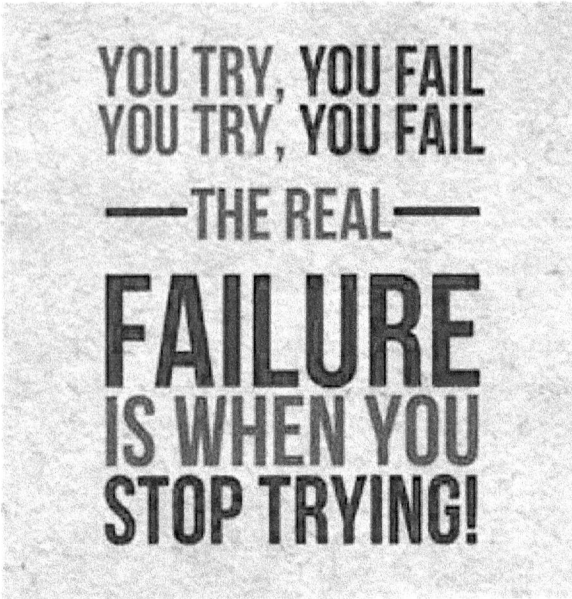

Figure 17; photo courtesy of pintrest.com

References

Abogunrin, S.O. ed., 2005. *Decolonization of biblical interpretation in Africa* (No. 4). Nigerian Association for Biblical Studies (NABIS).

Addison, T., Le Billon, P. and Murshed, S.M., 2002. Conflict in Africa: The cost of peaceful behaviour. *Journal of African Economies, 11*(3), pp.365-386.

Adebanwi, W., 2016. *Nation as Grand Narrative: The Nigerian Press and the Politics of Meaning.* University of Rochester Press.

Adeleke, T., 2015. *UnAfrican Americans: Nineteenth-century black nationalists and the civilizing mission.* University Press of Kentucky.

Adie, J.W., Duda, J.L. and Ntoumanis, N., 2008. Autonomy support, basic need satisfaction and the optimal functioning of adult male and female sport participants: A test of basic needs theory. *Motivation and Emotion, 32*(3), pp.189-199.

Agbenyega, J.S., 2006. Corporal punishment in the schools of Ghana: Does inclusive education suffer? *The Australian Educational Researcher, 33*(3), pp.107-122.

Ahmed, S., 2004. Affective economies. *Social text, 22*(2), pp.117-139.

Akyeampong, E., 2007. Indigenous knowledge and maritime fishing in West Africa: the case of Ghana. *Tribes and Tribals*, pp.173-182.

Alaga, E., Background brief "Pray the Devil Back to Hell:"

Alao, A., 2007. *Natural resources and conflict in Africa: the tragedy of endowment* (Vol. 29). University Rochester Press.

Alia, V., 2008. *Names and Nunavut: culture and identity in the Inuit homeland.* Berghahn Books.

Almond, P.C., 2008. *Adam and Eve in Seventeenth-Century Thought.* Cambridge University Press.

Anderson, B., 2013. Us and them. *The dangerous politics of immigration control.*

Anderson, L.P., 2008. A More Excellent Way: Moral Imagination & (and) the Art of Judging. *Notre Dame JL Ethics & Pub. Policy, 22*, p.399.

Anderson, W., 2009. From subjugated knowledge to conjugated subjects: science and globalisation, or postcolonial studies of science? *Postcolonial Studies*, *12*(4), pp.389-400.

Andrews, E.E., 2009. Christian missions and colonial empires reconsidered: A Black evangelist in West Africa, 1766–1816. *Journal of Church and State*, *51*(4), pp.663-691.

Annamalai, E., 2005. Nation-building in a globalised world: Language choice and education in India. *Decolonisation, globalisation: Language-in-education policy and practice*, pp.21-38.

Assembly, U.G., 1948. Universal declaration of human rights. *UN General Assembly*.

Ayittey, G. ed., 2016. *Africa unchained: The blueprint for Africa's future*. Springer.

Azam, J.P., 2001. The redistributive state and conflicts in Africa. *Journal of Peace research*, *38*(4), pp.429-444.

Badenhorst, S., 2010. Descent of Iron Age farmers in southern Africa during the last 2000 years. *African Archaeological Review*, *27*(2), pp.87-106.

Baderoon, G., 2012. The Provenance of the term 'Kafir'in South Africa and the notion of Beginning.

Baker, B.J. and Judd, M., 2012. Development of paleopathology in the Nile valley. *The Global History of Paleopathology*, pp.209-34.

Baldwin, J.R., Faulkner, S.L., Hecht, M.L. and Lindsley, S.L. eds., 2006. *Redefining culture: Perspectives across the disciplines*. Routledge.

Banja, O.N., 2008. Uganda martyrs: place and role of women.

Barkun, M., 1990. Racist apocalypse: Millennialism on the far right. *American Studies*, *31*(2), pp.121-140.

Barton, D., 2017. *Literacy: An introduction to the ecology of written language*. John Wiley & Sons.

Battersby, P. and Siracusa, J.M., 2009. *Globalization and human security*. Rowman & Littlefield Publishers.

Beale, A., 2014. Clash of Civilizations?

Bekerman, Z. and Zembylas, M., 2011. *Teaching contested narratives: Identity, memory and reconciliation in peace education and beyond*. Cambridge University Press.

Belasco, A., 2009. *Cost of Iraq, Afghanistan, and Other Global War on Terror Operations since 9/11*. Diane Publishing.

Belmonte, J.A., o1427273/01/0026-oool/s2. 50 G) 2001 Science History Publications Ltd. Belmonte, J.A., o1427273/01/0026-oool/s2. 50 G) 2001 Science History Publications Ltd.

Benhabib, S., 2004. *The rights of others: Aliens, residents, and citizens* (Vol. 5). Cambridge University Press.

Bergmann, W., 2008. Anti- Semitic Attitudes in Europe: A Comparative Perspective. *Journal of Social Issues*, *64*(2), pp.343-362.

Bernault, F., 2007. The shadow of rule: Colonial power and modern punishment in Africa. *Cultures of confinement: A history of the prison in Africa, Asia and Latin America*, pp.55-94.

Bidgood, S., 2001. Ethiopian artefacts made with plant materials: Vanishing wonders. In *Biodiversity Research in the Horn of Africa Region: Proceedings of the Third International Symposium on the Flora of Ethiopia and Eritrea at the Carlsberg Academy, Copenhagen, August 25-27, 1999* (p. 311). Kgl. Danske Videnskabernes Selskab.

Bishop, A.J., 1990. Western mathematics: The secret weapon of cultural imperialism. *Race & Class*, *32*(2), pp.51-65.

Blackstock, C., 2007. Residential schools: Did they really close or just morph into child welfare. *Indigenous LJ*, *6*, p.71.

Bonilla-Silva, E., 2009. Are the Americas 'sick with racism 'or is it a problem at the poles? A reply to Christina A. Sue. *Ethnic and Racial Studies*, *32*(6), pp.1071-1082.

Bonnet, C., Valbelle, D. and FIGS, C., 2008. *The Nubian pharaohs: black kings on the Nile*. American University in Cairo Press.

Bonsu, S.K. and Belk, R.W., 2003. Do not go cheaply into that good night: Death-ritual consumption in Asante, Ghana. *Journal of Consumer Research*, *30*(1), pp.41-55.

Bose, S., 2007. *Contested lands*. Harvard University Press.

Boshoff, N., 2009. Neo-colonialism and research collaboration in Central Africa. *Scientometrics*, *81*(2), p.413.

Bosman, F.G. and Poorthuis, M., 2015. Nephilim: The Children of Lilith. The Place of Man in the Ontological and Cosmological Dualism of the Diablo, Darksiders and Devil May Cry Game Series. *Online-Heidelberg Journal of Religions on the Internet*, *7*.

Boswell, C., 2003. The 'external dimension' of EU immigration and asylum policy. *International affairs*, *79*(3), pp.619-638.

Boulware, L.E., Cooper, L.A., Ratner, L.E., LaVeist, T.A. and Powe, N.R., 2016. Race and trust in the health care system. *Public health reports.*

Boyd, D., 2011. No taps, no toilets: First Nations and the constitutional right to water in Canada. *McGill Law Journal/Revue de droit de McGill, 57*(1), pp.81-134.

Bracken, H.M., 1978. Philosophy and racism. *Philosophia, 8*(2-3), pp.241-260.

Braverman, M., 2010. *Fatal embrace: Christians, Jews, and the search for peace in the Holy land.* Book Pros, LLC.

Brecht, B., 2015. *Life of Galileo.* Bloomsbury Publishing.

Brennan, J.R., 2011. Politics and business in the Indian newspapers of colonial Tanganyika. *Africa, 81*(1), pp.42-67.

Brennan, J.R., 2012. *Taifa: making nation and race in urban Tanzania.* Ohio University Press.

Brezinski, J.C., 2012. Promoting education for children in rural communities: a perspective of Burkina Faso.

Brounéus, K., 2008. Truth-telling as talking cure? Insecurity and retraumatization in the Rwandan Gacaca courts. *Security Dialogue, 39*(1), pp.55-76.

Brounéus, K., 2010. The trauma of truth telling: Effects of witnessing in the Rwandan Gacaca courts on psychological health. *Journal of conflict resolution, 54*(3), pp.408-437.

Brown, S.I., 2014. *Problem posing: Reflections and applications.* Psychology Press.

Bruner, J.S., 2009. *The process of education.* Harvard University Press.

Bueger, C., 2013. Practice, pirates and coast guards: The grand narrative of Somali piracy. *Third World Quarterly, 34*(10), pp.1811-1827.

Buncombe, A., 2010. Oldest university on earth is reborn after 800 years. *Independent,* 3 August (accessed July, 2017).

Burton, E., 2013. "… what tribe should we call him?" The Indian Diaspora, the State and the Nation in Tanzania since ca. 1850. *Stichproben-Vienna Journal of African Studies, 13*(25), pp.1-28.

Bush, K.D. and Saltarelli, D., 2000. The two faces of education in ethnic conflict: Towards a peacebuilding education for children.

Bustin, E., 2002. Remembrance of sins past: unraveling the murder of Patrice Lumumba. *Review of African Political Economy*, *29*(93-94), pp.537-560.

Butt, K.M. and Butt, A.A., 2014. UN Sanctions against Iraq: From ailment to chronic. *Journal of Political Studies*, *21*(2), p.271.

Byrne, S. and Irvin, C.L., 2000. *Reconcilable differences: Turning points in ethnopolitical conflict.* West Hartford, CT: Kumarian Press.

Byyny, R.L. and Houston-Ludlam, A., 2016. 10 On the problems of chatting with angels. *Pharos*, p.1.

Calame, C., 1999. Indigenous and modern perspectives on tribal initiation rites: Education according to Plato. *Bucknell Review*, *43*(1), p.278.

Caldas, M.M. and Perz, S., 2013. Agro-terrorism? The causes and consequences of the appearance of witch's broom disease in cocoa plantations of southern Bahia, Brazil. *Geoforum*, *47*, pp.147-157.

Cannon, B.J., 2016. Terrorists, Geopolitics and Kenya's Proposed Border Wall with Somalia. *Browser Download This Paper*.

Carney, S., Rappleye, J. and Silova, I., 2012. Between faith and science: World culture theory and comparative education. *Comparative Education Review*, *56*(3), pp.366-393.

Carpenter, K.E., Abrar, M., Aeby, G., Aronson, R.B., Banks, S., Bruckner, A., Chiriboga, A., Cortés, J., Delbeek, J.C., DeVantier, L. and Edgar, G.J., 2008. One-third of reef-building corals face elevated extinction risk from climate change and local impacts. *Science*, *321*(5888), pp.560-563.

Carter, J., Irani, G. and Volkan, V.D. eds., 2009. *Regional and ethnic conflicts: Perspectives from the front lines.* Routledge.

Carter, N. and Byrne, S., 2000. The dynamics of social cubism: A view from Northern Ireland and Québec. *Reconcilable differences: Turning points in ethnopolitical conflict*, pp.41-62.

Castles, S., 2009. World population movements, diversity, and education. *The Routledge international companion to multicultural education*, pp.49-61.

Castro, J.E., 2011. Gaddafi and Latin America. *Society*, *48*(4), pp.307-311.

Cattani, F., 2015. Songs and Verses of New Ethnicities: Resistance and Representation in Black British Culture. *Between*, *5*(10).

337

Chaliand, G. and Blin, A. eds., 2007. *The history of terrorism: from antiquity to al Qaeda*. University of California Press.

Chan, M.K., Louis, W.R. and Jetten, J., 2010. When groups are wrong and deviants are right. *European Journal of Social Psychology*, *40*(7), pp.1103-1109.

Cheldelin, S., Druckman, D. & Fast, L. (2003). *Conflict: From analysis to intervention*. New York: Continuum.

Cherry, K., 2014. Hierarchy of needs. *Retrieved Aug*, *16*, p.2014.

Chinn, P.W., 2007. Decolonizing methodologies and indigenous knowledge: The role of culture, place and personal experience in professional development. *Journal of research in science teaching*, *44*(9), pp.1247-1268.

Chirwa, G. and Naidoo, D., 2014. Curriculum change and development in Malawi: a historical overview. *Mediterranean Journal of Social Sciences*, *5*(16), p.336.

Chisholm, L. and Leyendecker, R., 2008. Curriculum reform in post-1990s sub-Saharan Africa. *International Journal of Educational Development*, *28*(2), pp.195-205.

Cikara, M., Bruneau, E.G. and Saxe, R.R., 2011. Us and them: Intergroup failures of empathy. *Current Directions in Psychological Science*, *20*(3), pp.149-153.

Clarence-Smith, W.G., 2006. *Islam and the Abolition of Slavery*. Oxford University Press, USA.

Cornelius, S., 2010. Ancient Egypt and the other. *Scriptura: International Journal of Bible, Religion and Theology in Southern Africa*, *104*(1), pp.322-340.

Cortés, J., Delbeek, J.C., DeVantier, L. and Edgar, G.J., 2008. One-third of reef-building corals face elevated extinction risk from climate change and local impacts. *Science*, *321*(5888), pp.560-563.

Crystal, D., 2012. *English as a global language*. Cambridge university press.

Culpepper, P.D., 2007. Eppure, non si muove: Legal change, institutional stability and Italian corporate governance. *West European Politics*, *30*(4), pp.784-802.

Czekalska, R, & Klosowicz, R., 2016. Satyagraha and South Africa: Part I: The Origins of the Relationship between the Idea and the Place in Mahatma Gandhi's Writings. *Politeja*, (40), p.31.

Danjibo, N.D., 2009. Islamic fundamentalism and sectarian violence: the 'Maitatsine' and 'Boko Haram' crises in northern Nigeria. *Peace and Conflict Studies Paper Series*, pp.1-21.

Deliovsky, K., 2008. Normative white femininity: Race, gender and the politics of beauty. *Atlantis: Critical Studies in Gender, Culture & Social Justice*, *33*(1).

Dellinger, D., 2013. *The mountaintop vision: Martin Luther King's cosmology of connection* (Doctoral dissertation, California Institute of Integral Studies).

Despeux, C. and Kohn, L., 2017. *Women in Daoism*. Lulu Press, Inc.

Diop, C.A., 1989. *The African origin of civilization: Myth or reality*. Chicago Review Press.

Draper, R., 2008. Black Pharaohs. *Nat Geogr*, *213*, pp.34-59.

Du Bois, W.E.B. and Akyeampong, E., 2014. *Africa, Its Geography, People and Products and Africa-Its Place in Modern History*. Oxford University Press.

Duprée, U.E., 2012. *Ho'oponopono: The Hawaiian Forgiveness Ritual as the Key to Your Life's Fulfillment*. Simon and Schuster.

Durrant, J.E., 2008. Physical punishment, culture, and rights: current issues for professionals. *Journal of Developmental & Behavioral Pediatrics*, *29*(1), pp.55-66.

Education Revisited: Contemporary Discourses for Democratic Education and Leadership, p.119.

Eijck, M.V. and Roth, W.M., 2007. Keeping the local local: Recalibrating the status of science and traditional ecological knowledge (TEK) in education. *Science Education*, *91*(6), pp.926-947.

El Hamel, C., 2008. Constructing a diasporic identity: Tracing the origins of the Gnawa spiritual group in Morocco. *The Journal of African History*, *49*(2), pp.241-260.

El-Malik, S.S., 2013. Critical pedagogy as interrupting Thingification. *Critical Studies on Security*, *1*(3), pp.361-364.

Encyclopaedia of Ancient Myths and Culture 2003.

Eriksson, J. and Norman, L., 2011. Political utilisation of scholarly ideas: the 'clash of civilisations' vs. 'Soft Power' in US foreign policy. *Review of International Studies*, *37*(1), pp.417-436.

Escobar, A., 2008. *Territories of difference: place, movements, life, redes.* Duke University Press.

Ethiopian Jews Hold Protest in Tel Aviv against Racism. *Al Jazeera,* 19 May, 2015.

Evans, C.H.R.I.S., 2015, March. BGuinea Rods^ and BVoyage Iron^: metals in the Atlantic slave trade, their European origins and African impacts. In *Economic History Society annual conference 2015.*

Fantina, R., 2010. Reade, Race, and Colonialism. In *Victorian Sensational Fiction* (pp. 147-160). Palgrave Macmillan, New York.

Faraday, M., 2013. "I shall be good health for you nevertheless, /and filter and fibre for your blood." Poetry, Health and the Body in Walt Whitman. *As Humanidades e as Ciências,* p.131.

Ferreira, M.E., 2006. Angola: Conflict and development, 1962-2002. *The Economics of Peace and Security Journal, 1*(1).

Fieldhouse, P., 2013. *Food and nutrition: customs and culture.* Springer.

Fielding, M. and Moss, P., 2010. *Radical education and the common school: A democratic alternative.* Routledge.

Fischer, S.R., 2004. *A history of reading.* Reaktion books.

Fisher, R., Ury, W.L. and Patton, B., 2011. *Getting to yes: Negotiating agreement without giving in.* Penguin.

Forsey, M. and Low, M., 2014. Beyond the production of tourism imaginaries: Student-travellers in Australia and their reception of media representations of their host nation. *Annals of Tourism Research, 44,* pp.156-170.

Foucault, M., 1984. *The Foucault Reader.* Pantheon.

Frantzman, S., 2015. Ethiopian Jews: Not Jewish enough. *Al Jazeera,* 4.

Fredrickson, G.M., 2015. Racism: A short history. Princeton University Press.

Freedman, S.W., Weinstein, H.M., Murphy, K. and Longman, T., 2008. Teaching history after identity-based conflicts: The Rwanda experience. *Comparative Education Review, 52*(4), pp.663-690.

Freeman, M., 2017. *Human rights.* John Wiley & Sons.

Fulford, T. and Kitson, P.J. eds., 2005. *Romanticism and colonialism: Writing and empire, 1780-1830.* Cambridge University Press.

Gade, C.B., 2012. What is Ubuntu? Different interpretations among South Africans of African descent. *South African Journal of Philosophy*, *31*(3), pp.484-503.

Gaertner, S.L. and Dovidio, J.F., 2014. *Reducing intergroup bias: The common ingroup identity model.* Psychology Press.

Gaffey, C., 2-016. 'Dogs and slaves': Egypt hits back over African racism allegations. *Newsweek*, 1.

Galilei, G., 1957. *Discoveries and opinions of Galileo: including The starry messenger (1610), Letter to the Grand Duchess Christina (1615), and excerpts from Letters on sunspots (1613), The assayer (1623)* (Vol. 94). Anchor.

Galtung, J. and Fischer, D., 2013. Positive and negative peace. In *Johan Galtung* (pp. 173-178). Springer, Berlin, Heidelberg.

George-Williams, D., 2006. Bite Not One Another. *Selected accounts of nonviolent struggle.*

Gerard, E. and Kuklick, B., 2015. *Death in the Congo: Murdering Patrice Lumumba.* Harvard University Press.

Gerrard, M.B., 2015. America's forgotten nuclear waste dump in the Pacific. *SAIS Review of International Affairs*, *35*(1), pp.87-97.

Giblin, J., 2012. Decolonial challenges and post-genocide archaeological politics in Rwanda. *Public Archaeology*, *11*(3), pp.123-143.

Gilbert, N., 2013. A hard look at GM crops. *Nature*, *497*(7447), p.24.

Gillborn, D., Rollock, N., Warmington, P. and Demack, S., 2016. Race, Racism and Education: inequality, resilience and reform in policy &.

Gilmore, S., 2015. Canada's Race Problem? It's Even Worse than America's. *Maclean's*, 22 January (accessed January 2016).

Gilstrap, D.L., 2007. Phenomenological reduction and emergent design: Complementary methods for leadership narrative interpretation and metanarrative development. *International Journal of Qualitative Methods*, 6(1), pp.95-113.

Ginty, R.M. and Williams, A., 2009. Conflict and development. *Abingdon: Routledge.*

Giomi, E., 2015. Tag femicide. Lethal violence against women in 2013 Italian press: quantitative and qualitative analysis. *Problemi dell'informazione*, *40*(3), pp.549-574.

Goeka, S.N, *Vol.15* No.5 May 23, 2005.

Golan, G.J., 2008. Where in the world is Africa? Predicting coverage of Africa by US television networks. *International Communication Gazette*, *70*(1), pp.41-57.

Goldman, M., 2007. Tracking wildebeest, locating knowledge: Maasai and conservation biology understandings of wildebeest behavior in Northern Tanzania. *Environment and Planning D: Society and space*, *25*(2), pp.307-331.

Goodhart, M. ed., 2013. *Human rights: politics and practice*. Oxford university press.

Goodhart, M. ed., 2016. *Human rights: politics and practice*. Oxford university press.

Goodwin, C. and Roach, J., Page| Printing| Abstract| Reviews| Contents| Text| E-mail

Gordon, R., 2015. (Sm) othering others? Post-millennial anthropology in Namibia. *Journal of Namibian Studies*, *18*.

Gordon, R., 2016. Moving targets: hunting in contemporary Africa.

Granville, J., 2008. The Nubians.

Green, E., 2010. Ethnicity and nationhood in precolonial Africa: The case of Buganda. *Nationalism and Ethnic Politics*, *16*(1), pp.1-21.

Grieves, V., 2007. What is indigenous wellbeing? In *Matauranga Taketake: Traditional Knowledge Conference* (p. 105).

Gruen, L. and Weil, K., 2012. Animal Others—Editors' Introduction. *Hypatia*, *27*(3), pp.477-487.

Gruenfeld, D.H., Inesi, M.E., Magee, J.C. and Galinsky, A.D., 2008. Power and the objectification of social targets. *Journal of personality and social psychology*, *95*(1), p.111.

Gupta, T.D. ed., 2007. *Race and racialization: Essential readings*. Canadian Scholars' Press.

Gurr, T.R., 2015. *Why men rebel*. Routledge.

Gurr, T.R., 2015. *Why men rebel*. Routledge.

Habashi, F., 2015. The pyramids of Egypt. *De re metallica (Madrid): revista de la Sociedad Española para la Defensa del Patrimonio Geológico y Minero*, (24), pp.81-89.

Hale, C.R., 2008. *Engaging contradictions: Theory, politics, and methods of activist scholarship*. University of California Press.

Hall, B.S., 2011. *A history of race in Muslim West Africa, 1600–1960* (Vol. 115). Cambridge University Press.

Haller, M., 2014. The East African Community (EAC). The difference between theory and practice based on the example of the free Movement of Goods and Services.

Harris, B. ed., 2015. *CCDA Theological Journal.* Wipf and Stock Publishers.

Hernandez, V., 2012. Jose Mujica: The world's 'poorest' president. *BBC News Magazine, 14.*

Holden, C.J. and Mace, R., 2003. Spread of cattle led to the loss of matrilineal descent in Africa: a coevolutionary analysis. *Proceedings of the Royal Society of London B: Biological Sciences, 270*(1532), pp.2425-2433.

Holt, M., Campbell, R.J. and Nikitin, M.B., 2012. *Fukushima nuclear disaster.* Congressional Research Service.

Houghton, A., 1972. Introduction to the. *The Wellesley Index to Victorian Periodicals*, 1824–1900 (2).

Hoyt Jr, C., 2012. The pedagogy of the meaning of racism: Reconciling a discordant discourse. *Social work, 57*(3), pp.225-234.

http://en.wikipedia.org/wiki/Johannes_Rebmann

https://www.youtube.com/watch?v=9VtIk1masqU

https://www.youtube.com/watch?v=wWl66V8pVH4

Hume, J., 1994. Acceptance of Diversity: The Essence of Peace in the North of Ireland. *Fordham Int'l LJ, 18*, p.1084.

Humphreys, M., 2005. Natural resources, conflict, and conflict resolution: Uncovering the mechanisms. *Journal of conflict resolution, 49*(4), pp.508-537.

Hurlbert, M.A. ed., 2011. *Pursuing justice: An introduction to justice studies.* Fernwood Pub.

Hurskainen, Arvi. "Early Records on Bantu." *Studia Orientalia Electronica* (2014): 65-76.

Hynd, S., 2008. Killing the condemned: the practice and process of capital punishment in British Africa, 1900–1950s. *The Journal of African History, 49*(3), pp.403-418.

Index, G.P., 2015. Measuring peace, its causes and its economic value (2015). *Institute for Economic & Peace, http://economicsandpeace.*

org/wp-content/uploads/2015/06/Global-Peace-Index-Report-2015_0.pdf.

Irving, J.A., Howard, C. and Matteson, J., 2004. Framing metanarrative: The role of metanarrative in leadership effectiveness through the production of meaning. *Proceedings of the American Society of Business and Behavioral Sciences*, *11*(1), pp.738-750.

Jafarian, T., Azizifar, A., Jamalinesari, A. and Gowhary, H., 2015. Investigating The Extent Of Familiarity Of Iranian ESP Teachers And ESP Course Learners With Academic Rhetoric Within A Systemic Functional Grammar Based Their Educational Level, Age And Gender. *Procedia-Social and Behavioral Sciences*, *192*, pp.213-219.

Jameson, F., 2013. The political unconscious: Narrative as a socially symbolic act. Routledge.

Jenkins, Brian Michael. Countering Al Qaeda: An Appreciation of the Situation and Suggestions for Strategy. Rand Corporation, 2002.

Jensen, S.Q., 2011. Othering, identity formation and agency. *Qualitative studies*, *2*(2), pp.63-78.

Jeong, H.W., 2005. *Peacebuilding in postconflict societies: Strategy and process* (p. 124). Boulder, CO: Lynne Rienner.

Jessop, B. (2008). Dialogue of the deaf: Some reflections on the Poulantzas-Miliband debate. In *Class, Power and the State in Capitalist Society* (pp. 132-157). Palgrave Macmillan, London.

Jinyuan, G., 1984. China and Africa: the development of relations over many centuries. *African Affairs*, *83*(331), pp.241-250.

Johannessen, C., 2006. *Kingship in Uganda. The Role of the Uganda Kingdom in Ugandan Politics*. Chr. Michelsen Institute.

Johnson, D.C., 2009. Ethnography of language policy. *Language policy*, *8*(2), pp.139-159.

Joseph, G.G., 2010. *The crest of the peacock: Non-European roots of mathematics*. Princeton University Press.

Joshi, S., 2012. Conflict Resolution-Means End and Methods. *The Indian Journal of Research*, *6*(1), p.47.

Justice, C., 2011. Criminology's Disney World: The Ethnographer's Ride of South. *What is Criminology?* p.125.

Kaiwar, V., 2007. Experiments in South Africa.

Kam, C.D. and Kinder, D.R., 2007. Terror and ethnocentrism: Foundations of American support for the war on terrorism. *Journal of Politics*, *69*(2), pp.320-338.

Kaplan, E.H. and Small, C.A., 2006. Anti-Israel sentiment predicts anti-Semitism in Europe. *Journal of Conflict Resolution*, *50*(4), pp.548-561.

Kasomo, D., 2010. The position of African traditional religion in conflict prevention. *International Journal of Sociology and Anthropology*, *2*(2), p.23.

Katan, D., 2014. *Translating cultures: An introduction for translators, interpreters and mediators.* Routledge.

Kellow, Christine L., and H. Leslie Steeves. "The Role of Radio in the Rwandan Genocide." *Journal of Communication* (1998): 107-128.

Kelm, M.E., 2011. *Colonizing bodies: Aboriginal health and healing in British Columbia, 1900-50.* UBC Press.

Kelsall, T., 2008. Going with the grain in African development? *Development Policy Review*, *26*(6), pp.627-655.

Khosroeva, A., 2013. Assyrian Massacres in Ottoman Turkey and Adjacent Turkish Territories. *Assyrian International News Agency.*

Kideghesho, J.R., 2009. The potentials of traditional African cultural practices in mitigating overexploitation of wildlife species and habitat loss: experience of Tanzania. *International Journal of Biodiversity Science & Management*, *5*(2), pp.83-94.

Killingray, D. and Plaut, M., 2012. *Fighting for Britain: African Soldiers in the Second World War.* Boydell & Brewer Ltd.

Kingma, K., 2016. *Demobilization in Subsaharan Africa: The Development and Security Impacts.* Springer.

Kipling, R., 2015. The white man's burden.

Kirsch, G.E. and Rohan, L. eds., 2008. *Beyond the archives: Research as a lived process.* SIU Press.

Kloor, K., 2014. The GMO-suicide myth. *Issues in science and technology*, *30*(2), pp.65-78.

Koehler, M. and Mishra, P., 2009. What is technological pedagogical content knowledge (TPACK)? *Contemporary issues in technology and teacher education*, *9*(1), pp.60-70.

Kopko, K.C., 2012. Religious Identity and Political Participation in the Mennonite Church USA. *Politics and Religion*, *5*(2), pp.367-393.

Kraidy, M., 2017. *Hybridity, or the cultural logic of globalization*. Temple University Press.

Krishna, S., 2013. 7 IR and the postcolonial novel. *Postcolonial Theory and International Relations: A Critical Introduction*, p.124.

Kuokkanen, R., 2011. *Reshaping the university: Responsibility, indigenous epistemes, and the logic of the gift*. UBC Press.

Kusurkar, R.A. and Croiset, G., 2015. Self-determination theory and scaffolding applied to medical education as a continuum. *Academic Medicine*, *90*(11), p.1431.

Lakshmi, R., 2016. Indian Mob Strips, Molests and Beats Tanzanian Student. *Washington Post*, 2.

Lalji, N., 2007. The resource curse revised: Conflict and Coltan in the Congo. *Harvard International Review*, *29*(3), p.34.

Lambert, J., 2009. Democratic foundations of social education. *Dewey's Democracy and Education Revisited: Contemporary Discourses for Democratic Education and Leadership*, p.119.

Landertinger, L., 2011. *The Biopolitics of Indigenous Reproduction: Colonial Discourse and the Overrepresentation of Indigenous Children in the Canadian Child Welfare System* (Doctoral dissertation).

Landsberg, C., 2006. South Africa's Global Strategy and Status. *Johannesburg, Friedrich Ebert Stiftung New powers for global change*.

Lanning, G. and Mueller, W.M., 1979. *Africa Undermined*. Penguin Books.

Larkin Jr, W.J., 2000. The recovery of Luke-Acts as" grand narrative" for the church's evangelistic and edification tasks in a postmodern age. *Journal of the Evangelical Theological Society*, *43*(3), p.405.

Laurie, P. and Wolfe, S.M., 2012. Unethical trials of interventions to reduce perinatal transmission of the Human Immunodeficiency Virus in developing countries. *Arguing About Bioethics, 479*.

Law, T.M., 2013. *When God Spoke Greek: The Septuagint and the Making of the Christian Bible*. Oxford University Press.

Le Billon, P., 2001. Angola's political economy of war: The role of oil and diamonds, 1975–2000. *African Affairs*, *100*(398), pp.55-80.

Lederach, J.P., 2005. *The moral imagination: The art and soul of building peace*. Oxford University Press.

Lederach, J.P., 2008. Cultivating peace: A practitioner's view of deadly conflict and negotiation. In *Contemporary Peacemaking* (pp. 36-44). Palgrave Macmillan, London.

Lehner, U.L., 2010. What is 'Catholic Enlightenment'? *History Compass*, *8*(2), pp.166-178.

Leijen, Ä., 2006. Pedagogical context of practical dance classes in higher education. *Danswetenschap in Nederland*, *4*, pp.91-97.

Leishman, N., 2017. Prof. Watson WRTG 150–sec 059 October 02, 2017.

Lema, E., Mbilinyi, M. and Rajani, R., 2004. Nyerere on education/Nyerere kuhusu elimu. *Dar es salaam: The Mwalimu Nyerere Foundation/HakiElimu.*

Lepore, J., 2009. *The name of war: King Philip's war and the origins of American identity.* Vintage.

Lesser, L.I., Ebbeling, C.B., Goozner, M., Wypij, D. and Ludwig, D.S., 2007. Relationship between funding source and conclusion among nutrition-related scientific articles. *PLoS Medicine*, *4*(1), p.e5.

Letseka, M., 2000. African philosophy and educational discourse. *African voices in education*, pp.179-191.

Levin, G., 2012. Critique of microcredit as a development model. *Pursuit-The Journal of Undergraduate Research at the University of Tennessee*, *4*(1), p.9.

Lexchin, J., Bero, L.A., Djulbegovic, B. and Clark, O., 2003. Pharmaceutical industry sponsorship and research outcome and quality: systematic review. *Bmj*, *326*(7400), pp.1167-1170.

Lombardo, P.A., 2008. *Three generations, no imbeciles: Eugenics, the Supreme Court, and Buck v. Bell.* JHU Press.

Loode, S., 2011. Navigating the unchartered waters of cross- cultural conflict resolution education. *Conflict Resolution Quarterly*, *29*(1), pp.65-84.

Łubowicz, A., 2002. Derived environment effects in Optimality Theory. *Lingua*, *112*(4), pp.243-280.

Luce, S., 2016. From Fanon to the Postcolonials: For a Strategic and Political Use of Identities. *Política Común*, *9*.

Luckham, R., Ahmed, I., Muggah, R. and White, S., 2001. Conflict and poverty in sub-Saharan Africa: an assessment of the issues and evidence.

Lugard, L.F.J., 2013. *The dual mandate in British tropical Africa.* Routledge.

Luke, A., 2005. Curriculum, ethics & metanarrative. *Struggles Over Difference: Curriculum, Texts, and Pedagogy in the Asia-Pacific, State University of New York Press, Albany, NY*, pp.11-24.

Lupyan, G., 2012. What do words do? Toward a theory of language-augmented thought. In *Psychology of learning and motivation* (Vol. 57, pp. 255-297). Academic Press.

Lütticken, S., 2010. Art and Thingness, Part Two: Thingification. *E-Flux Journal*, (15).

Lynn, S., 2010. The pastoral to agro-pastoral transition in Tanzania: Human adaptation in an ecosystem context. *Report to the Global Climate Adaptation Partnership. Available from: www. economics-of-cc-in-tanzania. org. Accessed on, 4.*

Lytle, E., 2016. Early Greek and Latin Sources on the Indian Ocean and Eastern Africa. In *Early Exchange between Africa and the Wider Indian Ocean World* (pp. 113-134). Palgrave Macmillan, Cham.

Maanga, G.S., 2015. Rewriting Chagga History: Focus on Ethno-Anthropological Distortions and Misconceptions. *Global Journal of Human-Social Science Research.*

Mabovula, N.N., 2011. The erosion of African communal values: a reappraisal of the African Ubuntu philosophy. *Inkanyiso: Journal of Humanities and Social Sciences*, 3(1), pp.38-47.

Mac Ginty, R., 2008. Indigenous peace-making versus the liberal peace. *Cooperation and conflict*, 43(2), pp.139-163.

MacDonald, D.B. and Hudson, G., 2012. The genocide question and Indian residential schools in Canada. *Canadian Journal of Political Science/Revue canadienne de science politique*, 45(2), pp.427-449.

MacFarlane, S.N. and Khong, Y.F., 2006. *Human security and the UN: A critical history.* Indiana University Press.

Mafabi, D., 2001. Death takes Africa's light: Chief Musamali Nangoli. *Daily Monitor, 5.*

Majani, F., 2016. Waafrika Wanaosoma India Waitwa Nyani, Sokwe.) (Africans Studying in India Are Called Monkeys, Chimps). *Mwananchi*. 14 February (accessed July 2016).

Makgoro, Y., 2017. Ubuntu and the law in South Africa. *Potchefstroom Electronic Law Journal/Potchefstroomse Elektroniese Regsblad*, *1*(1), pp.16-32.

Makoni, S.B., Dube, B. and Mashiri, P., 2006. Zimbabwe colonial and post-colonial language policy and planning practices. *Current issues in language planning*, *7*(4), pp.377-414.

Malcolm, J.R., Liu, C., Neilson, R.P., Hansen, L. and Hannah, L.E.E., 2006. Global warming and extinctions of endemic species from biodiversity hotspots. *Conservation biology*, *20*(2), pp.538-548.

Mamdani, M., 2007. Scholars in the Marketplace. *Kampala: Fountain Publishers*.

Mamdani, M., 2011. The importance of research in a university. *Pambazuka News*, *526*(21), pp.1-8.

Mariano, M., 2017. A History That" Dares Not Speak Its Name"? Atlantic History, Global History and the Modern Atlantic Space. *Journal of Transnational American Studies*, *8*(1).

Martin, G., 2017. *Understanding terrorism: Challenges, perspectives, and issues*. SAGE publications.

Martins, V., 2015. The plateau of trials: modern ethnicity in Angola.

Masanja, G.F., 2014. Human population growth and wildlife extinction in Ugalla ecosystem, western Tanzania. *Journal of Sustainable Development Studies*, *5*(2).

Mascarenhas, M., 2012. *Where the waters divide: Neoliberalism, white privilege, and environmental racism in Canada*. Lexington Books.

Matyok, T., Mendoza, H.R., Schmitz, C., Matyók, T., Mendoza, H.R. and Schmitz, C.L., 2014. Deep analysis: Designing complexity into our understanding of conflict. *InterAgency Journal*, *5*(2), pp.14-24.

Mawere, M., 2011. Epistemological and moral implications of characterization in African literature: A critique of Patrick Chakaipas Rudo Ibofu (love is blind). *International Journal of English and Literature*, *2*(1), pp.1-9.

Mearsheimer, J.J., 2014. China's unpeaceful rise. *The realism reader*, *105*(690), p.464.

Memmi, A., 2013. *The colonizer and the colonized*. Routledge. Meshesha, M. and Jawahar, C.V., 2005, August. Recognition of printed Amharic documents. In *Document Analysis and Recognition, 2005. Proceedings. Eighth International Conference on* (pp. 784-788). IEEE.

Meshesha, M. and Jawahar, C.V., 2007. Indigenous scripts of African languages. *Indilinga African Journal of Indigenous Knowledge Systems, 6*(2), pp.132-142.

Metz, S., 1994. *Disaster and Intervention in Sub-Saharan Africa: Learning from Rwanda*. Strategic Studies Institute, US Army War College.

Metz, T., 2007. Toward an African moral theory. *Journal of Political Philosophy, 15*(3), pp.321-341.

Mhango, N.N., 2015. *Africa Reunite or Perish*. Langaa RPCIG.

Mhango, N.N., 2017. *'Is It Global War on Terrorism' or Global War over Terra Africana?: The Ruse Imperial Powers Use to Occupy Africa Militarily for Economic Gains*. Rowman & Littlefield.

Milhizer, E.R., 2009. So help me Allah: An historical and prudential analysis of oaths as applied to the current controversy of the Bible and Quran in oath practices in America. *Ohio St. LJ, 70*, p.1.

Miller, A.N., Deeter, C., Trelstad, A., Hawk, M., Ingram, G. and Ramirez, A., 2013. Still the Dark Continent: A content analysis of research about Africa and by African scholars in 18 major communication-related journals. *Journal of International and Intercultural Communication, 6*(4), pp.317-333.

Millon, T., Millon, C.M., Meagher, S.E., Grossman, S.D. and Ramnath, R., 2012. *Personality disorders in modern life*. John Wiley & Sons.

Mintah, J. K. *Akan Amambra mu bi. Bureau of Ghana Languages*, 1996.

Moghaddam, A.A., 2011. *A metahistory of the clash of civilisations: us and them beyond orientalism*. Columbia University Press.

Molander, B., 2013. Attentiveness in Musical Practice and Research. *Music & Practice, 1*.

Monnin, A., 2009, July. Artifactualization: Introducing a new concept. In *InterFace 2009: 1st International Symposium for Humanities and Technology*.

Moore, M., Brugnatelli, E. and Colombo, M., 2003. *Stupid white men*. Mondadori.

Morey, R.A., Hinduism Exposed. *Faith Defenders*.

Morkot, R.G., 2013. Thebes under the Kushites. *Tombs of the South Asasif Necropolis: Thebes, Karakhamun (TT 223), and Karabasken (TT 391) in the Twenty-fifth Dynasty.*

Mose, C., 2014. Continuities of Heroism on the African Political Landscape. *Hip Hop and Social Change in Africa: Ni Wakati, 3.*

Mozaffar, S., 2007. The Politicization of Ethnic Cleavages: Theoretical Lessons with Empirical Data from Africa. In *ECPR Workshop on Politicizing Socio-Cultural Structures: Elite and Mass Perspectives on Cleavages.*

Mudimbe, V.Y., 2010. Discourse of power and knowledge of otherness. *Perspectives on Africa: A reader in culture, history and representation,* pp.55-60.

Müller, J., 2015. Exploring 'nostalgia' and 'imagination' for Ubuntu-research: A postfoundational perspective. *Verbum et Ecclesia, 36*(2), pp.1-6

Muller, J.Z., 2008. Us and them: The enduring power of ethnic nationalism. *Foreign Affairs,* pp.18-35.

Munishi, E.J., 2013. *Rural-urban Migration of the Maasai Nomadic Pastoralist Youth and Resilience in Tanzania: Case Studies in Ngorongoro District, Arusha Region and Dar Es Salaam City* (Doctoral dissertation, Institut für Umweltsozialwissenschaften und Geographie).

Murithi, T., 2006. African approaches to building peace and social solidarity. *African Journal on Conflict Resolution, 6*(2), pp.9-33.

Murithi, T., 2006. Practical peacemaking wisdom from Africa: Reflections on Ubuntu. *The journal of Pan African studies, 1*(4), pp.25-34.

Mutamba, C., 2012. 21st Century African Philosophy of Adult and Human Resource Education in Southern Africa. *Online Submission.*

Mwakikagile, G., 2015. *Western Involvement in Nkrumah's Downfall.* New Africa Press.

Nauriya, A., 2006. *The African Element in Gandhi.* National Gandhi Museum.

Navarro, V., Muntaner, C., Borrell, C., Benach, J., Quiroga, Á., Rodríguez-Sanz, M., Vergés, N. and Pasarín, M.I., 2006. Politics and health outcomes. *The Lancet, 368*(9540), pp.1033-1037.

Ndegwah, D.J., 2007. *Biblical Hermeneutics as a Tool for Inculturation in Africa: A Case Study of the Pökot People of Kenia.* Nairobi: Creations Enterprises.

Ndembwike, J., 2006. *Tanzania: The land and its people.* New Africa Press.

Ndenecho, E.N., 2011. *Local livelihoods and protected area management: Biodiversity conservation problems in Cameroon.* African Books Collective.

Neocosmos, M., 2010. *From Foreign Natives to Native Foreigners. Explaining Xenophobia in Post-apartheid South Africa: Explaining Xenophobia in Post-apartheid South Africa: Citizenship and Nationalism, Identity and Politics.* African Books Collective.

Nhemachena, A., 2014. *Knowledge, chivanhu and struggles for survival in conflict-torn Manicaland, Zimbabwe* (Doctoral dissertation, University of Cape Town).

Nichols, J.D., Boulinier, T., Hines, J.E., Pollock, K.H. and Sauer, J.R., 1998. Estimating rates of local species extinction, colonization, and turnover in animal communities. *Ecological applications, 8*(4), pp.1213-1225.

Nivola, C.A., 2008. *Planting the trees of Kenya: The story of Wangari Maathai.* Farrar Straus & Giroux.

Nussubaun, B., 2003. Ubuntu: Reflections of a South African on our common humanity. *Reflections: The SoL Journal, 4*(4), pp.21-26.

Nyamnjoh, F.B., 2012. 'Potted plants in greenhouses': A critical reflection on the resilience of colonial education in Africa. *Journal of Asian and African Studies, 47*(2), pp.129-154.

Nzongola-Ntalaja, G., 2014. *Patrice Lumumba.* Ohio University Press.

O'conor, M.R., 2010. Maasai Herders Now Dar Security Guards. *Global Post,* May 30 (accessed January, 2016).

O'hare, B.A. and Southall, D.P., 2007. First do no harm: the impact of recent armed conflict on maternal and child health in Sub-Saharan Africa. *Journal of the Royal Society of Medicine, 100*(12), pp.564-570.

Okonta, P. and Rossouw, T., 2013. Prevalence of scientific misconduct among a group of researchers in Nigeria. *Developing world bioethics, 13*(3), pp.149-157.

Omarova, S.T., 2011. Wall Street as community of fate: Toward financial industry self-regulation. *University of Pennsylvania Law Review, 159*(2), pp.411-492.

Omboki, A., 2016. Students Torch Dorm over Euro Match Miss Out. *Daily Nation*, 27 June, 2016 (accessed August, 2017).

Onuoha, C.C., 2013. The Quality of Justice is Strained: The Death Penalty in Nigeria.

Oppenheimer, L., 2006. The Development of Enemy Images: A Theoretical Contribution. *Peace*

Oraegbunam, I.K., 2009. The principles and practice of justice in traditional Igbo jurisprudence. *OGIRISI: a New Journal of African Studies, 6*(1), pp.53-85.

Oreskes, N. and Conway, E.M., 2011. *Merchants of doubt: How a handful of scientists obscured the truth on issues from tobacco smoke to global warming.* Bloomsbury Publishing USA.

Orr, D., 1991. What is Education for? *Context 27*: 52-55.

Orr, D., 2016. Still an African Anomaly: Politicised Ethnicity in Tanzania. *Co-Managing Editors Alexandra Green & Emma Jones*, p.13.

Orwell, G., 2010. *Animal farm* (Vol. 31). Random House.

Osborn, E.L., 2003. 'Circle of iron': African colonial employees and the interpretation of colonial rule in French West Africa. *The Journal of African History, 44*(1), pp.29-50.

Oyefara, J.L., 2007. Food insecurity, HIV/AIDS pandemic and sexual behaviour of female commercial sex workers in Lagos metropolis, Nigeria. *SAHARA: Journal of Social Aspects of HIV/AIDS Research Alliance, 4*(2), pp.626-635.

p'Bitek, O., 1984. *Song of Lawino & Song of Ocol* (No. 266). Heinemann.

Paffenholz, T., 2010. Civil society and peacebuilding. *A Critical Assessment.*

Parpart, J. and Stichter, S. eds., 2016. *Women, employment and the family in the international division of labour.* Springer.

Patil, P.N., 2012. *Discoveries in pharmacological sciences.* World Scientific.

Pearce, M.E., Christian, W.M., Patterson, K., Norris, K., Moniruzzaman, A., Craib, K.J., Schechter, M.T. and Spittal, P.M., 2008. The Cedar Project: Historical trauma, sexual abuse and

HIV risk among young Aboriginal people who use injection and non-injection

Pennycook, A., 2017. *The cultural politics of English as an international language.* Taylor & Francis.

Pennycook, A., 2017. *The cultural politics of English as an international language.* Taylor & Francis.

Phillips, J. and Whatman, S.L., 2007. Decolonising Preservice Teacher Education-reform at many cultural interfaces.

Phillips, J. and Whatman, S.L., 2007. Decolonising Preservice Teacher Education-reform at many cultural interfaces.

Pingel, F., 2014. The Holocaust in textbooks: From a European to a global event. *Holocaust education in a global context,* p.77.

Pinter, H., 2013. *Art, Truth and Politics: The Nobel Lecture.* Faber & Faber.

Poggo, S.S., 2009. Ethnicity and Race in Modern Sudan. In *The First Sudanese Civil War* (pp. 9-20). Palgrave Macmillan, New York.

Poncian, J., 2015. The persistence of western negative perceptions about Africa: Factoring in the role of Africans.

Post, K.W., 1968. Is there a case for Biafra? *International Affairs (Royal Institute of International Affairs 1944-), 44*(1), pp.26-39.

Power, E.M., 2008. Conceptualizing food security for Aboriginal people in Canada. *Canadian Journal of Public Health/Revue Canadienne de Sante'e Publique,* pp.95-97.

Prins, H.H., 1992. The pastoral road to extinction: competition between wildlife and traditional pastoralism in East Africa. *Environmental Conservation, 19*(2), pp.117-123.

Ramose, M.B., 2001. An African perspective on justice and race. In *Polylog: Forum for Intercultural Philosophy* (Vol. 3, p. 14).

Ramsamy, E., BETWEEN BELONGING AND ALIENATION. *Minorities and the State in Africa,* p.51.

Ranga Rao, G.V., Sahrawat, K.L., Rao, C.S., Das, B., Reddy, K.K., Bharath, B.S., Rao, V.R., Murthy, K.V.S. and Wani, S.P., 2009. Insecticide residues in vegetable crops grown in Kothapalli Watershed, Andhra Pradesh, India: A case Study. *Indian Journal of Dryland Agricultural Research and Development, 24*(2), pp.21-27.

Ravitch, S.M., 2014. The Transformative Power of Taking an Inquiry Stance on Practice: Practitioner Research as Narrative and

Counter-Narrative. *Penn GSE Perspectives on Urban Education*, *11*(1), pp.5-10.

Razack, S., 2004. *Dark threats and white knights: The Somalia affair, peacekeeping, and the new imperialism.* University of Toronto Press.

Ricento, T., 2012. Political economy and English as a 'global' language. *Critical Multilingualism Studies*, *1*(1), pp.31-56.

Rizvi, S.A.H., Hypothesis of Great Flood: Lake Lisan Deluge.

Roberts, S.A., 2012. The Rise & Fall of the Nephilim. *Genesis*, *6*, pp.1-4.

Robinson, M., 2013. *African Humanity: Shaking Foundations: A Sociological, Theological, Psychological Study*, Xlibris.

Roca, E., 2010. The exercise of moral imagination in stigmatized work groups. *Journal of business ethics*, *96*(1), pp.135-147.

Rollins, J., 2010. *Al Qaeda and affiliates: historical perspective, global presence, and implications for US policy.* DIANE Publishing.

Rosillon, F., Vander Borght, P. and Sama, H.B., 2005. River contract in Wallonia (Belgium) and its application for water management in the Sourou valley (Burkina Faso). *Water science and technology*, *52*(9), pp.85-93.

Rutgers, M.R., 2010. The oath of office as public value guardian. *The American Review of Public Administration*, *40*(4), pp.428-444.

Said, E.W., 2012. *Culture and imperialism.* Vintage.

Samuelson, B.L. and Freedman, S.W., 2010. Language policy, multilingual education, and power in Rwanda. *Language Policy*, *9*(3), pp.191-215.

Sangmpam, S.N., 2012. *Comparing apples and mangoes: the overpoliticized state in developing countries.* SUNY Press.

Sashidharan, S.P., 2001. Institutional racism in British psychiatry. *The Psychiatrist*, *25*(7), pp.244-247.

Schaap, A., 2006. Agonism in divided societies. *Philosophy & Social Criticism*, *32*(2), pp.255-277.

Schabas, W.A., 2005. Genocide trials and gacaca courts. *Journal of International Criminal Justice*, *3*(4), pp.879-895.

Schatzberg, M.G., 2014. Transformation and Struggle. *The Politics of Governance: Actors and Articulations in Africa and Beyond*, *3*, p.25.

Schaul, J.C., 2013. Human-Wildlife Conflict: An Interview with Dr. Michael Hutchins. *National Geographical*, *9*.

Schmid, W.T., 1996. The definition of racism. *Journal of Applied Philosophy*, *13*(1), pp.31-40.

Schniedewind, W.M., 2005. *How the Bible became a book: The textualization of Ancient Israel.* Cambridge University Press.

Scolnicov, S., 2013. *Plato's metaphysics of education.* Routledge.

Seehausen, O., 2004. Hybridization and adaptive radiation. *Trends in ecology & evolution*, *19*(4), pp.198-207.

Selasi, T., 2013. African Literature Doesn't Exist. *Opening Address, 13th International Literature Festival Berlin.*

Shaltout, M. and Belmonte, J.A., 2005. On the orientation of ancient Egyptian temples: (1) Upper Egypt and Lower Nubia. *Journal for the History of Astronomy*, *36*(3), pp.273-298.

Shimron, A., 2010. *"All Human Beings are Born Free and Equal": Women's Human Rights and the International Criminal Tribunals* (Master's thesis).

Skinner, G., 2008. Nuremberg's Legacy Continues: The Nuremberg Trials' Influencing on Human Rights Litigation in US Courts under the Alien Tort Statute. *Alb. L. Rev.*, *71*, p.321.

Smith, L.T., 2013. *Decolonizing methodologies: Research and indigenous peoples.* Zed Books Ltd.

Smith, R., 2007. *Being human: Historical knowledge and the creation of human nature.* Columbia University Press.

Smith, R.J., 2012. The geography of the death penalty and its ramifications. *BuL rev.*, *92*, p.227.

Soske, J., 2009. *'Wash Me Black Again': African Nationalism, the Indian Diaspora, and Kwa-Zulu Natal, 1944-1960.* University of Toronto.

Soudien, C., 2010. "What to Teach the Natives": A Historiography of the Curriculum Dilemma in South Africa. In *Curriculum Studies in South Africa* (pp. 19-49). Palgrave Macmillan, New York.

Sparks, A. and Tutu, M., 2011. *Tutu: Authorized.* Harper Collins.

Stone, J. H. "MK Gandhi: Some Experiments with Truth." *Journal of Southern African Studies 16.4* (1990): 721-740.

Stone, P., 2004. Presenting the past. *Heritage, museums and galleries: an introductory reader*, p.215.

Streck, M.P. and Wasserman, N., 2016. On Wolves and Kings. Two Tablets with Akkadian Wisdom Texts from the Second Millennium Bc. *IRAQ*, *78*, pp.241-252.

Strother, Z.S., 2013. Looking for Africa in Carl Einstein's Negerplastik. *African arts, 46*(4), pp.8-21.

Super, G., 2011. Punishment and the body in the 'old' and 'new' South Africa: A story of punitivist humanism. *Theoretical Criminology, 15*(4), pp.427-443.

Sutherland, E., 2011. Coltan, the Congo and your cell phone.

Swami, V. and Barrett, S., 2011. British men's hair color preferences: An assessment of courtship solicitation and stimulus ratings. *Scandinavian Journal of Psychology, 52*(6), pp.595-600.

Takyi, B.K. and Broughton, C.L., 2006. Marital stability in sub-Saharan Africa: Do women's autonomy and socioeconomic situation matter? *Journal of Family and Economic Issues, 27*(1), pp.113-132.

Taylor, M.S., 2011. Buffalo hunt: International trade and the virtual extinction of the North American bison. *American Economic Review, 101*(7), pp.3162-95.

Teo, T., 2010. What is epistemological violence in the empirical social sciences? *Social and Personality Psychology Compass, 4*(5), pp.295-303.

Terrebonne, R., 2008. Fulla, the veiled Barbie: An analysis of cultural imperialism and agency. *MAI Review, 2*, p.1.

Tewkesbury, P., 2011. Keeping the Dream Alive: Meridian as Alice Walker's Homage to Martin Luther King and the Beloved Community. *Religion and the Arts, 15*(5), pp.603-627.

Thompson, A. ed., 2007. *The media and the Rwanda genocide.* IDRC.

Tremain, S.L., 2015. *Foucault and the Government of Disability.* University of Michigan Press.

Tripp, A.M., 2005. Legislative quotas for women: Implications for governance in Africa. In *African Parliaments* (pp. 48-60). Palgrave Macmillan, New York.

Tuck, E. and Yang, K.W., 2012. Decolonization is not a metaphor. *Decolonization: Indigeneity, education & society, 1*(1).

Turner, B., 2013. Burkina Faso. In *The Statesman's Yearbook* (pp. 249-252). Palgrave Macmillan, London.

Tutu, D. and Tutu, N., 2006. *The Words of Desmond Tutu.* Newmarket Press.

Tyler, I., 2013. Naked protest: the maternal politics of citizenship and revolt. *Citizenship studies, 17*(2), pp.211-226.

Uzgalis, W., 2002. An inconsistency not to be excused: On Locke and racism. *Philosophers on race: Critical essays*, pp.81-100.

Vaden, V.C. and Woolley, J.D., 2011. Does God Make It Real? Children's Belief in Religious Stories from the Judeo-Christian Tradition. *Child development*, *82*(4), pp.1120-1135.

Vandenberghe, F., 2008. Deleuzian capitalism. *Philosophy & Social Criticism*, *34*(8), pp.877-903.

Vargas, O., 2014. The Face of the Morally Responsible Scholar–Practitioner. *Educational Leadership and Moral Literacy: The Dispositional Aims of Moral Leaders*, p.93.

Villafana, F.R., 2011. *Cold war in the Congo: the confrontation of Cuban military forces, 1960-1967*. Transaction Publishers.

Viriri, A. and Mungwini, P., 2010. African cosmology and the duality of Western Hegemony: The search for an African identity. *The Journal of Pan African Studies*, *3*(6), pp.24-42.

Wa Thiong'o, Ngugi. *Decolonising the Mind: The Politics of Language in African Literature*. East African Publishers, 1994.

Washington, R.E., 1990. Brown racism and the formation of a world system of racial stratification. *International Journal of Politics, Culture, and Society*, *4*(2), pp.209-227.

West, M.S. and Curtis, J.W., 2006. *AAUP faculty gender equity indicators 2006* (p. 85). Washington, DC: American Association of University Professors.

Whitford, D.M., 2009. *The curse of Ham in the early modern era: the Bible and the justifications for slavery*. Ashgate Publishing, Ltd.

Wierzynski, A., 2004. Consolidating democracy through transitional justice: Rwanda's Gacaca courts. *NYUL Rev.*, *79*, p.1934.

Williams, C., 2013. Explaining the Great Ear in Africa: How Conflict in the Congo Became a Continental Crisis. *Fletcher F. World Aff.*, *37*, p.81.

Williams, E., 2011. Language policy, politics and development in Africa. *Dreams and realities: Developing countries and the English language*, pp.39-55.

Wolfe, P., 2006. Settler Colonialism and the Elimination of the Native. *Journal of genocide research*, *8*(4), pp.387-409.

Wong, C.Y., Boon-Itt, S. and Wong, C.W., 2011. The contingency effects of environmental uncertainty on the relationship between supply chain integration and operational performance. *Journal of Operations management, 29*(6), pp.604-615.

Woolford, A., 2009. Ontological destruction: genocide and Canadian aboriginal peoples. *Genocide Studies and Prevention, 4*(1), pp.81-97.

Wright, C.J., 2013. *The mission of God: Unlocking the Bible's grand narrative.* InterVarsity Press.

Wright, S.C. and Lubensky, M.E., 2009. The struggle for social equality: Collective action versus prejudice reduction. *Intergroup misunderstandings: Impact of divergent social realities*, pp.291-310.

Wynne-Jones, S., 2016. *A Material Culture: Consumption and Materiality on the Coast of Precolonial East Africa.* Oxford University Press.

Yang, C., 2011. The quality of narrative research: On a theoretical framework for narrative inquiry. *STUT Journal of Humanities and Social Sciences, 6*, pp.195-241.

Zami, M.S. and Lee, A., 2007, March. Earth as an alternative building material for sustainable low cost housing in Zimbabwe. In *7th International Postgraduate Research Conference.*

Zhang, R., El-Mashad, H.M., Hartman, K., Wang, F., Liu, G., Choate, C. and Gamble, P., 2007. Characterization of food waste as feedstock for anaerobic digestion. *Bioresource technology, 98*(4), pp.929-935.

Zubieta Calvert, L.F., 2010. *The rock art of Chinamwali: material culture and girls' initiation in south-central Africa* (Doctoral dissertation).

www.ingramcontent.com/pod-product-compliance
Lightning Source LLC
Chambersburg PA
CBHW060022030426
42334CB00019B/2142